RED CLOUD
AND THE SIOUX PROBLEM

Books by James C. Olson

J. STERLING MORTON (1942)
HISTORY OF NEBRASKA (1955)

Red Cloud
and the Sioux Problem

JAMES C. OLSON

University of Nebraska Press / Lincoln and London

FOR VERA,

ELIZABETH, AND SARAH

Foreword

A number of years ago, while serving as Director of the Nebraska State Historical Society, I became interested in a body of materials relating to the history of the Sioux which the Society, under the leadership of Dr. Addison E. Sheldon, its Superintendent for more than thirty years, had accumulated. Knowing that Dr. Sheldon had hoped to use these materials to write a biography of Red Cloud, it seemed to me that it would be appropriate for his successor to try to carry on the work. It soon became evident, however, that I, at least, would not be able to prepare a biography, in the strict sense of the word, from the sources available in the Historical Society and elsewhere. For voluminous as they are, these sources provide only a sketchy record of Red Cloud's activities, particularly during the first half of his life, and virtually no insight into his mind. To be sure, I have quoted him frequently, but it must be remembered that the words I have used have come to us through interpreters, who frequently, as M. Simonin said of Pierre Chene and John Richard, "translated the eloquent discourses of the day into bad English."* Most of what we know about Red Cloud, then, comes to us from others, many of whom were involved with the chief in one way or another as a problem. As I worked with the sources, it occurred to me that the most worthwhile contribution I could make would be to use them primarily to try to provide an objective account of Red Cloud's role in the life of his people during the years when they were making the transition from warriors to wards of the Government. The sources have dictated that while the study would be focused on Red Cloud, the point of view would be that of the white citizens of the United States. Hence, the title of the book.

Anyone who studies Sioux history is conscious of the debt he owes to the pioneering work of George E. Hyde. The reader who is familiar with *Red Cloud's Folk*, *Spotted Tail's Folk*, and *A Sioux Chronicle* will be aware that I have traveled the trail which Hyde pioneered. At certain points along the way I have not seen things as he did, but this study

---

* Wilson O. Clough, ed., *Fort Russell and Fort Laramie Peace Commission in 1867*, State University of Montana, *Sources of Northwest History*, No. 14, p. 8.

should be thought of as a supplement to Hyde's work rather than as an effort to revise it. I have followed Hyde's practice of using the English plural in writing tribal names; the spelling of all Indian names follows F. W. Hodge, *Handbook of the American Indians North of Mexico*.

Military rank poses a difficult problem for anyone working in the years immediately after the Civil War. Many officers had earned wartime brevets, and until 1870 they were entitled to wear the uniform and bear the title of their highest brevet grade. Beginning in 1870, they were required to wear the insignia of their regular rank (although the brevet rank could be shown on the collar), and only actual rank could be referred to in orders. Except in quotations or in certain contexts, I have followed the military rule: brevet rank until 1870, actual rank after 1870. Thus, for example, Bvt. Maj. Gen. John E. Smith becomes Col. John E. Smith, except that sometimes he is referred to by others as "General Smith." The Army could establish regulations, but in common usage, even within the military establishment, once a man attained the rank of general, even by brevet, he remained a general. In matters of rank, I have followed F. B. Heitman, *Historical Register of the United States Army* (Washington: The National Tribune, 1890).

My debts are legion. Mari Sandoz encouraged me to undertake the work. The Nebraska State Historical Society made it possible for me to conduct the research, and various members of its staff, notably Myrtle D. Berry, Helen D. Boehmer, Donald F. Danker, Marvin F. Kivett, William F. Schmidt, and John B. White, provided assistance far beyond the call of duty. A Montana Heritage grant enabled me to spend time at the State Historical Society of Montana; for hospitality and assistance during two summers in Helena, I am grateful to K. Ross Toole, Michael Kennedy, and Virginia Walton. A Woods Faculty Fellowship from the University of Nebraska provided the time and freedom which enabled me to organize my notes and begin the first draft. The Research Council of the University of Nebraska assisted with funds for the purchase of microfilm and the typing of manuscript. The staff of the University of Nebraska Libraries, and particularly Mrs. Leona Mason and Mrs. Virginia Trautman, patiently responded to innumerable requests for help. Henry G. Waltmann of Purdue University read all of the manuscript; Preston Holder of the University of Nebraska and James T. King of Wisconsin State University, at River Falls read parts of it. All contributed valuable suggestions. Mrs. Donna McCarthy typed the manuscript. Others whom I wish to thank for help along the way are: Oliver W. Holmes, Jane F. Smith, and Richard

Wood of the National Archives; Merrill J. Mattes, Don Rickey, and Robert M. Utley of the National Park Service; Mrs. Margaret Cook of Agate, Nebraska; Father Lawrence Edwards, S.J. of Holy Rosary Mission on the Pine Ridge Reservation in South Dakota; Lola Homsher of the Wyoming State Department of History and Archives; Wayland Magee of Bennington, Nebraska; Watt Marchman of the Rutherford B. Hayes Library, Fremont, Ohio; Will G. Robinson of the State Historical Society of South Dakota; Leland Sage of the State College of Iowa; and Everett Sterling of the State University of South Dakota.

Finally, special thanks must go to my wife and daughters, to whom this book is dedicated, for cheerfully accepting the fact that vacations are times for visiting libraries, Indian reservations, and abandoned forts.

JAMES C. OLSON

Contents

List of Illustrations and Maps

Red Cloud and the Sioux Problem

Abbreviations in Footnotes

AAAG Acting Assistant Adjutant General
AAG Assistant Adjutant General
AGO Agent General's Office
CO Commanding Officer
Com. Commissioner
LR Letters Received
LS Letters Sent
NARS National Archives and Records Service
RG Record Group
TR Telegrams Received
TS Telegrams Sent

CHAPTER 1

The Problem

The unleashing of the pent-up forces of western expansion at the end of the Civil War brought the knotty problem of Indian affairs in the West to a crisis. Stripped to its essentials, the problem was the ancient one that always arose when one people attempted to dispossess another of their lands. Since it was as old as European colonization in North America and no satisfactory solution had been found for it, the history of Indian affairs had been replete with crises. But in the past the process of dispossession had been gradual, and the dispossessed had always had some place to go. Now, however, in the words of Bvt. Maj. Gen. John Pope, commanding the Military Division of the Missouri, the nation was "at one grasp seizing the whole region of country occupied by the Indians and plunging them without warning into suffering and starvation." As a result:

> The Indian, in truth, has no longer a country. His lands are everywhere pervaded by white men; his means of subsistence destroyed and the homes of his tribe violently taken from him; himself and his family reduced to starvation, or to the necessity of warring to the death upon the white man, whose inevitable and destructive progress threatens the total extermination of his race. . . . The Indians, driven to desperation and threatened with starvation, have everywhere commenced hostilities against the whites, and are carrying them on with a fury and courage unknown to their history

hitherto. There is not a tribe of Indians on the great plains or in the mountain regions east of Nevada and Idaho of any consideration which is not now warring on the whites.[1]

Among the tribes most bitterly at war with the whites were the Oglala and Brulé Sioux, the Northern Cheyennes, and the Arapahoes. The hostility of these tribes was critical in the extreme. They were among the most warlike Indians in the West, and the country through which they roamed—the area between the Platte and the Yellowstone, the Upper Missouri and the Rockies—was in a very real sense the highroad of western expansion. Here ran the great emigrant roads, the transcontinental telegraph, and the stage and freight lines. Here were the gold fields of Colorado, Dakota, and Montana and the routes thereto. Here was where the transcontinental railroad would soon be built. The development of the West would be stifled so long as the tribes inhabiting this area were hostile and able to implement their hostility—and at the end of the Civil War they were both.

Actually, these tribes—particularly the Sioux—had given trouble almost from the day the overland emigration began, and the frustrating futility of efforts to deal with them had provided both a pattern for subsequent negotiations and a reason for subsequent difficulties.

In 1845 Col. Stephen Watts Kearny, accompanied by five companies of well-equipped and well-mounted dragoons and seventeen wagon-loads of provisions and presents, met with about a thousand Sioux at Fort Laramie, then a fur-trading post belonging to the American Fur Company.[2] He told them of the tender love the Great White Father in Washington had for his red children and of his desire that they be happy and content. He warned them against the white man's whiskey. He warned them particularly that the emigrant road must remain open and the whites who traveled it must not be disturbed. The Sioux, eyeing the wagonloads of presents, readily promised that they would heed the words of the Great Father; the roads would remain open and the white children would not be disturbed. Kearny rewarded their easy acquiescence by ordering a distribution of presents—blankets, cloth, beads, knives, tobacco, and knickknacks—fired three rounds from a couple of

[1] Pope to Col. R. M. Sawyer, Military Division of the Mississippi, August 1, 1865, *War of the Rebellion, Official Records*, Ser. I, XLVIII, Pt. 2, 1149–1153.

[2] For an account of Fort Laramie, which played such an important role in Indian affairs, see LeRoy R. Hafen and Francis M. Young, *Fort Laramie and the Pageant of the West, 1834–1890* (Glendale: Arthur H. Clark Co., 1938).

mountain howitzers and marched away, confident that his mission had been a success.[3]

Just a year later, however, Francis Parkman, visiting Fort Laramie, observed the "perturbation on the part of the emigrants" and the "dangerous spirit on the part of the Dacotah." In his judgment, "a military force and military law are urgently called for in that perilous region; and unless troops are speedily stationed at Fort Laramie, or elsewhere in the neighborhood, both immigrants and other travellers will be exposed to most imminent risks."[4]

The noted mountain man Thomas Fitzpatrick, who had been appointed United States agent for the tribes of the Upper Platte and Arkansas, was of the same opinion. In 1847 he advised the Army that "a post at or in the vicinity of Laramie is much wanted. It would be nearly in the vicinity of the buffalo range, where all the most formidable Indian tribes are fast approaching, and near where there will eventually (as the game decreases) be a great struggle for ascendancy. . . ."[5]

In 1849 the Government purchased Fort Laramie from the American Fur Company and turned it into a military post. It seemed ideally located to protect the emigrant road from the Sioux. For years the Indians had traveled through the region and gathered on the rich bottomlands for hunting and feasting. After the establishment of the trading post in 1834, many had taken to residing more or less permanently in the area. This was where the emigrants encountered them; this was where the protection was needed.

The need for protection had grown with each passing year as the volume of emigration through the Platte Valley had increased from a trickle of less than a hundred in 1841 to a flood of more than fifty

[3] S. W. Kearny, "Report of a Summer Campaign to the Rocky Mountains, &c., in 1845," 29th Cong., 1st Sess., S. Ex. Doc. 1, pp. 210–213; see also Louis Pelzer, *Marches of the Dragoons in the Mississippi Valley* (Iowa City: State Historical Society of Iowa, 1917), pp. 120–133.

[4] Francis Parkman, *The Oregon Trail* (4th ed.; Boston: Little, Brown and Co., 1891), pp. 108–109. *The Oregon Trail* appeared serially in the *Knickerbocker* during the years 1847–1849. In his Journal, Parkman wrote of the Sioux: "Never so turbulent as this year. Declare that if the emigrants continued to pass through, they would rob them and kill them if they resisted . . ." (Mason Wade, ed., *The Journals of Francis Parkman* [New York and London: Harper & Brothers, 1947], II, 468–469). Parkman's comments on the Sioux's reaction to Kearny are also of interest (*ibid.*).

[5] LeRoy R. Hafen and W. J. Ghent, *Broken Hand: The Life Story of Thomas Fitzpatrick, Chief of the Mountain Men* (Denver: The Old West Publishing Co., 1931), p. 131; cf. Hafen and Young, *Fort Laramie*, p. 139.

thousand in 1850, when the California Gold Rush was at its height.[6] Fort Laramie might have been equal to the growing danger had it been properly manned, but the size and composition of the force stationed there seemed more likely to incite than to prevent trouble. Fitzpatrick had recommended three hundred mounted men; the initial garrison consisted of but three companies, of which only two were mounted,[7] and there seemed little likelihood of improvement.

Under these circumstances Fitzpatrick, who as agent was the government official closest to the problem, concluded that the growing emigration could be protected only if a pledge could be secured from the Indians to keep the peace. This fit in nicely with the views of his superiors. For some time, Thomas H. Harvey, Superintendent of Indian Affairs at St. Louis, had been urging a grand council of the western Indians as a solution to the problems of dealing with them. In his report for 1847, he confidently wrote:

> The civilization of the Indians is no longer a mere speculative idea. Remove from among them bad white men and their contaminating influence, and substitute an efficient administration among them, aided by energetic missionaries, with the manual school system, and it will be found entirely practicable.

Moreover, the prospect of increased intertribal wars loomed as a threat to the security and development of the country:

> An opinion prevails that the buffalo must soon disappear, and thereby cut off the support of the several tribes that are at present subsisted by them. As they become scarce, hostile tribes will be necessarily forced to pursue them into each other's country, and deadly wars may be expected to follow. . . .[8]

Accordingly, in September, 1851, the tribes of the northern plains— or such of them as could be persuaded to come in[9]—assembled at Horse Creek, a few miles below Fort Laramie, for a great treaty council. Here, after eighteen days of feasting, smoking, visiting, and parleying,[10] the assembled tribes—including such intransigent enemies

[6] Statistics on emigration are only approximations. See Hafen and Young, *Fort Laramie*, pp. 120–130; Merrill J. Mattes, "Roubidoux's Trading Post at 'Scott's Bluffs,' and the California Gold Rush," *Nebraska History*, XXX (June, 1949), 108.

[7] Hafen and Young, *Fort Laramie*, pp. 140–143.

[8] Supt. of Indian Affairs, Report, October 29, 1847, 30th Cong., 1st Sess., Ex. Doc. 8, II, 840–841.

[9] For the difficulties involved in securing attendance at the council, see George E. Hyde, *Red Cloud's Folk* (Norman: University of Oklahoma Press, 1957), p. 65.

[10] An excellent description of the gathering at Horse Creek will be found in David Lavender, *Bent's Fort* (New York: Doubleday and Company, 1954), pp. 319–323.

as the Sioux and the Crows—agreed "to abstain in future from all hostilities whatever against each other, to maintain good faith and friendship in all their mutual intercourse, and to make an effective and lasting peace." They further agreed to lay off the country into separate tracts, with each tribe claiming a specific area for its own. Within these territories they recognized "the right of the United States Government to establish roads, military and other posts." And finally they bound themselves "to make restitution or satisfaction for any wrongs committed . . . by any band or individual of their people, on the people of the United States, whilst lawfully residing in or passing through their respective territories."

In return for all this, D. D. Mitchell (who had succeeded Harvey) and Fitzpatrick, Commissioners for the Government, pledged the United States to protect the Indians against depredations by whites and to distribute among the tribes the sum of fifty thousand dollars per year for fifty years, "in provisions, merchandise, domestic animals, and agricultural implements."[11]

The treaty was hailed by Father Pierre J. De Smet, the famed Jesuit missionary, as "the commencement of a new era for the Indians —an era of peace."[12] Actually, the "era of peace" ended when the conference broke up. The Sioux went back to fighting the Crows with their old enthusiasm, and everywhere there seems to have been a general disregard of the treaty, if not an actual hostility to it.[13] The arrangement was hardly adequate in the first place—as Mitchell put it, "fifty thousand dollars . . . [was] a small amount to be distributed among at least fifty thousand Indians"[14]—and then the Senate confused matters by reducing the period from fifty years to fifteen.[15] The traders were opposed to the treaty because they were afraid the

[11] C. J. Kappler, ed., *Indian Affairs, Laws and Treaties*, 58th Cong., 2d Sess., S. Doc. 319, II, 594–596. The signatory tribes were the Sioux, Cheyennes, Arapahoes, Crows, Assiniboins, Gros Ventres, Mandans, and Arickaras.

[12] Hiram Martin Chittenden and Alfred Talbot Richardson, eds., *Life, Letters and Travels of Father Pierre-Jean De Smet, S.J., 1801–1873* (New York: Francis P. Harper, 1905), II, 684.

[13] Hyde, *Red Cloud's Folk*, pp. 65–66.

[14] D. D. Mitchell to Com. of Indian Affairs, November 11, 1851, in Com. of Indian Affairs, *Annual Report*, 1851, pp. 27–29; cf. Lillian B. Shields, "Relations with the Cheyennes and Arapahoes in Colorado to 1861," *The Colorado Magazine*, IV (August, 1927), 148.

[15] For an interesting discussion of the Senate amendment, see Harry Anderson, "The Controversial Sioux Amendment to The Fort Laramie Treaty of 1851," *Nebraska History*, XXXVII (September, 1956), 201–220.

distribution of goods would hurt their business;[16] they had great
influence over the Indians and may have encouraged them in their
hostility. Some of the tribes on the upper Missouri even refused to
come in for their goods.[17]

Ironically enough—since the treaty's principal objective was to
protect the emigrant road—it was on the Platte that the main difficulties occurred. There was constant unrest among both red men and
white, and incidents enough to keep the embers of suspicion steadily
smoldering. Some of these incidents struck sparks which threatened to
set the prairies afire. One of the most serious was that of the Mormon
cow.

On August 17, 1854, a footsore cow belonging to a party of Mormons
en route to Utah strayed into a camp of the Brulé Sioux east of Fort
Laramie. The cow was killed and promptly eaten. The next day the
Mormons reported the incident to the commandant at Fort Laramie,
who sent a detachment of men under twenty-one-year-old John
Grattan, fresh from Vermont and West Point and as ignorant of the
Indians as he was contemptuous of them. The Bear (sometimes called
Conquering Bear), chief of the Brulés, tried to reason with the young
lieutenant, but the conversation had to be carried on through a drunken
interpreter, and Grattan, becoming impatient, withdrew and opened
fire on the encampment, killing The Bear. In the ensuing struggle,
Grattan and his entire force of twenty-nine men were killed.[18]

Throughout the next year the Sioux terrorized travelers on the
Platte Valley trail. In August, 1855, Brig. Gen. William S. Harney set
out from Fort Leavenworth with twelve hundred men and orders to
restore peace to the trail. At Ash Hollow on September 3, coming
upon Little Thunder's band of Brulés, Harney and his forces killed
one hundred and thirty-six and dragged the rest to Fort Laramie in
chains. From Fort Laramie he went to Fort Pierre, where he spent the
winter. On his own authority, he assembled the Sioux at Fort Pierre
and forced them to agree to a treaty restating their willingness to
permit white travel along the Platte Valley trail and agreeing to the
establishment of a military road from Fort Laramie to Fort Pierre.[19]

[16] See, e.g., John Tutt, Fort Laramie, to John Dougherty, April 14, 1852, Dougherty
papers, Missouri Historical Society.

[17] Hyde, *Red Cloud's Folk*, pp. 65–66.

[18] An excellent account of the Grattan massacre will be found in Lloyd E. McCann,
"The Grattan Massacre," *Nebraska History*, XXXVII (March, 1956), 1–25.

[19] For the Grattan massacre and the Harney campaign, see Hafen and Young,
Fort Laramie, pp. 221–246.

The Oglalas reacted to the Harney campaign by leaving the Fort Laramie region—the Bear people, or southern group, going south to hunt on the Republican, and the Smoke people going to the Powder River country to join the northern bands. The Bear people came up to the Platte occasionally to trade, but for the most part they remained well south of the river. There were traders in the Powder River country—even Agent Thomas S. Twiss had moved up to Deer Creek—so the northern bands who wanted to trade could avoid the Platte. Such warfare as both groups engaged in was intertribal (against the Pawnees and the Crows primarily).[20] Harney, it seemed, had cleared the emigrant road.

Thus when the Civil War broke out the tribes on the plains were generally peaceful. The riders of the Pony Express were seldom bothered, and the overland telegraph was completed in 1861 with relatively little interference. By the summer of 1863, however, the Platte road again was being ravaged by Indian attacks—stages ambushed, telegraph operators killed, emigrants murdered, ranches burned, cattle run off, and freighting caravans robbed. It was thought at first that this was the work of irresponsible bands and that the tribes would eventually disavow and punish the outlaws who were causing the trouble.[21] Perhaps so, but by 1863 pressures in the Platte country had built up to such a point as to give the Indians still living in the region—primarily the Cheyennes and the Arapahoes—cause for serious alarm. With the outbreak of the Civil War, the overland stage had been transferred to the Platte, and in 1861 daily service was established. Emigration continued apace—many, both North and South, went west to escape the draft—and the discovery of gold in Montana in 1862 created still additional pressures. Moreover, westerners, nervous as a result of the Minnesota massacres and convinced that the Indians would take advantage of the Civil War to launch a full-scale attack, were in no mood to wait and see whether the troublemakers eventually would be punished by their own people. The West wanted action, and wanted it fast.

In response to these pressures, the Government sent troops west as rapidly as the exigencies of the War in the South permitted. Escorts

[20] The best account of the activities of the Sioux during this period is in Hyde, *Red Cloud's Folk*, pp. 88–98. For Sioux-Pawnee warfare, see Alexander Lesser, *The Pawnee Ghost Dance Hand Game* (New York: Columbia University Press, 1933), pp. 1–33 *passim*.

[21] Edward B. Taylor, Report of Northern Superintendency, September 15, 1865, 39th Cong., 1st Sess., H. Ex. Doc. 1, pp. 581–584.

were provided for travelers west of Fort Kearny, Fort McPherson was established near the junction of the North and South Platte,[22] and the garrison at Fort Laramie was augmented by the 11th Ohio Cavalry. Unfortunately, for the most part the Army had to put its third team in the West. The men—some of whom were former Confederates, or "galvanized yanks"—were poorly disciplined, and many of the officers seemed both inexperienced and unable to learn.[23] Yet it is doubtful that even the wisest officers and best-disciplined men could have averted difficulty in the 1860's. The tide of western expansion was rolling into the Indians' last, best hunting grounds, and trouble was inevitable. By 1864 the Platte Valley was aflame with war, and before the year was out it was apparent that the sporadic attacks of 1863 had given way to a general, well-organized war.

In the spring of the year, Brig. Gen. Alfred Sully was sent out to clear the route to the Montana gold fields. Leading a well-equipped force of four thousand cavalry and eight hundred mounted infantry, he went up the Missouri to the Cannonball and thence across country to the Heart River and the Little Missouri. At Killdeer Mountain he encountered the Sioux, and in a three-day running battle sent them packing toward the south.[24] There seems to have been little need for the whole expedition. There were difficulties on the routes to Montana, to be sure, but even on the new Bozeman Trail, which ran through the heart of the Sioux country, they did not begin to compare with the trouble travelers were having in the Platte Valley.[25] Moreover, the expedition, by forcing the Powder River Indians to the south, was responsible for increasing the pressure in the Platte Valley, where conditions steadily were worsening.

[22] For a history of Fort McPherson, see Louis A. Holmes, *Fort McPherson, Nebraska, Fort Cottonwood, N.T.* (Lincoln: Johnsen Publishing Co., 1963).

[23] Hyde, *Red Cloud's Folk*, pp. 102–113, contains a vigorous denunciation of the Army in the West during this period.

[24] Grace Raymond Hebard and E. A. Brininstool, *The Bozeman Trail* (Cleveland: The Arthur H. Clark Co., 1922), I, 125–126.

[25] The Montana Historical Society has a number of typescripts of diaries of persons who went over the Bozeman Trail in 1864, and from these one gathers the impression that there were relatively few difficulties. See, e.g., "Diary of Cornelius Hedges on Journey to Montana from Iowa—1864"; E. A. Maynard, "My Trip to Montana," Montana Historical Society, Helena; "Diary of the Travels of Richard Owen from Omaha, Nebraska to the Gold Regions of Idaho," *ibid.* However, Benjamin Williams Ryan, "The Bozeman Trail to Virginia City, Montana in 1864: A Diary," *Annals of Wyoming*, XIX (July, 1947), 88–89, reports a skirmish with the Indians on Powder River.

On August 8, after a summer of scattered raids, the Cheyennes, Arapahoes, and Southern Sioux launched a series of concerted attacks on stage stations, emigrant trains, and ranches all the way from Denver to the Little Blue Valley in eastern Nebraska. Travel in the Platte Valley stopped completely and settlers in central Nebraska left their homes to find shelter at fortified points such as Grand Island.[26] Whatever the situation before, the attacks of August 8 seemed to provide convincing evidence that the Indians were disposed to wage a general war.[27] The military had been able to offer little effective resistance, and when a retaliatory blow was struck it was so inept that it increased rather than reduced the danger. The blow came in the form of an attack by Col. H. M. Chivington on a band of defenseless and peaceable Cheyennes who had assembled at Sand Creek, Colorado Territory, at the request of the commandant of Fort Lyon.[28]

Chivington's barbarous and ill-conceived action destroyed every hope of peace. Samuel G. Colley, agent for the Cheyennes, reported bitterly:

> I was in hopes our Indian troubles were over. I had 250 lodges near this place under my protection and that of Fort Lyon. All the chiefs and their families were in camp and doing all they could to protect the whites and keep the peace, when Colonel Chivington marched from Denver, surprised the village, killed one-half of them, all the women and children, and then returned to Denver. Few if any white men can now live if an Indian can kill them. . . .[29]

The Army, too, was aware of the Chivington problem. Maj. Gen. Henry W. Halleck, chief of staff, in telegraphing Bvt. Maj. Gen. S. R. Curtis, commanding the Department of the Missouri, to order an investigation, commented: "Statements from respectable sources have been received here that the conduct of Colonel Chivington's command toward the friendly Indians has been a series of outrages calculated to make them all hostile."[30]

[26] The best account of these troubles is Leroy R. Hagerty, "Indian Raids Along the Platte and Little Blue Rivers, 1864–1865," *Nebraska History*, XXVIII (September, December, 1947), 176–186, 229–260.

[27] See, e.g., John Evans, Supt. of Indian Affairs, *Annual Report*, October 15, 1864, 38th Cong., 2d Sess., S. Ex. Doc. 91.

[28] Stan Hoig, *The Sand Creek Massacre* (Norman: University of Oklahoma Press, 1961), contains a full account of the Chivington massacre and events leading thereto.

[29] December 20, 1864, *War of the Rebellion, Official Records*, Ser. I, XLVIII, Pt. 1, 511.

[30] Telegram, Halleck to Curtis, January 13, 1865, *War of the Rebellion, Official Records*, Ser. I, XLVIII, Pt. 1, 489. Curtis apparently was not as much concerned as

Whatever the cause—and it is difficult to overemphasize the effects of the Chivington massacre—it was apparent that the situation on the plains was daily growing more critical. The Indians continued their attacks on stage and telegraph stations, emigrant and supply trains. The mail service was paralyzed and the mountain communities actually faced shortages of food.[31] Unless the West were to be given up entirely, something would have to be done, and quickly.

To breathe life into the flagging campaign, Maj. Gen. Grenville M. Dodge was ordered to Fort Leavenworth to relieve the ineffectual Curtis, and Bvt. Maj. Gen. Patrick E. Connor, an Indian fighter in whom many westerners had great confidence, was moved from Salt Lake City to Denver to take command of a newly created District of the Plains.[32] Determined to solve the problem during the summer, Dodge made plans to take the offensive all the way from the Arkansas to the Yellowstone. For a variety of reasons, these plans failed to materialize. To facilitate the negotiations of the Doolittle Committee, conducting a Congressional investigation of the Chivington affair, the campaign against the southern Indians was called off before it got well under way. In the north, General Connor, plagued by poor communications, bad weather, low morale, and serious supply shortages, failed to achieve a decision in his much publicized Powder River campaign, and before he could pursue such minor successes as he had enjoyed, the Government decided to call the whole thing off in favor of negotiation.[33]

Sentiment for negotiation had long been building up. Most officials of the Bureau of Indian Affairs, looking forward to the day when the Indians would abandon their nomadic habits for a peaceful existence as farmers, favored it as the best means to that end. They argued that military pressure only increased the hostility of the tribes and that no lasting peace could be secured unless the Indians themselves could be convinced that their best interests would be served by maintaining the

---

Halleck. In response to Halleck's telegram, he wrote Col. Thomas Moonlight, commanding the District of Colorado: "I suppose a commission of officers better be ordered. . . . If the colonel did attack that camp, knowing it to be under the instructions of the commander at Lyon, or the Indian agent, he committed a grave error, and may have very much embarrassed our Indian affairs. But I have written General Halleck that such reports must be taken with great allowance . . ." (Curtis to Moonlight, January 13, 1865, *ibid.*).

[31] The best account of the attacks of the winter of 1864–65 is George B. Grinnell, *The Fighting Cheyennes* (Norman: University of Oklahoma Press, 1956), pp. 181–203.

[32] The changes in command are detailed in Fred B. Rogers, *Soldiers of the Overland* (San Francisco: The Grabhorn Press, 1939), pp. 146–153.

[33] *Ibid.*, pp. 244–246.

peace. This conviction, they reasoned, could be developed only by a policy of kindness in which the Government, through gifts and annuities, indicated its willingness both to compensate the Indians for the abandonment of their old ways and to assist them in the development of new ones. Contractors, and others who stood to gain from Indian business, were always ready to use their very considerable influence on behalf of the humanitarian ends of the Indian Bureau. The more cynical, pointing to the tremendous cost of maintaining troops on the plains, argued that it was cheaper to feed the Indians than to fight them. Most military men disagreed. They argued that the trouble lay in the vacillating policy of the Government, the mismanagement of the Indian Bureau, and the treaty system. As General Dodge put it:

> ... instead of dealing with these Indian tribes as with foreign nations, or recognizing them as treaty-making powers, the Government should regard and treat them as subjects, take care of and protect their rights and interests, make laws and prescribe rules for their government, compel obedience, punish offenses, and, in fact, adopt all necessary measures for their government, protection, support, and future welfare as subjects or wards.

But even this policy could not succeed until the Indians "were punished for the outrages they have committed, and made to feel, respect, and fear the power of the Government."[34]

Whatever the officers might think, the great expense of the military campaign, added to the financial burdens of the Civil War and the costs of Reconstruction, made many impatient; and when the expenditures failed to produce the desired results the impatience grew. When the Chivington massacre, which outraged public opinion throughout all of the East and part of the West,[35] brought only increased hostilities, the military was forced to accept a secondary role in Indian affairs. Senator J. R. Doolittle, who went west in the spring of 1865 as head of a commission to investigate Indian affairs and at whose instance the campaign against the southern tribes was called off, was given authority to make "such treaties and arrangements" as in his judgment would suspend hostilities and establish peace with the Indians.[36] Meanwhile, in the north, Governor Newton Edmunds of

[34] Dodge to Lt. Col. Joseph McBell, AAG, Department of the Missouri, November 1, 1865, *War of the Rebellion, Official Records*, Ser. I, XLVIII, Pt. 1, 344–346.

[35] Some westerners, it should be kept in mind, praised Chivington. E.g., the *Montana Post*, Virginia City, January 21, 1865, wrote: "Col. Chivington will be received on his return like David after the death of Goliath. His is the true way to settle Indian difficulties." See also Hoig, *The Sand Creek Massacre*, pp. 163–164.

[36] Telegram, Secretary of War E. M. Stanton to Doolittle, June 15, 1865, *War of the Rebellion, Official Records*, Ser. I, XLVIII, Pt. 2, 895–896.

Dakota Territory, long an opponent of the military policy, secured authority to treat with the Sioux on the upper Missouri. General Pope was dead set against talking to the Sioux until they had been chastised and flatly informed Edmunds that he would not cooperate in his venture.[37] Edmunds got the ear of the President, however, and in the end General Curtis and Bvt. Brig. Gen. Henry H. Sibley were appointed to the Edmunds ·Commission.[38] All told, the Commission negotiated nine treaties with as many different bands of Sioux, representing, it was claimed, more than sixteen thousand persons. Not one chief who had been engaged in hostilities along the Platte or in the Powder River country signed the treaty, and yet the Commission and the Bureau of Indian Affairs blandly announced that peace had been made with the hostiles and that they had agreed to allow the establishment of roads through their country.[39]

As instruments of peace, the Edmunds treaties were not worth the paper they were written on—to say nothing of the cost of their negotiation and implementation. But fraudulent as they were, they set a pattern of negotiation which, with luck, might be applied to the hostiles themselves. The Indian Bureau moved rapidly to see what could be accomplished with the hostiles, and in so doing it ran into *Makhpíya-lúta*, Red Cloud, the Oglala, already famous in war and soon to become known as a wily, obdurate negotiator, a man who for many epitomized the unsolved and seemingly insoluble Indian problem.

[37] Pope to Edmunds, May 3, 1865, *ibid.*, pp. 357–358.

[38] William S. Waddel, "The Military Relations Between the Sioux Indians and the United States Government in the Dakota Territory, 1860–1891" (Master's thesis, University of South Dakota, 1931), p. 37, describes the manner in which Edmunds acquired his authority.

[39] For a summary of the treaties, see *Report of the Commissioner of Indian Affairs for the Year 1866*, pp. 4–5; for a blistering comment on them, see Hyde, *Red Cloud's Folk*, pp. 134–137. See also Cora Hoffman Parrish, "The Indian Peace Commission of 1867 and the Western Indians" (Master's thesis, University of Oklahoma, 1948), pp. 20–21.

CHAPTER 2

The Rise of a Leader

On one occasion an old Indian at Pine Ridge was asked to tell something of the youth of Red Cloud. He simply shrugged his shoulders and said, "All great men were once boys." [1]

One is tempted to let it go at that, for though Red Cloud—*Makhpíya-lúta*, or *Makhpía-sha*, to his own people—was one of the most celebrated members of his race, better known among both red men and white than almost any other Sioux, his early life remains veiled in obscurity. We do not know for sure when or where he was born, who his parents were, or how he got his name. The white man's records are concerned only with his role as warrior, politician, diplomat, and above all, as a "problem"; the red man's, at best, are little more than tradition, reminiscence, and conjecture. The modicum of information we do have is contradictory and confused. We can only guess, therefore, at the facts of Red Cloud's early life, and how it was that he grew to a position of leadership among his people.

With respect to his birth, the authoritative *Handbook of American Indians North of Mexico*, edited by F. W. Hodge, states that Red Cloud was born in 1822 at the forks of the Platte River. The date but not the place is confirmed by the Dakota Winter Counts, which generally mention that Red Cloud was born during the winter of 1822. [2] In old

[1] Warren K. Moorehead, *The American Indian in the United States* (Andover: The Andover Press, 1914), p. 174.

[2] Cf. Garrick Mallery, "Pictographs of the North American Indians," Bureau of

age, Red Cloud told his friend Charles W. Allen that he was born in May, 1821, on the banks of Blue Water Creek near the spot where it empties into the Platte.[3] This statement to Allen—which is the most precise as well as the earliest date assigned to his birth—was but one of many assertions by Red Cloud that he was born in the Platte River country. In 1870, he told officials of the Department of the Interior in Washington that he was born at the forks of the Platte,[4] and in 1897 he told the Senate Committee on Indian Affairs: "There is a branch of the Platte River called Bluewater Creek. It is only 15 miles from where Harney killed some of the Rosebud Indians. I was born on that creek." [5]

George E. Hyde, eminent historian of the Sioux, disputes this assertion, declaring it to be "a political prevarication of the type this chief often indulged in. He said what he did hoping that it would convince the officials that he had a right to live on the Platte." Hyde insists that there is no evidence that the Sioux had gone as far south as the Platte by the time of Red Cloud's birth.[6] Hyde's evidence regarding the migrations of the Sioux is no more convincing, however, than Red Cloud's own statements—unless, of course, you accept his strictures on the old chief's character, which, on the whole, seem a little gratuitous.

The facts of Red Cloud's parentage are as obscure as those of his birth. The *Handbook* contents itself with saying that he was a member of the Snake family. Capt. James H. Cook, the noted frontiersman and

---

American Ethnology, *Fourth Annual Report*, pp. 111, 136–137; and Mallery, "Picture Writing of the American Indians," *ibid.*, *Tenth Annual Report*, p. 317.

[3] Addison E. Sheldon, "Red Cloud, Chief of the Sioux," Ms., Nebraska State Historical Society. This manuscript is based in part upon Red Cloud's reminiscences secured by Charles W. Allen, postmaster at Pine Ridge Agency, who, in the 1890's, persuaded the old chief to tell him stories of his life. Unfortunately, we do not know what happened to the originals. Sheldon used them as sources but he did not preserve their wording. In the absence of the originals, the manuscript is frustrating to use, but I have had recourse to it at times simply because there was nothing else. Moreover, it seems to be as reliable as most sources based on reminiscences or tradition—and, except for the winter counts and the results of archeological research, virtually all sources of Indian history in the period prior to white contact are so based. C. W. Allen, "Red Cloud, Chief of the Sioux," *The Hesperian*, I (November, 1895; December, 1895; January, 1896), 144–147, 173–178, 211–216, Allen's own account, is similar to Sheldon's.

[4] Transcript of Interviews with Red Cloud in Washington, June 3, 7, 1870, NARS, RG 75, LR, Red Cloud Agency.

[5] 55th Cong., 1st Sess., S. Ex. Doc. 61, pp. 9–12. The reference to Harney alludes to the Battle of Ash Hollow, 1855.

[6] George E. Hyde, *Red Cloud's Folk* (Norman: University of Oklahoma Press, 1957), p. 34.

one of Red Cloud's closest friends, identified his father only as "a big chief." [7] Hyde, using the authority of Red Cloud's nephew, He Dog, states that his father was Lone Man, a Brulé chief, and his mother was Walks-as-She-Thinks, a Saone and a sister of Old Smoke. [8] Sheldon, however, asserts that the chief's father was named Red Cloud, as was his father before him. [9] This is supported by American Horse, an Oglala chief and contemporary of Red Cloud. [10]

In the matter of the origin of the name, confusion is compounded with controversy. The *Handbook*, while admitting that the origin is in dispute, repeats Dr. V. T. McGillycuddy, long-time agent at Pine Ridge, to the effect that the name "Red Cloud" referred "to the way in which his scarlet-blanketed warriors covered the hillsides like a red cloud." George P. Belden provides an earlier account of the same version. His authority was a cook at Fort Kearny. [11] Hyde calls all this "childish nonsense," and he is equally contemptuous of the suggestion that Red Cloud was a family name. He prefers to find the name's origin in the ball of fire meteorite which passed over the Sioux country from west to east on the night of September 20, 1822. The meteorite was observed at Fort Snelling in Minnesota, and by tribes far out on the plains. Hyde cites a number of instances in which names were bestowed on boys in commemoration of this phenomenon. [12]

Hyde's explanation ignores the fact that among tribes which do not have the clan or gens system—as the Sioux do not—a child is not named ceremoniously and often does not have a name until adolescence or until he earns it. This would tend to support the Belden-McGillycuddy theory—which, incidentally, was held by many Oglalas—but Red Cloud had his name before he had many warriors in his entourage.

[7] James H. Cook, *Fifty Years on the Old Frontier* (New Haven: Yale University Press, 1923), p. 234. Royal B. Hassrick, *The Sioux: Life and Customs of a Warrior Society* (Norman: University of Oklahoma Press, 1964), p. 14, states: "In spite of . . . [his] distinguished career, Red Cloud, because of modest family background, was never able to command the kind of reverence among the Sioux which someone from an important family might have received." This is not documented, and is not supported by any evidence I have seen.

[8] Hyde, *Red Cloud's Folk*, p. 317.

[9] Sheldon, "Red Cloud," p. 4.

[10] E. S. Ricker, Interview with American Horse, Ricker Mss., Tablet No. 15, Nebraska State Historical Society.

[11] George P. Belden, *Belden, The White Chief* (Cincinnati and New York: C. F. Vent, 1871), p. 421.

[12] Hyde, *Red Cloud's Folk*, pp. 316–317. The meteorite was noted in the Dakota Winter Counts.

This brings us to Sheldon's rather overdrawn account, based apparently on information furnished by Red Cloud himself.

Sheldon, it will be recalled, contends that Red Cloud was a family name, pointing out that not only was it borne by the great chief's father and grandfather, but that it had been given to a cousin ten years his senior. The cousin was killed by the Pawnees at the age of twenty-six, and shortly thereafter a retaliatory party was organized. The young Red Cloud—sixteen years old and as yet unnamed—joined this party much against the wishes of his mother, who tried in every way to dissuade him from taking such a hazardous journey. When the boy failed to show up at the appointed time and place, the story went around that he had listened to his mother, that "his heart had failed him." Sheldon goes on:

> Much sport was being indulged in at his expense as the party started, when a shout arose from among the bystanding women, "he is coming."
> "Who is coming?"
> Then it seems to have occurred to the people of the village that the young man was without a name, when some one answered, "Red Cloud's Son!"
> "Red Cloud!" shouted another, and then the shout became general. "Red Cloud comes, Red Cloud comes!" and the young man dashed up, mounted upon a fine spotted horse decked with all the paint and feathers that belong to a warrior's equipment, leading a splendid bay. Amid shouts of congratulations he joined the party having thus ridden to his name. . . .[13]

None of the foregoing accounts is particularly satisfactory. Fortunately for this study, which is concerned primarily with Red Cloud's career vis-à-vis his white antagonists, the question is of small moment. Perhaps those who feel that such things are important in Indian history, should be referred to George E. Hyde's trenchant statement on the subject:

> If one thing is clear it is the fact that Red Cloud, Man-Afraid-of-His-Horse, and the other old chiefs were not much interested in the origin of their own names. It is their descendants who are attempting to ennoble the families by devising these queer explanations of the origin of the names. These tales all exhibit a lamentable ignorance of the customs and living conditions in the old days.[14]

Information about Red Cloud's boyhood is as inadequate and frustrating as that about his birth, parentage, and name. Dr. Charles

[13] Sheldon, "Red Cloud," pp. 4–5.
[14] Hyde, *Red Cloud's Folk*, p. 317.

A. Eastman, a full-blood Sioux, wrote in some detail about the early life of Red Cloud and other chiefs, largely from Indian sources, but his work has been generally discredited.[15] Doane Robinson, long-time secretary of the South Dakota State Historical Society, published an article, "The Education of Red Cloud," but this is merely an effort to apply specifically to Red Cloud general information about the education of young Sioux, and it is not particularly convincing.[16]

Perhaps in the end the best that one can do is to assume that Red Cloud's boyhood was spent much like that of other Sioux boys—that he was taught to hunt and to fight, to shoot and to ride—that, in short, he learned those arts which made the Sioux superb horsemen and difficult adversaries.

It is apparent, also, that year by year the young man's reputation grew. He took his first scalp on that expedition against the Pawnees.[17] Thereafter, he was always ready to join the war parties, and almost always distinguished himself. In later years, the old Oglalas who had fought by his side as young men proudly recounted his exploits.[18] American Horse once told of a raid on the Crows in which Red Cloud killed the boy who was herding the horses and ran off with fifty head, and the next day killed the chief of the pursuing Crows. He told also of a raid on the Pawnees in which Red Cloud killed four men with his own hand, and of another time when they were out against the Utes. A Ute, crossing a stream on a wounded horse, was about to drown. Red Cloud rode out, grabbed the man by the hair and brought him to shore. When they reached the shore, he took his knife, slashed off the Ute's scalp, and let him fall to the ground.[19] Incidents such as this support Captain Cook's statement that Red Cloud "was a terror in war with other tribes."[20] They also support the charge that cruelty was one of his marked characteristics.[21]

The exploit which perhaps did the most to establish young Red Cloud's position among his people was the killing of Bull Bear. For

[15] Charles A. Eastman, *Indian Heroes and Great Chieftains* (Boston: Little, Brown, and Co., 1920). For an estimate of Eastman, see Hyde, *Red Cloud's Folk*, p. 54.

[16] Doane Robinson, "The Education of Red Cloud," *Collections*, South Dakota Department of History, XII (1924), 156–178.

[17] Sheldon, "Red Cloud," p. 5.

[18] Cook, *Fifty Years on the Old Frontier*, p. 234.

[19] Ricker, Interview with American Horse (above, n. 10).

[20] Cook, *Fifty Years on the Old Frontier*, p. 234.

[21] See, e.g., Ricker, Interview with Dr. J. R. Walker, Pine Ridge, Nov. 21, 1906, Ricker Mss., Tablet No. 17.

years there had been bickering between the followers of Bull Bear, known as the Koyas, and the Bad Faces, who were under the leadership of Old Smoke. Red Cloud's mother, it will be recalled, was a sister of Old Smoke. Shortly after Red Cloud was born, his father died, and the boy was taken to live with the Smoke people. After the traders came to the Laramie region in 1834, both the Koyas and the Bad Faces—as well as most of the rest of the Oglalas—fell into the habit of spending most of their time in this region, where they soon became the victims of a bitter rivalry between the American Fur Company and its competitors. Long experience had taught the traders that their most potent weapon in the struggle for the Indian trade was liquor, and they used it without stint.[22] Under the influence of the white man's firewater, the Indians became irritable and quarrelsome, and petty differences often were magnified into sources of serious trouble. The difficulties between the Koyas and the Bad Faces were accentuated by Old Smoke's jealousy of Bull Bear, who, largely by the force of a domineering personality, was easily the most powerful chief among the Oglalas. Indeed, the Smoke people seem to have lost their identity when they followed Bull Bear to the Platte.[23]

The trouble came to a head in the fall of 1841 when a young Bad Face, much disliked by Bull Bear, stole a Koya woman. Determined on revenge and well fortified with firewater, Bull Bear led a force to the Bad Face camp on the Chugwater (a branch of the Laramie). The Koyas shot the father of the young man who had stolen the girl and apparently were prepared to wipe out the entire village. At this juncture, the young men, among whom was Red Cloud, charged the intruders. They opened fire on the Koyas, and a shot struck Bull Bear in the leg, bringing him to the ground. Red Cloud, never one to give quarter in a battle, rushed up and shot him through the head, killing him instantly. The young Bad Faces then dashed off to the Koya camp, but the demoralized Koyas had fled, leaving only a few women, children, and ponies as the spoils of battle.[24]

The killing of Bull Bear opened a breach that remained unhealed

---

[22] Hyde, *Red Cloud's Folk*, pp. 52 ff., is a particularly good discussion of the effect on the Indians of competition among the traders. For an account of the establishment of the various posts in the Laramie region, see Hafen and Young, *Fort Laramie*, pp. 17–94.

[23] Hyde, *Red Cloud's Folk*, p. 40.

[24] This version of the killing of Bull Bear follows Sheldon, "Red Cloud," pp. 31–34. Allen, "Chief of the Sioux" (above, n. 3), is similar. Hyde, *Red Cloud's Folk*, pp. 52–55, contains a different version, apparently based on the accounts of Francis Parkman and Rufus B. Sage; cf. Wade, ed., *Journals of Francis Parkman*, II, 461.

for many years. The Koyas, soon to become known as the Kiyuksas or Cut-Off band, reorganized under the leadership of Bull Bear's son, known as Bull Bear the Younger.[25] Gradually they drifted off to the south and east, occupying the lands between the Platte and the Smoky Hill, and ultimately associating themselves with the Southern Cheyennes. The Bad Faces moved to the Powder River country where they had close associations with the Northern Cheyennes and the Miniconjous. The associations were more geographical than political, and there is no hint of the formation of what might be called an alliance. Each little group acted independently, "and when the people came together in large camps to decide upon some important action, it was only to quarrel and separate again, each band going off hating all the others."[26] The bad blood between the Cut-Offs and the Bad Faces persisted throughout the wars with the whites, and even down into the reservation period, although Sheldon states that Red Cloud's action after the Treaty of 1868—in which he was recognized by the Government as chief of the Sioux—in elevating Little Wound, one of the Bear people, to a sub-chieftaincy did much to mend the breach.[27] Red Cloud may have furthered Little Wound's interest, but chiefs and sub-chiefs among the Sioux were not made by "appointment," and Little Wound, as we shall see, did not always act in concert with Red Cloud.[28]

In later years, Dr. William F. Girton, who knew the Sioux well, intimated that Red Cloud not only killed Bull Bear, but plotted the whole affair in the belief that with Bull Bear out of the way he might be in a position to assume the old chief's position of leadership.[29] There is

[25] Sheldon, "Red Cloud," p. 35. Hyde, *Red Cloud's Folk*, p. 55, states that Whirlwind was selected to succeed Bull Bear. There are two versions of the origin of the name "Kiyuksa." Sheldon, "Red Cloud," pp. 34–35, states that at the council held for the purpose of electing a new chief, the Koyas decided to change their name. "Several names were proposed and there was much discussion but at last an old man seeing a little garter snake wriggling through the grass, caught it up and holding it by the head and tail bit it in two in the middle, exclaiming, 'This shall be our name—Ki-ya-ksa,' meaning literally 'bitten in two;' the general translation however, is incorrectly 'cut-off' by which the band has ever since been known." According to Philip F. Wells, long a resident at Pine Ridge and well versed in Indian lore, "The band got this name from a young warrior chief of considerable following at the time, who had violated a pledge. He was sentenced by his followers to bite a live snake in two, which he did, and they all went by this name, growing into a prominent band" (Ricker, Interview with Philip F. Wells, Ricker Mss., Tablet No. 3, pp. 71–77).

[26] Hyde, *Red Cloud's Folk*, p. 55; see also pp. 85–86.

[27] Sheldon, "Red Cloud," p. 35.   [28] See below, pp. 273, 277.

[29] Ricker, Interview with William Girton, Ricker Mss., Tablet No. 18, pp. 69–70.

no denying that Red Cloud was ambitious, even at an early age,[30] but there is little basis for believing that his part went beyond firing the shot that killed the old chief. A young man of twenty—and accepting the earliest stated date for Red Cloud's birth, he would have been only that—was hardly in a position to aspire to leadership of the nature Bull Bear exercised. Nevertheless, it seems quite certain that Red Cloud came out of the affray with a greatly enhanced reputation; a short time later he was leading his first war party, a sure sign of growing importance in the tribe.

This expedition almost ended the young Red Cloud's career. It began as just another horse-stealing foray against the Pawnees, who were then camped on the Middle Loup River. But the Sioux underestimated their old foes and barely escaped annihilation. For a time there was fear that Red Cloud had been killed. He was found with an arrow through his body just below the ribs. One of the older men pulled it out, and somehow the bleeding was stopped before life ebbed away. By the next morning Red Cloud was able to eat a little and ride a short distance on a hastily made travois. Surprisingly, the Pawnees did not press their advantage, and the war party returned unmolested to the main camp. For two months the young warrior's life hung in the balance, but gradually he regained his strength and vigor. As long as he lived, however, the wound continued to trouble him.[31]

Shortly after his recovery, according to Sheldon, Red Cloud was married. Of all aspects of the chief's life, the domestic side is that about which we have the least—and the most confusing—information. Sheldon identifies the wife as Pretty Owl, and asserts that Red Cloud, unlike many other prominent Sioux, was monogamous.[32] These latter statements are contradicted by notes kept by Mrs. James H. Cook of an

[30] See, e.g., Mari Sandoz, *Crazy Horse* (New York: Hastings House, 1958), p. 134.

[31] Sheldon, "Red Cloud," pp. 35–39. Cook, *Fifty Years on the Old Frontier*, mentions what presumably was this wound.

[32] Sheldon, "Red Cloud," pp. 42–43. We do not know exactly when Pretty Owl died; she may even have outlived her famous husband. With respect to Red Cloud's monogamous life, Sheldon states that the young man had decided to take a second wife, Pine Leaf, about a month after he married Pretty Owl, but Pine Leaf not knowing of this and grieving over her loss of Red Cloud, committed suicide during the night of the marriage ceremony, and that "this occurrence made an impression upon Red Cloud that caused him to resolve never to have but one wife, and he never did" (*ibid.*, pp. 45–48). A generally unreliable source, Julia McGillycuddy, *McGillycuddy: Agent* (Stanford: Stanford University Press, 1941), pp. 206–207, describes an attempt by Red Cloud in the 1880's to take a young wife—an attempt which was foiled by Pretty Owl's threat to kill the intruder.

interview with one of Red Cloud's daughters, whose mother is identified as Good Road. These notes further state that Red Cloud had six wives and married the last of them when he was twenty-four years old.[33] All accounts I have seen state that Red Cloud had five children, although some identify them as a boy and four daughters, and others as two sons and three daughters. The only one of his children to acquire any standing in the tribe was Jack, who lived about sixty years, and who, though prominent, never achieved his father's position of leadership.[34]

In addition to fame as a warrior, Red Cloud seems to have enjoyed a fleeting reputation as a medicine man. Melvin R. Gilmore reports that in 1849–1850, when the Sioux were being ravaged by the Asiatic cholera, Red Cloud developed a concoction of cedar leaves which was said to have effected a cure. Apparently it was both drunk and used for bathing.[35]

Even if this story is true, Red Cloud's growing reputation rested not on his "medicine" but upon his success as a warrior—against the Pawnees, the Crows, the Utes, and the Shoshonis.[36] By the time he was forty, perhaps earlier, he was a leading warrior among the Bad Faces.

This brings us to the problem of Red Cloud's status among the Sioux. It is not an easy one to deal with. The whites were soon calling him a chief—Col. Henry E. Maynadier, for example, in March, 1866, wrote of Red Cloud and Spotted Tail, "they two rule the nation"[37]—but he was not a chief in the sense that the whites used the term. (Indeed, chieftainship as the whites persisted in thinking of it, involving a leader who could speak for his followers and direct their actions, probably did not exist among the Sioux before the treaty-making process began and the Government insisted that someone be able to talk for the tribe.)[38]

[33] Notes of an interview with one of Red Cloud's daughters by Mrs. James H. Cook, Cook Mss., Agate Springs Ranch, Agate, Nebraska. These notes were called to my attention by Mrs. Harold Cook, who kindly made them available to me.

[34] See below, pp. 339–340.

[35] Melvin R. Gilmore, "Uses of Plants by the Indians of the Missouri River Region," *Bureau of American Ethnology, 33rd Annual Report*, 1911–1912, p. 64. See also Hyde, *Red Cloud's Folk*, p. 64, and Stanley Vestal, *New Sources of Indian History, 1850–1891* (Norman: University of Oklahoma Press, 1934), p. 325.

[36] As an old man, Red Cloud on occasion went to the Shoshoni agency to visit. See below, pp. 291, 338–339.

[37] Maynadier to D. N. Cooley, March 9, 1866, *Report of the Commissioner of Indian Affairs, 1866*, pp. 207–208.

[38] For a good discussion of chieftainship among the Sioux, see Robert Pennington, "An Analysis of the Political Structure of the Teton-Dakota Tribe of North America," *North Dakota History*, XX (July, 1953), 146–147.

He may not even have been a "shirt-wearer" or head soldier. George Hyde states that Red Cloud was a "shirt-wearer" in 1865,[39] but Mari Sandoz, working largely from Sioux sources, writes that he was passed over in the Oglala ceremonials of that year. In part, this may have been because the Bad Faces, of whom Red Cloud was the recognized leader, failed to cooperate with the rest of the Oglalas, and Miss Sandoz indicates that he was recognized as a leading Oglala, shirt-wearer or not.[40] Reporting an interview with Clarence Three Stars, E. S. Ricker wrote:

> Three Stars says that Red Cloud was not elected a chief, but he was a head warrior, and because of his devotion to the cause of his people from the standpoint of patriotism, his ability to do and his courage and self assertion in acting for them he came to be recognized on account of his force of character and the need of it in their behalf, as their chieftain. The government also in the same way, by a sort of natural selection, recognized him as a chief.[41]

This is not very precise, but Three Stars' evidence seems to be as good as any available, and it may explain what happened.

In any event, it is clear that Red Cloud was one of those who were developing a stiffening attitude against the whites. This change, for all the Sioux, came slowly, and involved some curious distinctions in attitudes towards various groups of white men who invaded their country. They had welcomed the traders, and once the trading house was established at Fort Laramie, many of them forsook their old life to dwell almost permanently around the fort.[42] They became dependent upon the goods in the traders' wagons—the guns, the blankets, the beads, and especially the whiskey—and they even let their old warrior societies decay.[43] It is difficult to know when their attitude began to stiffen, but it can be traced to the coming of the emigrants. The Sioux continued to tolerate even the worst of the traders, and Red Cloud in later life frequently championed their cause; but from the beginning— partly, perhaps, as the result of the influence of the traders who saw a

[39] Hyde, *Red Cloud's Folk*, p. 97.

[40] Sandoz, *Crazy Horse*, pp. 174–178. For a discussion of Oglala organization, including shirt-wearers, see Clark Wissler, "Societies and Ceremonial Associations in the Oglala Division of the Teton-Sioux," *Anthropological Papers of the American Museum of Natural History*, XI (1916), 1–99.

[41] Ricker Mss., Tablet No. 25.

[42] See above, p. 20.

[43] Sandoz, *Crazy Horse*, pp. 174–175.

danger to their profits in the growing emigration [44]—they resented the emigrants, these strange, unfriendly men who brought no trade goods in their white-topped wagons and who filled the trail along the Platte with their women, their children, and their cattle. At first, the Sioux were content to stand by the trail each year and watch the wagons roll by, certain that soon the white man's country would be drained of its people; but as the whites continued to come, spreading disease and driving away the game, the Indians' resentment developed into hostility—hostility engendered, in part at least, by the timidity and churlishness of the emigrants. The cholera, brought west by the Forty-Niners, took a heavy toll in the Indian camps and compounded hostility with frustration. When the soldiers arrived to make sure that the roads would stay open, many among the Sioux began to feel that they must now resist. [45]

Organized resistance was more than a decade away but it might have developed earlier if the Sioux had possessed strong leadership. Without it they seemed, as Hyde put it, "incapable of breaking the spell that held them on the Platte, where they drifted here and there and every year became more entangled in the web of events which Fate seemed to be weaving for their ruin." [46] As we have seen, the Oglalas left the Platte Valley sometime after the Harney campaign of 1855, [47] and this removal reduced the pressures of white contact. Those pressures increased again with the discovery of gold in Montana, and particularly with the opening of the Bozeman Trail. The Oglalas seem to have remained peaceable throughout 1864, even though great struggles were going on both to the north and south of them, [48] but by the spring of 1865 they were ready to take the warpath. [49]

Although Red Cloud was one of those who advocated war in the spring of 1865, we have little specific information about either his activities or his influence. Hyde and J. W. Vaughn, using the authority of George Bent, who was with the Southern Cheyennes, state that Red Cloud and Young-Man-Afraid-of-His-Horse participated in the May council of the Sioux and Cheyenne soldier societies on the

[44] See Hyde, *Red Cloud's Folk*, pp. 61–63.

[45] For a moving account of the reaction of the Sioux to the coming of the whites, see Sandoz, *Crazy Horse*, pp. 3–6.

[46] Hyde, *Red Cloud's Folk*, p. 63.

[47] See above, p. 9.

[48] See above, p. 10.

[49] For a good discussion of the process by which the Oglalas were drawn into the war, see Hyde, *Red Cloud's Folk*, pp. 114–118.

Tongue River at which summer war plans were made, and that both men were in the Platte Bridge fight of July 25–26.[50] On the other hand, George Bird Grinnell, who also relied heavily upon Bent, does not mention Red Cloud in connection with either event.[51] Both agree, however, that Red Cloud took a leading role in the mid-August harassment near Pumpkin Buttes of James A. Sawyer's party which was surveying a wagon road from the mouth of the Niobrara River to Virginia City, Montana, and that it was he who made the decision to allow the party to continue on its way after they had given the Indians some food and tobacco.[52]

Whatever his precise role during the summer of 1865, by the spring of 1866, when the Government began to hope that the Sioux and Cheyennes would come in off the warpath and make peace, Red Cloud was a key element in those hopes.

[50] *Ibid.*, pp. 117–118, 123–126; J. W. Vaughn, *The Battle of Platte Bridge* (Norman: University of Oklahoma Press, 1963), pp. 37–39.

[51] George Bird Grinnell, *The Fighting Cheyennes* (Norman: University of Oklahoma Press, 1956), pp. 216–229.

[52] Hyde, *Red Cloud's Folk*, pp. 128–129; Grinnell, *Fighting Cheyennes*, pp. 208–209. Dull Knife apparently served as spokesman for the Cheyennes. Sawyer, in his official report, identifies the Indians only as "mostly Cheyennes and Sioux" (James A. Sawyer to James A. Harlan, Secretary of the Interior, January 19, 1866, 39th Cong., 1st Sess., H. Doc. 58, VIII, 22–23; cf. Elsa Spear Edwards, "A Fifteen Day Fight on Tongue River, 1865," *Annals of Wyoming*, X [April, 1938], 51–58). See also LeRoy R. Hafen and Ann W. Hafen, eds., *Powder River Campaigns and Sawyers Expedition of 1865* (Glendale: Arthur H. Clark Co., 1961), *passim*.

CHAPTER 3

"*A Lasting Peace*"—
Fort Laramie, 1866

The hope that the Powder River Sioux would come in and that peace might be secured set everyone atwitter. On January 16, 1866, Dodge telegraphed Pope: "Big Ribs has returned with a large delegation of Sioux Indians to Fort Laramie. The prospects of peace with the Sioux Nation good." Later that same day he got off another wire to Pope. "Please telegraph me what you consider I should say to the Sioux, what to promise them and what to demand from them," he asked. "They want to hear from me and demand to treat with a soldier. If we manage this matter right, we will settle all troubles in the North. . . ."[1] The next day Pope advised Secretary of the Interior James Harlan that he had instructed Dodge to arrange with the Sioux Indians to meet in council early in the spring, with commissioners appointed by the President, for the conclusion of a final treaty of peace.[2]

It seemed, indeed, that a miracle was about to happen; that the Sioux, who the year before had frustrated General Connor's efforts to open the Powder River road, were willing to call it quits and come in

[1] NARS, RG 75, LR, Upper Platte Agency.
[2] Telegram, Pope to Harlan, January 17, 1866, *ibid.*

for a conference; that the "successes" of the Edmunds Commission on the upper Missouri were to be repeated on the Platte.

The Army had taken the initiative in the events that had led up to this happy prospect[3]—and it had done so even though most high-ranking officers on the plains had been opposed to a treaty with the Indians until they had been soundly punished and made to feel the power of the Government. The reason for the abrupt change in attitude can be found in the Army's impossible position vis-à-vis the Indians: It had been unable to defeat them with the forces available in 1865, and now even those forces were to be reduced.[4] As Pope wrote Bvt. Maj. Gen. Frank Wheaton, assigned to command the District of Nebraska (which included the Platte and Powder River country), it was hoped that Connor's campaign would bring an end to hostilities, but "In any event . . . it is the purpose to return to a purely defensive arrangement for the security of the overland routes . . . and I desire especially, General, to impress upon you the absolute necessity of the strictest economy in your expenditures. It is essential that you return without delay to a peace basis, and to the economical arrangements which obtained before the rebellion. . . ."[5]

In a sense, conditions were about what they had been fifteen years earlier: with the Army unable to coerce the Indians, the only hope for peace and security lay in persuading the tribes themselves to keep the peace. Accordingly, when General Wheaton visited Fort Laramie in October he ordered Col. Henry E. Maynadier, commandant of the post and of the West Sub-District of Nebraska, to send messengers to the hostile Sioux "to inform them that other tribes were making peace and an opportunity would be offered them to do the same."[6] The prospects of success were not very bright; the mission was so dangerous

[3] As late as October 17, 1865, D. N. Cooley, Commissioner of Indian Affairs, wrote Vital Jarrot, newly appointed agent for the Indians of the Upper Platte: "I . . . do not think proper at this juncture . . . to give you other direction than that you repair at once to the agency at Fort Laramie and there await the further developments of the proceedings of the military authorities and be ready at any time to communicate and cooperate with them. The instructions given you by my predecessor to endeavor to negotiate a treaty with the tribes in question, you will hold in suspense until further advised . . ." (NARS, RG 75, LS, Upper Platte Agency).

[4] *War of the Rebellion, Official Records*, Ser. I, Vol. XLVIII, contains voluminous correspondence on the subject of reducing the military force on the plains.

[5] Letter, Pope to Wheaton, August 23, 1865, *ibid.*, Pt. 2, pp. 1206–1208.

[6] Maynadier to D. N. Cooley, Com. of Indian Affairs, January 25, 1866, NARS, RG 75, LR, Upper Platte Agency. A slightly edited version of this letter appears in Com. of Indian Affairs, *Annual Report*, 1866, pp. 204–206.

that no white man could be found who would try it. Maynadier, however, had finally persuaded Big Ribs, one of the "Laramie Loafers," and four others to undertake the mission.[7] After three months, during which Maynadier despaired of ever seeing his envoys again, they returned. They brought the great news that had so excited Dodge: Red Cloud would soon be in with some two hundred and fifty lodges. They also brought Swift Bear and his band of Brulés.[8]

Maynadier was elated. He told Swift Bear that his people could have peace if they wanted it—and peace would mean presents and the right to camp where they could get game and live quietly. All they had to do was to abstain from hostilities and commit no more depredations on the whites. Swift Bear was ready. He had wanted peace all along, but his people had been afraid to come into the fort for fear of being killed. Now they were glad to be able to come and get something for their women and children, who were naked and starving. After reporting all this to the Commissioner of Indian Affairs, Maynadier wrote:

> As soon as I have completed all arrangements with the Brules and Ogallalas, I will direct them to go to the Black Hills, 80 miles north, and establish their camps until Spring. This is their favorite ground, but for three years they have not been permitted to occupy it.

The Sioux were not the only ones with whom peace would be secured: "The band of Northern Cheyennes affiliate with the Sioux and I have good reason to suppose that they will ask to be allowed to come in." The Arapahoes were on the Big Horn and the Yellowstone, some seven hundred miles away, and could not be communicated with until spring, but, "If they should continue to be hostile, the aid of the Sioux can be obtained next summer to chastise them."[9]

All that spring the plains were bathed in hope. E. B. Taylor, head of the Northern Superintendency, who had been appointed president of the commission to treat with the tribes, busied himself at Omaha in preparation for the trip to Fort Laramie, where the final treaty was to be

[7] George E. Hyde, *Red Cloud's Folk* (Norman: University of Oklahoma Press, 1957), p. 137, erroneously identifies Big Mouth as the leader of the group. He was along, but, according to Maynadier (letter to Cooley, January 25, 1866), Big Ribs was the leader.

[8] Swift Bear was no catch. He had long been friendly, and apparently had been forced by the hostiles to leave the whites. He was ready to rejoin them as soon as he could be assured of protection against his own people (Hyde, *Red Cloud's Folk*, pp. 137–138).

[9] Maynadier to Cooley, January 25, 1866 (above, n. 6).

concluded.[10] And from Fort Laramie good news arrived steadily. On March 3, couriers from Red Cloud reported that he was on his way, and that he wanted the Northern Cheyennes and the Arapahoes to join the Sioux in making peace.[11] A few days later there was word from Spotted Tail, chief of the Brulés. He had had long association with the whites and for the most part had been friendly; alienated by mistreatment, however, for the past several years he had been with the hostiles.[12] Now he had with him the body of his daughter who had died from disease and exposure and who had begged to have her grave among those of the whites. Would Colonel Maynadier permit it? Maynadier, seeing an opportunity to bring Spotted Tail back into the fold, not only replied that he would permit it but rode out to meet the sorrowing chief and personally escorted him to his headquarters. He was honored that the great chief would entrust to him the remains of a daughter whom he knew Spotted Tail deeply loved. Everything would be prepared to have her funeral at sunset, "and as the sun went down it might remind him of the darkness left in his lodge when his beloved daughter was taken away; but as the sun would surely rise again, so she would rise, and some day we would all meet in the land of the Great Spirit." Maynadier also talked of peace, saying that in a few months commissioners from the Great Father would come to treat with the Indians and that everything would be settled on a permanent basis of peace and friendship. Spotted Tail was overwhelmed. Tears fell from his eyes, and as he grasped Maynadier's hand, he said:

> This must be a dream for me to be in such a fine room and surrounded by such as you. Have I been asleep during the last four years of hardship and trial and am dreaming that all is to be well again, or is this real? Yes, I see that it is; the beautiful day, the sky blue, without a cloud, the wind calm and still to suit the errand I come on and remind me that you have offered me peace. We think we have been much wronged and are entitled to compensation for the damages and distress caused by making so many roads through our country, and driving off and destroying the buffalo and game. My heart is very sad and I cannot talk on business; I will wait and see the counsellors the Great Father will send.

[10] The other members were: Maynadier, R. N. McLaren of Minnesota, and Thomas Wistar of Philadelphia. Charles E. Bowles of the Department of the Interior was secretary, and Frank Lehmer of Omaha, assistant secretary (Com. of Indian Affairs, *Annual Report*, 1866, p. 211).

[11] Telegram, Wheaton to Dodge, March 3, 1866, NARS, RG 48, LR, Dept. of the Platte.

[12] For an account of the relations of Spotted Tail with the whites, see George E. Hyde, *Spotted Tail's Folk* (Norman: University of Oklahoma Press, 1961), *passim*.

Maynadier was quite overwhelmed, too. The scene was "one of the most impressive" he ever saw, and its ramifications could hardly be overemphasized. "I attach great importance to this ceremony as rendering beyond a doubt the success of the efforts I have made to restore peace," he concluded. "It satisfies me of the entire trustiness of Pegaleshka, who is always with Red Cloud, and they two rule the nation. . . . The occurrence of such an incident is regarded by the oldest settlers, men of most experience in Indian character, as unprecedented, and as calculated to secure a certain and lasting peace." [13]

But this was not all that augured for peace. On March 12, four days after the funeral, Red Cloud himself arrived. He, Spotted Tail, and two hundred warriors were escorted into the fort with great pomp and ceremony for a council with Maynadier and Vital Jarrot, agent for the Indians of the Upper Platte. This was to be no ordinary conference. Maynadier would use the talking wires so that the chiefs could counsel with the man whom the Great Father was sending to Fort Laramie. At first, Red Cloud refused to enter the telegraph office, but finally his objections were overcome, and between the chiefs at Laramie and Taylor at Omaha, the telegraph carried messages of peace and good will. Taylor sent the following message to Red Cloud:

> The Great Father at Washington has appointed Commissioners to treat with the Sioux, the Arapahoes and Cheyennes of the Upper Platte, on the subject of peace. He wants you all to be his friends and the friends of the White Man. If you conclude a treaty of peace, he wishes to make presents to you and your people as a token of his friendship. A train loaded with supplies and presents cannot reach Fort Laramie from the Missouri River before the first of June and he desires that about that time be agreed upon as the day when his commissioners shall meet you to make a treaty.

The message was interpreted to the Indians and they seemed to approve. Taylor's next concern was whether peace would be imperiled by delaying the conference until June 1. Maynadier thought the chiefs would consent to wait:

> Red Cloud says now our horses are very poor and the Indians are scattered and will take some time to gather up all the Indians. Will do it as soon as possible. He will stay and hear what we have to say for two months and all will be quiet and peaceable.

To protect himself, Taylor stated that June 1 was the earliest possible date, and that he could more certainly have the presents with him if

[13] Maynadier to Cooley, March 9, 1866, Com. of Indian Affairs, *Annual Report*, 1866, pp. 207–208.

the conference were delayed until June 30. The chiefs apparently were agreeable. Maynadier reported, "Red Cloud says he will be five or six days going to his village but he will tell them how he has been received and will assemble all the Indians to come in here at the time the commissioners will be here. He knows now that everything is right and they can be better to wait and get traps and beaver between now and the first of June."[14]

Taylor was jubilant. That same day he wrote D. N. Cooley, Commissioner of Indian Affairs: "There is every reason to hope and no cause to doubt that a lasting peace will be easily effected with the hitherto hostile tribes of the Upper Platte, including the Sioux, Arapahoes and Cheyennes."[15]

That hopeful phrase, "a lasting peace," seemed to be the watchword on the plains during the spring of 1866. Apparently it was based solely on the supposition that with the disappearance of buffalo and other game the Indians had become so destitute that they were willing to agree to anything in return for presents and subsistence. Of their desperate condition, there was ample and heart-rending evidence; Maynadier wrote of Red Cloud's people: "Nothing but occular demonstration can make one appreciate their destitution, and near approach to starvation."[16] Of their willingness to agree to anything, the evidence was not quite so clear, although Maynadier thought them "thoroughly subdued" and believed that "the wildest spirit will only have to remember last winter to make him forgo any depredations."[17]

The critical question, of course, was the willingness of the Indians to permit the use of the Powder River road to Montana. Swift Bear and other friendlies had said that they would not object if they were paid for it.[18] This was a foregone conclusion; the friendlies had never really objected. The important consideration was the attitude of Red Cloud and others who had carried on the war during 1865. Apparently, no one bothered to find out what it was. At least, there is no record to show that at any time during the pre-conference parleys Taylor, Maynadier, or Jarrot intimated to Red Cloud that a condition of peace

[14] The telegrams are in NARS, RG 75, LR, Upper Platte Agency. For a further report of the conference, see Letter, Maynadier to Com. of Indian Affairs, March 24, 1866, NARS, RG 75.

[15] E. B. Taylor to Com. of Indian Affairs, March 12, 1866, NARS, RG 75, LR, Upper Platte Agency.

[16] Maynadier to Cooley, March 24, 1866 (above, n. 14).

[17] *Ibid.*

[18] Jarrot to Cooley, February 11, 1866, NARS, RG 75, LR, Upper Platte Agency.

and presents would be the maintenance of the Powder River road. Subsequent events would indicate that the failure was no mere oversight, but that it was based on the assumption that the best policy was to keep the Indians content with presents until the Commissioners could reach Fort Laramie, and then hope that their situation really was so desperate that they would agree to anything and could be held to that agreement with a minimum force.

The Army certainly operated on the assumption that a minimum force would be sufficient, and its plans for protecting the Powder River road consisted almost entirely of an administrative reorganization. In April, the Department of the Platte was established, with headquarters at Omaha, to afford, as Maj. Gen. William T. Sherman stated, "the best possible protection to . . . the region of Montana, and the routes thereto."[19] Almost simultaneously, Col. Henry B. Carrington was placed in command of a newly created "Mountain District" and ordered to take the Second Battalion of the 18th Infantry from Fort Kearny to occupy it.[20] No fighting was expected.[21] Carrington was a garrison officer with no experience in Indian warfare, and his little force consisted almost entirely of raw recruits—but more of that later.[22]

Meanwhile, in Omaha, Taylor busied himself with plans for the conference, and out at Fort Laramie, Maynadier and Jarrot tried to keep the Indians content until the Commissioners could arrive. It was not an easy task.

After the conference of March 12, Maynadier gave his visitors a small amount of powder and lead and urged them to go off and hunt until the council was called.[23] By May 8, however, they were all back at Fort Laramie, desperately in need of provisions. Maynadier wrote Cooley that they were "grateful and patient and have implicit confidence in promises made them,"[24] but Jarrot wired Taylor that the chiefs were very impatient and that if he wanted to meet with them he had better arrive by the twentieth or they would all have dispersed.[25]

[19] Sherman to James Wright, Secretary of the State of Iowa, April 7, 1866, in *Omaha Weekly Herald*, April 27, 1866.

[20] 50th Cong., 1st Sess., S. Ex. Doc. 33, p. 2.

[21] For the assumptions on which the Mountain District was created see Edward Jay Hawken, "The Military Problem on the Powder River Road, 1865–1868" (Master's thesis, University of California, 1938), pp. 35–38.

[22] See below, pp. 44–45.

[23] Maynadier to Cooley, March 24, 1866 (above, n. 14).

[24] Maynadier to Cooley, May 8, 1866, NARS, RG 75, LR, Upper Platte Agency.

[25] Jarrot to Taylor, *ibid*.

That, Taylor replied, was impossible, although he would try to reach Laramie by the twenty-sixth. Jarrot and Maynadier would have to explain the whole matter to the chiefs and hold them together if possible.[26]

Somehow—largely through issuing rations and making promises—the two men managed to keep the Indians in the vicinity of Fort Laramie. Taylor and his associates finally arrived on May 30, and on June 5 the conference that was to bring "a lasting peace" formally opened.

Taylor was pleased at the prospect. Red Cloud, Red Leaf, Man-Afraid-of-His-Horse, and Spotted Tail were all there, and many of their people were with them. There was also a small representation of Cheyennes and Arapahoes. Taylor told the assembled Indians that "it was not the desire of the government to purchase their country, but simply to establish peaceful relations with them and to obtain from them a recognition of the rights of the government to make and use through their country such roads as may be deemed necessary for the public service and for the emigrants to mining districts of the West."[27] Taylor was not being altogether candid. E. B. Chandler, who was sent to Fort Laramie in December, 1866, to investigate Indian problems there, wrote that Taylor had intimated to the Indians that travel on the Powder River road "should be confined strictly to the line thereof, and that emigrants and travellers generally should not be allowed to molest or disturb the game in the country through which they passed." This impossible promise, Chandler charged, "was well calculated, and . . . designed to deceive" the Indians.[28]

The next day, Red Cloud, Spotted Tail, Red Leaf, and Man-Afraid-of-His-Horse responded for the Sioux. We have no direct translation of their speeches, but Taylor—apparently lacking candor in his reports to his superiors as well as in his representations to the Indians[29]—wrote that they

> were marked by moderation and good feeling; and at the conclusion of the council, these chiefs expressed the opinion that a treaty could and would be made and asked for time to bring in their people who are encamped in

[26] Telegram, Taylor to Jarrot, May 9, 1866, *ibid.*

[27] Unless otherwise indicated, for the early part of the conference I am following Letter, Taylor to Cooley, June 9, 1866, *ibid.*

[28] Letter, Chandler to H. B. Denman, January 13, 1867, 40th Cong., 1st Sess., S. Ex. Doc. 13, pp. 11–12.

[29] *Ibid.* Chandler reported that the Indians "were indisposed to comply" with the request that they permit the use of the Powder River road.

large numbers on the head waters of White River, some fifty or sixty miles distant from Fort Laramie. . . . The general feeling of all these tribes is very conciliatory and friendly and I have no doubt that satisfactory treaties will be effected with each and all, if their attendance can be secured.

Taylor, of course, had the chiefs who really counted, and while it was a truism of Indian negotiations that you had to get common consent of all to make an agreement binding, it is difficult to see how much more authoritative representation could have been achieved than was already present. Nevertheless, he agreed to adjourn the council until the thirteenth, meanwhile persuading Colonel Maynadier to issue supplies to the chiefs for the trip to White River and to keep on issuing rations to the Indians who remained behind.[30]

On the thirteenth the council convened again—and immediately exploded. The charge was unwittingly detonated by the arrival of Colonel Carrington who for the past several weeks had been plodding up the Platte bringing troops to provide protection for travelers who would use the road that was to be opened by the peace commissioners at Fort Laramie.

There are many stories as to just what happened on that fateful day;[31] and, in the absence of a detailed, official report, various writers have accepted uncritically one or another of the yarns. Perhaps the most spectacular account is Cyrus Townsend Brady's. Brady has it that Carrington approached in advance of his troops and was introduced to the members of the council. "Red Cloud, noticing his shoulder straps, hotly denounced him as the 'White Eagle' who had come to steal the road before the Indian said yes or no. In full view of the mass of Indians who occupied the parade ground he sprang from the platform under the shelter of pine boughs, struck his tepees and went on the warpath."[32] This story is to a degree confirmed by Frances C. Carrington, who wrote:

Red Cloud himself, it is officially reported, when he saw Colonel Carrington at his visit to the council, upon his arrival threw his blanket around himself, refused an introduction, and left with this announcement of his

[30] The Commissioners were somewhat embarrassed because their own treaty supplies had not arrived. They had to depend on the supplies the Army had available at Fort Laramie, and apparently these were not very good: "the shoulders and hard bread are damaged and scarcely fit for issue," Taylor complained.

[31] Stanley Vestal, *Warpath and Council Fire* (New York: Random House, 1948), p. 92, incorrectly gives the date of arrival as June 16.

[32] Cyrus Townsend Brady, *Indian Fights and Fighters* (Garden City: Doubleday, Page and Company, 1904), pp. 7–8.

views, pointing to the officer who had just arrived, "The Great Father sends us presents and wants us to sell him the road, but White Chief goes with soldiers to steal the road before the Indians say Yes or No.[33]

Frances Carrington was then the wife of Lt. George W. Grummond of Colonel Carrington's command. She arrived at Fort Laramie after Carrington, and was not an eyewitness of the events she described, but she included in her story a reminiscence of William Murphy, an enlisted man in the 18th Infantry who apparently was an observer:

Our expedition reached Fort Laramie on June 13, in time for Colonel Carrington to participate in the council being held with Red Cloud, Man-Afraid-of-His-Horses, [*sic*] and other Indian chiefs to secure the Indian's consent to the construction of a road and the erection of the promised forts, the Indians protesting vigorously against this.

Red Cloud made a dramatic and effective speech. He claimed that the Peace Commissioners were treating the assembled chiefs as children; that they were pretending to negotiate for a country which they had already taken by Conquest. He accused the Government of bad faith in all its transactions with Indian tribes.

In his harangue to the Indians he told them that the white men had crowded the Indians back year by year and forced them to live in a small country north of the Platte and now their last hunting ground, the home of their people, was to be taken from them. This meant that they and their women and children were to starve, and for his part he preferred to die fighting rather than by starvation.

Red Cloud promised that if the combined tribes would defend their homes they would be able to drive the soldiers out of the country. He said it might be a long war, but as they were defending their last hunting grounds they must in the end be successful.

The powwow continued for some time, until finally the hostile Sioux under Red Cloud withdrew, refusing to have any further counsel or to accept any presents.[34]

Margaret I. Carrington, who was with her husband, describes the council chamber, but writes only in a general way of Red Cloud as protagonist, saying that he and Man-Afraid-of-His-Horse "made no secret of their opposition," and that Red Cloud, "with all his fighting men, withdrew from all association with the treaty-makers, and in a very few days quite decidedly developed his hate and his schemes of mischief."[35]

[33] Frances C. Carrington, *Army Life on the Plains* (Philadelphia: J. B. Lippincott Company, 1910), pp. 46–47.

[34] *Ibid.*, pp. 291–292

[35] Margaret I. Carrington, *Ab-Sa-Ra-Ka; or, Wyoming Opened* . . . (Philadelphia: J. B. Lippincott Company, 1890), pp. 78–79.

Finally, there is the tale that when Red Cloud was informed that the soldiers had come to open the Bozeman Road, he "leaped from the platform, caught up his rifle, saying, 'In this and the Great Spirit I trust for the right.'"[36]

Whatever happened—and Murphy's story seems to be the most viable—it was apparent that with the withdrawal of Red Cloud, the great council at Fort Laramie was not going to bring peace to the plains. Later, officials of the Indian Bureau would blame Carrington's arrival in the midst of negotiations for the failure of the treaty,[37] but Taylor went ahead as though nothing had happened; he had been heard to say that he had been sent by the Government to make peace and it should be accomplished if made with but two Indians.[38] Treating the departure of Red Cloud and Man-Afraid-of-His-Horse as of no consequence, he busied himself with signing up the friendly chiefs. They were not a very impressive lot: Big Mouth and Blue Horse, of the Laramie Loafers; Swift Bear, who had been with the hostiles only against his wishes; and a few others of even less importance.[39] The biggest catch of all was Spotted Tail, but even he had a long history of friendship with the whites. Moreover, his people, preferring to live south of the Platte, had little interest in the Powder River country. Essentially, of course, what it boiled down to was that those who had no stake in the Powder River area were perfectly willing to sign a treaty granting a right-of-way through it. The inducements, it might be noted, were substantial: annuities in the amount of seventy thousand dollars a year for twenty years.[40] Taylor also managed to sign up a few Cheyennes—they were to get fifteen thousand dollars a year for twenty

[36] Doane Robinson, "Tales of the Dakota," *South Dakota Historical Collections*, XIV (1928), 536–537.

[37] Com. of Indian Affairs, *Annual Report*, 1867, p. 269. Carrington's arrival was unfortunate, and it undoubtedly triggered Red Cloud's flare-up. It is difficult to believe, however, that Red Cloud was prepared at this time to sign a treaty permitting a road through the Powder River country—notwithstanding the hopeful estimates of the effect of the winter's privations on the spirit of the Sioux. Moreover, Taylor and Cooley were fully aware of Carrington's proposed movement and there seems to be no record of any protest on their part against it. Carrington probably would have been beyond Fort Laramie when the council began had not his departure from Fort Kearny been delayed by General Cooke because of the weather and the condition of his command (Brig. Gen. Philip St. George Cooke to Maj. Gen. W. T. Sherman, April 26, 1866, NARS, RG 98, LS, Dept. of the Platte).

[38] 40th Cong., 1st Sess., S. Ex. Doc. 13, p. 12.

[39] The names of the chiefs who signed will be found in *ibid.*

[40] *Ibid.*, pp. 11–12.

years[41]—and on June 29 he triumphantly wired the Commissioner of Indian Affairs: "Satisfactory treaty concluded with the Sioux and Cheyennes. Large representations. Most cordial feeling prevails."[42]

It was not long, however, before disturbing rumors began to filter back to Washington. The Indians, it seemed, were as hostile as they had been before the treaty, and travel on the Powder River road was as hazardous as it had ever been. The Commission, back in Omaha, telegraphed President Johnson: "Satisfactory treaties of peace have been concluded with the Upper Platte Sioux and Cheyennes at Fort Laramie. Contradictory reports are without foundation."[43] Still the rumors would not down. The *Omaha Herald*, which was frequently quoted by eastern papers on Indian affairs, wrote on July 27:

> Much doubt prevails concerning the late so-called Treaty with the Indians at Fort Laramie. From all we can gather we do not believe it will prove of the least value to our interests. Long-winded speeches and the deal out of powder and lead, bogus kinnikinnick, small trinkets, rations, and other similar traps, to a set of blind and antiquated Indian chiefs, amounts to nothing. . . . We have ceased to hope anything from the Laramie abortion. . . .

By August 22, Cooley was calling on Taylor, now in Washington, for a special report.[44] Taylor had a ready answer. There had been depredations, but these were the work of "about two hundred fifty Bad Faces, composed of Oglalas and desperate characters of various tribes of Sioux . . . [who] refused to recognize the authority of the tribe." The depredations would not lead to a general war, and alarmist news to the contrary could be attributed "to the fertile imagination of some enterprising gentleman who cares more for army contracts than the public peace."[45]

Taylor continued to play on this theme. In his report as president of the treaty commission, he wrote that "although the Indians, as might naturally be expected, were reluctant to allow the proposed road to pass through the best of their remaining hunting grounds, yet when

[41] *Ibid.*

[42] Telegram, Taylor to Cooley, June 29, 1866, NARS, RG 75, LR, Upper Platte Agency.

[43] Telegram, E. B. Taylor, R. N. McLaren, Thomas Wistar, to the President of the United States, July 16, 1888, *ibid.*

[44] Cooley to Taylor, August 22, 1866, NARS, RG 75, LS, Upper Platte Agency.

[45] Taylor to Cooley, August 23, 1866, NARS, RG 75, LR, Upper Platte Agency.

informed of the wishes of the government, and of our disposition to give a liberal equivalent, they acquiesced in our request in a full council. . . ." Those who were trying to cast doubt on the permanence of the treaty were "evil-disposed persons, actuated by malice or cupidity."[46] In his annual report as head of the Northern Superintendency, written October 1, he took cognizance of the difficulties with Red Cloud, but hardly in a way to describe what had actually happened:

> A band numbering perhaps three hundred warriors, headed by Red Cloud, a prominent chief of the Ogalallahs, refused to come in. They are known as Bad Faces, and are composed of the most refractory and desperate characters of the tribe, who, having committed some serious infraction of the internal policy of the tribe, have congregated themselves together, and refuse to be governed by the will of the majority.

They were of no consequence, because "at least seven-eighths of the Ogalallahs and Brulés" had signed the treaty.[47]

Moreover, it soon appeared that even these "refractory and desperate characters" would be brought to terms. On October 18, M. T. Patrick, who had succeeded Jarrot as agent for the Indians of the Upper Platte, wired Taylor that Red Leaf's band was on the way to Fort Laramie to make peace, and that Red Cloud himself was coming in to sign the treaty.[48] On November 19, Patrick solemnly announced that he was "about to move Red Cloud, Red Leaf and Man-Afraid-of-His-Horses, Sioux bands of Indians, now north of Powder River, to Mr. Bordeaux Ranche, nine miles east of this place, and there negotiate a peace treaty with them."[49] Taylor, the same day, advised his superiors in Washington that all hostile bands of Sioux wanted to sign the treaty.[50]

This continuing optimism evidently made an impression at the highest levels of government. On December 5, President Johnson, in his annual message on the state of the union, assured the country that

[46] Com. of Indian Affairs, *Annual Report*, 1866, pp. 208–209. This report was signed only by Taylor and Maynadier. McLaren and Wistar, the other commissioners, seem to have taken little part in the proceedings, although, as was noted, they did join with Taylor in signing the telegram of July 16 to the President.

[47] *Ibid.*, p. 211.

[48] NARS, RG 75, LR, Upper Platte Agency.

[49] Patrick to Maj. James Van Voast, Fort Laramie, November 19, 1866, NARS, RG 48, LR, Dept. of the Platte.

[50] Telegram, Taylor to Lewis V. Bogy, November 19, 1866, NARS, RG 75, LR, Upper Platte Agency.

the Indians had "unconditionally submitted to our authority and manifested an earnest desire for a renewal of friendly relations."[51]

A little more than a fortnight later, these same Indians inflicted upon Colonel Carrington's command the worst defeat the Army had yet suffered in Indian warfare.

[51] James D. Richardson, comp., *Messages and Papers of the Presidents, 1789–1897* (Washington: Government Printing Office, 1897), VI, 454.

CHAPTER 4

Carrington Reaps the Whirlwind

While Commissioner Taylor was busy assuring the country that the Treaty of Fort Laramie was a complete success, Colonel Carrington was at work trying to carry out his particular responsibilities in connection with opening the Powder River road. It was obvious that he would not have an easy task; shortly after Red Cloud and Man-Afraid-of-His-Horse pulled out of the Laramie council, some of the friendly chiefs who signed the treaty warned that those who wanted to venture into the Powder River country should "go prepared and look out for their hair." [1] Carrington was aware of possible difficulties, but he was cautiously—and characteristically—optimistic. On June 16, the day before he left Fort Laramie, he wrote:

> All the commissioners agree that I go to occupy a region which the Indians will only surrender for a great equivalent; even my arrival has started among them many absurd rumors, but I apprehend no serious difficulty. Patience, forbearance, and common sense in dealing with the Sioux and Cheyennes will do much with all who really desire peace, but it is indispensable that ample supplies of ammunition come promptly. [2]

[1] 40th Cong., 1st Sess., S. Ex. Doc. 13.

[2] Carrington to Lt. Col. H. G. Litchfield, AAAG, Dept. of the Platte, June 16, 1866, 50th Cong., 1st Sess., S. Ex. Doc. 33, p. 6. This document, which was not published until 1887, contains the testimony and accompanying papers presented by Colonel Carrington to an investigating committee at Fort McPherson in the spring of 1867. It is the basic source for virtually all accounts of Carrington's activities in

It was not long before the pattern of his problem began to evolve. He reached the Little Piney, where he planned to build his principal post, without having seen an Indian, although while he was at Fort Reno a herd of mules belonging to the sutler had been driven off. The next day he had a message from the Cheyennes asking, "Does the white chief want peace or war?" Carrington replied that he wanted peace, of course: "The Great Father at Washington wishes to be your friend, and so do I and all my soldiers. I tell all the white men that go on the road that if they hurt Indians or steal their ponies I will follow and catch them and punish them. I will not let white men do hurt to the Indians who wish peace." After two sleeps they could come and talk.[3]

On July 16, the Cheyenne chiefs came in as directed—Dull Knife, Black Horse, and several others. They wanted peace, but they were afraid of the Sioux, and the Sioux, they warned Carrington, were prepared to fight.[4] Red Cloud and Man-Afraid-of-His-Horse were the leading spirits. They were full of talk about the treachery of the whites at the Fort Laramie council, and they were insisting that the Cheyennes unite with them to prevent the whites from using the road. They were camped on the Tongue River, about a day's march away, and they were now engaged in a Sun Dance. Red Cloud had five hundred warriors with him, and he had sent some of them south toward the Powder River to cut off further travel. The Cheyennes wanted none of this, but they were weak and could not fight the Sioux. If Carrington would give them provisions, they would make a lasting peace and go wherever he told them, "away from the Sioux and away from this road." Also, they would let him have one hundred of their young men to help fight the Sioux. Carrington declined the offer; he had "men enough to fight the Sioux, but if they [the Cheyennes] kept good faith with the white men and had trouble with the Sioux near by . . . [he] would help them." He gave them some presents of food and tobacco and sent them away, armed with certificates of good behavior.[5]

1866—a good, recent example is Dee Brown, *Fort Phil Kearny: An American Saga* (New York: Putnam, 1962)—and unless otherwise indicated, citations in this chapter are from it.

[3] Carrington to "The Great Chief of the Cheyennes," July 14, 1866.

[4] I have not been able to find a satisfactory reason for the change in the attitude of the Cheyennes from their warlike attitude of a year earlier.

[5] Carrington's testimony. Margaret I. Carrington, *Ab-sa-ra-ka, Home of the Crows* (Philadelphia: J. B. Lippincott Co., 1869), pp. 110–118, gives a detailed account of the conference. Another good account of the council will be found in J. Cecil Alter, *James Bridger* (Salt Lake City: Shepard Book Co., 1925), pp. 445–446. Bridger served as a guide for Carrington.

The Cheyennes went from Carrington's camp to the nearby trading house of Pete Gasseau. During the evening a party of Sioux chiefs rode up to ask what the white chief had told them and whether he was going back to the Powder River. When Black Horse answered that he was not going back, but was going on, and that he had told them "to tell ... all the Indians in the Tongue River Valley that the Great Father had left at Laramie presents for them all, and they could get them whenever they went and signed the treaty," the Sioux unslung their bows, whipped the Cheyenne chiefs over their backs and faces, and left. The humiliated Cheyennes then fled, warning Gasseau that he had better take refuge with Carrington to avoid being killed by the Sioux. Gasseau tried to heed their advice but was killed the next morning while enroute. Later in the day, the Sioux attacked one of Carrington's wagon trains, running off one hundred and eighty-seven head of stock, killing two men, and wounding two others;[6] and from that time forward, as Hebard and Brininstool put it, "there was never a day, never an hour, but that the Indians attacked, or would have attacked if not properly watched...."[7]

Meanwhile, Colonel Carrington went doggedly ahead with the work of building his headquarters post, named Fort Philip Kearny.[8] After a reconnaissance of some sixty-six miles, he selected a high plateau between the forks of the Piney, and here he built a stout stockade of pine. Despite the aggressive attitude of the Indians, he worked rapidly, and in ten days had hauled a thousand logs from the nearby pineries.[9] By the end of the month he could assure General Sherman, "I am located so as to defy thousands when I get ammunition."[10] His pride in the post was justified. Bvt. Maj. Gen. W. B. Hazen, on a tour of inspection, called it the best stockade he had ever seen, "except one built by the Hudson's Bay Company."[11] To provide protection

[6] Carrington's testimony.

[7] Grace Raymond Hebard and E. A. Brininstool, *The Bozeman Trail* (Cleveland: Arthur H. Clark Co., 1922), I, 271.

[8] The post was named for Maj. Gen. Philip Kearny, who lost his life in the Civil War. It usually was referred to as "Fort Phil Kearny," and, as was true of Fort Kearny on the Platte, named for Maj. Gen. Stephen Watts Kearny, the name was frequently misspelled, even in official correspondence. See *ibid.*, I, 272, and James C. Olson, "Along The Trail," *Nebraska History*, XXIX (September, 1948), 294–295.

[9] Carrington to Litchfield, August 9, 1866, NARS, RG 98, LR, Dept. of the Platte.

[10] Carrington to Sherman, July 31, 1866, *ibid.*

[11] Hazen to Litchfield, August 29, 1866, *ibid.* The *Army and Navy Journal*, IV (November 24, 1866), 215, contains a description of the post. See also Hebard and Brininstool, *Bozeman Trail*, I, 263–296.

further along the road, Carrington sent Bvt. Lt. Col. N. C. Kinney with two companies of infantry ninety-one miles north to the Big Horn, where on August 12 they began the construction of Fort C. F. Smith.[12] This would complete the fortifications Carrington had planned for the Montana road. The three posts were located so as to command the most hazardous section of the route,[13] and Carrington was confident that they would provide more than adequate bases from which to carry out his mission.

He was not as confident of his men and material—and with good reason. His total force consisted of only eight companies of infantry, mostly recruits from the general depot. He had managed to mount two hundred of them, but, as he sorrowfully observed, "infantry make poor riders,"[14] and by fall his horses were so broken down that they were next to useless. Most of the troops were armed with old, muzzle-loading Springfields, inferior at best to the Indian arms, and wholly unsuited for use while mounted. There was so little ammunition that the recruits could not even engage in target practice; at one time the command at Fort C. F. Smith was reduced to ten rounds per man, that at Fort Reno to thirty, and that at Fort Phil Kearny to forty-five.[15] Including himself and his staff, Carrington had only twelve officers in his entire command, and two of these were detached for recruiting duty.[16] The officers were brave enough, but none of them had had experience in Indian fighting, and all of them had contempt for their foe. There was much talk about "having Red Cloud's scalp,"[17] and Lt. Col. W. J. Fetterman was heard to remark that given eighty men he could ride through the whole Sioux nation.[18]

Carrington called repeatedly for reinforcements, but with little effect. Brig. Gen. Philip St. George Cooke, aging commandant of the newly created Department of the Platte and Carrington's immediate

[12] Edgar I. Stewart, *Custer's Luck* (Norman: University of Oklahoma Press, 1955), pp. 36–39, contains a good brief account of the construction of all the Bozeman forts. On Fort C. F. Smith, see also Merrill J. Mattes, *Indians, Infants and Infantry: Andrew and Elizabeth Burt on the Frontier* (Denver: Old West Publishing Co., 1960), pp. 123–171.

[13] There was little danger around Fort Laramie, and once travelers got north of the Big Horn they were in the land of the Crows, who, if not above a little stealing, were in no mood to join their hereditary enemies the Sioux in open hostilities.

[14] Carrington to Litchfield, July 30, 1866.

[15] 40th Cong., 1st Sess., S. Ex. Doc. 13, p. 63.

[16] Carrington to Litchfield, July 30, 1866.

[17] Frances C. Carrington, *Army Life on the Plains* (Philadelphia: J. B. Lippincott Co., 1910), p. 132.

[18] Struthers Burt, *Powder River* (New York: Farrar and Rinehart, 1939), p. 127.

superior, seems to have attached no great sense of urgency to these calls.[19] Requisitions for ammunition and supplies were routinely processed to higher headquarters, and the garrison at Fort Laramie, normally a four-company post, was maintained at twelve companies, even though there was not a hostile Indian for miles around. On August 9, Lt. Gen. William T. Sherman, commanding the Military Division of the Mississippi, ordered the posts in Carrington's district supported "as much as possible" and announced that a regiment was on its way from St. Louis.[20] This was more than Carrington had requested. He had maintained all along that if he had left Fort Laramie with two battalions (sixteen companies) instead of one he could have accomplished his mission.[21] As it developed, however, these reinforcements were not to arrive in time to do him any good.[22] All he received was a company of cavalry and another of infantry, temporarily detached from Fort Laramie. Both consisted entirely of raw recruits—the cavalrymen did not even know how to mount![23]

Carrington maintained that Cooke could have given him adequate support during the summer of 1866 from the twelve companies available at Fort Laramie. Cooke, however, seems to have had other plans for these troops. Maj. James Van Voast, who had succeeded Maynadier as commandant at Fort Laramie, was anxious to undertake a winter campaign against the hostiles,[24] and Cooke had given tentative approval, although he later withdrew it because he felt that Van

[19] For an account of the establishment of the Department of the Platte and the designation of Cooke as commandant, see Robert G. Athearn, *William Tecumseh Sherman and the Settlement of the West* (Norman: University of Oklahoma Press, 1956), pp. 38–39.

[20] Telegram, Cooke to Carrington, August 9, 1866.

[21] See, e.g., Carrington to Litchfield, August 19, 1866.

[22] See below, p. 51.

[23] He also received authority to enlist fifty Indian scouts, but this did not help him much either. As has been noted, he turned down a Cheyenne offer to furnish men. Later, he rejected a similar offer from the Crows, preferring instead to use Pawnees or Winnebagoes who had served under him the year before at Fort Kearny on the Platte. George E. Hyde, *Red Cloud's Folk* (Norman: University of Oklahoma Press, 1957), p. 144, calls this preference "almost unbelieveable foolishness." In justice to Carrington, however, it should be pointed out that when the Cheyenne offer was made he did not have the authority to accept it; and by the time he learned of the Crow offer he had already dispatched an agent to eastern Nebraska to enlist Pawnees or Winnebagoes. Moreover, as he testified later, "the necessary delay in procuring their arms would defeat the object of their employment" (Carrington's testimony).

[24] Van Voast to Litchfield, November 2, 3, 21, 1866, NARS, RG 98, LR, Dept. of the Platte.

Voast's force was too small and the risks too great.[25] In sharp contrast, Cooke seems to have been sure that Carrington, with a much smaller force than Van Voast, could conduct a successful winter campaign. On September 27 he telegraphed Carrington that it would be impossible to assume the offensive during the current season unless Carrington could manage to surprise Red Cloud in his winter camp by using infantry. "Two or three hundred infantry," he added, "with much suffering, perhaps, might thus accomplish more than two thousand troops in summer."[26] On November 12 the order was repeated, with the reminder that Carrington had "a large arrears of murderous and insulting attacks by the savages upon emigrant trains and troops to settle."[27]

Cooke seems to have had little confidence in either Carrington or his mission. In mid-July he sent General Hazen out to inspect the Mountain District. He was not at all certain that the posts were being located at the best possible sites, and told Hazen to avail himself "of the information of residents best acquainted with the military view of the subject" and recommend any necessary changes.[28] Cooke even vacillated between abandoning and continuing Fort C. F. Smith on the Big Horn.[29] Hazen reassured him with respect to the soundness of the general plans for the Mountain District—including Fort C. F. Smith—but he probably confirmed any doubts Cooke may have had about Carrington. He wrote from Fort Phil Kearny:

> Indian depredations, so far, have been of a desultory, thieving nature. With care, nothing should have occurred, and the whole character of affairs here has been greatly exaggerated, resulting greatly from the fault of not communicating promptly and regularly with department headquarters, Col. Carrington appearing to think only of building his post.[30]

Cooke's doubts were reinforced by the irregularity with which reports were received from Carrington, and at one time he even threatened a

[25] Cooke to Bvt. Maj. Gen. J. A. Rawlins, C/S Washington, December 27, 1866, 40th Cong., 1st Sess., S. Ex. Doc. 13, pp. 29–30.

[26] Telegram, Cooke to Carrington, September 27, 1866, *ibid.*, p. 31.

[27] Litchfield to Carrington, November 12, 1866.

[28] Litchfield to Hazen, July 18, 1866, NARS, RG 98, LS, Dept. of the Platte.

[29] See, e.g., Hazen, Fort Reno, to Carrington, August 20, 1866. To have abandoned the post on the Big Horn, as Carrington remarked in his testimony, would have surrendered the purpose of his entire movement and subjected him "to compliance with the very demands the Sioux had made." As Hyde, *Red Cloud's Folk*, p. 144, puts it: "the result would have been a road leading from Fort Laramie to Piney Fork and there ending in the heart of a hostile Indian country."

[30] Hazen to Litchfield, August 29, 1866, NARS, RG 98, LR, Dept. of the Platte.

court-martial. The difficulty, however, lay with the mails rather than with Carrington. He reported regularly enough, but the mails just did not get through on schedule; the same courier who brought the threat of a court-martial brought an acknowledgment that the reports in question had been received.[31] More serious than their irregularity was the conflicting nature of the reports. All through the summer and fall, they alternated between complacency and concern. On August 9, for example, Carrington complained that "there is at Laramie, as elsewhere a false security, which results in immigrants' trains scattering between posts and involving danger to themselves and others . . . it is a critical period with the road and many more outrages will injure it." Yet he wanted to make it clear that the situation, though critical, was not desperate; and if the immigrants would arm properly and keep together, they could get through with little trouble.[32] By September 17, with attacks mounting in ferocity, concern seemed completely over-come by complacency. In a letter made public by Cooke's headquarters, Carrington announced:

> No women nor children have been captured or injured by Indians in the District since I entered it. No train has passed without being cared for and protected to their full satisfaction. No post has been besieged or so threatened that it could not drive off offensive Indians and at the same time protect itself. While more troops are needed, I can say that I am in the heart of the hostile district, and that most of the newspaper reports are gross exaggerations. I gather and furnish you as requested all the bad news, neither coloring nor disguising facts.[33]

Colonel Carrington has been much berated for his failures in 1866,[34] and his conflicting reports give some justification for the strictures leveled against him. In justice, however, it should be pointed out that no one unequivocal statement could describe the situation in the Mountain District. The press could charge that "the lines of travel are wholly interrupted to Montana, and the military garrisons are in a condition of virtual siege,"[35] and the depredations gave color to the charges. At the same time, it could be shown that much of the difficulty was the result of carelessness and foolishness—as Carrington insisted—

[31] Carrington's testimony.

[32] Carrington to Litchfield, August 9, 1866, NARS, RG 98, LR, Dept. of the Platte.

[33] Carrington to Litchfield, September 17, 1866, in *Omaha Weekly Herald*, October 5, 1866.

[34] Cf. Hyde, *Red Cloud's Folk*, pp. 143–149; Stanley Vestal, *Warpath and Council Fire* (New York: Random House, 1948), pp. 92–106.

[35] *Omaha Weekly Herald*, October 19, 1866.

and that a number of trains, unescorted and not particularly well defended, did get through with relatively little trouble.[36]

Central to the confusion was uncertainty about the status of the treaty and the nature of the opposition. Officially, the treaty was a success, binding all except a small and inconsequential band of "refractory and desperate characters" who would soon be brought to terms.[37] From the beginning, Carrington had had little faith in the treaty, but he scrupulously avoided any action which might detract from its effectiveness. Without knowing what it provided or with whom it had been negotiated, this was difficult at best. A rather plaintive letter of June 30 illustrates the confusion in the situation as well as in Carrington's mind:

> The Indian commissioners before they adjourned passed a resolution which they sent me by the courier who brought my mail, advising me that a treaty had been signed by them and left at Laramie, with certain presents for Arapahoes and Cheyennes, requesting me to inform such tribes within my command of the fact that they might go and sign and receive their presents. Having received no copy of that treaty and no names of chiefs who have already signed it, I do not see how I can give to the Indians (if they wish peace) any indication of what they are to sign or receive. The commissioners announce "a satisfactory treaty" with the "Ogallallas" and Brule "bands," and yet some of those Sioux are in my command, hostile.
>
> The Indians who are about me, who are most interested in this route and who carry barbarity as far as almost any savage precedent, either have not signed a treaty or fight me with the donations of the United States. . . .
>
> If "Red Cloud" and "The-man-afraid-of-his-horses" signed the treaty they have the power to restore much stolen stock. The commissioners did all they could, but, as when I left I wrote you so, since my impressions derived from closest scrutiny of the Indians I saw are confirmed that I shall have to whip the Indians, and they have given me every provocation. My policy has been to treat them kindly . . . but the present status is one of war. . . .[38]

Had Carrington been willing to believe the Cheyennes in his interview of July 16, he would have had no uncertainty about the relationship of Red Cloud and Man-Afraid to the treaty. As the summer wore

[36] See, e.g., Robert G. Athearn, ed., "From Illinois to Montana in 1866: The Diary of Perry A. Burgess," *Pacific Northwest Quarterly*, XLI (January, 1950), 46–65; George W. Fox, "George W. Fox Diary," *Annals of Wyoming*, VIII (January, 1932), 580–601; James C. Olson, ed., "From Nebraska City to Montana, 1866: The Diary of Thomas Alfred Creigh," *Nebraska History*, XXIX (September, 1948), 208–237.

[37] See above, pp. 38–39.

[38] Carrington to Litchfield, July 30, 1866.

on and as their position was made increasingly clear, he appears to have acted more and more without reference to what was or was not accomplished at Fort Laramie. Even so, he persisted in the belief that he faced nothing that approached an organized, general war. The Indians' only interest, he assured Cooke on August 29, was in plunder, and while the young warriors were "repugnant to the surrender" of the Powder River road, there was "no possibility . . . of any Indian alliance that will bring on a general war."[39] In a sense, Carrington was right. There would be no grand alliance to prosecute a general war—the Indians did not fight that way; and among these particular Indians, there were some who were inclined to sign the treaty and see what presents could be obtained. Red Leaf sent emissaries to Fort Laramie,[40] and even Man-Afraid appears to have considered going back for further negotiations.[41] Red Cloud seems to have been the only hostile leader who remained unshakeable in his determination to carry on the war to the bitter end.

By fall, Carrington recognized the nature of Red Cloud's opposition, but he had little fear of it. "Red Cloud," he solemnly asserted, "does not comprehend the idea of a year's supplies, nor that we are now prepared to not only pass the winter, but next spring and summer, even if he takes the offensive."[42] Carrington was not alone in his contempt for Red Cloud. Major Van Voast told Red Leaf's emissaries to tell Red Cloud that he did not want him to come in,

> That I wanted him to stay and fight this winter. . . . That Red Cloud had made fools of a good many, and that if any began to see they were fools, and wanted to leave Red Cloud, they could come. But, the soldiers had given them all summer to make peace—but they had no ears—that soon the soldiers would give them ears. That all who wanted to fight must join Red Cloud—that all who were friendly must leave him at once.[43]

Van Voast discounted a report from Jim Bridger that the Sioux were organizing for war and were trying to form alliances with other tribes in the north: "I do not believe much of what Mr. Bridger says. He exaggerates about Indians."[44]

[39] Carrington to Litchfield, August 29, 1866.

[40] See above, p. 39.

[41] Carrington to Litchfield, November 5, 1866.

[42] *Ibid.*, November 9, 1866.

[43] Van Voast to Litchfield October 18, 1866, NARS, RG 98, LR, Dept. of the Platte.

[44] Note appended to Letter, Bridger to W. G. Bullock, November 5, 1866, *ibid.*

Higher headquarters seemed to share the feeling that there were no really serious problems on the Powder River road. The perfunctory way in which Cooke dealt with the problem has been mentioned. General Sherman (who had urged the officers with Carrington to take their wives along) [45] at no time seemed to feel that the operation was more than routine, even though he did send a regiment to reinforce Colonel Carrington's command. General Grant also was quite unconcerned, and he was sure that additional troops were not needed in the West. As late as December 11 he wrote Secretary Stanton:

> A standing army could not prevent occasional Indian outrages, no matter what its magnitude. It is to be hoped, however, that the number of these outrages will materially diminish from this time forward, until travel will finally be as safe through the "Far West" as through the old States. . . .[46]

The outrages were not to "diminish," at least for a while. On December 6, five days before General Grant penned his optimistic estimate of the situation, the Indians had attacked a wood train about two miles from Fort Phil Kearny. Such attacks were nothing new; the Indians had been mounting them regularly for weeks. This time, however, the escorting troops panicked, and it was all the officers could do to save them from annihilation. The Indian victory was not spectacular, but it certainly justified the belief that with luck and good management they could overpower any force sent out against them.[47] There was great fear that they might attack Fort Phil Kearny itself, but evidently they felt that its defenses would be too much for them. So for several days they contented themselves with menacing forays in the vicinity of the fort, just waiting for an opportunity to strike a telling blow. That opportunity came on the cold winter morning of December 21, and they made the most of it. It came when Lt. Col. W. J. Fetterman and eighty men—the number with which Fetterman had said he "could ride through the whole Sioux nation"—were sent out to relieve a beleaguered wood train. Ignoring Carrington's orders to stay with the

---

[45] Frances C. Carrington, *Army Life on the Plains*, p. 61. For accounts of the distaff side of the expedition, see this and Margaret I. Carrington, *Ab-sa-ra-ka*.

[46] *Omaha Weekly Herald*, January 18, 1867.

[47] Carrington's report of the battle will be found in Carrington to Litchfield, December 6, 16, 1866, NARS, RG 98, LR, Dept. of the Platte; the report of Lt. Col. W. J. Fetterman, who had command of the relief forces, will be found in Fetterman to Capt. W. H. Bisbee, December 7, 1866, 40th Cong., 1st Sess., S. Ex. Doc. 13, pp. 37–38, that of Lt. G. W. Drummond, in Drummond to Adj., Fort Phil Kearny, December 9, 1866, NARS, RG 98, LR, Dept. of the Platte; see also Carrington's testimony.

train, Fetterman dashed off in pursuit of the Indians—and to his death, taking his eighty men with him.

The Fetterman massacre—the greatest disaster to befall the Army in the West up to that time—provided a tragic climax to a season of indecision and uncertainty. Its causes, its details, and its implications have been much debated. One aspect of the debate concerns Red Cloud's participation. In old age, he asserted that he was present and had command of the forces fighting Colonel Fetterman.[48] The monument erected on the site of the battle proclaims the same thing. Much Indian testimony, however, has it that Red Cloud, far from leading the Indians on that fateful day, was not even present.[49] As Hyde suggests, this is difficult to credit, but Indian fighting being what it was, there is little hope of discovering just where the truth lies. For the purposes of this account, it is unimportant. Whoever was in command of the Indians, the Fetterman massacre demonstrated that the problem posed by Red Cloud's refusal to sign the treaty was far from solved.

Reaction to the massacre was immediate and vigorous. As soon as General Cooke heard the news, he relieved Colonel Carrington as commanding officer of the Mountain District and ordered Bvt. Brig. Gen. Henry W. Wessells, enroute to Fort Phil Kearny with the long-awaited reinforcements, to take command.[50] "Colonel Carrington," Cooke wrote in justification of his action, "is very plausible; an energetic, industrious man in garrison; but it is too evident that he has not maintained discipline and that his officers have no confidence in him."[51] When Carrington's official report of the disaster came in, Cooke, in his own hand, dashed off a bitter endorsement to Sherman's headquarters:

> This report put off for thirteen days, until notice of his being relieved was received. That seems to have given color to it.
> An officer of high rank in letter of January 7th from Phil Kearny gives us the following version:

[48] James H. Cook, *Fifty Years on the Old Frontier* (New Haven: Yale University Press, 1923), pp. 228–230.

[49] See, e.g., N. B. Buford to Secretary of War, June 6, 1867, 40th Cong., 1st Sess., S. Ex. Doc. 13, p. 59; George B. Grinnell, *The Fighting Cheyennes* (New York: Charles Scribner's Sons, 1915), p. 225; Hyde, *Red Cloud's Folk*, p. 149; Vestal, *Warpath and Council Fire*, pp. 64–68.

[50] Telegrams, Cooke to Bvt. Maj. Gen. John A. Rawlins, C/S, December 26, 1866, Cooke to Wessells, December 27, 1866, NARS, RG 98, LS, Dept. of the Platte.

[51] Cooke to Rawlins, December 27, 1866, NARS, RG 98, LS, Dept. of the Platte, also in 40th Cong., 1st Sess., S. Ex. Doc. 13, pp. 29–30.

The men, as usual when the wood train was known to be corraled by the Indians, rushed out helter-skelter, some leaping over the stockade, which is in no place over eight feet high. What probability there is of their having had with them a proper supply of ammunition you can judge. No reinforcements ever assured Colonel C. failed to be sent. . . .[52]

Sherman's reaction was equally vigorous. Upon hearing of the disaster, he wired Cooke:

Of course, this massacre should be treated as an act of war and should be punished with vindictive earnestness, until at least ten Indians are killed for each white life lost. You should prohibit all leaves of absence and put whom you please in command of the sub-districts. But, at once, there should be organized a strong force under your best commander and sent into the Indian country to avenge with terrible severity this and past acts of the Sioux. You must be fully prepared now, but if you need more men, let me know. If Indians can act in Winter, so can our troops and so they will if properly led. You should not allow the troops to settle down on the defensive, but carry the war to the Indian camps, where the women and children are, and should inflict such punishment that even Indians would discover they can be beaten at their own game. Of course, it is useless to find fault with officers there, but the truth should be ascertained and reported, but this should not delay the punishment of the Indians as a people. It is not necessary to find the very men who committed the acts, but destroy all of the same breed.[53]

Cooke responded by forwarding plans for a punitive campaign to begin about March 1, and by reiterating the need for more troops.[54] Although Cooke earlier had looked forward sanguinely to the prospect of a winter campaign, there was doubt now that even the March 1 date would be feasible. Lt. Col. Innis N. Palmer, who had succeeded Major Van Voast as commandant at Fort Laramie, wrote that his command, consisting largely of recruits, was wholly unprepared for a strenuous

[52] Endorsement, Cooke, January 22, 1867, to Carrington to AAG., Dept. of the Platte, January 3, 1867, NARS, RG 98, LR, Dept. of the Platte, also in 49th Cong., 2d Sess., S. Ex. Doc. 97, pp. 1–6. Later Cooke apologized to Carrington, saying: "The country was greatly excited, and the government very urgent so I endorsed the papers for transmission by one of my staff. I do not remember which. I can do nothing more than to express my deep pain at what transpired. My memory recalls nothing of the details, except that it was hurried off to Gen. Sherman, and you must take my regrets as sincere, and my congratulations, that in the end you were finally vindicated" (Hebard and Brininstool, *Bozeman Trail*, I, 340–341; cf. Otis E. Young, *The West of Philip St. George Cooke* [Glendale: The Arthur H. Clark Company, 1955], pp. 346–353).

[53] Sherman to Cooke, December 28, 1866, NARS, RG 98, LR, Dept. of the Platte.

[54] Cooke to AAG, Military Division of the Missouri, January 3, 1867, NARS, RG 98, LS, Dept. of the Platte.

campaign: "half of our cavalrymen would fall off their horses in a charge, more than half the horses would run away with the men at a firing drill."[55] In any event, before Cooke's plans for a winter campaign could be developed he was relieved as commanding general, Department of the Platte, to be succeeded by Maj. Gen. Christopher C. Augur.[56] Sherman wrote Augur that he hoped Congress would give the Army exclusive management of the Indians, but, pending that, he should consider all Sioux near the Powder River and Yellowstone as hostile and "punish them to the extent of utter extermination if possible."[57]

Congress, however, was in no mood to turn the Indians over to the Army. It had called for an investigation of the Fetterman massacre even before Sherman had expressed the hope that it would do so, and the President had appointed a commission consisting of Generals Alfred Sully, J. B. Sanborn, and N. B. Buford, Col. E. S. Parker, Judge J. F. Kinney, and G. P. Beauvais. Although it was dominated by military men, it was to work under the direction of the Secretary of the Interior.[58] Officials of the Department of the Interior, it should be noted, responded to the Fetterman massacre with as much vigor as did the military. For weeks they had been trumpeting the success of the Fort Laramie negotiations, assuring the country that Red Cloud and the other hostiles were not important, and that they would soon be in to sign the treaty anyway. The Fetterman massacre had exploded both assertions, and Interior as well as War was obliged to do some explaining.[59] Their explanation was very simple: the policy of the military was the cause of all the trouble.

[55] Palmer to Cooke, January 18, 1867, NARS, RG 98, LR, Dept. of the Platte.

[56] Hebard and Brininstool, *Bozeman Trail*, I, 340, contains a statement from Carrington, dated June 6, 1902 (repeated in Young, *Cooke*, p. 352) which declares that Sherman relieved Cooke because of his endorsement to Carrington's report of the Fetterman disaster. This obviously is incorrect, because Cooke was relieved before the endorsement was sent, and, according to Robert G. Athearn, Sherman, far from relieving Cooke, was not even consulted on the action, which was taken by General Grant (Athearn, *William Tecumseh Sherman and the Settlement of the West*, pp. 99–100). Cooke, incidentally, objected bitterly to being relieved, and in a letter to the Adjutant General demanded a court of inquiry. Calling attention to his former successes in fighting Indians, he wrote: "I was allowed to do little in the late war; it happened that a youthful Commander in Chief, his classmates and favorites, jealously excluded me from all important opportunity . . ." (January 19, 1867, NARS, RG 98, LS, Dept. of the Platte).

[57] Sherman to Augur, February 19, 1867, NARS, RG 98, LR, Dept. of the Platte.

[58] 40th Cong., 1st Sess., S. Ex. Doc. 12.

[59] Perhaps the most positive recognition that the treaty had failed was a rather plaintive letter, dated December 26, 1866, in which M. T. Patrick, agent for the

Although Special Agent E. B. Chandler had charged that the terms of the treaty and particularly Taylor's technique in presenting it had been largely responsible for the ill will which drove the Indians into hostility,[60] Lewis V. Bogy, Commissioner of Indian Affairs, in transmitting the report to the Secretary of the Interior generally ignored Chandler's charges—even though he had expressed himself as opposed to the ratification of the treaty[61]—and declared instead that the hostility could be traced to the aggressive attitude of high-ranking officers on the plains and their refusal to court the friendship of the Indians. He even charged that the Indians involved in the fight of December 6 actually were well disposed and had been attacked while on a friendly visit to Fort Phil Kearny! Specifically, the root of all the evil was an order issued by General Cooke, July 31, prohibiting the sale of arms and ammunition to the Indians:

> such orders are not only unwise, but really cruel, and therefore calculated to produce the very worst effect. Indians are men, and when hungry will, like us, resort to any means to obtain food; and as the chase is their only means of subsistence, if you deprive them of the power of procuring it, you certainly produce great dissatisfaction. If it were true that arms and ammunition could be accumulated by them to war against us, it certainly would be unwise to give it to them; but this is not the fact. No Indian will buy two guns. One he absolutely needs; and as he has no means of taking care of powder, he necessarily will take, when offered to him, but a very limited quantity. It is true that formerly they hunted with bows and arrows, . . . but to hunt successfully with bow and arrows requires horses, and as the valleys of that country are now more or less filled with white men prospecting for gold and silver, their means of subsisting their horses have passed away, and they now have but few horses.[62]

Colonel Fetterman and his men were killed by arrows, shot by well-mounted Indians.[63] Moreover, Bogy's reaction is curious in view

---

Indians of the Upper Platte, recommended that the goods which had been reserved for Red Cloud and Man-Afraid-of-His-Horse, "who are now with the hostile Indians and refuse to come in . . . be given to those Indians that have remained peaceable and are camped at this post and vicinity, as they have kept their treaty faithfully and are in need of clothing" (Patrick to H. B. Denman, Supt. of Indian Affairs, Omaha, December 26, 1866, NARS, RG 75, LR, Upper Platte Agency).

[60] See above, p. 34.

[61] Bogy to Augur, January 14, 1867, NARS, RG 75, LR, Dept. of the Platte.

[62] Bogy to Secretary of the Interior, February 4, 1867, 40th Cong., 1st Sess., S. Ex. Doc. 13, pp. 7–11.

[63] Vestal, *Warpath and Council Fire,* pp. 96–106.

of the language of Cooke's order: "the Commissioner of Indian Affairs has instructed Indian agents to prohibit traders from selling . . . [arms and ammunition] to the Indians, and all commanders of troops within the department will cooperate in the enforcement of these instructions. . . ."[64] Officials of the Interior Department appear to have paid no attention to the implication in Cooke's order that he was merely buttressing the position of the Commissioner of Indian Affairs, but rather went ahead on the assumption that the order was in opposition to their policy and was a basic cause of all the trouble. Secretary Browning's instructions to the Phil Kearny Commission specifically charged them with investigating the effect of the order. They also were to determine whether the Indians participating in the massacre "were on a friendly visit to the fort"—Bogy had said nothing about the "friendliness" of those involved on December 21, confining his remarks only to those engaged on December 6—and, above all, they were "to prevent, if possible, a general Indian war." They were not to make treaties with the Indians, but they were to "hold friendly talks" and, if necessary, pass out presents.[65]

The Commission assembled at Omaha in March, and spent several days taking testimony at the Herndon House, the city's leading hostelry.[66] They then traveled to Fort McPherson, where, among others, they examined Colonel Carrington.[67] They visited with a few friendlies at the Old California Crossing and at Fort Sedgwick, and then went on to Fort Laramie, where they proposed to have a grand council with all the Indians. They even sent a message to Red Cloud asking why he was at war and whether he wished to come in and talk with the representatives of the Great Father, or to send them some

[64] Hq., Dept. of the Platte, Gen. Order No. 10, July 31, 1866, 39th Cong., 2d Sess., S. Ex. Doc. 16, p. 8.

[65] O. H. Browning, February 18, 1867, 40th Cong., 1st Sess., S. Ex. Doc. 13, pp. 55–56.

[66] *Omaha Weekly Herald*, March 15, 1867.

[67] Carrington's testimony, which was finally published in 1887 and which has been referred to above, apparently was taken at this time. Carrington was sent to Fort Casper from Fort Phil Kearny, and then to Fort McPherson. Augur explained his action thus: "I am unacquainted, personally, with Colonel Carrington and it is possible that an injustice may be done him, but right, or wrong, his reputation in the upper country is such for inefficiency and unfitness for command that I regard it as unsafe and unjust to leave him in charge of any post in that country. It is for these reasons I have brought him to Fort McPherson where the effects of his incapacity, if it exists, may be readily controlled" (Augur to AAG, Military Division of the Missouri, February 19, 1867, NARS, RG 98, LS, Dept. of the Platte).

word.[68] The message was wholly disregarded,[69] and again the best the Commissioners could do was to talk with a few friendlies. Meanwhile, Judge Kinney was sent on to Fort Phil Kearny, and General Sully went back to his old stamping grounds on the upper Missouri. Sully, accompanied by Parker, had conferences at Forts Rice and Berthold, but with no one who really counted.[70]

The Commission did not get around to submitting a joint report. Before the party divided at Fort Laramie, Buford, Sanborn, and Beauvais agreed upon a draft and wanted all to support it, but, as Buford complained to Secretary Stanton, they "could not induce Generals Sully and Parker and Judge Kinney to give the matter their attention." It was agreed, therefore, that Buford and Sanborn should go to Washington and report individually. This they did early in June.[71] Evidently the Commission had not particularly concerned itself with Secretary Browning's specific questions. Sanborn wrote at length on the Fetterman massacre, but aside from "reporting" that all the Indians around Fort Phil Kearny had been in a state of war since June 20 and charging that the basic difficulty was that Carrington had been furnished no more troops and supplies for a state of war than for a state of peace, his comments were peculiarly inconclusive. The Commission found no living officer of those immediately concerned "deserving of censure"; and of the dead, "even if evidence justifies it, it would ill become us to speak evil . . . or censure." Of those higher in authority, the Commission left it to the President and the Secretary of the Interior "to determine where the censure must fall."

The Commission seemed much more interested in the larger aspects of its charge. Continued warfare, it held, could be avoided only if the invasion of the Indians' territory—contrary to law as interpreted by the Supreme Court—were abandoned. It made a number of specific recommendations—the setting aside of a separate tract of land for the Sioux; the establishment of a special, federal tribunal to deal with Indian wrongs; the organization of the Indian Bureau as a separate department of government—but for the immediate future it urged "that aggressive war by the government against the Indians at once cease, and . . . that commissioners be sent at once to counsel with them."

[68] J. F. Kinney to N. G. Taylor, June 4, 1867, NARS, RG 75, LR, Upper Platte Agency.

[69] *Ibid.*, June 17, 1867.

[70] Sully to Taylor, June 28, 1867, NARS, RG 75, LR, Upper Platte Agency.

[71] These reports will be found in 40th Cong., 1st Sess., S. Ex. Doc. 13, pp. 57–74.

These recommendations were in line with what investigating committees had been saying ever since the Chivington massacre.[72] In short, the country badly needed a new policy, not only for the Sioux, but for all the western tribes.

[72] For a brief discussion of the Chivington and related investigations, see Stan Hoig, *The Sand Creek Massacre* (Norman: University of Oklahoma Press, 1961), pp. 163–176; see also pp. 11–12, above.

CHAPTER 5

Red Cloud Signs the Treaty

Congress responded to the demand for a new Indian policy by creating an Indian Peace Commission. The act, approved July 20, 1867, provided nothing that was particularly new either in its concept of the problem or in its methods of solution.[1] The Commission was to call together the warring chiefs, try to find out why they were hostile, and if possible negotiate treaties with them which would (1) remove the causes of war, (2) provide for the safety of the frontier settlements and the Pacific railroads, and (3) inaugurate some plan for the civilization of the Indians. It was assumed that these objectives could best be secured by persuading the tribes to abandon their nomadic ways and settle down on one or more reservations. This was quite an order, involving as it did the renunciation by the hostiles of virtually all they had been fighting for, and the act recognized the possibility of failure by providing that if the Commission was unsuccessful the President could call out four regiments of mounted troops "for the purpose of conquering the desired peace."[2]

The dichotomy evident in the hopes for the Peace Commission was reflected in its membership. Congress, in line with its postwar policy of restricting the Executive wherever possible, named four members of the

[1] See, e.g., Martha L. Edwards, "A Problem of Church and State in the 1870's," *Mississippi Valley Historical Review*, XI (June, 1924), 42–43.

[2] "Report to the President by the Indian Peace Commission, January 7, 1868," Com. of Indian Affairs, *Annual Report*, 1868, pp. 26–27; U. S. *Statutes at Large*, XV, 17.

Commission in the legislation establishing it; the President was permitted to add three general officers of the Army. The congressional appointees were all well-known opponents of force in dealing with the Indians: N. G. Taylor, Commissioner of Indian Affairs, a former Methodist minister dedicated to redressing the wrongs inflicted on the aborigines; Senator J. B. Henderson of Missouri, chairman of the Senate Committee on Indian Affairs; S. S. Tappan of Colorado, a loyal follower of Taylor; and Gen. John B. Sanborn, who had endeared himself to the peace party by his work on the Phil Kearny Commission. The presidential appointees, by contrast, were all vociferous advocates of the military position that peace without punishment was impossible: General Sherman, Maj. Gen. William S. Harney, and Maj. Gen. Alfred H. Terry.[3] Later, when Sherman was called to Washington temporarily, General Augur was added to the Commission.[4]

From the beginning it was apparent that the Commission would have to exercise the highest order of statesmanship to achieve even partial success. The Sioux, emboldened by good luck and fattened by treaty supplies and robbery, were in no mood to accept overtures of peace on any but their own terms;[5] Red Cloud, it will be recalled, had even refused to send word to the Phil Kearny Commission.[6] All spring, news from the Indian country emphasized the seriousness of the situation. On May 4, Lt. Col. Innis N. Palmer, commandant at Fort Laramie, wrote that many attacks had been made on the line between Forts Sedgwick and C. F. Smith, and that "no train, escort, herd or party of any description has escaped between this place and Fort P. Kearney for a month."[7] On May 18, Augur telegraphed Sherman: "I

[3] A detailed description of the men composing the Commission, taken from the *Cincinnati Commercial* (n. d.), will be found in *Yankton Union and Dakotaian*, October 19, 1867; see also Stanley Vestal, *Warpath and Council Fire* (New York: Random House, 1948), pp. 114–115. A good general discussion of the work of the Commission will be found in Cora Hoffman Parrish, "The Indian Peace Commission of 1867 and the Western Indians" (Master's thesis, University of Oklahoma, 1948).

[4] Telegram, Grant to Augur, October 5, 1867, NARS, RG 98, LR, Dept. of the Platte. Vestal, *Warpath and Council Fire*, p. 116, gives the impression that Sherman was removed from the Commission, presumably for plain-speaking. This was not the case. He was absent a considerable part of the time, but he continued to be a member.

[5] For an estimate of the Indian position, see Brig. Gen. Philip St. George Cooke to AAG, Military Division of the Missouri, January 3, 1867, NARS, RG 98, LS, Dept. of the Platte; Brig. Gen. Alfred Sully to L. V. Bogy, March 9, 1867, NARS, RG 75, LR, Upper Platte Agency.

[6] See above, pp. 55–56.

[7] Palmer to Litchfield, May 4, 1867, NARS, RG 98, LR, Dept. of the Platte.

have not reported the many instances of Indian hostilities . . . hoping they were the result of temporary excitement and would soon cease. But they are becoming almost a daily occurrence at some point."[8]

The Indians were in complete command of the Powder River country, and the Bozeman Road, for all practical purposes, was closed. A representative of Wells Fargo in North Platte, Nebraska, predicted that not a pound of freight would go overland to Montana during 1867.[9] This was confirmed by General Augur, who informed Sherman that there would "be no travel this season over the Powder River route, except our own trains."[10] Indeed, the Army was finding it troublesome to maintain its own trains. Freight rates skyrocketed, and even then it was difficult to get freighters to accept contracts for supplying the Powder River posts.[11]

To the south, in the Platte Valley, conditions were equally critical. There were depredations at Brady's Island, at Ash Hollow, on the Lodgepole, and on the South Platte.[12] The noted correspondent Henry M. Stanley wrote from North Platte: "Murders are getting to be so tame from their plurality, that no one pays any attention to them, though reports come to headquarters every day."[13] Most disturbing of all was word that the Pacific railroad was imperiled. Thomas C. Durant wrote General Grant that the Indians were interfering seriously with the construction of the Union Pacific, "and unless some relief can be afforded . . . immediately . . . the entire work will be suspended."[14]

Further complicating the situation was the disposition on the part of westerners to take matters into their own hands. In April, Thomas F. Meagher, acting governor of Montana Territory, predicted "the utter inability of the troops garrisoning Forts Smith and Phil Kearny to do more than hold their ground, even should they be competent to do as much as this,"[15] and, excited about the killing of John Bozeman and

[8] NARS, RG 98, LS, Dept. of the Platte.

[9] D. Sweet to Louis McClain, May 21, 1867, NARS, RG 98, LR, Dept. of the Platte.

[10] Augur to Sherman, May 22, 1867, NARS, RG 98, LS, Dept. of the Platte.

[11] Edward Jay Hawken, "The Military Problem on the Powder River Road, 1865–1868" (Master's thesis, University of California, 1938), pp. 119–120.

[12] Sherman to Bvt. Lt. Col. G. K. Leet, AAG, War Dept., July 1, 1867, NARS, War Dept., LR, AGO.

[13] Henry M. Stanley, *My Early Travels and Adventures in America and Asia* (New York: Charles Scribner's Sons, 1895), I, 119.

[14] Durant to Grant, May 23, 1867, NARS, War Dept., LR, AGO.

[15] *Montana Post*, April 27, 1867, quoted in Robert E. Albright, "The Relations of

the reported movement of Sioux into the Gallatin Valley, he called for volunteers to clear the Indians out of Montana.[16] In Colorado, a mass meeting of citizens subscribed five thousand dollars for the purpose of buying Indian scalps, with the proviso that twenty-five dollars each was to be paid "for scalps with the ears on." Governor A. C. Hunt approved the action and called for volunteers to defend the territory.[17] It appeared, as the *New York Times* put it, that the Army was going to have "quite as much difficulty in repressing the whites as in keeping the Indians quiet."[18]

The Army was embarrassed by the volunteer activity,[19] but even more by its own inability to conduct an offensive campaign, and by confusion as to just what it should do with the troops available. Lack of capability had been a primary cause of the Fetterman disaster and of the failure to carry out a quick retaliation. General Augur's forces were increased somewhat during the winter and spring, but he never developed sufficient strength to take the offensive. As he stated in his annual report:

> The Montana route alone, between Laramie and C. F. Smith, near the Yellowstone, has occupied two regiments of infantry . . . and half a regiment of cavalry . . . and they have merely maintained themselves upon it and kept it open for their own supplies. . . .[20]

Moreover, the Montana route was but a part of his responsibility. As the *Omaha Herald* put it:

> We say now what we have said before, that Gen. Augur is set to command an extensive region of country with forces totally inadequate to the end proposed. He is expected to protect the Great Road, the Mail and the Telegraph as well as the growing commerce of the Plains, and at the same time make an expedition against the Indians in a remote region with a force numbering less than 5,000 men. When it is remembered that these lines requiring protection are several hundred miles in extent, and that the

---

Montana with the Federal Goverment, 1864–1889" (Ph. D. dissertation, Stanford University, 1933), pp. 116–117.

[16] For an account of Meagher's activities and the volunteer movement, see Robert G. Athearn, "The Montana Volunteers of 1867," *Pacific Historical Review*, XIX (May, 1950), 127–136.

[17] *New York Times*, June 23, 1867.

[18] *Ibid.*, June 25, 1867.

[19] See, e.g., Telegrams, Sherman to Augur, May 6, 9, 1867, Sherman to Augur, May 23, 1867, NARS, RG 98, LR, Dept. of the Platte.

[20] Secretary of War, *Annual Report*, 1867, 40th Cong., 2d Sess., H. Ex. Doc. 1, Serial 1324, p. 58.

campaign against Red Cloud is to be made hundreds of miles in an entirely different direction; the causes of the coming failure to accomplish any practical result from the Indian expedition will be made pretty clearly manifest.[21]

As the spring wore on it became evident that any campaign against Red Cloud to open the Powder River road might have to take a secondary place. On January 26, Grant had written Sherman: "Now that the government has assumed the obligation to guarantee the bonds of the Pacific Railroad, it becomes a matter of great pecuniary interest to see it completed as soon as possible. Every protection practicable should be given by the military both to secure the rapid completion of the road and to avoid pretext on the part of the builders to get further assistance from the government."[22] As construction crews were subjected to increasingly frequent attacks, railroad officials brought strong pressures on the War Department to divert all forces on the plains to the line of the road.[23] Sherman admitted that the progress of the railroad was "more important than any other single thing," but he believed that more effective protection would be provided by attacking the Sioux in the Powder River country "than by attempting to defend the line in its whole length."[24] He ordered Augur to proceed as rapidly as possible with his projected operation (generally referred to as the Yellowstone campaign) and warned him not to "be diverted from the main object by these incursions on the railroad."[25]

More distressing than confusion as to where the limited forces should be used was uncertainty as to whether they should be used at all. Sherman was anxious for an aggressive campaign against the hostile Sioux and was hopeful that Congress would turn the Indians over to the Army so that they could be brought to terms without interference from civilian officials.[26] The appointment of the Phil Kearny Commission had put a damper on these plans—Sherman wrote Augur, "I infer we are bound to defer action until they have had a chance to talk"[27]—

[21] *Omaha Weekly Herald*, May 31, 1867.

[22] Grant to Sherman, January 26, 1867, NARS, RG 98, LR, Dept. of the Platte.

[23] Durant to Grant (above, n. 14), made such a suggestion; Sweet (above, n. 9) charged that Senator Evans and other influential Coloradoans had joined with Union Pacific officials in trying to force an abandonment of the campaign in the Powder River country.

[24] Telegram, Sherman to Augur, May 27, 1867, NARS, RG 98, LR, Dept. of the Platte.

[25] *Ibid.*, May 28, 1867.

[26] See above, p. 53.

[27] February 25, 1867, NARS, RG 98, LR, Dept. of the Platte.

and by the time it became evident that this Commission would fail to accomplish anything with Red Cloud, plans were under way for sending another. The Army, therefore, was to bide its time, as indeed it had been doing all year, despite Sherman's bellicose telegrams.[28]

Moreover, it appeared that peace might break out. The Phil Kearny Commission had emphasized the importance of its talks with Spotted Tail and other friendly chiefs, and on July 28 the *New York Times* carried a story that Spotted Tail had used his influence with Red Cloud to persuade him to listen to overtures of peace, and that "the quietness now reigning in the Powder River country is a faithful witness to his work." The "quietness," it soon developed, was just the calm before the storm, and Red Cloud, instead of listening to overtures of peace, was planning for more war.[29] At a Sun Dance in June the Sioux and the Cheyennes had pondered attacks on troops at the northern forts but had not agreed on whether they should concentrate on those at Fort C. F. Smith on the Little Big Horn or those at Fort Phil Kearny on the Little Piney.[30] As it turned out, they decided to attack both, and as the members of the Peace Commission were preparing to head west, the "quietness" was shattered by the most severe attacks the Indians had launched since they massacred Colonel Fetterman's command.

On August 1 a band of perhaps four hundred and fifty to five hundred Cheyennes and Arapahoes with a few Sioux mixed in, attacked a haying party near Fort C. F. Smith. Capt. Sigeman Sternberg, commanding the detachment, and two privates were killed, but a relief party from the fort, armed with new breech-loading rifles, managed to drive the Indians off without further loss of life.[31] The

[28] The *Omaha Weekly Herald*, August 22, 1867, in reporting Sherman's order to Augur to hold his troops on the defensive pending the outcome of the Peace Commission's discussion, commented, "If entirely in order, we should like to enquire when they have been on the offensive."

[29] M. T. Patrick, agent for the Indians of the Upper Platte, wrote H. B. Denman that Dog Hawk, a chief from the Powder River country, had arrived at Fort Laramie with news that Red Cloud's band "were determined to make war this summer more actively than last" (Patrick to Denman, July 28, 1867, NARS, RG 75, LR, Upper Platte Agency).

[30] Capt. T. B. Burrows, commandant, Fort C. F. Smith, to AAG, Mountain District, Fort Phil Kearny, July 12, 16, 1867, NARS, RG 98, LR, Dept. of the Platte; cf. George E. Hyde, *Red Cloud's Folk* (Norman: University of Oklahoma Press, 1957), pp. 158–159.

[31] Burrows to Post Adj., Fort C. F. Smith, August 3, 1867, NARS, RG 98, LR, Dept. of the Platte.

next day Red Cloud's Oglalas, accompanied by some Miniconjous and perhaps a few Sans Arcs, swept down upon an improvised wagon-box corral which Capt. James Powell had constructed near Piney Island, about five miles from Fort Phil Kearny, to guard a woodcutting party. Powell had only one officer beside himself—Lt. John C. Jenness, who was killed—twenty-six enlisted men, and four citizens. Again, the Army carried the day. Powell's men, also armed with new breech-loaders, were able to stand off the attacking Indians until they were dispersed by a relief party from the fort. Powell's losses, in addition to Lieutenant Jenness, were five enlisted men killed and two wounded.[32]

These two heroic stands, coming after months of inaction and/or disaster, provided a ray of hope to a country which had begun to wonder whether its Army would ever be able to stand up to the Indians. The Wagon Box fight in particular—probably because it took place near the site of the Fetterman massacre and because Red Cloud was involved—created much excited interest, and inevitably, perhaps, a great deal of nonsense was written about it. The primary sources for much of it were Cyrus Townsend Brady and Bvt. Col. Richard I. Dodge. Brady, who labeled his account "The Thirty-two Against the Three Thousand," described a grand battle in the classical tradition with Red Cloud throwing his hordes against the little redoubt time and time again, only to fail and to leave the field strewn with the bodies of his fallen warriors.[33] Dodge wrote a similar story, and in addition reported the number of Indian casualties as 1,137.[34] These tales were repeated by some who should have known better,[35] and soon acquired the force of legend. Red Cloud himself contributed to the legend: Fred M. Hans reported that Red Cloud told him that he had lost "nearly six hundred" of his warriors in the battle;[36] E. A. Brininstool repeated, but did not credit, an assertion by the chief in old age that he "went into that fight with three thousand of his choicest fighting

[32] Powell to Post Adj., Fort Phil Kearny, August 4, 1867, *ibid.*

[33] Cyrus Townsend Brady, *Indian Fights and Fighters* (Garden City: Doubleday, Page and Co., 1940), pp. 40–58.

[34] Richard I. Dodge, *Our Wild Indians* (Hartford: A. D. Worthington Co., 1890), pp. 480–489.

[35] Cf. J. Cecil Alter, *James Bridger* (Salt Lake City: Shepard Book Co., 1925), pp. 465–468; Grace Raymond Hebard, *The Pathbreakers from River to Ocean* (Chicago: Lakeside Press, 1912), pp. 186–188.

[36] Fred M. Hans, *The Great Sioux Nation* (Chicago: M. A. Donohue & Co., 1907), p. 505.

warriors and came out with but half of them." [37] The old chief perhaps came nearest the truth when he told E. S. Ricker in 1906 that he did not remember the Wagon Box fight at all! [38]

Captain Powell estimated that there were three thousand Indians engaged, but was much more conservative with respect to losses: "not less than 60 Indians were killed on the spot and about 120 wounded severely." Even these figures seem fantastically high. Stanley Vestal, using the authority of White Bull, a participant, states that not more than a thousand Indians could have been involved, and goes on to say that the Indians simply would not have kept fighting if their losses had approached fifty percent, that they seldom tolerated losses of more than one or two percent.[39] Doane Robinson quotes Red Feather, also a participant, as saying that there were only five Indians killed and five wounded.[40] George Sword, another participant, said in old age that there were only three hundred Indians in the battle and that only two were killed.[41]

Accompanying an exaggerated estimate of the numbers involved in the battle has been an exaggeration of its significance: the defeat was decisive; Red Cloud's influence began to wane and he never fought again.[42] Actually, the Indians do not appear to have regarded the Wagon Box fight as a defeat; their losses had been slight, and they had captured many horses and mules.[43] They scattered after the fight, but they probably would have done so had they wiped out Powell's entire command, for such was their way of carrying on war. They continued to attack isolated parties and to make the road as hazardous as it had ever been.[44] They gave particular trouble to the troops attempting to establish Fort Fetterman, about eighty miles from Fort Laramie, to

[37] E. A. Brininstool, *Fighting Red Cloud's Warriors* (Columbus: Hunter-trapper-trader Co., 1926), p. 74.

[38] Ricker, Interview with Red Cloud, Ricker Mss., Tablet No. 25, Nebraska State Historical Society.

[39] Stanley Vestal, *Warpath* (Boston: Houghton Mifflin Company, 1934), pp. 70–82.

[40] Doane Robinson, "The Education of Red Cloud," *Collections*, South Dakota Department of History, XII (1924), 156–178.

[41] Ricker, Interview with George Sword, April 29, 1907, Ricker Mss., Tablet No. 16.

[42] See, e.g., Grace Hebard and E. A. Brininstool, *The Bozeman Trail* (Cleveland: Arthur H. Clark Co., 1922), I, 180–181; Struthers Burt, *Powder River* (New York: Farrar & Rinehart, 1939), p. 134.

[43] Hyde, *Red Cloud's Folk*, p. 159.

[44] For an account of these minor engagements, see Charles Griffin Coutant, *The History of Wyoming* (Laramie: Chapin, Spafford and Mathison, 1899), I, 593.

provide further protection for the Bozeman Road.[45] Farther south, they also continued to harass the railroad. On August 7 they attacked a Union Pacific freight train near Plum Creek, Nebraska (about halfway between Forts Kearny and McPherson). This attack, in a region occupied by supposed friendlies, created much excitement. Oliver Ames, acting president of the Union Pacific, wrote Secretary of War Stanton that the railroad would have to suspend work altogether unless the Government could provide adequate protection;[46] the *Omaha Herald*, ever sensitive to the interests of the Union Pacific, wrote: "The attack upon the trains near Plum Creek opens up a new chapter in Indian depredation. It may be considered as the beginning of actual war."[47]

Into this situation the Commissioners moved to bring peace to the plains.[48] Holding their organizational meeting in St. Louis on August 7, they decided to try to negotiate two treaties, one with the southern tribes and the other with the Powder River Sioux; they would meet the former at some point near Fort Larned, Kansas, on October 13, and the latter at Fort Laramie on September 13. While waiting for the tribes to gather they would visit the upper Missouri, and enroute to Fort Laramie they would meet with Spotted Tail and other friendly chiefs at North Platte, Nebraska.

They soon learned that they could expect trouble, particularly with the Sioux. When their steamboat stopped at Omaha, General Augur told the Commissioners that he was receiving regular accounts of hostilities in the Powder River country and that he rather expected a general war, a war which would require at least twenty thousand men in his own command and perhaps as many as one hundred thousand in the entire West. He was sure that Red Cloud was on the warpath to the death, and would not even come in to talk to the Commissioners. G. P. Beauvais, the old-time Sioux trader who was attached to the Commission for the purpose of rounding up the hostiles, was of the same opinion.[49] The Commissioners nevertheless dispatched Beauvais to the Sioux, and proceeded up the Missouri. After friendly but inconclusive talks with

---

[45] Telegrams, Bvt. Brig. Gen. William Dye to Augur, Bvt. Brig. Gen. N. P. Sweitzer to Augur, August 23, 1867, NARS, RG 98, LR, Dept. of the Platte.

[46] Ames to Stanton, August 7, 1866, copy *ibid.*

[47] August 15, 1867.

[48] Unless otherwise indicated, for the rest of this chapter I am following 40th Cong., 2d Sess., H. Ex. Doc. 97, and "Record of the Meetings of the United States Peace Commission with Certain Hostile Tribes of Indians in 1867," copy in Ricker Mss., Tablets No. 86B–90.

[49] *New York Times*, August 25, 27, 1867.

the up-river tribes, who were no longer hostile, the Commissioners returned to Omaha on September 11. This was a little late to keep their September 13 date with the Sioux, and General Sherman wired the commandant at Fort Laramie: "Telegraph me if we should make undue haste to reach your fort. Are the Indians assembling, or should we delay a few days to give them more time. We can be ready to start tomorrow evening. Give all notice that we are here and are coming." [50] There was no need to hurry; the word from Fort Laramie was that the hostile Sioux were not there and that runners just in from their camps reported that they would not be in at all. [51]

On September 14 the Commissioners boarded the Union Pacific for North Platte, where on September 19–20 they met with the Sioux and Cheyennes who had been living around Fort McPherson. [52] The situation at the boisterous little railroad town was not conducive to calm deliberation. The Indians got hold of a barrel of whiskey, and for a time it looked as though there would be no council at all. Things calmed down enough for the conference to proceed only after General Sherman invoked martial law. [53] The chiefs, even though ostensibly friendly, did not seem to be particularly tractable. Spotted Tail, their principal spokesman, complained about the Powder River road and demanded that it be closed. He had signed the Treaty of 1866 which had provided that he would accept a reservation and go to farming, but he was in no hurry to begin. He much preferred hunting to farming, and if the Commissioners wanted to make him happy they would provide guns and ammunition for his people. Sherman, in reply, lectured the Indians on the futility of trying to continue to live by the chase, and warned them that the Commission was a War Commission as well as a Peace Commission, that roads and railroads would be built, and that if the Indians attempted to interfere, "the Great Father,

[50] Telegram, Lt. Gen. W. T. Sherman to CO, Fort Laramie, September 11, 1867, NARS, RG 98, TS, Dept. of the Platte.

[51] Telegram, A. G. Litchfield, AAG, Dept. of the Platte, to Bvt. Maj. Gen. C. C. Augur, end of track, U.P.R.R., September 12, 1867, NARS, RG 98, TS, Dept. of the Platte.

[52] The Commission was accompanied by a number of newspaper reporters. For good journalistic accounts of the North Platte councils, see Stanley, *Early Travels*, I, 190–216; *New York Times*, September 23, 27, 1867.

[53] A. S. H. White, commenting upon the incident, wrote: "The problem, how to live at peace with the Indians, would be of easy solution if the white thieves, murderers and scoundrels were driven out of the Indian country; I believe that to them can be traced all the causes of our Indian troubles" (White to O. H. Browning, October 2, 1867, NARS, RG 75, Indian Division, Misc. Papers, Box No. 747).

who out of kindness for you, has heretofore held back the white soldiers and people, will let them out, and you will be swept out of existence." He said that they could not have guns and ammunition until they had demonstrated that they could live in peace. Later, however, N. G. Taylor, president of the Commission, announced that guns and ammunition would be available so that they could hunt on the Republican until the treaty council was held at Fort Laramie.

Postponing their visit to Fort Laramie in the hope that Red Cloud might yet be persuaded to come in, the Commissioners went from North Platte to Medicine Lodge Creek, about seventy miles from Fort Larned, where in mid-October they spent a week with certain of the Apaches, Arapahoes, Cheyennes, Comanches, and Kiowas. They passed out presents and got the chiefs to agree to treaties of peace involving the acceptance of reservations. The presents were fine, but the treaties proved to be wholly unsatisfactory and were soon rejected by the Indians.[54] Taylor nevertheless telegraphed Secretary O. H. Browning, "Please congratulate the President and the country upon the entire success of the Indian Peace Commission thus far," reporting that the Commissioners were now on their way to Fort Laramie where they would "meet the Crow, Sioux, Northern Arrapahoes, and all the Northwestern Indians."[55]

Arriving at Fort Laramie on November 9, the Commissioners found only a few Crows waiting to meet with them.[56] Although disappointed, they went through the formality of holding a council and talking peace. It was a veritable love-feast; at one point, Bear's Tooth took off his moccasins and gave them to Taylor, saying, "I have nothing else to give you. It is cold weather, but take them," and

[54] See Le Roy R. Hafen and C. C. Rister, *Western America* (New York: Prentice Hall, 1941), pp. 522–527.

[55] *New York Times*, November 3, 1867. Taylor should not be confused with E. B. Taylor of the 1866 Commission, although their actions were in many respects similar.

[56] For interesting contemporary comments on the Fort Laramie council, see Stanley, *Early Travels*, I, 262–274; Wilson O. Clough, ed., *Fort Russell and Fort Laramie Peace Commission in 1867*, State University of Montana, *Sources of Northwest History*, No. 14. The Crows complained about the distance to Fort Laramie, and the Commissioners promised to hold their next conference at Fort Phil Kearny or at some other point more convenient than Fort Laramie (see also Telegram, C. C. Augur to W. T. Sherman, November 18, 1867, NARS, RG 98, TS, Dept. of the Platte). This promise seems generally to have been ignored in planning for the council of 1868. Red Cloud, of course, would have nothing to do with a meeting at Phil Kearny; indeed, the abandonment of that post remained one of his conditions precedent to any council.

Taylor, accepting them, said, "I will borrow the warmth of your blood to make me warm."

Talking peace with the peaceable Crows was one thing; making peace with the Sioux was quite another. With respect to that, the Commissioners, disappointed but hopeful, reported:

> Red Cloud, the formidable chief of the Sioux, did not come to this council. . . .
>
> We greatly regret the failure to procure a council with this chief and his leading warriors. If an interview could have been obtained, we do not for a moment doubt that a just and honorable peace could have been secured. Several causes operated to prevent his meeting us. The first, perhaps, was a doubt of our motives; the second results from a prevalent belief amongst these Indians that we have resolved on their extermination; and third, the meeting was so late that it could not be attended in this cold and inhospitable country without great suffering. . . .

These causes may all have been operative, but the Commission, continuing, gave the real reason why Red Cloud had refused to negotiate:

> He sent us word, however, that his war against the whites was to save the valley of the Powder River, the only hunting ground left to his nation, from our intrusion. He assured us that whenever the military garrison at Fort Phil. Kearney and Fort C. F. Smith were withdrawn, the war on his part would cease. As we could not then, for several reasons, make any such agreement, and as the garrisons could not have been safely removed so late in the season, the commission adjourned, to meet in Washington. . . .

When the Peace Commissioners went back to Washington they left A. T. Chamblin and H. M. Mathews, special agents of the Indian Bureau, at Fort Laramie to try to establish contact with the hostile leaders. They were to send word to Red Cloud that the Commissioners would like to meet him next summer, and that they hoped he would agree to a cessation of hostilities until the council could be held. The prospects were mixed. The Commission reported on January 7, 1868, "we are gratified to be informed that Red Cloud has accepted our proposition to discontinue hostilities and meet us in council next spring or summer,"[57] but the Army's word was that the chief was still hostile

[57] 40th Cong., 1st Sess., H. Ex. Doc. 97. This may have been based on H. B. Denman, Supt., Omaha, to Com. of Indian Affairs, December 16, 1867, NARS, RG 75, LR, Upper Platte Agency, which stated: "Red Cloud sends word that he has received the tobacco of peace and that he will smoke it, and that as soon as he can gather his young men in there will be no more war parties sent out, and that he will come in to Laramie and see the Agent. . . ."

and had no intention of talking peace.[58] Moreover, there were rumors that the tribes were being encouraged by outsiders to continue the war. Lt. Col. L. P. Bradley, commandant at Fort C. F. Smith, had sent couriers to Red Cloud in December, and they had returned with the news that white men from north of the Missouri had been to see the chief with presents of powder and tobacco and with advice that he should not make peace because they would provide him powder and lead with which to carry on the war.[59]

It developed that even if this information were correct—and it seemed to be, although rumors of interference from "across the border" were endemic in the Indian country—it was not particularly alarming. On January 2, while Bradley was still awaiting the return of his couriers, Mathews had met a number of Bad Faces, including one identified as a brother of Red Cloud, at Fort Phil Kearny. Red Cloud, it seemed, was willing to make peace. All the Government had to do was abandon the Powder River road and evacuate the forts. Mathews made some sort of commitment—enough, at least, to extract a promise that Red Cloud would hold his warriors off the warpath until commissioners could come and talk—and hurried off to Washington with his news.[60]

"News" is hardly the proper word. The Government could have had peace with Red Cloud on these terms at any time during the past two years. The real "news" was that the Government now decided to accept the terms. This complete about-face at a time when the Army was in a stronger position in the Powder River country than it had been since the beginning of hostilities has been the subject of much caustic comment by historians of Indian affairs.[61] Actually, the Army's strength in the West was more apparent than real. It simply did not have a force adequate to keep the Bozeman Road open and at the

[58] See, e.g., Bvt. Maj. Gen. John E. Smith, Fort Phil Kearny, to Maj. Gen. C. C. Augur, December 24, 1867, NARS, RG 98, LR, Dept. of the Platte.

[59] Bradley to Litchfield, January 7, 1868, *ibid.*

[60] Mathews to N. G. Taylor, January 13, February 18, 1868, NARS, RG 75, LR, Upper Platte Agency. At one point, Mathews seems to have been trying to arrange to take the principal chiefs to Washington with him, and Headquarters, Department of the Platte, even sent out word that Red Cloud was reported en route to the East with Mathews (Telegram, Litchfield to Augur, who was in Washington, January 22, 1868, NARS, RG 98, LS, Dept. of the Platte).

[61] See, e.g., Hyde, *Red Cloud's Folk*, pp. 161–163; Vestal, *Warpath and Council Fire*, pp. 129–132, 143–146; Charles E. DeLand, "The Sioux Wars," *South Dakota Historical Collections*, XV (1930), 203; Doane Robinson, "A History of the Dakota or Sioux Indians," *ibid.*, II (1904), Pt. II, 140.

same time protect the construction of the Union Pacific,[62] and as long as troops were necessary in the South there was little likelihood that an economy-minded Congress would provide a larger force for the West.[63] Moreover, Congress was moving steadily toward acceptance of the view that war with the Indians was as unnecessary as it was unthinkable. The mere fact that the pressures of expansion were depriving the red men of their homes and destroying their way of life weighed heavily upon the conscience of a Christian nation, and when accompanied by such outrages as the Chivington massacre, the burden became insupportable. Then, too, warfare with the Indians was not only repugnant to the conscience, it was hard on the pocketbook. Pointing to the great cost of carrying on the Indian wars, the advocates of the peace policy argued that feeding the Indians was much cheaper than fighting them and also more effective. Peace, then, was a necessity in 1868— and peace had to include Red Cloud. This chief's capacity and authority had been so widely advertised since the Fetterman massacre that it was obvious that the country would insist upon having his name on a treaty before recognizing its validity. The Government, therefore, was prepared to accept his terms. Moreover, with the completion of the Union Pacific it would be possible to break a new road to Montana from some point west of Fort Laramie, thus making the Powder River road unnecessary. Furthermore, the Northern Pacific Railroad had been chartered in 1864, and its construction would provide easy access to Montana from the east. Peace with Red Cloud would facilitate both of these projects as well as the development of the West generally, and the Powder River road was not worth a continuation of war.

The Army was not overly enthusiastic about the new policy. On March 2, Grant wrote Sherman with resignation and a trace of bitterness:

> I think it will be well to prepare at once for the abandonment of the posts Phil Kearney, Reno, and Fetterman and to make all the capital with the Indians that can be made out of the change. In making this removal, it may be necessary to establish a new line of posts to protect travel from the railroad north from some point west of Cheyenne; your knowledge of the

[62] Sherman had argued that the best way to provide protection for the railroad was to keep pressure on the Indians of the north (see above, p. 62), but the Cheyennes and the Arapahoes to the south rather than the Sioux were the ones who were giving trouble to the construction crews.

[63] Democratic editors in the West complained bitterly of a policy which provided troops to enforce Radical reconstruction in the South and denied them to protect the interests of the West (see, e.g., *Omaha Weekly Herald*, August 22, 1867).

country will enable you to fix this to the best advantage; I would advise that but little confidence be placed in the suggestions of citizens who have made their homes in the territories, in selecting points to be occupied by troops.

My experience is, and no doubt it is borne out by your own, that these people act entirely from selfish and interested motives. We will have, hereafter, to rely upon inspections by competent officers to govern us in our disposition of troops and dealings with the Indians. This advice is probably more applicable to myself than to you. I am where a President, a Secretary of War, a Secretary of the Interior and Superintendent of Indian Affairs can all be approached by politicians in the interests of traders and speculators. I will try to embarrass you as little as possible by their suggestions.

I recommend this early movement in the abandonment of the posts referred to because by delay the Indians may commence hostilities and make it impossible for us to give them up.[64]

The next day Grant telegraphed Sherman to add Fort C. F. Smith to the list of posts to be abandoned. Sherman forwarded the letter to Augur, with the comment: "You may consider the thing as settled and may proceed as soon as you please to draw off your troops from that line and let the Montana people know that it is done by superior authority and that the road had not been of practical use to them, notwithstanding the great cost to the government." He did not advise haste, however, but directed that the withdrawal of the troops "should be made with the utmost deliberation, for at best I fear the Indians may attribute the withdrawal to the wrong motive." He was sure that General Grant did not intend to include Fort Fetterman (which was true), and advised Augur to ignore that part of the order. Also, Augur should wait a while before beginning work on a new line of posts to the west: "I don't believe in the necessity or policy of banishing our men to that wild Mountain region until it is demonstrated to be of some practical use."[65]

Augur reluctantly went ahead with the implementation of the order; as we shall see, he carefully followed Sherman's injunction to proceed "with the utmost deliberation." The peacemakers, however, moved with alacrity. Taylor telegraphed Augur that the Commission would be at Fort Laramie on April 7;[66] runners were sent to Red Cloud and the other hostiles to advise them of the Government's decision to abandon the Powder River road and to invite them in for a grand council with

---

[64] Grant to Sherman, March 2, 1868, NARS, RG 98, LR, Dept. of the Platte.

[65] Sherman to Augur, March 7, 1868, *ibid.*

[66] Augur to Nichols, March 13, 1868, *ibid.*

representatives of the Great White Father. They were bringing with them a treaty more generous than any that had ever been offered to the Indians. In addition to yielding to their demands for abandonment of the Powder River forts, it set aside a large tract of land for their exclusive use (from the Missouri River on the east to the Big Horns on the west, from the northern boundary of Nebraska on the south to the 46th parallel on the north), and further gave them the right to hunt on any lands north of the North Platte River and on the Republican. Rations and annuities were to be provided for thirty years.[67] Peace, at last, seemed to be in sight. Soon enough, however, the Peace Commission found that making peace with Red Cloud was almost as difficult as fighting him.

While the Commission prepared to return to Fort Laramie, Mathews and Chamblin set about trying to collect the Indians and to keep those who arrived in a tractable frame of mind. Neither task was easy. On March 18, Mathews telegraphed that he did not think the Indians could all be brought in before the end of April, but that meanwhile those who had arrived were becoming impatient, and some had already left.[68] There also were disturbing reports of continued depredations, both along the line of the railroad and in the Powder River country.[69] Augur tried to reassure Dodge, who continued to bombard the War Department with demands for protection for his railroad construction crews, telling him that the situation was improving and that there would be no general Indian trouble. It was uncertain yet what could be done with the northern bands, but the prospects looked good, and if the Commission could just get an opportunity to meet with them, peace was likely: "not an Indian that the commission treated with last year has made trouble since," he reminded Dodge.[70] Dodge hoped Augur's estimate of the situation was correct, "but," he complained, "it is impossible to hold men to work when Indians are seen and when depredations grow ten times every mile it travels."[71]

[67] The text of the treaty will be found in Appendix A.

[68] Mathews to Augur, March 18, 1868, NARS, RG 98, LS, Dept. of the Platte. Augur forwarded the telegram to Taylor.

[69] Telegram, Bvt. Brig. Gen. H. W. Wessells to AAG, Dept. of the Platte, March 19, 1868, NARS, RG 98, LR, Dept. of the Platte; *Omaha Weekly Herald*, April 8, 15, 1868.

[70] Telegram, Augur to G. M. Dodge, April 16, 1868, NARS, RG 98, LS, Dept. of the Platte.

[71] Telegram, Dodge to Augur, April 17, 1868, NARS, RG 98, LR, Dept. of the Platte.

Indeed, many people in the West seemed wholly pessimistic. As the *Cheyenne Leader* put it on the eve of the proposed conference:

> the old residents, travelers, freighters and miners of the plains and mountains, can have no hope of peace. . . . They will continue to rely upon their own vigilance, their stout hearts and strong arms for protection, and this meeting of Chiefs shall be unto them as nothing. . . .[72]

It was not long before events seemed to justify the fears of the pessimists. When the Commissioners arrived at Fort Laramie on April 10, they found none of the hostile leaders there to meet them. Disappointed but undaunted, they sent runners out to ask the chiefs in and reported to the Secretary of the Interior that they hoped soon to meet with both Red Cloud and Man-Afraid-of-His-Horse.[73] April passed, however, without word from either chief, and the Commissioners decided to hold a conference with Spotted Tail and his head men, whom they had met at North Platte and persuaded to come to Laramie for the grand council. The situation was little short of grotesque. Here were representatives of the President—the intrepid Indian fighters Sherman, Harney, Terry, and Augur; the distinguished peace advocates Taylor, Henderson, Sanborn, and Tappan. They had come west with wagon-loads of presents and a treaty which conceded everything Red Cloud had demanded, and they could not even get him to come in and talk to them. All they could do was to meet with a set of superannuated chiefs who for the past two years had been willing to sign anything put before them, and who had no power whatever for peace or war. Swallowing their pride, the Commissioners on the twenty-ninth met in a full-dress conference with Spotted Tail and other head men of the Brulés, explained the treaty to them, and obtained their marks on the paper.[74]

On May 1, after the Brulés had returned to the Republican Valley to spend the summer hunting, Mathews arrived from the Powder River country with assurances that Red Cloud and Man-Afraid had promised him to come to Fort Laramie and that the Commissioners could expect them in ten days.[75] Before that time had passed, however, word came from Red Cloud that he would not come in until the forts had actually been abandoned. "We are on the mountains looking down on the soldiers and the forts," he is reported to have said. "When we see the

[72] *Cheyenne Leader*, April 3, 1868.

[73] Telegrams, A. S. H. White to O. H. Browning, April 11, 14, 1868, NARS, RG 75, LR, Upper Platte Agency.

[74] *Ibid.*, May 2, 1868. The signatures to the treaty will be found in Charles J. Kappler, ed., *Indian Affairs, Laws and Treaties*, II, 998–1007. For text, see Appendix.

[75] *Ibid.*

soldiers moving away and the forts abandoned, then I will come down and talk."[76]

Thus humiliated, the majority of the Commission determined to leave, although Harney and Sanborn remained behind to meet with any Indians who might still come in. They concluded treaties with the Crows, Northern Cheyennes, and Arapahoes,[77] and on May 20 Sanborn reported that Man-Afraid-of-His-Horse would "be in tomorrow."[78] Sanborn and Harney did manage to collect the signatures of a substantial number of Oglalas, Miniconjous, and Yanktonnais on the twenty-fifth and twenty-sixth, but it is not at all certain that Man-Afraid's was among them.[79] Sanborn and Harney then went to Cheyenne to take the Union Pacific to Omaha, where they boarded a steamboat waiting to take them to Fort Rice to negotiate with the tribes of the Upper Missouri. Sanborn reported the council as "eminently successful in all respects,"[80] but as at Fort Laramie, the Commissioners had done little more than confirm the peaceable disposition of the friendlies.[81]

When Sanborn and Harney departed Fort Laramie they left the treaty with Bvt. Brig. Gen. A. J. Slemmer, post commandant, with instructions to obtain Red Cloud's signature, if possible. Seth E. Ward, the post trader, was authorized to make presents to the Indians after they had signed the treaty, and Charles E. Geren, the Commission's special interpreter, was left behind to help out in any way possible.[82] It

[76] *Omaha Weekly Herald,* June 10, 1868. This was based on an interview with Harney. The *Cheyenne Leader,* May 13, 1868, reported substantially the same thing after an interview with Sherman, Augur, Terry, and Tappan.

[77] Sanborn to Taylor, May 20, 1868, NARS, RG 75, LR, Upper Platte Agency.

[78] *Ibid.*

[79] Kappler, *Indian Affairs,* II, 1004–1006. There is considerable confusion as to just when Man-Afraid signed the treaty. Charles E. Geren, interpreter for the Commission, wrote Taylor, July 1, 1868, that Man-Afraid had signed the treaty before Harney and Sanborn left Fort Laramie (Com. of Indian Affairs, *Annual Report,* 1868, pp. 252–254). The official copy of the treaty, however, shows that Man-Afraid signed it on November 6. There is similar confusion with respect to the time at which certain other signatures were secured. Geren reported that Tall Wolf, Mad Elk, and Sitting Bear signed early in June. Their signatures appear on the treaty under the date of May 26. It is strange, if Man-Afraid signed in May, that his name should not appear under an earlier date than November 6.

[80] Sanborn to Browning, July 9, 1868, NARS, RG 75, LR, Upper Platte Agency.

[81] For an account of the Fort Rice negotiations, see Hyde, *Red Cloud's Folk,* pp. 165–166.

[82] Sanborn and Harney to Slemmer, May 27, 1868, NARS, RG 75, Old Misc. Records. Hyde, *Red Cloud's Folk,* pp. 164–165, overemphasizes the role of Geren.

was evident that all concerned would have a long wait. There were the usual stories that Red Cloud was about to come in—the one current during the summer was that the chief was organizing an expedition against the Snakes to avenge the death of his son, after which he would come in and sign the treaty [83]—but it was apparent that there would be no action until after the Powder River forts were abandoned.

The process of abandonment was proceeding slowly, even more slowly than originally intended. The Army tried to negotiate with the Bureau of Indian Affairs for the sale of supplies at the posts, but that failed, and some of the supplies were put on public sale. This, too, was unsuccessful; bidders, it seemed, were reluctant to come to Fort C. F. Smith, where the sales were being held, for fear of the Indians! [84] Finally, the freighting firm of McKenzie and Story bought some of the supplies at C. F. Smith, some were hauled away, and the rest were issued to the Crows or abandoned. On July 29 the troops at Fort C. F. Smith marched away, [85] and at dawn the next morning Red Cloud and his warriors swept down on the post and set it afire. They were concerned only with destroying the hated symbol of the white man's invasion of their country, and they did not molest the McKenzie and Story freight train still camped in the vicinity. [86] A few days later, Forts Phil Kearny and Reno were abandoned, and Phil Kearny was burned. [87]

By early August, then, Red Cloud's demands had been met: the forts had been abandoned; the Bozeman Road had been closed. The stage was set for his long-awaited visit to Fort Laramie: the treaty was drawn up, the presents were ready, and Francis La Framboise, Father Pierre J. De Smet, and Reverend Samuel D. Hinman had been sent back to the fort to help explain matters to the chief and bolster his faith in the intentions of the Government. But Red Cloud was in no hurry. He would make his winter's meat first, and then perhaps he would come in and see what the white men had to say.

[83] See, e.g., Telegram, Litchfield to Augur, June 16, 1868, NARS, RG 98, LS, Dept. of the Platte; Denmer to Litchfield, July 5, 1868, LR.

[84] Maj. A. S. Burt, CO, Fort C. F. Smith, to Adj., 27th Infantry, Fort Phil Kearny, June 1, 1868; Burt to Litchfield, June 16, 1868; telegram, Bvt. Maj. Gen. John E. Smith, CO, Fort Phil Kearny, to AAG, Dept. of the Platte, June 7, 1868; telegram, Augur to Litchfield, June 12, 1868, NARS, RG 98, LR, Dept. of the Platte.

[85] Burt to Adj., 27th Infantry, July 27, 1868, *ibid.*, sets forth the moving schedule.

[86] Ricker, Interview with Baptiste Pourier, Ricker Mss., Tablet No. 15, pp. 113–118.

[87] Bvt. Maj. Gen. C. C. Augur, Report, Dept. of the Platte, October 14, 1868, Secretary of War, *Annual Report*, 1868, pp. 21–24; Hyde, *Red Cloud's Folk*, pp. 166–167.

Red Cloud's failure to come in after the forts had been abandoned was disquieting, to say the least. Indeed there was some fear that he might not come in at all, and that hostilities would be renewed. An officer who was providing escort for the Army paymaster on his last trip to the Powder River forts wrote, "From signs on the road, I deem the Indians hostile."[88] General Augur was not especially optimistic, either. On August 29, in a circular directing all troops under his command to be "particularly careful not to interfere with the rights of the Indians," he warned, "In the present state of Indian affairs, all parties of Indians will be regarded with the greatest suspicion and precautions taken accordingly."[89] Perhaps the most pessimistic view was that expressed by Col. D. S. Stanley, who wrote from Fort Sully that in his opinion there was "a large body of Sioux which can only be brought to peace by killing." He continued:

> As a peace measure the withdrawal of the troops from the Powder River country was worth the experiment but I fully believe that the concession has persuaded the Indians that by keeping up the war they can now force the abandonment of all posts on the Missouri.[90]

Pessimism pervaded even the Peace Commission. In addition to Red Cloud's broken promises there were new troubles in the south—depredations committed by Indians who apparently had signed the treaties at Medicine Lodge—and it seemed that despite the work and the expenditures peace was far from being achieved. When the Commission met in Chicago, October 9, therefore, the peacemakers were on the defensive, and the military members—particularly General Sherman—completely took over. Sherman had some harsh words with Tappan, who insisted that the Government was the aggressor and that the Indians had no alternative but war,[91] but in the end he managed to push through a resolution dissolving the Commission and adopting a final report to the President which consisted of six short resolutions. The Government should recognize treaties already made, and should feed and supply all Indians who abided by them. No longer, however, should the United States treat the Indian tribes as "domestic dependent

[88] Capt. E. T. P. Shirrley to Capt. Thomas A. DeWeise, August 2, 1868, NARS, RG 98, LR, Dept. of the Platte.

[89] Hqs., Dept. of the Platte, Circular to Commanding Officers, August 29, 1868, NARS, RG 98, LS, Dept. of the Platte.

[90] Bvt. Maj. Gen. D. S. Stanley to Bvt. Brig. Gen. O. D. Greene, AAG, U.S. Army, October 3, 1868, NARS, RG 98, LR, AGO.

[91] Sherman to Sheridan, October 15, 1868, *ibid.*

nations," entering into treaties with them and allowing the tribes jurisdiction over their members. Indians should be held individually subject to the laws of the United States. Moreover, those Indians who refused to go to the reservations should be compelled to do so by military force. Finally, the Bureau of Indian Affairs should be transferred from the Department of Interior to the Department of War.[92] In other words, the Peace Commission concluded its efforts by recommending force as a major ingredient in the formula of peace with the Indians.

In the Indian country, military force had already supplanted civilian authority. Congress, in appropriating funds for carrying out treaty stipulations, had provided specifically that the money should be distributed under the direction of Lieutenant General Sherman.[93] In response to a request for advice, Secretary Browning wrote Sherman that the Army's function would be limited to the supervision of disbursements, and that "the relations between the department [of the Interior] and the Indians remain unchanged."[94] Sherman thought otherwise. He issued an order creating two military districts, one for the Sioux under General Harney, and another for the Cheyennes, Arapahoes, Kiowas, and Comanches under Bvt. Maj. Gen. W. B. Hazen. Moreover, military commanders would construe themselves as the "agents" of all Indians not on reservations and in that capacity "afford them temporary support to conduct them to their reservations." When the Indians were actually on reservations with civilian agents, "no interferences will be made, but military commanders may note any neglect or irregularities on the part of said Indians or their agents, and will report the same for the information of the government."[95]

At Fort Laramie, General Slemmer interpreted Sherman's order to mean that inasmuch as the Indians there were not on a proper reservation—the Peace Commission and later the Army designated Fort Randall on the Missouri as the Sioux agency—he was to consider himself as their agent. This resulted in one of those military-civilian squabbles which continually cropped up in Indian affairs. The Indian Bureau had appointed J. P. Cooper as a special agent for the Indians in the vicinity of Fort Laramie. When he arrived at the post, Slemmer

[92] Com. of Indian Affairs, *Annual Report*, 1868, pp. 371–372.

[93] U. S. *Statutes at Large*, XV, 222.

[94] Browning to Sherman, August 6, 1868, Com. of Indian Affairs, *Annual Report*, 1868, pp. 82–184.

[95] Hqs., Military Division of the Missouri, General Order No. 4, August 10, 1868, in *ibid.*, pp. 85–86.

refused to let him deal with the Indians. The Peace Commission, he told Cooper, had left the treaty with him, and as soon as Red Cloud came in and signed the document no more Indians would be allowed around Fort Laramie; they would all have to go to Fort Randall.[96] For all practical purposes, as H. B. Denman, Superintendent of the Northern Superintendency, put it in his annual report, "the action of Congress in withholding appropriations from the department for the Indians of this agency, and placing money to subsist them and to carry out the stipulations of the recent treaties in the hands of Lieutenant General Sherman, virtually places these Indians under the care and control of the military."[97]

Meanwhile, what of Red Cloud, whose intentions had been a source of anxiety all year?

By the end of October, he apparently decided that he had "made enough meat" to take care of his needs for the winter and would go down to Fort Laramie to see what the representatives of the Great White Father had to say.

The decision created considerable consternation at Fort Laramie. On November 2, Bvt. Brig. Gen. William Dye, who had succeeded Slemmer as commandant, telegraphed General Augur that Red Cloud and a large band of Sioux were expected soon, and asked what he should do. Augur replied that the Peace Commission had dissolved and that Dye was to "tell Red Cloud he should go to General Harney who is prepared to take care of all Northern Indians this winter and who is the only one authorized to do so."[98]

At ten o'clock on the morning of the fourth, Red Cloud came in for a conference. He had an impressive group with him, including many of the leading men of the Hunkpapas, Blackfeet, Brulés, and Sans Arcs. Altogether there were about one hundred and twenty-five chiefs and head men, including Red Leaf, Brave Bear, and others who had already signed the treaty. Man-Afraid-of-His-Horse was present also.[99] If

---

[96] Cooper to H. B. Denman, August 27, 1868, in *ibid.*, pp. 250–252.

[97] Com. of Indian Affairs, *Annual Report*, 1868, p. 231.

[98] Dye to Bvt. Brig. Gen. G. D. Ruggles, November 20, 1868, NARS, RG 75, Old Misc. Records. This is Dye's report of the conference, and my account is taken from it.

[99] See above, note 79. Dye's report does not indicate that Man-Afraid was one of those who had signed earlier, but rather leaves the impression that he had not signed. The only reference to Man-Afraid's earlier visit is in connection with a request from Red Cloud that no liquor be introduced into his camp, "he no doubt having in view the drunkenness of Man-afraid-of-his horses, when here last summer."

there was any doubt about Red Cloud's standing among his people, his position as the recognized leader of this group should have dispelled it.

The conference did not get off to a very auspicious beginning. While the other chiefs rose and shook hands with apparent cordiality, Red Cloud remained seated and sulkily gave the ends of his fingers to the officers who advanced to shake hands with him. He then opened the proceedings by saying that were the Commissioners or anyone in high authority present, he would talk to them frankly, but as long as no one was there but officers of the Army, the result of the council could not be satisfactory to either party. Dye responded by telling Red Cloud that the treaty, which already had been signed by many of his people, had been left at Fort Laramie by the Commission and that the post commander had authority to have it signed by himself and any others who wished to do so.

This satisfied Red Cloud for the moment, and he began asking questions about the treaty. In answering him, Dye went through the document point by point. When he got to the long and complicated sections about the reservation and farming, Red Cloud said that he had learned from others all he cared to know about that.[100] His people had no desire to leave their country for a new one, nor were they interested in abandoning the chase for farming. Moreover, he did not wish to receive his rations from General Harney—his father knew General Harney and he did not like him.[101] What Red Cloud wanted the white men to understand was that he had come, not because he had been sent for, but because he wanted to hear the news and get some powder and lead with which to fight the Crows. The Crows had received arms which they had used against his people, and it was only right that he should be similarly supplied.

The conference—as would be true of many a later meeting with Red Cloud—was bogging down in irrelevancies and misunderstandings. Dye pointed out that powder and lead could not be issued to Indians who were at war, and that in any case General Harney was the only person who had authority to make issues to the Sioux. The Government would supply all their necessities, but they must go to the reservation. He advised Red Cloud to think the matter over during the night, and,

[100] This is of some importance in connection with Red Cloud's frequently repeated assertion that the treaty had never been explained to him. See e.g., below, p. 107.

[101] If this is true, it upsets the generally held assumption that Red Cloud's father died while Red Cloud was a small boy. Harney had no contact with the Sioux until 1855. Could Red Cloud have been referring to his uncle, Old Smoke?

as he put it, "we facilitated a favourable result, by gladdening, during the day, their bellies with a feast."

The next morning Dye again explained the provisions of the treaty, emphasizing the benefits that would accrue to the Indians if they signed it. He told Red Cloud that the whites were particularly anxious to be in friendly relations with him because they regarded him as a big chief; he should think about this one more night and return the next morning with his mind fully made up as to peace or war.

The next morning Red Cloud began by reiterating his desire for powder and lead, requesting Dye to telegraph General Augur about it. At this point, Dye read Augur's telegram stating that the Indians would have to receive all of their supplies from Harney. Red Cloud then went on to other matters, asking further questions about the treaty, particularly the provisions covering the extent of the territory provided for them and excluding white men from the area. Finally, Red Cloud, "with a show of reluctance and tremulousness washed his hands with the dust of the floor" and put his mark on the treaty. The others followed. Red Cloud asked all of the white men present to touch the pen. When this was done, he shook hands all around, and then launched into a long speech. The speech did not bode well for the future.

To be sure, he was now ready for peace. The great cause of the war had been the establishment of the Powder River road without the consent of the Indians, and now that the road was abandoned there was no need for further fighting.[102] It might be difficult for a time to control his young braves, but he would live up to the treaty as long as the white man.

There is grave doubt, however, that he knew what was meant by "living up to the treaty." He was not sure that he would go to the reservation to accept rations and presents; he would have to see what they were before he could make up his mind. He was much interested in visiting Fort Laramie from time to time, and he hoped that the officers now there would treat his people as they had been treated in years past, and that the old traders would be allowed to trade with them again. For the time being, he, Man-Afraid-of-His-Horse, and Brave Bear, with their lodges, would go to the Powder River where they would remain among the buffalo during the winter and make war on

[102] He recalled that when he was at Fort Laramie in 1866 a heavy cloud hung in the heavens portending war. The cloud had now cleared away. (In reporting this, Dye remarks that the days Red Cloud was at Fort Laramie were cloudless and pleasant.)

the Crows. They had no desire at all to abandon the chase and their country which abounded in game for the lands of the reservation. They did not know how to farm, and so long as there was game they did not care to learn.

Dye apparently did not try to correct the chief's misapprehensions—possibly, after three days, he decided that there was no point in trying. He issued rations for the use of the Indians on the journey to the Powder River, Ward gave them the presents which had been left by the Commission, and the Indians departed, "apparently well pleased."

It was obvious, nonetheless, that there was trouble ahead.

CHAPTER 6

What Does the Treaty Mean?

Red Cloud had given ample evidence during his conference with General Dye that he had only the vaguest notion of what the treaty meant, and that he intended to interpret it as he saw fit. By the time the Senate ratified the document (February 16, 1869), some of the difficulties the Government would face in enforcing its provisions on its most celebrated signatory were already apparent. Others soon developed.

The Peace Commission had selected Fort Randall on the Missouri River as the site for the Sioux agency, and as soon as the various bands of Sioux signed the treaty they were instructed to move to the new agency, where General Harney would be prepared to issue rations and annuities as provided in the agreement.[1] Fort Randall was satisfactory to none of the Sioux. It was located in the extreme southeast corner of the reservation, far from their accustomed haunts, and it was wholly devoid of game. Even so, the friendly Indians were persuaded to go to the Missouri by the simple expedient of cutting off their subsistence on the Platte, and by November 23 Harney could report that he had located the Laramie Loafers at the mouth of Whetstone Creek and Spotted Tail's band at the forks of the White River. He was confident

[1] See above, p. 78. This action, approved by Congress in the appropriations act of July 27—passed before the treaty had even been presented to the Senate, much less ratified—indicates how far the treaty-making process had deteriorated as an instrument for dealing with the Indians.

that the plan adopted would "effectually settle our difficulties with the Sioux bands of Indians for all time to come."[2]

The facts do not support Harney's optimism. Red Cloud had announced at Fort Laramie that he was unalterably opposed to the Missouri River site, and even before he came in to Fort Laramie there was reason to doubt that any of the northern people would go to the Missouri.[3] Even some of the Platte River Indians refused to make the journey;[4] these Indians, under Pawnee Killer and Whistler, eventually caused so much consternation in Nebraska and Kansas that an expedition was sent in the summer of 1869 under Bvt. Maj. Gen. E. A. Carr to force them out of the Republican Valley and onto the reservation.[5] There were rumors during the winter that Red Cloud would come to see Harney at Fort Randall in the spring "to definitely arrange an enduring peace with the white man,"[6] but his actions gave no indication that he had in any way ameliorated his opposition, expressed repeatedly at Fort Laramie, to moving to the Missouri River.

Red Cloud's principal objective in signing the treaty, it soon became evident, had been to create a situation which would make possible the resumption of trade at or near Fort Laramie; he had told Dye that he "hoped that the officers now at Laramie would treat them as they were treated in years gone by, and that the old traders would again be allowed to trade with them."[7] This the Government, or at least the Army, strenuously opposed. On November 16 Sherman wrote Augur that Red Cloud "should be made to go forthwith over to General Harney about Fort Sully," adding, "I would not allow him to hang around Laramie or Fetterman this winter."[8] A short time later he wrote:

> I reiterate my orders that there must be no trade with the Sioux outside of Harney's reservation. All of these Indians have had plenty of time to go

[2] Harney to Sherman, November 23, 1868, NARS, RG 98, LR, AGO.

[3] See, e.g., Cooper to Denman, August 27, 1868, Com. of Indian Affairs, *Annual Report*, 1868, pp. 250–252.

[4] M. T. Patrick to Denman, September 16, 1868, NARS, RG 75, LR, Upper Platte Agency.

[5] See James T. King, "The Republican River Expedition, June, July, 1869," *Nebraska History*, XL (September, December, 1960), 165–200, 281–298. See also James T. King, *War Eagle: A Life of General Eugene A. Carr* (Lincoln: University of Nebraska Press, 1963), pp. 94–119.

[6] *Omaha Weekly Herald*, December 16, 1868.

[7] See above, p. 81.

[8] NARS, RG 98, LR, Dept. of the Platte.

there. If any are likely to suffer for tobacco or flour, you may authorize the commanding officers to issue out of their public stores, if on hand, and to take the furs and skins to be sold at Omaha for their benefit, viz. to reimburse the commissary and the balance to go to the Indians, provided no trader gets a cent of profit. . . . If those Sioux make the least trouble, by spring we will give them our attention. Sheridan has knocked the Cheyennes, Arapahoes and Kiowas all to pieces and they are running for Hayes reservation. I think the same process will have to be applied to those Powder River Sioux and by early spring we will have the troops available.[9]

Augur passed the word on to Dye with the admonition that "this order must be strictly enforced and should you find any person violating it, you will arrest him and seize his goods."[10] Dye assured Augur that he was enforcing the order, that, indeed, he was keeping the Sioux strictly on the north side of the North Platte, away from Fort Laramie: "We have been so particular, that . . . only a single Indian is permitted to cross and go to the lodge of the interpreter and inform him what is wanted; . . . the post commander . . . decides whether the business is of sufficient importance to justify their entering the post or whether it is a new pretext to see and beg." He was not at all sure, however, that the Sioux would continue to put up with these restraints, and he had come "from their manner of talk about the trading prohibitions to look upon a war as probable, if not inevitable."[11]

Three days later Grass, one of the chiefs who had signed with Red Cloud, showed up at Fort Fetterman with about forty young warriors. He was in a belligerent mood. Recalling that Red Cloud had told the commanding officer at Fort Laramie "that he had come in without invitation to sign the treaty, that he intended to keep it all his life, but that before he signed it he wanted it understood that he and his people were to be treated as white men, to be allowed to go where they pleased and there was but one thing that he objected to and that was Fort Fetterman," Grass asserted that inasmuch as Red Cloud had been allowed to sign the treaty after making this declaration, all of the Sioux assumed that his wishes were to be complied with. Further, the Commissioners themselves had assured the Sioux that if they signed the treaty, Fort Laramie would be the only post left north of the railroad and it would be a trading post. Also, the whites should

---

[9] Sherman to Augur, December 4, 1868, *ibid.*

[10] Augur to CO, Fort Laramie, December 8, 1868, NARS, RG 98, LS, Dept. of the Platte.

[11] Dye to AAG, Dept. of the Platte, NARS, RG 98, LR, Dept. of the Platte.

understand that he, Red Cloud, Red Leaf, and Man-Afraid would never go to the Missouri River.[12]

Although there is no record that Red Cloud specifically mentioned Fort Fetterman in his conversations with Dye, he complained again and again that he had understood that it was to be abandoned and held that failure to do so was a violation of the treaty.[13] For the moment, however, the trading problem was the critical one. On February 3, Dye reported that Red Cloud had sent him word that he would be at Fort Laramie in the spring and that he expected to trade.[14] On March 22 Red Cloud appeared across the river from the post. He had about a thousand of his people with him, and had he been hostile, Dye would have faced a real crisis. But the old belligerence had disappeared; Red Cloud was simply on a begging mission. The winter had been hard in the north country and game was scarce. His people were hungry. Dye permitted six of the Indians to come in for a conference. He told them that if they would go to the Missouri he would permit them to trade for sufficient provisions to get them there. There is no record of what they promised, but they got their provisions and went away.[15]

This anticlimactic encounter was by no means the last of the trading problem. Although Red Cloud spent the summer in the Wind River Valley,[16] he continued to press for the right to trade at Fort Laramie. He found willing allies in the white traders who were as fond of the Laramie region as were the Indians, and who apparently had assumed with them that trading at Fort Laramie would be one of the fruits of the treaty.

On February 24, John Richard, Jr., half-breed son of the old-time Sioux trader, appeared in General Augur's office in Omaha with a license from the Commissioner of Indian Affairs to trade with the northern Indians in the Powder River country. The license, he repre-

[12] Bvt. Lt. Col. C. H. Carlton, CO, Fort Fetterman to AAG, Dept. of the Platte, January 19, 1869, *ibid.*

[13] See below, p. 105.

[14] Dye to AAG, Dept. of the Platte, February 3, 1869, NARS, RG 98, LR, Dept. of the Platte.

[15] Dye to AAG, Dept. of the Platte, March 26, 1869, *ibid.* A number of western newspapers carried a story that Red Cloud slipped into Fort Laramie during the night and when the garrison awoke it found the parade ground occupied by the chief and five hundred of his warriors "with bows strung and mounted on ponies"! See, e.g., *Cheyenne Leader*, March 29, 1869; *Denver News*, April 1, 1869; *Montana Post*, April 23, 1869.

[16] Com. of Indian Affairs, *Annual Report*, 1869, p. 24.

sented, had been drawn up under the supervision of General Sanborn, who had assured him that he would not be interfered with by the military. It was accompanied by a permit signed by General Harney.[17] Harney later complained that he had been "tricked" into signing the permit and urged that everything possible be done to stop Richard from trading with the Powder River Sioux; as long as they could trade outside the reservation, there certainly was no hope of getting them to move onto it.[18] Augur, however, had already let Richard go. The trader had promised that he would locate near the mouth of Horsehead and Beaver creeks, and would take no arms, ammunition, or liquor with him.[19] It is a little hard to determine what Richard would have used for trading stock if he omitted these commodities—as two irate citizens of Cheyenne complained, "If he trades, he must trade powder, lead and guns, or the Indians would make no trade"[20]—and, as Augur soon learned, he was well supplied with all of them.[21] Moreover, Richard soon gave evidence that he had no intention of going where he had promised, but instead established himself on Raw Hide Creek, only a few miles from Fort Laramie.[22] He also had the wood and hay contracts for Fort Fetterman. Although little is known about his activities during that summer, he must have been a busy man. Augur reported that Richard had not been allowed to trade in the vicinity of Fetterman and that his goods were confiscated,[23] but there is considerable evidence that he traded throughout the summer and that his goods were not confiscated until September.[24] In any event, all of his business activities abruptly came to an end on September 9 when he killed a corporal who

[17] Augur to Sherman, February 25, 1869, Augur to AG, U.S. Army, March 13, 1860, MARS, RG 98, LS, Dept. of the Platte.

[18] Harney, Washington, to Augur, April 12, 1869, NARS, RG 98, LR, Dept. of the Platte. Harney wrote: "The permit was read to me when I had company at my rooms and I did not notice the 'Headwater' being mentioned (a trick). I had intended to allow him to go as far as the forks from the mouth of the Big Cheyenne River and when I discovered from the copy of his permit what his object was, I determined to revoke his license and to do all in my power to have him stopped. It was distinctly understood that he was to go up the Missouri River."

[19] Augur to AG, U.S. Army, March 13, 1869.

[20] Alexander DuBois and Henry Brant to Sherman, March 6, 1869, NARS, RG 98, LR, Dept. of the Platte.

[21] Annual Report, Dept. of the Platte, October 23, 1869, 41st Cong., 2d Sess., H. Ex. Doc. 1, pp. 70-75.

[22] Augur to Harney, April 7, 1869, NARS, RG 98, LS, Dept. of the Platte.

[23] Augur, Report, October 23, 1869 (above, n. 21).

[24] Ricker, Interview with Baptiste Pourier, January 7, 1906. Ricker Mss., Tablet No. 15, pp. 118–125, Nebraska State Historical Society.

had been his rival for the affections of one of the ladies living around the fort, and fled to the Indians.[25]

Richard took refuge with Red Cloud, from whose camp, it was reported, he busied himself with trying to unite all of the northern Indians in a war against the whites.[26] Whether or not Richard had any such grandiose scheme—and he probably did not—he managed to keep Red Cloud stirred up about the trading problem. On March 11, Col. Franklin F. Flint, who had succeeded Dye, telegraphed: "Report has been received here from John Richard through his father that Man Afraid of His Horses and Red Cloud will visit this post about the last of this month with a large body of Sioux warriors 1500 or 2000 to trade here in accordance with late treaty with General Sherman, Harney and others, or to fight if not allowed to trade." The report was "credited by old residents" and had caused great apprehension among the settlers of the region, many of whom had applied for permission to move to the post. Flint wanted a strong force of cavalry, "prepared for any emergency."[27] By March 18, however, the threat had subsided somewhat. Red Cloud and Man-Afraid were on their way to Fort Laramie, but they wanted peace and wondered if they would be permitted to trade in small parties at Fetterman or Laramie.[28]

It was obvious that the Indians were simply on a begging mission as they had been the year before, and that they probably could be satisfied again by being given some food and rations, and then sent on their way. But this would not solve the problem of the treaty or quiet the constant uproar created in the West by Red Cloud's refusal to go on the reservation. Something would have to be done, but no one seemed to know just what. Lt. Gen. Philip Sheridan, who had taken command of the Military Division of the Missouri when Grant brought Sherman to Washington as chief of staff, telegraphed Augur that he was "inclined to the opinion that it is best not to grant the request of Red Cloud and others to trade at Fetterman and Laramie, but leaves the subject to be

25 *Ibid.*; Augur, Report, October 23, 1869 (above, n. 21); Ricker, Interview with William Garnett, January 10, 1907, Ricker Mss., Tablet No. 1, p. 41.

26 Augur, Report, October 23, 1869 (above, n. 21); *Omaha Weekly Herald*, December 8, 1869. The *Herald* even reported that Richard had arranged a treaty of peace between the Crows and the Sioux, "the main object of which is to wage a terrible and continued war against the whites."

27 Telegram, Flint to AAG, Dept. of the Platte, March 11, 1870, NARS, RG 98, TR, Dept. of the Platte.

28 Telegram, Maj. Alexander Chambers, CO, Fort Fetterman, to AAG, Dept. of the Platte, March 18, 1870, *ibid.*

decided according to your best judgement."[29] In desperation, the Secretary of War took the matter before the President's Cabinet. That body decided that the Government should hold firm and not give in to Red Cloud's request, that he should be told to move inside the reservation where agents would be appointed to give his people the benefits of the treaty and to protect them from the whites who were flocking into Montana and Wyoming.[30] Shortly after this ruling had been sent, the Commissioner of Indian Affairs got it modified to provide that Red Cloud should be told that while for the present he must trade at one of the agencies on the Missouri, as soon as possible the Government would provide trading houses "at such point in the Indian Territory as Red Cloud may select as his camp."[31]

This provision—apparently the first break in the Government's determination to consolidate the Indians on the Missouri—opened a whole new realm of possibilities for continued negotiation. Before discussing these, we should look briefly at another problem connected with the interpretation of the treaty which was coming to a head at the same time. This problem arose not from the Indians, but from the whites.

From the beginning of negotiations there was strong opposition in the West to any solution which would give the Indians a large tract of land from which whites would be excluded. The *Yankton Union and Dakotaian*, for example, called the idea of two great reservations "the most foolish and puerile invention that ever emanated from the brain of a full grown man."[32] For many of those who wanted to develop the resources of the new country wherever they might be found, the Indian was simply a nuisance to be got rid of as expeditiously as possible. These people had no solution to the Indian problem save extermination, and they looked forward to the day when, as a Montana paper put it, the country would be cleared of "every sign of Indians but their graves."[33]

When it became apparent that the Peace Commission was planning to set aside a large reservation for the Sioux there was immediate

[29] Telegram, AAG, Military Division of the Missouri, to Augur, March 19, 1870, *ibid.*

[30] *Ibid.*, March 24, 1870. [31] *Ibid.*, March 29, 1870.

[32] August 24, 1867. Henry Fritz, *The Movement for Indian Assimilation, 1860–1890* (Philadelphia: University of Pennsylvania Press, 1963), pp. 109–119, is an excellent summary of attitudes of westerners toward Indian affairs.

[33] *New North-West*, Deer Lodge, August 20, 1869.

protest, particularly from Dakota. Already there were rumors of gold in the Black Hills and Dakotans were dreaming of the great wealth that could be had from exploiting the area. To have the region reserved for the Indians was unthinkable. On August 17, 1867, the *Yankton Union and Dakotaian* wrote with alarm:

> We have heard it intimated that a large portion of western Dakota, embracing the wealthy Black Hills region, was looked upon as a favorable section for the location of the wild tribes, and though we can hardly credit the report, it may be true, and if so will call for prompt and forcible action on the part of our people to prevent it. No greater calamity could befall Dakota than to have that portion of our Territory closed to exploration and settlement by the whites. . . .

Governor Andrew J. Faulk and Moses K. Armstrong used their influence to dissuade the Commission from including any part of Dakota in the reservation—Faulk, with the keen localism that frequently characterized western patriotism, suggested instead the country north of the 45th parallel, embracing the valleys of the Yellowstone and the Little Missouri, "the best game country in the world"[34]—but their efforts were of no avail. Convinced that "Dakota will not be a State until this miserable farce is 'played out,' and the Government has had an opportunity to witness and appreciate its failure,"[35] Dakotans kept agitating the Black Hills question until it erupted into a major crisis.[36] For the moment, however, threats of trouble over the treaty came not from Dakota, but from Wyoming.

The people of Wyoming were no happier with the Peace Commission and the treaty than were the people of Dakota. The valleys of the Wind River, the Sweetwater, and the Big Horn beckoned temptingly. There was gold along the Sweetwater and, possibly, the Wind River and the Big Horn. Settlers and prospectors who were anxious to develop the region were kept from doing so only by the Indians. In his annual report as Superintendent of Indian Affairs for 1869, Governor J. A. Campbell wrote:

> It will be seen that the Sioux [by terms of the treaty] are thus in actual possession of nearly one-third of this Territory, and come up to the very borders of the Sweetwater mining settlements and the Shoshone reservation before they are discovered. This fact has enabled them to successfully make three raids this year on these settlements, in which they have murdered

---

[34] *Ibid.*, October 5, 1867; see also issue of April 4, 1868.
[35] *Ibid.*, October 5, 1867.
[36] See below, pp. 171–174, 199–201.

eight men and stolen a number of horses and mules. . . . As these Sioux have repeatedly violated the terms of their treaty, it appears to me that adherence to it on the part of the government is suicidal and unjust to ourselves. I am very much inclined to believe that a rigorous enforcement of the present policy of the Indian department would be the proper course to pursue with the Sioux, and that they should be compelled to go on their reservation and stay upon it. The unceded lands in this Territory would then be no longer used simply as a vantage ground from which murderous and plundering raids could be made on the white settlers . . . .[37]

There was a strong disposition in Wyoming to force the Government's hand rather than await its decision. During the winter of 1869–1870, a group in Cheyenne organized the "Big Horn Mining Association" for the express purpose of sending an expedition of prospectors and settlers into that part of Wyoming given to the Sioux by the treaty. W. L. Kuykendall, chairman of the group, admitted that he had "no assurance of what action the administration will take in the premises." He continued:

I can only say that from the best information obtained, we confidently believe that such an expedition will be allowed to go unmolested, as it must have been the intention of congress in organizing this territory to secure its speedy settlement and development, that having always been the policy of the government with other territories. It now remains to be seen whether the general government will give us territorial organization and then prevent us from carrying out its true interest.[38]

Kuykendall's arguments were almost as old as the West itself. They had been used by the Scotch-Irish against the Penns;[39] they had been used by almost every other western group bent on taking the law in its own hands, or, at the least, restive under governmental restrictions which prevented them from doing as they wished.[40] They were not

[37] Com. of Indian Affairs, *Annual Report*, 1869, p. 272.

[38] *Omaha Weekly Herald*, January 26, 1870.

[39] See, e.g., Amelia C. Ford, *Colonial Precedents of our National Land System as it Existed in 1800*, Bulletin, University of Wisconsin, No. 352, p. 434.

[40] Complaining of the proposal to establish the Sioux reserve in Dakota, the *Yankton Union and Dakotaian*, October 5, 1867, wrote: "The people of Dakota were invited here by the Government of the United States. They came here to make homes for themselves and their children and to lay the foundations of a future state. After years of toil, privation and hardship, incident to the settlement of every new country, and just as they are beginning to anticipate brighter days and reap the reward of toil, this Indian Commission comes along and proposes to rob them of the fairest and wealthiest portions of their Territory, and dedicate the same to the cause of barbarism forever. . . . we claim that the people of Dakota . . . have rights, which if not guaranteed

unattractive. As General Augur observed after a hurried trip to Cheyenne to investigate the rumor that an expedition was being planned to go to the Big Horn country, the Government could hardly expect the citizens of Wyoming to acquiesce in a policy which cut them off from a third of their territory for the benefit of hostile tribes.[41] Yet to allow the Big Horn expedition to start would mean the scuttling of the treaty even before it had been put into effective operation. As Governor Campbell himself admitted: "We can have little hope that they [the Sioux] will believe any future promises when they find promises solemnly made by our most eminent citizens acting under a special law of Congress are totally disregarded."[42]

This question, like the trading problem, was put before the Cabinet, whose decision was not particularly helpful. Augur was to "use his discretion and prevent an invasion of the Indian country and consequent Indian war." If the expedition was only for parts of Wyoming which could be visited without preventing a collision, he could let it proceed; otherwise, he would have to stop it.[43] For a time, there was uncertainty as to what the Government could or would do. Strong pressures were brought on Governor Campbell to permit the expedition to start, and there was a suggestion from one quarter that if the necessary permission could not be obtained, "why let the expeditionists go when they please and how they please."[44] Moreover, the trading problem remained unsettled, and there was fear that the Sioux might make serious trouble before the summer was out.[45]

It seemed that the second summer after the treaty was to be no better than its predecessors, that the familiar pattern of confusion, controversy, and threats of war was to be continued. In late April, however, word came that transformed the whole aspect of Indian affairs: Red Cloud wanted to visit the Great White Father in Washington; he wanted to talk about the treaty and perhaps about going on a reservation.[46]

to them by the *lex scripta* which brought this Indian Commission into existence, are at least secured by the law of common justice and common decency. . . ."

[41] Augur to AG, U.S. Army, March 12, 1870, NARS, RG 98, LS, Dept. of the Platte.

[42] Campbell to J. D. Cox, March 23, 1870, NARS, RG 75, Indian Office, Wyoming.

[43] Telegram, AAG, Military Division of the Missouri, to Augur, March 31, 1870, NARS, RG 98, TR, Dept. of the Platte.

[44] *Yankton Union and Dakotaian*, March 31, 1870.

[45] Telegram, Maj. Alexander Chambers, CO, Fort Fetterman, to AAG, Dept. of the Platte, April 2, 1870, NARS, RG 98, TR, Dept. of the Platte.

[46] *Ibid.*, April 28, 1870.

The origin of this unusual request is clouded in obscurity. John Richard, Jr., seems to have had a good deal to do with it, but it is difficult if not impossible to determine his exact role in the matter, and, indeed, his total relationship to the Government. Although a grand jury in Cheyenne had indicted Richard for the murder at Fort Fetterman,[47] the authorities had made no serious effort to arrest him and he was able to enlist some powerful support in his behalf. Gen. John B. Sanborn, late of the Peace Commission, agreed to serve as his attorney, arguing that in addition to extenuating circumstances which mitigated the crime, Richard should not be prosecuted because of the great services he had rendered the Government during the Powder River wars of 1866: Sanborn claimed that Richard had saved the garrison at Fort C. F. Smith from starvation and capture after the Phil Kearny massacre.[48] From Whetstone Agency, Spotted Tail addressed a petition to the President asking that Richard be pardoned. This petition, which contained the signature of H. B. Denman as well as those of a number of Army officers, urged the desirability of a pardon for quite different reasons than those given by Sanborn: Richard had great influence with the Indians, and if prosecuted might use it to bring on a war against the whites![49] Richard visited Fort Fetterman several times during the winter and spring and he may have worked out a scheme to secure a pardon if he could persuade Red Cloud and others to go to Washington.[50] On the other hand, he may have persuaded Red Cloud, who apparently had assumed certain responsibilities for the renegade's safety, that by going to Washington to see the Great White Father he could secure Richard's pardon.[51] In any event, when Red Cloud's request came in, it was accompanied by the further request that Richard go with him.[52]

[47] J. A. Campbell to E. S. Parker, May 2, 1870, NARS, RG 75, LR, Upper Platte Agency.

[48] Sanborn to Parker, January 6, 1870, NARS, RG 98, LR, AGO. Sanborn, it will be recalled, had helped Richard with his trading permit (see above, pp. 86–87).

[49] Spotted Tail *et al.* to the President, January 10, 1870, *ibid.*

[50] William Garnett, who was at Fort Fetterman at the time, held this view (Ricker, Interview with William Garnett, January 10, 1907, Ricker Mss., Tablet No. 1, p. 41).

[51] Campbell to Parker, May 2, 1870 (above, n. 47).

[52] Chambers to AAG, Dept. of the Platte, April 28, 1870, (above, n. 46). George Hyde, *Red Cloud's Folk* (Norman: University of Oklahoma Press, 1957), p. 173, points out that the Indian Bureau had been considering the advisability of bringing Red Cloud to Washington, and Richard's negotiations may have been pursuant to that. It is hard to believe, as Hyde intimates, however, that the whole affair was a put-up job designed to fool both the Indians and the American public.

Maj. Alexander Chambers, commandant at Fort Fetterman, urged that the request be granted. He believed it would "stop, in a short time, all Indian depredations in this section of the country." [53] Sherman had an entirely different view. Upon receipt of the recommendation, he telegraphed Sheridan:

> The President and Secretary of the Interior are away, but I know their views so well that I think I need not wait their return to answer about Red Cloud and the Sioux about Fort Fetterman. They should be told plainly and emphatically that they are expected to occupy that reservation north of Nebraska and to trade down the Missouri River. That General Augur may take a delegation of them around by rail and river to see and confer with Spotted Tail and others already located. After the return of the President, we will see about some of them coming to Washington, but as a general rule, this does more harm than good. Still I must leave this to the Indian Bureau. . . . [54]

Sherman was mistaken in his estimate of the attitudes of President Grant and Secretary of the Interior Cox. The matter was laid before the Cabinet on May 3 and that body decided that Red Cloud should be brought in. He could bring Man-Afraid-of-His-Horse and others of his own choosing, not to exceed twelve in all. Richard could also come along, "with the understanding that he is fully to abide the decision of the War Department in reference to the killing of the soldier at Fort Laramie [*sic*]." [55] At the same time, it was decided to bring Spotted Tail to Washington so that he, too, could visit with the Great White Father. [56]

The son of Man-Afraid was at Fort Fetterman when the word from Washington arrived, and he rushed off to take the news to his father and Red Cloud. [57] Chambers soon had a reply. Red Cloud and Man-Afraid would be at Fort Fetterman on May 14, ready to go. There was fear, however, that the whole business would be for naught if the Big Horn expedition were allowed to proceed. [58] With peace dangling so

[53] Chambers to AAG, *ibid.*

[54] Sherman to Sheridan, April 29, 1870, transmitted by telegram, Sheridan to Augur, April 29, 1870, NARS, RG 98, TR, Dept. of the Platte.

[55] *Ibid.*, May 4, 1870.

[56] Parker to John A. Burbank, Yankton, South Dakota, May 3, 1870, NARS, RG 75, LS, Com. of Indian Affairs.

[57] Chambers to AAG, Dept. of the Platte, May 6, 1870, NARS, RG 98, TR, Dept. of the Platte.

[58] Telegram, J. A. Campbell to E. S. Parker, May 12, 1870, NARS, RG 75, LR, Upper Platte Agency.

alluringly, nothing like a prospecting excursion was going to be allowed to interfere, and President Grant directed that the Big Horn party be prevented from leaving Cheyenne.[59] Sherman warned Augur to take every precaution to protect the Indians while they were in the neighborhood of Cheyenne, "for it would be an infamous outrage if Indians in custody of agents should be molested."[60]

When Red Cloud did not arrive at Fort Fetterman on time, there was momentary concern that he might not come at all.[61] But on May 16 he appeared at the fort prepared for the trip and with five hundred of his people to see him off.[62]

The stage was set for one of the most bizarre scenes yet enacted in the tortured drama of negotiations with the man who had come to be recognized as the most powerful chief of all the Sioux.

[59] Telegram, Sherman to Augur, May 13, 1870, NARS, RG 98, TR, Dept. of the Platte. Bvt. Maj. Gen. John H. King wired from Cheyenne that the expedition had been abandoned; "in fact, it never could have started with any chances of success, being only 200 strong" (King to AAG, Dept. of the Platte, May 15, 1870, *ibid.*).

[60] Telegram, Sherman to Augur, May 12, 1870, *ibid.*

[61] Telegram, Campbell to Parker, May 17, 1870, NARS, RG 75, LR, Upper Platte Agency.

[62] Telegram, Chambers to AAG, Dept. of the Platte, NARS, RG 98, TR, Dept. of the Platte.

CHAPTER 7

Red Cloud Visits the Great White Father

On May 18, Red Cloud left Fort Fetterman to go down to Fort Laramie to meet Col. John E. Smith, who was coming out from Washington to provide escort for the chief and his party on their epochal journey to see the Great White Father.[1] Everything possible was done to impress Red Cloud with both his own importance and that which the Government attached to his mission. Colonel Smith originally had planned to meet the Indians at Fort Sanders, near Cheyenne, but at Red Cloud's request he came to Laramie. When the Indians arrived at the fort, on May 24, they were escorted with great pomp and ceremony to the commanding officer's residence, and W. G. Bullock, the post sutler, provided handsomely for their needs.[2] Not since 1868,

[1] Telegram, Smith to E. S. Parker, May 19, 1870, NARS, RG 75, LR, Upper Platte Agency. The journey was conducted under the auspices of the Commissioner of Indian Affairs, and Colonel Smith was placed on temporary duty with that official by the War Department. His instructions were very broad. He was given a drawing account of $2,500, from which he was authorized to purchase clothing or anything else the Indians might need. In particular, he was to "see that every precaution is taken to prevent the party from being molested in any way while in Cheyenne or when passing through that or any other place" (Parker to Smith, May 14, 1870, NARS, RG 75, LS, Com. of Indian Affairs).

[2] Telegram, Col. F. F. Flint, CO, Fort Laramie, to AAG, Dept. of the Platte, May 24, 1870, NARS, RG 98, TR, Dept. of the Platte; *Omaha Weekly Herald*, June 8, 1870.

when he had come in to sign the treaty, had Red Cloud been treated with such deference at Fort Laramie.

He soon learned that there were definite limits to what the Government would do. He had hoped to take twenty of his chiefs and head men with him, and seven of them insisted upon bringing their wives. This, Colonel Smith told him, could not be permitted.[3] The original authorization had provided for a party of twelve;[4] an increase had been authorized, but under no circumstances was the delegation to exceed twenty in number.[5] After much discussion, the party was cut to twenty-one, identified by Colonel Smith as follows: Red Cloud, Red Dog, Brave Bear, Little Bear, Sitting Bear, Bear Skin, Long Wolf, Brave, Afraid, Red Fly, Rocky Bear, Swing Bear, Yellow Bear, Black Hawk, Sword, The-One-That-Runs-Through, and the wives of the last four, who refused to come without them. John Richard, of course, was also along; W. G. Bullock and James McCloskey accompanied the group as interpreters. Later, Jules Ecoffey, at Red Cloud's request, was added to the party.[6] Man-Afraid-of-His-Horse, who was to have been a member of the delegation, took sick at Fort Fetterman and had to be left behind.[7] Red Cloud, it seems, had decided not to take his wife, because he had been told that, as a general rule, the wives of congressmen and other great men did not accompany them on trips to Washington.[8]

Colonel Smith and his charges left Fort Laramie on May 26.[9] For fear that there might be trouble in Cheyenne, where there was a good deal of resentment against the Government's action in stopping the Big Horn Expedition, the group boarded the Union Pacific at Pine Bluffs, forty miles east of the Wyoming capital.[10] Nightfall of the twenty-seventh saw them comfortably ensconced in a special coach

[3] Smith to Parker, July 15, 1870, Com. of Indian Affairs, *Annual Report*, 1870, pp. 324–326.

[4] Telegram, Lt. Gen. P. H. Sheridan to Gen. C. C. Augur, May 4, 1870, NARS, RG 98, TR, Dept. of the Platte.

[5] Telegram, Parker to J. A. Campbell, May 16, 1870, NARS, RG 75, LS, Com. of Indian Affairs.

[6] Smith to Parker, July 15, 1870 (above, n. 3).

[7] Telegram, Flint to AAG, Dept. of the Platte, May 24, 1870 (above, n. 2).

[8] *New York Times*, June 2, 1870.

[9] Telegram, Flint to AAG, Dept. of the Platte, May 26, 1870, NARS, RG 98, TR, Dept. of the Platte.

[10] Smith to Parker, July 15, 1870 (above, n. 3). Interestingly enough, both Red Cloud and the people of Cheyenne objected to this arrangement (*Omaha Weekly Herald*, June 8, 1870).

and speeding eastward on the iron horse. We do not know what Red Cloud's thoughts and feelings were as he rode away from the land of his fathers, past the farms and villages of the white man and through his cities. We do know that many people, particularly in the East, had high hopes for the journey. The *New York Times* wrote:

> The visit of Red Cloud to Washington cannot but do good. . . . Red Cloud is undoubtedly the most celebrated warrior now living on the American Continent . . . a man of brains, a good ruler, an eloquent speaker, an able general and fair diplomat. The friendship of Red Cloud is of more importance to the whites than that of any other ten chiefs on the plains. Let every care be taken of him while in the East and no efforts spared to win his good will and create in his mind a favorable impression. He is a savage, but a powerful and wise man withal. . . .[11]

Westerners were not so enthusiastic. A citizen of Cheyenne commented sarcastically: "Rumor has it that he [Red Cloud] is to become a member of the Cabinet, *vice* Fish, to resign, and thus have a voice in our national affairs equal to the power which he has so far exercised."[12]

From the beginning the Army, which up to this time had had more dealings with Red Cloud than had any other branch of the government, had been only lukewarm about the visit,[13] and as the party passed through Omaha, General Augur felt called upon to remind his superiors of the realities of the situation. He wrote:

> While I think it very desirable that Red Cloud should be confirmed in what seems to be his present friendly disposition, I feel it my duty to state my opinion that however successful the government may be in doing this, it will by no means stop Indian depredations on the plains. I do this as I see by the papers that an impression prevails in the East that Red Cloud is the head and front of all the hostile bands. Nothing can be further from the truth. His band is not a large one and I have reasons to believe that during the past year has not been a very troublesome one. I cannot, of course, be certain of this, but I am almost certain that most of the Indian troubles in this department for the past two years have come from Minneconjous, the Northern Cheyennes, the regular bands heretofore on the Republican under Pawnee Killer, Whistler and others, and probably part of the Northern Arapahoes, with a sprinkling of Uncpapas and others from the North.
>
> Red Cloud cannot control any of these bands and his influence with them

[11] June 1, 1870.
[12] *Omaha Weekly Herald,* June 8, 1870.
[13] See above, p. 94.

will be no greater than that of Spotted Tail. I think it will be found that any chief or head man who becomes friendly to the whites will cease to exert any influence over the hostiles, unless of his immediate family. . . .

I have taken the liberty to write the above that no undue expectations may be formed from any amicable arrangement made with Red Cloud, but while I doubt the possibility to do much good, there is no question that he can do a great deal of harm, if so disposed, and if by any arrangement this can be prevented and he be induced to exert any influence that he has for peace, a great deal will have been accomplished.[14]

As subsequent events would show, General Augur had assessed the situation with more than a little perspicacity. Officials of the Interior department, however, and almost everyone else in the country, were convinced that peace with Red Cloud would mean peace on the plains, and they were going to bend every effort to secure it.

The Indians arrived in Washington on June 1, at six o'clock in the morning, and were taken immediately to the Washington House on Pennsylvania Avenue.[15] Here they found Spotted Tail and a delegation of Brulés from Whetstone Agency who had been in the capital since May 24 and already were growing weary of its sights and anxious to return to their homes.[16] It was feared that there might be some awkwardness when the two chiefs met. There had been bad blood between them since 1866, when Spotted Tail had signed the treaty and Red Cloud had refused. The ill feeling was increased when Spotted Tail, in self-defense, killed Big Mouth, an Oglala and chief of the Laramie Loafers.[17] And of course the fact that the whites persisted in looking upon Spotted Tail as the leader of the friendlies and Red Cloud as the leader of the hostiles augmented the rivalry between them.

[14] Augur to Brig. Gen. E. D. Townsend, May 28, 1870, NARS, RG 98, LS, Dept. of the Platte.

[15] *New York Times*, June 2, 1870. The government paid the Washington House $954.50 for boarding the Oglala and Brulé Sioux, and $281.65 "for furnishing lemonade, cigars, tobacco, oranges, nuts, etc." (W. F. Kady, Acting Commissioner of Indian Affairs, to Mrs. A. F. Beveridge and B. F. Beveridge, June 15, 1870, NARS, RG 75, LS). Among other expenses incident to the trip were $204 for furnishing carriages (Kady to J. P. Allcott and Sons, June 28, 1870, *ibid.*) and $730 for medical services (Kady to Dr. W. W. Potter, July 5, 1870, *ibid.*).

[16] *New York Herald*, May 31, 1870; *New York Times*, May 31, 1870. A good account of Spotted Tail's visit to Washington will be found in D. C. Poole, *Among the Sioux of Dakota* (New York: D. Van Nostrand, 1881), pp. 151–208. Poole was in charge of the Whetstone Agency and accompanied Spotted Tail on the trip.

[17] For a discussion of the killing of Big Mouth, see George E. Hyde, *Spotted Tail's Folk* (Norman: University of Oklahoma Press, 1961), pp. 149–153.

Spotted Tail heightened the suspense by saying that he had no desire to meet Red Cloud,[18] but those who were looking for trouble between the two chiefs were doomed to disappointment. When they met in the lobby of the hotel, "they shook hands and talked together for some time, seemingly burying all unfriendly feelings in a common understanding to exert whatever influence each possessed with the white rulers in behalf of their respective Indian tribes."[19]

When the Indians arrived, G. P. Beauvais, who had been added to the party to assist with the interpreting and with the management of the Indians generally, reported that they were very tired from their long journey and needed several days' rest.[20] Beauvais underestimated the recuperative power of his charges, for within twenty-four hours Red Cloud was insisting that he be allowed to see the representatives of the Great White Father, and an interview was hastily arranged for Friday, June 3, in the office of the Secretary of the Interior.[21] After the Indians had filed through a large crowd of curious onlookers and had found chairs, Secretary J. D. Cox and Commissioner Ely S. Parker came in. They were introduced to Red Cloud and all the members of his delegation; earlier they had met Spotted Tail, who was present also. Commissioner Parker opened the proceedings with a few innocuous words of welcome:

> "I am very glad to see you today. I know that you have come a long way to see your Great Father. . . . You have had no accident, have arrived here all well, and should be very thankful to the Great Spirit, who has kept you safe. The Great Father got Red Cloud's message that he wanted to come to Washington and see him, and the President said he might come. We will be

[18] *New York Herald*, May 31, 1870; *New York Times*, May 31, 1870.

[19] *New York Times*, June 3, 1870. I find no evidence to support Hyde's assertion that the two chiefs were locked in a room to have it out and that Spotted Tail gave way by agreeing to let Red Cloud be recognized as the head of the nation (George E. Hyde, *Red Cloud's Folk* [Norman: University of Oklahoma Press, 1957], pp. 175–176). The two men were rivals, and the Washington visit, particularly because the Indian Bureau gave Spotted Tail precedence in recognition of his having been the first to sign the treaty, produced a number of potentially explosive situations. These two unlettered red men from the plains, however, seem to have handled these difficulties over precedence with considerably more discretion than some of their more sophisticated white brethren have exhibited under similar circumstances. The *New York Times* reporter in Washington, in common with his colleagues generally, was inclined to be something of a supercilious smart aleck when writing about the Indians, but in this instance he seems to have reported the situation carefully and correctly.

[20] *New York Times*, June 2, 1870.

[21] *Ibid.*, June 4, 1870.

ready at any time to hear what Red Cloud has to say for himself and his people."[22]

He then introduced Secretary Cox, who continued in the same vein, but with emphasis on the Government's great desire for peace. In concluding his remarks, Cox addressed a few words to Spotted Tail, thanking him for being present and expressing appreciation for the good will he had toward the whites. Apparently it was assumed that this would bring the day's proceedings to an end, but Red Cloud got up and announced that he had something to say:

> My friends, I have come a long ways to see you, but some how or other you don't look at me. I had to come to see you.
>
> When I heard the words of my Great Father permitting me to come I was glad and came right off. I left my women and children at home and want you to give them more rations and wish you would send my people some ammunition to kill game and telegraph to them that I have arrived all right.

Secretary Cox tried to get off the hook. "When they arrived we knew they were tired," he lamely explained. "We thought they wanted to rest and we treated them as we thought would most gratify them." He would send a telegram to Red Cloud's people saying that their chief had arrived safely, but they would have to consider the other requests. Right now he had to leave "to go to Council of the President." After Cox had departed, Parker told the Indians that tomorrow he wanted to show them the city. The next day was Sunday and the whites did no business on that day. On Monday evening, however, the President would have them all at his house so that he could meet them, and then on Tuesday they would hold another conference.

The sight-seeing began on Friday afternoon, when the Indians were escorted on a tour of the Capitol. Just like any other tourists, they were taken to the top of the dome for a view of the city and surrounding countryside, and then were ushered into the Senate gallery. The Senate, they were told, was at that very moment considering legislation for their welfare.[23] If this made any impression upon the visitors as they

[22] Transcript of Interviews with Red Cloud in Washington, June 3, 7, 1870, NARS, RG 75, LR, Upper Platte Agency. This transcript is neither complete nor well organized, but unless otherwise indicated, I am using it as the source for the conferences, supplemented by the *New York Herald* and the *New York Times*, both of which carried very full accounts of the proceedings.

[23] The Senate was debating the Indian Appropriation Bill (*Congressional Globe*, 41st Cong., 2d Sess., Pt. V, pp. 4042–4061).

sat fanning themselves and impassively watching the proceedings, they gave no sign of it. Indeed, the only part of the Capitol which elicited any show of interest whatever was the Marble Room where they commented among themselves about the huge chandelier, the mirrors, and the busts of two Indian chiefs.

Saturday's excursion, which included visits to the Arsenal and the Navy Yard, was designed to impress the Indians with the power of the Great White Father. No effort was spared, but somehow the show did not come off quite as expected. The Indians were interested enough— in marked contrast to the stoical indifference they had exhibited the day before at the Capitol—but the surprise and awe which the weapons were supposed to evoke on the countenances of the savage visitors did not materialize. When the cannon at the Arsenal were fired, for example, the women put their hands to their ears in advance of the shots, indicating that they knew all about such things. Perhaps the biggest disappointment was the effect created by the fifteen-inch coastal defense gun. To be sure, it was a mighty weapon. Red Cloud gravely measured the diameter of the barrel on his face and hand (not with his fan, as is usually reported),[24] and the huge grains of powder used to fire the monster elicited much comment, as did the big shell which went ricocheting four or five miles down the Potomac. But of what good was all this? The Indians knew they could ride all around the big gun and far away while it was being loaded; besides, the gun was so heavy it could not be moved—and who would be fool enough to sit near it and wait to be killed?

At the Navy Yard a regiment of Marines put on a full-dress parade for the entertainment of the visitors. All the equipment for the manufacture of howitzers and ammunition was running and its operation was carefully explained to them, but the Indians betrayed no more than polite interest. Their reaction was quite different, however, when they saw the bright ringlets of brass which fell from a lathe which was turning out a howitzer, and they were delighted when they were told to help themselves. They were also much interested in an ironclad monitor lying at the wharf; they doubted, though, that it was made of iron because anyone knew that iron would not float. Red Cloud and Spotted Tail were invited to try to cut the deck with their knives, and found to their astonishment that the ship really was made of iron. It took a good deal of persuasion to get them to go aboard, but they

[24] See, e.g., Hyde, *Red Cloud's Folk*, p. 176; Stanley Vestal, *Warpath and Council Fire* (New York: Random House, 1948), p. 187.

finally consented to make a short inspection of the ship. It was lying low in the water and when they got below deck they were sure they were under water and insisted on going back up. They all seemed relieved when they stepped ashore again. At the conclusion of the tour, the wife of Admiral John A. Dahlgren, commandant of the Navy Yard, invited them to lunch, but Red Cloud respectfully declined, saying he had come for business and not for pleasure.

On Monday evening the Indians were all taken to the White House to meet the Great Father. As Saturday's proceedings had been designed to impress them with the Great Father's power, this occasion was calculated to dazzle them with the splendor in which he lived. After the Indians had been ushered into the East Room and seated in chairs ranged along the walls, servants came in to light the great chandeliers. This apparently excited as much interest as anything the Indians had seen. When the room was ablaze with light, President and Mrs. Grant entered, followed by members of the Cabinet, representatives of the diplomatic corps, officials of the Indian Bureau, and a number of congressmen. Many of the dignitaries were accompanied by their wives. After all had been introduced, and after the British Minister had tried unsuccessfully to converse with Red Cloud in English, the throng moved on to the State Dining Room, where they found tables loaded with the white man's delicacies. The savage guests ate the strawberries and ice cream with relish, but drank sparingly of the wine. Spotted Tail remarked that the white men surely had many more good things to eat and drink than they sent to the Indians. When told that this was because the white men had quit the warpath and gone to farming, he replied that he would be glad to farm, too, "if you will always treat me like this and let me live in as big a house." All in all, it was quite an evening. The *New York Times* commented that "in every respect the entertainment was as elegant as that given to Prince Arthur last summer."[25]

The Indians had come through the ordeal very well. They had been bewildered and embarrassed, but they had behaved with decorum throughout the day of being impressed and the day of being dazzled. Moreover, they demonstrated their mettle as diplomats by showing, when the conference finally got down to business on Tuesday, that they had not been in the least daunted by the Great Father's might or splendor.

Secretary Cox opened the conference by reviewing the events of the

[25] June 7, 1870.

past few days. Because of what they had seen, "Red Cloud and his people . . . will now know that what the President does is not because he is afraid but because he wants to do that which is right and good." When the number of whites grew so fast that they had to move out onto the plains, the President wanted to find a place where the Indians could live by themselves and not be disturbed—"for that reason our great soldier, General Sherman, made the treaty to give them the country where they now are and take our people out of it so that they could be there alone." Cox reminded the Indians, with an obvious reference to the Big Horn expedition, that lately some of the whites had wanted to go into the Indian country but that the President had refused to let them go, saying he had given the country to the Sioux. He said further that the President had considered Red Cloud's request of the other day, and while he would continue to give them plenty to eat, he could not give them powder and lead because the whites on the frontier were afraid, and so long as any Indians were at war none of them could have powder and lead. When all of the Indians had abandoned the warpath and were living at peace on the reservations, the President would see what he could do. Meanwhile he wanted Red Cloud to try to learn the ways of the white man and to persuade others to do so. Referring to Felix R. Brunot, chairman of the newly created Board of Indian Commissioners, who was present at the meeting, Cox said that later in the summer the President was going to send him out to visit the Indians: "When he goes he will ask what is the best thing we can do for them—if anybody has done them any wrong they can tell him—and when he comes back we will try to do what he will say they need to have done."[26] Cox concluded his address to the Indians with this warning: "The first thing we want to say to them is they must keep the peace and then we will try to do for them as is right."

After a few moments, Red Cloud got up and walked to the table where Cox and the other officials were sitting. He shook hands with them very

[26] The Board of Indian Commissioners was created by an act approved April 10, 1869. It will be recalled that in 1868, Congress had provided that the Army should supervise the expenditure of funds under the Fort Laramie treaty (see above, pp. 78–79). This was wholly unsatisfactory to the Department of the Interior, and strenuous efforts were made to return full control of all the Indians to the Department. Congress was agreeable, but the Indian service was so suspect that some sort of safeguard had to be established to revive public confidence. The Board of Indian Commissioners was created to provide that safeguard. Consisting of eminent civilians, who served without pay, the Board was given general supervision over the management of the Indians. (A brief historical sketch of the Board will be found in *Twenty-Fifth Annual Report of the Board of Indian Commissioners, 1893*, pp. 3–15.)

solemnly, and said, "I came from where the sun sets. You were raised on a chair; I want to sit where the sun sets." He then sat down on the floor and delivered his reply.

The Great Spirit has received me naked and my Great Father I have not fought against him. I have offered my prayers to the Great Spirit so I could come here safe. Look at me. I was a warrior on this land where the sun rises, now I come from where the sun sets. Whose voice was first sounded on this land—the red people with bows and arrows. The Great Father says he is good and kind to us. I can't see it. I am good to his white people. From the word sent me I have come all the way to this house. My face is red yours is white. The Great Spirit taught you to read and write but not me. I have not learned. I came here to tell my Great Father what I do not like in my country. You are close to my Great Father and are a great many chiefs. The men the President sends there have no sense no heart. What has been done in my country, I do not want do not ask for it. White people going through my country. Father have you or any of your friends here got children. Do you want to raise them. Look at me I come here with all these young men. All are married have children and want to raise them.

The white children have surrounded me and have left me nothing but an island. When we first had this land we were strong, now we are melting like snow on the hillside while you are growing like spring grass.

Now I have come to my Great Father's house, see if I leave any blood in his land when I leave. Tell the Great Father to move Fort Fetterman away and we will have no more troubles. I have two mountains in that country (Black Hills and Big Horn Mountains). I want Great Father to make no roads through.

I have told these things three times now. I have come here to tell them the 4th time.

I don't want my reservation on the Missouri. This is the fourth time I have said no. Here are some people from Missouri now. Our children are dying off like sheep. The country does not suit them.

I was born at the Forks of the Platte and I was told that the land belonged to me. From N.E.S.W. the red men have come to the Great Father's house. These Oglallas are the last who come here but I came here to hear and listen to the Great Father's words. They have promised me traders, but we have none. At the mouth of ——— creek they had a treaty in 1862 [*sic*], and the man who made the treaty is the only one who has told me truth.

When you send goods to me they would steal all along the road so when it reaches me it was only a handful. They hold a paper for me to sign and that is all I get for my goods.

I know now the people you sent out there are all liars, and Mr. Bullock may now have some of the orders along with him. Look at me, I am poor and

naked. I do not want war with my government. The railroad passing
through my country now. I have received no pay for the land, not even a
[two words illegible]. I want you to tell all this to my Great Father.

This young man is mine (Richard). The whites have taken him away from us.
Richard took away all his stock and shot at him. At Fort Fetterman Richard
was a contractor there cutting hay for Government. Indians took all he had.
He was going to kill them. He has done something and he wants to tell the
Great Father and has brought him here. General Smith is the only gentle-
man who has told us everything straight and I know he is good &c &c.[27]

Red Cloud was followed by Grass, who made a short speech endors-
ing all that the chief had said. Spotted Tail confined himself to a
plea for Richard. Cox replied that all that had been said would be
reported to the President, and that later the President himself would
meet with the chiefs. Parker concluded the conference by inviting them
all to attend an entertainment at a deaf and dumb asylum, but Red
Cloud declined, saying that if he was to see the Great Father again he
wanted time to think about what to say.

Whatever he might say to the Great Father, he had said enough
already to put the Indian Bureau on the spot and to dramatize the folly
of trying to overawe the Indians into an abandonment of what they
considered to be their rights. The *New York Times* wrote:

We might search in vain through a month's file of the Congressional *Globe*
for a speech so interesting as that delivered by Red Cloud at the Indian
Council yesterday. . . .

A plain and dispassionate statement of the Indian view of the standing
problem between barbarism and civilization, is precisely what most people
required, and it is what this oration of Red Cloud, endorsed as it was by his
companions, affords. It is not a little startling to hear this bold reminder of
the Chief, "You are the people who should keep peace," and one-sided as
it is, there is in it much matter for reflection. The clear conception which this
unlettered savage possesses of what he claims as his rights, and what he is
disposed to resent in his wrong, shows very plainly the necessity for treating
with the leaders of the aboriginal "nations" on some straightforward and
intelligible principle. The attempt to cajole and bamboozle them, as if they
were deficient in intelligence, ought to be abandoned, no less than the
policy of hunting them down like wild beasts. Whatever may be the theories
we hold about the ultimate future of a decaying race, we cannot fail to
recognize the wisdom of meeting Red Cloud and his people in a spirit of
frankness and firmness. In this respect we need not be above learning a
lesson, even from the savage.[28]

The *New York Herald* said that Red Cloud combined "the logic and

[27] I have followed the original transcript, cited in note 22, above.
[28] June 8, 1870.

pathos of Logan with the indomitable pluck of Red Jacket and Bow-legs," and expressed the hope that his speech had convinced the Secretary of the Interior "that palaver has very little effect on the Indian character, . . . that faithlessness on our part in the matter of treaties, and gross swindling of the Indians by our agents and their tools—the contractors—are at the bottom of all this Indian trouble." [29]

The eagerly awaited interview with the President brought little more than a reiteration of Red Cloud's complaints and of the Government's desire to do what was right by the Indians. In speaking to the President, Red Cloud concentrated on Fort Fetterman, demanding that it be abandoned. Grant replied that his authority would always be used for the protection of both the whites and the Indians, and that Fort Fetterman could not be abandoned because it was used for both. On the next day, June 10, the Indians assembled again at the Department of the Interior for what was to be their final interview with the Secretary. Red Cloud repeated all of his old complaints, this time reserving special fire for the Army officers sent to the plains; they were all whiskey drinkers, except General Smith, who "does not drink their whiskey, and therefore he can talk with our Great Father." This created consternation among the military,[30] and there were more fireworks to come. After Secretary Cox, hoping to wind up the long conference, had gone over the provisions of the Treaty of 1868 and had explained that this was the basis of the Government's dealings with the Indians, Red Cloud provided the real bombshell of the meeting. "This is the first time I have heard of such a treaty," he announced. "I never heard of it and do not mean to follow it." Cox, showing no sign that he was aware of the implications of Red Cloud's statement, now made a patient effort to explain the work of the Commission, reminding Red Cloud that General Sherman and the others who met with the Indians "would not tell a lie to save their lives." To this Red Cloud—who had brushed aside Major Dye's efforts to explain the treaty[31]—replied: "I do not say the Commissioners lied, but the interpreters were wrong. I never heard a word, only what was brought to my camp. When the forts were removed, I came to make peace. You had your war-houses, or forts. When you removed them, I signed a treaty of peace. We want to straighten things up."

It seemed indeed as though there was much that needed to be

[29] June 9, 1870.

[30] See, e.g., Telegram, Maj. Alexander Chambers, CO, Fort Fetterman, to AAG, Headquarters, Dept. of the Platte, June 25, 1870, NARS, RG 98, TR, Dept. of the Platte.

[31] See above, pp. 80–82.

straightened up. There would have to be yet another meeting—the much-heralded journey to Washington simply could not end on this note. The prospects for another meeting, however, were not very encouraging. When Cox offered Red Cloud a copy of the treaty so that he could have it explained to him, the chief angrily replied, "I will not take the paper with me. It is all lies." In desperation, the interpreters and agents were given copies in the hope that they could persuade the chief to listen to an explanation, and another meeting was set for the following day.

It was all the interpreters and agents could do to persuade the Indians, who were so disheartened that some of them wanted to commit suicide, to attend another conference. When they arrived at the Interior building on the eleventh, however, they found that the Government was willing to place a new interpretation on the treaty: the Sioux would not have to go to the reservation to receive their goods; the Government would let them live on the headwaters of the Big Cheyenne River, northeast of Fort Fetterman. This concession was followed by a request that the Indians let the Commissioner know the names of the men whom they wanted for their agent and traders so that the Government could find out "whether they were good men and could be trusted."[32]

Red Cloud had won an important point. He came forward, shook hands with Cox and Parker, seated himself on the floor, and responded with that directness of which he was sometimes capable:

> What I said to the Great Father, the President, is now in my mind. I have only a few words to add this morning. I have become tired of speaking. Yesterday, when I saw the treaty and all the false things in it, I was mad. I suppose it made you the same. The Secretary explained it this morning, and now I am pleased. . . .

Then, despite the fact that he was "tired of speaking," he launched into another long discussion of the wrongs of his people and the history of their relations with the white man. He interrupted his harangue to point to Fanny Kelly, who had achieved fame because of her captivity by the Sioux: "Look at that woman. She was captured by Silver Horn's party. I wish you to pay her what her captors owe her. I am a man true to what I say, and want to keep my promise. The Indians robbed that lady there, and through your influence I want her to be paid."[33]

---

[32] Red Cloud had said several times that he wanted B. B. Mills for agent and W. G. Bullock for trader.

[33] *New York Times*, June 12, 1870; cf. Fanny Kelly, *Narrative of My Captivity Among the Sioux Indians* (Hartford, Conn.: Mutual Publishing Co., 1871), pp. 252–254.

When Red Cloud had finished, Cox expressed satisfaction at his change in attitude and promised the Sioux that they could look forward to the future with hope. He added that General Smith would take them to New York on their way home so that they could spend a day buying presents. Red Cloud immediately objected, saying: "I do not want to go that way. I want a straight line. I have seen enough of towns. There are plenty of stores between here and my home. . . . I want to go back the way I came. The whites are the same everywhere. I see them every day." Cox replied that he would be guided by General Smith as to the route home, that he was not particularly anxious that the Indians should go to New York.

This ended the conference. Later in the day, Senator Lot M. Morrill of Maine called on Red Cloud to urge him to accept the invitation to visit New York, to see his many friends in the north. Red Cloud decided to make the trip, but before he would leave Washington he wanted still another conference, so on Sunday, June 12, Cox and Parker again met with the chief.

Red Cloud had come to say good-bye; before he left he wanted to know whether the men he had requested would be sent as his agents and traders. He did not want military men for agents, and he did not want men who were poor, who were sent out to fill their pockets. He wanted B. B. Mills for agent and W. G. Bullock for trader. He also wanted seventeen horses "to take us back home from the railroad." He concluded by saying that he intended to make a speech in New York.

Cox responded with his usual equivocation. They were not ready to name agents and traders yet, but Red Cloud could rest assured that they would send him good and honest men. As he had said before, they were prepared to let Red Cloud and his people live north of Fort Fetterman, but the idea of sending an agent there was "a new thing," and it would depend upon "seeing that you are willing to live there in peace." Red Cloud must understand that "this new arrangement was made out of kindness," and that the treaty provided that trading should be done on the Missouri River. What Red Cloud had said about the forts was entitled to serious consideration, but the Great Father could not remove the troops from Fort Fetterman; they were needed to protect the Indians as well as the whites. Finally, about the presents, he was sorry to say that the Great Council had not yet given them all of the money they had asked for, so he could not say now just what they would be able to do, particularly about the horses. General Smith had money, however, and he would buy the Indians fine presents; and later, if the Sioux kept the peace, there would be more presents. As time went on, Red Cloud would see how friendly the white people were toward the Indians. He could rest assured that they would remember all that he had said.

Red Cloud was disappointed. When Cox had finished, he said:

> I know you will remember what I have said, for you have good memories. If I had not been for peace I should not have come to my Great Father's house. Tell your children to keep the peace. . . . If you had kept your people across the Platte you never would have had any trouble. You have your land fenced in and do not want us to come on it. We have our land fenced in and do not want you to intrude on us. All nations are around us. I do not want to make war with the Great Father. I want to show I go away peaceably. I want to raise my children on my land, and therefore I want my Great Father to keep his children away from me. . . . I want good horses, the same as you gave to Spotted Tail. I am not mad with you. I have got a better heart. I am going home. If you will not give me horses, very well. God Almighty raised me naked. I am much pleased with your offer to give me presents, but I do not want any.

With this the council terminated. Red Cloud and his warriors shook hands with Cox and Parker, then quickly left the room.

When the Indians got to New York on the evening of June 14, Red Cloud was in a surly mood. He went straight to his room in the St. Nicholas Hotel and refused to see anyone, even Peter Cooper and members of the Indian Peace Commission who called to make arrangements for the public meeting scheduled for the Cooper Institute on the sixteenth. There was grave danger that he would not put in an appearance at all. As Colonel Smith explained to the Commissioners, Red Cloud held the view that if he could accomplish nothing with the Great Father there was no use trying anywhere else.[34]

By the next morning his humor had improved somewhat, and he decided that he would see the Commissioners. When they were ushered in by Colonel Smith, they found the whole delegation present. Most of the men were decked out in their gaudiest ornaments, but Red Cloud was dressed in austere simplicity. After Smith had assured him that these men were his friends, that the people and government of the United States were his friends, Red Cloud arose with the dignity for which he was becoming famous and set forth his grievances in the simple, direct language for which he was also becoming famous:

[34] *New York Times*, June 15, 1870.

My Friends. The Great Spirit placed me and my people on this land poor and naked. When the white men came we gave them our lands, and did not wish to hurt them. But the white men drove us back and took our lands. Then the Great Father made us many promises, but they are not kept. He promised to give us large presents, and when they came to us they were small; they seemed to be lost on the way. I came from my people to lay their affairs before the Great Father and I tell him just what I mean and what my people wish, and I gain nothing. I asked him for seventeen horses for my young men to ride from the border to our camps, and he does not give them. I wish no stock and no presents. [Smith had told Red Cloud that he had a present of goods for him.] The Great Spirit placed me here poor and naked. I appear so before you, and I do not feel sorry for that. I am not mad—I am in good humor—but I have received no satisfaction. I am disappointed. I cannot change my claims. I am not Spotted Tail. What I say I stick to. My people understand what I come here for, and I should lose my power if I did not stick to one course. You are my friends. You always talk straight to me and I am not blaming you.

Smith replied that the present Great Father and his assistants were not the ones who had made the treaty, and that while they were required to live up to it, if the Indians would remain peaceable they would try to get it changed. He also thought that he could get the horses Red Cloud desired, but he could not positively promise it. At this juncture Peter Cooper spoke up and said that if the Government would not supply the horses, he would do so.

This seemed to change things. Red Cloud assured the Commissioners that he wanted to be friendly, and that if the presents and horses were offered to him "together, and freely," he would take them. Colonel Smith then outlined the wishes of the visitors. They wanted to show Red Cloud and his friends around the city and take them to the theater in the evening. Tomorrow they wished him to meet with the people of the city and talk to them. Red Cloud agreed. He would do what his friends wanted him to.

So that afternoon the Indians rode up Fifth Avenue and through Central Park, ogled by thousands of curious New Yorkers. Somehow, the plans for the evening went awry. The Commissioners had intended to take the Indians to the Jubilee for an elevated entertainment, but Jim Fisk got the party diverted to the Grand Opera House to see the "Twelve Temptations." As the *Times* reported, "they . . . sad to say, appeared to take especial delight in the fantastic gambols of the semi-nude coryphees and the gorgeous display of parti-colored fustian, glittering tinsel and red fire." [35]

[35] *Ibid.*, June 15, 1870.

By noon the next day the great hall at Cooper Institute was packed, and Red Cloud entered to a tumultuous ovation. Many, of course, had come simply to see a real wild Indian; but many others, and particularly the leaders, were motivated by the belief that justice and understanding would solve the Indian problem. Peter Cooper made that clear in his address of introduction. The Indians, he said, "do not question the right of eminent domain vested in our Government," but unless the Government was to behave like bandits they would have to be given just compensation. Any other policy would lead inevitably to war: "If you refuse to pay this equivalent amicably, and seek by force to wrest it from them, you will inaugurate a war that will cost so many millions that the interest alone will more than equal the price at which you can now purchase it."

It was now Red Cloud's turn. Amidst deafening applause, he arose and drew his blanket around him. Pointing his finger to the ceiling, he began: "My Brothers and my Friends who are before me today: God Almighty has made us all, and He is here to hear what I have to say to you today." Then followed the familiar recitation of the relationship between white man and red—"When the Almighty made you, He made you all white and clothed you. When He made us, He made us with red skins and poor. . . . The Great Spirit made us poor and ignorant. He made you rich and wise. . . . The Good Father made you to eat tame game and us to eat wild game. . . ." He recounted his grievances and reiterated his desire for peace:

> We came to Washington to see our Great Father that peace might be continued. The Great Father that made us both wishes peace to be kept; we want to keep peace. Will you help us? In 1868 men came out and brought papers. We could not read them, and they did not tell us truly what was in them. We thought the treaty was to remove the forts, and that we should then cease from fighting. But they wanted to send us traders on the Missouri. We did not want to go to the Missouri, but wanted traders where we were. When I reached Washington the Great Father explained to me what the the treaty was, and showed me that the interpreters had deceived me. All I want is right and just. I have tried to get from the Great Father what is right and just. I have not altogether succeeded. I represent the whole Sioux nation, and they will be bound by what I say. I am no Spotted Tail, to say one thing one day and be bought for a pin the next. Look at me. I am poor and naked, but I am the Chief of the nation. We do not want riches, but we want to train our children right. Riches would do us no good. . . . The riches that we have in this world, Secretary Cox said truly, we cannot take with us to the next world. Then I wish to know why Commissioners are sent

out to us who do nothing but rob us and get the riches of this world away from us? I was brought up among the traders, and those who came out there in the early times treated me well and I had a good time with them. They taught us to wear clothes and to use tobacco and ammunition. But, by and by, the Great Father sent out a different kind of men; men who cheated and drank whisky; men who were so bad that the Great Father could not keep them at home and so sent them out there. I have sent a great many words to the Great Father but they never reached him. They were drowned on the way, and I was afraid the words I spoke lately to the Great Father would not reach you, so I came to speak to you myself; and now I am going away to my home.[36]

The speech had been made with great difficulty. Red Cloud spoke rapidly and in a high key. After each sentence he stood impassively facing the audience while an interpreter relayed the words to Rev. Howard Crosby, who in turn passed them on to the audience. How much Crosby added to Red Cloud's words we do not know, but he did give them the benefit of his not inconsiderable oratorical powers.[37] Red Cloud's gestures and manner, though, were his own, and it was suggested that they "might be imitated with advantage by civilized and highly educated pale faces."[38] In any event, the speech made a great hit. The crowd applauded after almost every sentence, and there was sustained applause at the end.

Red Cloud had ended his tour in triumph. In years to come, the white man's histories would say that his influence began to slip after this trip to Washington and New York, but as he rode westward with the white man's applause ringing in his ears, he could reflect that he was the most celebrated member of his race, and the key to peace or war between the Government and his people.

[36] *Ibid.*, June 17, 1870.
[37] *Ibid.*
[38] *New York Herald*, June 17, 1870.

CHAPTER 8

The Government Gives In

It was difficult for the nation to determine how successful the excursion had been because no one really knew precisely what it was to accomplish. The Government was simply applying a formula that had been used since the days of Washington: keep peace on the frontier by bringing influential Indian chiefs in to see the Great White Father to impress them with his power and wealth and with the futility of waging war on him.[1]

Colonel Smith thought the formula had worked. During the journey home, he spent much time with Red Cloud, reviewing what had happened and explaining the wishes and intentions of the Government. He was sure that Red Cloud now had a much clearer idea of the relative position of the whites and the Indians, and that the chief was "convinced that it is useless to contend with the whites with any chance of success." The trip, Smith believed, would "not only be profitable to the Government, in averting war and its consequences, but prove highly beneficial to the Indians."[2] Secretary Cox, too, was certain that the visit had produced the desired effect; he assured the

[1] For a good general discussion of Indian visits to the President, including Red Cloud's visit, see Katherine C. Turner, *Red Men Calling on the Great White Father* (Norman: University of Oklahoma Press, 1951).

[2] Col. John E. Smith to E. S. Parker, July 15, 1870, Com. of Indian Affairs, *Annual Report*, pp. 324–326.

Toll of Time
The Changing Face of Red Cloud

Courtesy Smithsonian Institution, Bureau of American Ethnology

About 1872

About 1875

Courtesy Smithsonian Institution, Bureau of American Ethnology

About 1880

Courtesy Smithsonian Institution, Bureau of American Ethnology

About 1890

Undated

About 1895

About 1900

President that "an impending war, with all its unnumbered horrors—its waste of blood and treasure—has been averted." [3]

Others were not so sure. The *New York Herald*, which had followed the trip with much interest, called it "a fruitless failure":

> They [the Indians] found the department filled with the sweetmeats and pastry of palaver, but when they called for the substantial articles they were not forthcoming. It was very nice thought Red Cloud for the oily-tongued secretary to cause his eyes to make several affectionate revolutions toward the despoiled chiefs and to cause his tongue to vibrate like the continuous mechanical oscillation of the pendulum. But the Indian is sharp. He understands the lath and plaster of flattery too well. [4]

The *Herald* had "no doubt" that Red Cloud would organize war "on a greater scale than ever as soon as he reaches his people, and all because the Secretary has been trying to deal evasively with him." [5] The *Nation*, also much interested in Indian affairs, was equally pessimistic, but for different reasons. It commented: "Any one who reads the reports of speeches delivered at Washington by 'Red Cloud' and the other chiefs could see well enough that these men will not keep the peace except on their own impossible terms." [6] Out west, the *Yankton Union and Dakotaian* was "at a loss to imagine" what good could come of the conference; the only solution to the Indian problem, in its view, was for the government to give Red Cloud "a dose of terrible war." [7] The *Omaha Herald* was willing to concede that Red Cloud might be well disposed toward the whites as a result of his excursion but warned that no chief could control the young men who still sought war. [8] The *Cheyenne Daily Leader* exclaimed with contempt, "Lo! the conquering hero comes! . . . This autocratic savage and suite . . . will leave the line of the road at Pine Bluffs . . . and will not come via Cheyenne. The renegade Richard is with him, and doubtless the two have many scruples against coming where the western character of white people abound too thickly." [9] The whole reason for the trip, according to the *Leader*, was to clear Richard of his crimes, and though Red Cloud had been rebuffed on his other demands, in this respect he had been

[3] Secretary of the Interior, *Annual Report*, 1870.

[4] *New York Herald*, June 15, 1870.

[5] *Ibid.*, June 14, 1870.

[6] *The Nation*, X (June 16, 1870), 389–390.

[7] *Yankton Union and Dakotaian*, June 16, 1870.

[8] *Omaha Weekly Herald*, June 29, July 6, 1870.

[9] *Cheyenne Daily Leader*, June 22, 1870.

successful: Richard was returning with "a written pardon" from the President.[10]

Red Cloud had given no public sign that he was overawed by evidence of the Great Father's power, but there was some basis for hope that he was returning home in a reasonably peaceable frame of mind. The enthusiastic reception in New York helped to dim the memory of frustration in Washington, and all of the Indians were pleased with the promise of horses.[11] The *Omaha Herald* commented that Red Cloud, waiting in Omaha for the horses, seemed satisfied with the situation. He was still "reticent and reserved, although not to such an extent as while on his way to Washington."[12] As a matter of fact, Red Cloud seemed quite euphoric and inclined to exercise the political arts he undoubtedly had observed in the capital. He even commented that he was disposed to make peace with the Pawnees, although he couldn't stop now to make a treaty; he had to hurry home to his people.[13]

When the Indians arrived at Pine Bluffs, Wyoming, where they were to leave the railroad, their coach was switched off and the train was backed past it, giving the other passengers a chance to see the delegation. The passengers responded to the opportunity by waving hats, handkerchiefs, and hands in gestures of friendship. The Indians remained in their coach while their baggage was being loaded onto wagons sent from Fort Laramie.[14] Then they went out to a corral where Colonel Smith delivered the promised horses and saddles, "not in consideration of any treaty made, or hereafter to be made, but merely as a token of good will." The Indians saddled their horses and headed for Fort Laramie. An escort had been provided, but Colonel Smith dismissed it when Red Cloud complained that the presence of soldiers indicated a lack of faith in his honor.[15]

On June 26, after a journey of a day and a half, the delegation arrived

10 *Ibid.* See above, p. 93. The Richard case created a good deal of confusion. He had not been tried for his alleged crime, so he could hardly have been pardoned. Apparently there was an agreement of some kind that the Government would not pursue the matter further if Richard would use his influence for peace.

11 Telegram, John E. Smith to E. S. Parker, June 15, 1870, NARS, RG 75, LR, Upper Platte Agency.

12 *Omaha Weekly Herald*, June 29, 1870.

13 *New York Times*, June 28, 1870.

14 Some idea of the nature of the baggage can be gained from a bill for $1,032.20 submitted by a New York firm for goods furnished the Indians, including shirts, cloth, vests, satchels, and umbrellas (Buckley, Welling and Co. to Parker, June 18, 1870, NARS, RG 75, LR, Upper Platte Agency).

15 *Omaha Weekly Herald*, June 29, 1870, describes the departure from Pine Bluffs.

at Fort Laramie, to be met by their families and friends. Indeed, the Oglalas had been gathering at the fort for days, impatiently awaiting Red Cloud's return. At one time there were a thousand lodges encamped across the Platte under the leadership of American Horse, who came into the fort frequently to inquire about the travelers. The Indians had their robes with them, and it was obvious that they assumed that one of the fruits of Red Cloud's visit to the Great White Father would be permission to trade at Fort Laramie.[16] This was one of the practices the treaty was designed to prevent, but on the advice of Colonel Smith, who urged that the Indians should be allowed to trade, "with the understanding that it should not be a precedent,"[17] the President had consented to allow the Indians to trade at Laramie for ten days.[18] This genuflection to expediency apparently had little effect, for by the time Red Cloud arrived most of the Indians had become weary of waiting and had wandered off to Raw Hide Buttes, forty miles to the north.[19]

Conditions, nevertheless, seemed to augur for peace. Red Cloud went to the Powder River country to hold a general council with the Sioux, and on July 14 he was reported as having left Fort Fetterman "with the determination of inducing all Indians in this country to make peace."[20] At the same time, Col. Franklin F. Flint sent word from Fort Laramie that Yellow Eagle, brother of Man-Afraid-of-His-Horse, had been in to report that Red Cloud was "calling the Sioux together for a grand council on Powder River with a view to peace with the whites." He was also using his influence for peace with the Cheyennes and the Arapahoes. Indeed, according to Flint, "large numbers" of Sioux had visited the post since Red Cloud's return, and all were "desirous of peace." He had furnished them with rations—again in violation of at least the intent of the treaty—and had sent small supplies of tobacco out to the various tribes to be used in council; "this course," he explained, "seems necessary and proper, in view of the friendly and hospitable treatment extended to them recently by the

[16] Telegram, Bvt. Brig. Gen. F. F. Flint to Gen. George D. Ruggles, AAG, Omaha, June 19, 1870, NATS, RG 98, TR, Dept. of the Platte.

[17] Telegram, Smith to Parker, June 22, 1870, NARS, RG 75, LR, Upper Platte Agency.

[18] Telegram, Parker to Smith, June 22, 1870, NARS, RG 75, LS, Upper Platte Agency.

[19] Smith to Parker, July 15, 1870 (above, n. 2).

[20] Telegram, Maj. Alexander Chambers, CO, Fort Fetterman, to Parker, July 14, 1870, NARS, RG 75, LR, Upper Platte Agency.

government." He was optimistic, but with reservations. "It remains to be seen," he concluded, "whether these Indians are sincere in the profession of friendship and whether peace or war will be the result of the coming grand council on Powder River." [21]

We have no direct report of the "grand council," but presumably it was held sometime during the last week of July. [22] Although there were disturbing reports that the Sioux were attacking the Crows [23] and a warning from Brig. Gen. Alfred Sully, veteran Indian fighter who was now Superintendent of Indian Affairs for Montana, that the Sioux were threatening to take over the buffalo ranges of the Milk River Country and wipe out the unfortunate Crows, [24] Red Cloud seemed to be working assiduously and effectively for peace. On August 1, Colonel Flint telegraphed that Yellow Bear, one of the chiefs who had been to Washington, had told him that Red Cloud was visiting all bands of the Sioux, "using his authority and influence for peace," and that he hoped to persuade the Cheyennes and the Arapahoes to keep the peace also. Moreover, the young braves were listening and there were no war parties out. Flint also reported that the Sioux inquired frequently about the commissioners who were supposed to come out from Washington, and he, too, hoped that they would come soon: "The Indians must steal, involving loss of life, or be fed by the government and arrangements should be made at once." [25]

In a general way, arrangements had been made while Red Cloud was in Washington. Felix Brunot, chairman of the Board of Indian Commissioners, had been introduced to him with the promise that later in the summer he would be sent to visit the Indians. [26] Whether or not

[21] Telegram, Flint to Ruggles, AAG, Omaha, July 15, 1870, NARS, RG 98, TR, Dept. of the Platte.

[22] On July 27, 1870, Maj. Alexander Chambers, CO, Fort Fetterman, telegraphed Gen. George D. Ruggles, AAG, Omaha: "The Yellow Bear, one of the Ogallala chiefs from Washington came in and reported a runner having reached his camp from the vicinity of Bear Butte who says the Sioux are all collecting for a Grand Council, and that they are all for peace." On August 2, he telegraphed: "Man-afraid-of-his-horses with fifteen hundred lodges of various tribes of Sioux near the Cheyennes; they all make professions of peace, and have by this time had their grand council" (NARS, RG 98, TR, Dept. of the Platte).

[23] Gov. J. A. Campbell, Wyoming Territory, to Parker, August 1, 1870, NARS, RG 75, LR, Upper Platte Agency.

[24] Sully to Parker, NARS, RG 75, LR, Montana Superintendency.

[25] Telegram, Flint to Ruggles, AAG, Omaha, August 1, 1870, NARS, RG 98, TR, Dept. of the Platte. Yellow Bear apparently had gone directly from Fort Fetterman to Fort Laramie (see note 22, above).

[26] See above, p. 104.

pressure from the Sioux country had anything to do with fixing the schedule—and it probably did not—on August 5 General Augur was advised that Brunot would leave for the West immediately and that Robert Campbell of St. Louis, a member of the Board, would accompany him.[27]

Between them, Brunot and Campbell possessed all of the experience, insights, and talents one would think necessary to work out a just and satisfactory solution to the problem of Red Cloud. Brunot was a prominent Pittsburgh businessman, churchman, and philanthropist who had long been interested in Indian problems and who had been chairman of the Board of Indian Commissioners almost from the date of its organization. He believed that the nation's Indian policy should be designed to lead the red men as rapidly as possible toward civilization and Christianity, and that this could be accomplished only through education and the abandonment of the reservation life. He had had very little direct contact with either the Indians or the West, but a trip through the Indian Territory in the summer of 1869 had given him an opportunity to get a look at some of the western Indians in their native habitat.[28] Campbell, on the other hand, probably knew as much about the Indians and the West as any man in the country. He had been with William H. Ashley's second fur-trading expedition in 1825, and had spent ten years in the mountains, associating with such men as Thomas Fitzpatrick, Jedediah Smith, and Jim Bridger. He had established Fort Laramie in 1834 with William Sublette, and he had been one of the government commissioners at the great council of 1851.[29]

It was apparent from their instructions that the two men would not have an easy assignment; they were to persuade Red Cloud to abandon the idea of an agency near Fort Laramie or Fort Fetterman and to agree to a location at Raw Hide Buttes, about forty miles north of Fort Laramie. Acting Indian Commissioner W. F. Kady, who wrote the instructions, admitted that there might be some difficulty in overcoming the chief's preference for the Laramie-Fetterman area, but he added, somewhat fatuously, "It is however hoped that you will succeed in inducing him to yield and cheerfully accept the country which the government prefers should be the home of his people

---

[27] Telegram, E. D. Townsend to C. C. Augur, August 5, 1870, NARS, RG 98, TR, Dept. of the Platte.

[28] Charles Lewis Slattery, *Felix Reville Brunot, 1820–1898* (New York: Longmans, Green and Co., 1901), pp. 121–160.

[29] There is no adequate biography of Campbell. For a brief sketch, see *Dictionary of American Biography*, III, 462–463.

hereafter." Kady also wanted Brunot and Campbell to inquire into the characters of Ben Mills, whom Red Cloud wanted for his agent, and Ecoffey and Bullock, the chief's choices for traders. Finally, they were to visit Spotted Tail and locate his people somewhere on the White River. No trouble was anticipated here.[30]

While the Commissioners prepared to head west, runners went out to Red Cloud urging him to come to Fort Laramie for a conference.[31] Brunot arrived at Omaha on August 22, and Campbell, coming up the Missouri River by steamboat from St. Louis, arrived the next day. On the twenty-fourth, the two men called on General Augur, who assured them that transportation and two companies of cavalry would be available at Cheyenne, but who had had no word from Red Cloud. Augur got off telegrams to Major Chambers at Fetterman and Colonel Flint at Laramie, wondering what had happened to the runners and urging haste. Flint replied that his messenger had been out twelve days and that he had had no word from him; Chambers was able to report that "the principal chief of Red Cloud" had just arrived with information that Red Cloud was at Bear Butte and was coming in. The same day (August 25) a telegram came from W. G. Bullock saying that some of Red Cloud's chiefs had appeared at Fort Laramie the day before, and that Red Cloud would come in when he heard of the arrival of the Commissioners. He did not want to get there early because game was so scarce in the area that it would be difficult for his people to live there for a long period.

If the Commissioners wondered why Flint had not had this information, they gave no sign in their report, but with this assurance they took the Union Pacific for Cheyenne, arriving shortly after noon on the twenty-seventh—it was a twenty-four hour run in 1870. Here they met with J. A. Campbell, governor of Wyoming Territory, who had word that Red Cloud was now counseling on the Powder River and would be at Fort Laramie about the middle of September with a large delegation

---

[30] W. F. Kady, Acting Com. Indian Affairs, to Felix R. Brunot and Robert Campbell, August 11, 1870, NARS, RG 75, LS.

[31] The best account of the activities of Brunot and Campbell will be found in the hitherto unused Report of United States Special Indian Commission, August 22, 1870—October 10, 1870, Wm. Fayel, Clerk, NARS, RG 75, LR, Upper Platte Agency. Unless otherwise indicated, my account is based on this report. An abbreviated version appears in Felix R. Brunot and Robert Campbell to J. D. Cox, Secretary of the Interior, October 29, 1870, Com. of Indian Affairs, *Annual Report*, pp. 384–388. The *Omaha Weekly Herald*, October 19, 1870, contains an extended account from its correspondent "O. K." See also Slattery, *Brunot*, pp. 164–168.

to hear what the Commissioners had to say. The Commissioners were not happy at the prospect of killing two weeks before they could meet the chief, and they were somewhat alarmed at the intimation that they would be faced with the problem of caring for a large number of Indians; they had telegraphed earlier that they wanted only to meet Red Cloud and the principal chiefs. They decided to fill in their time by going to Denver to meet with a delegation of Utes who were calling on Governor Edward McCook of Colorado Territory; the problem of numbers was solved by the purchase of three hundred sacks of flour in Omaha and an offer from the Army to issue beef and other necessities from the commissary at Fort Laramie.

The Commissioners were back in Cheyenne on September 10 and left for Fort Laramie on the seventeenth. They were accompanied by Governor Campbell and a military escort which, in view of the large number of Indians expected, General Augur had increased from two companies of cavalry to ten. On the afternoon of the twenty-first they arrived at Fort Laramie. Their journey had served to impress them with the importance of their mission. They had traveled over country "pre-eminent for stock-raising" and even susceptible of considerable agricultural development if there could be instituted "a system of irrigation such as is being attempted in the neighboring territory of Colorado." All that stood in the way was the Indian menace—"the assurance of an exemption from marauding Indians will result in filling up the country."

At Fort Laramie they found about three hundred and fifty Cheyennes under Dull Knife and Little Crow, plus a few Brulés, encamped about the post and receiving rations from the quartermaster. The Cheyennes wanted to talk, but they were told that there would be no general talk until Red Cloud arrived. As for Red Cloud, he was reported to be on the Cheyenne River, more than one hundred miles away, awaiting word that the Commissioners actually had arrived at Fort Laramie. On the twenty-fifth John Richard came in with news that Red Cloud had started, and on the twenty-seventh the Commissioners were assured that the chief would be at the fort by October first or second. On October 1, not Red Cloud, but Man-Afraid-of-His-Horse arrived. Red Cloud, he said, was waiting at the forks of Lance Creek to hear further news of the Commissioners. This was almost too much for even the Christian forbearance of Felix Brunot. "We came a long way to see you and have been waiting a good while," he told Man-Afraid. "We came not so much because we belong to the government at Washington but because we are your friends and we think you ought not to keep us waiting."

Man-Afraid replied that he too had come a long way, that his stock was poor and he had traveled as fast as he could. He wondered if the Commissioners had any ammunition to give. Brunot responded with an emphatic "No," and tried to change the subject by expressing regret that Man-Afraid had not been able to come to Washington.[32] Colonel Flint came forward to say that two of the horses which had been given Red Cloud at Pine Bluffs and which had strayed had been recovered and were now waiting for him. This seemed to please Man-Afraid. He said that he wanted the Commissioners to open their hearts to his people, and that as soon as he got his rations he would leave for Red Cloud's camp and come in with him. He still hoped, however, that the Commissioners would be able to give him some ammunition. He was told again that this was impossible. Moreover, the Commissioners were becoming impatient. This was Saturday; Red Cloud must be in by Tuesday or Wednesday at the latest.

There were some at the fort who thought that this ultimatum would end the conference, that Red Cloud simply would not come in at the bidding of the Commissioners. On Tuesday morning, however, word was received that he was encamped but twelve miles out. According to William Fayel, clerk of the Commission: "His coming disappointed the predictions of some persons, but the Commissioners had confidence in the good faith of Red Cloud and were satisfied that his tardiness was owing to the desire he felt that all the Indians whose influence was of any importance should be present at the councils." The next day the Oglalas went into camp on the Platte, about three miles above the post. They constituted a vast throng—just how large we do not know[33]— and many of the curious from Fort Laramie went out to see them make camp. About four o'clock in the afternoon some two hundred warriors came galloping into the fort in the midst of a terrific dust storm. Red Cloud was not with them—he had sent word that he was fatigued and would see the Commissioners the next day—but the assembled warriors had a fine feast in front of the sutler's store before returning to their camp, and the inhabitants of Fort Laramie settled down to await the opening of the conference on the morrow.

[32] It will be recalled that Man-Afraid took sick at Fort Fetterman just before the delegation started for Washington. See above, p. 97.

[33] The *Omaha Weekly Herald*, October 19, 1870, reported that there were approximately seven thousand; this seems high, but it is the only figure we have.

The next morning Red Cloud came in for a preliminary interview. He immediately objected to holding the conference in the large tent which the quartermaster had erected for the purpose a short distance below the fort; he did not want to talk in a tent, he wanted to hold the council where all his people could be present and hear what was said. Colonel Flint thereupon hastily made arrangements to hold the council on the porch of his residence, and shortly after noon the parley opened. Assembled on the porch were the Commissioners, Colonel Flint, the officers of the post and of the cavalry escort, and "the ladies of the garrison"; representing the Indians, besides Red Cloud, were Man-Afraid-of-His-Horse, Red Dog, and Grass; spread out on the ground in front of the porch was a large crowd of Indians, soldiers, and visitors. John Richard was on hand to serve as interpreter.

Colonel Flint spoke first. After welcoming the Indians to Fort Laramie, he told them that the Commissioners were good men and that the Indians should follow their advice. Brunot then came forward and announced that inasmuch as nothing could prosper without the blessing of the Great Spirit, he would open the council with a prayer. It was a long prayer, an incongruous mixture of piety and nonsense. He thanked God that He had "put into the hearts of the rulers of our land to do justly, and love mercy in their dealings with all people." He went on:

> We beseech Thee to bless the efforts of Thy servants who are here . . . to promote peace and friendship with the aborigines of this land; may our words and counsels be tempered with wisdom, may the hearts of these Indians be made sincere and their words truthful and may savage warfare cease. Grant that they may be lead into the way of peace and civilization, and in Thy own time may these heathens be claimed for the inheritance of our Lord and Savior. . . .

At the conclusion of his prayer, Brunot turned to Red Cloud and said that he and Campbell had come "because the Great Spirit commands us," and that the Great Father in Washington had sent them to hear what Red Cloud had to say after seeing his people.

Red Cloud then arose. He, too, would pray to the Great Spirit. He touched his hands to the ground and all the Indians rose to their feet. With one hand pointing toward the sky, Red Cloud prayed:

> Oh Great Spirit, I pray you to look at us, we are your children and you placed us first in this land. We pray you to look down on us so nothing but the truth will be spoken in this council. We don't ask for anything but what is right and just. When you made your red children O Great Spirit, you

made them to have mercy upon them. Now we are before you today praying you to look down on us and take pity on your poor red children. We pray nothing but the truth will be spoken here, we hope these things will be settled up right. You are the protector of the people who use the bow and arrow, as well as of the people who wear hats and garments and I hope we don't pray to you in vain. We are poor and ignorant. Our forefathers told us we would not be in misery if we asked for your assistance. O Great Spirit look down on your children and have pity on them.[34]

When he finished praying, Red Cloud returned to his seat and began a long speech, professing friendship and reciting grievances. He had no sooner begun, however, than he noticed a photographer about to take a picture of the assemblage. He stopped his speech and asked that the man be ordered to withdraw. Colonel Flint had the camera removed, and Red Cloud went on. He had been told in 1852 that the Great Father would give him annuities for fifty-five years, but he had received them for only ten;[35] he had been told in 1868 that the white man should not pass through his country, but he continued to do so. He did not like these things; they made him ashamed of his words.

Brunot replied that there was a mistake about the boundary line and they wanted to work it out. The Great Father desired to have the old California road kept open. It went along the north side of the Platte for only a few miles; white men on the road would not interfere with Red Cloud's use of his country. Red Cloud said that he did not understand it that way, that when he was in Washington the Great Father told him that Fort Fetterman was there to watch his interests as well as those of the white man, and that this apparently was an untruth because in addition to people on the road, men from Fort Laramie had gone across the Platte to cut hay on his land. Brunot remarked that Red Cloud ought not to object to that little piece of road, but he promised to talk to the Great Father about it.

Red Cloud then turned to the question of trading posts. He said that he wanted his trading post at Mr. Ward's house, ten miles above Fort Laramie on the Platte. "I want to know also, what kind of presents you have brought me here, what you have come to see me with." Brunot ignored the question of presents but reminded Red Cloud that in signing the Treaty of 1868 he had agreed to go to the Missouri. He

---

[34] A slightly different version of this prayer will be found in Gibson Clark, "Red Cloud's Prayer," *Annals of Wyoming*, XV (October, 1943), 403–404.

[35] Red Cloud undoubtedly was referring to the council of 1851, in which he certainly was not a major participant; perhaps, as was his habit, he was using the first person singular to refer to his people. See above pp. 6–8.

noted that when Red Cloud had objected, the Great Father had said that he would establish a trading post somewhere north of the Platte in his own country, but that it could not be on the Platte—he thought that some place in the vicinity of Raw Hide Buttes would be a good location. Red Cloud was adamant; he would have his trading post on the Platte and nowhere else.

Dropping the question of the trading post, Brunot talked about the presents the Commissioners had brought with them. Red Cloud wanted to know what they were. They were good things, he was assured—blankets, calico, flannel, clothes, butcher knives, axes, and tobacco. Red Cloud was not impressed; he said that he had told the Great Father he had wanted ammunition, that it was the only thing he had to live upon. Unhappily, Brunot was forced to say that the Great Father had not sent ammunition. He was not sure that Red Cloud really wanted peace. What did Red Cloud think about it?

"If the Great Father looks after my interest, and keeps white men out of the country," Red Cloud replied, "peace will last forever, but if they disturb us there will be no peace."

This put it clearly and simply. Brunot responded, somewhat lamely:

> We want Red Cloud to be satisfied about passing on the California Road and cutting hay for the fort on their lands. We will tell the Great Father about these matters, but he must not allow a little thing like that to create trouble in the heart or war with the Great Father's people.

Red Cloud agreed that he would not go to war about a little thing like that, "but," he added, "I want you to understand that the Great Father has made us ashamed before my people because he told what was not so."

After Colonel Flint explained about the hay-cutting and Brunot remarked that the Great Father intended that all parts of the treaty should be carried out, Red Dog arose and said that he agreed with the Great Father, that he had something to say, and that he wanted Leon Palladay, who had been with General Harney on the Missouri, to interpret his words. This broke up the conference. No sooner had Palladay started to interpret than Sitting Bear rushed forward, seized him by the shoulders, and said he would not allow him to speak because he belonged on the Missouri River. Others joined in. Little Wound stepped up and said that Sitting Bear had a right to complain about Palladay—he had lied to the Indians before and was the cause of all their trouble. Palladay withdrew, and Little Wound, having the floor, turned to Red Cloud and said:

During the war I was strong hearted, but now I am poor, and have nothing, but I did not listen to the words of the Great Father and his soldiers cleaned us out. Now we have no houses or nothing. If you go to war with the whites you have no country to go to. Now it is our duty and interest to be peaceable and mind what our friends here have to tell us.

He wanted the council postponed until the next morning. Others attempted to speak, but Red Cloud suggested that it would be best to adjourn until the next day so that the Indians could adjust their differences before proceeding. The Commissioners agreed to the adjournment, although before the day was out they assembled Red Cloud, Man-Afraid-of-His-Horse, Red Dog, and Grass in Bullock's residence for a private conference. After a talk with the chiefs, the interpreter, John Richard, told the Commissioners that they were determined to have their trading post on the south side of the Platte, and that it would be advisable to go slowly on this matter as perhaps in a year or two they might agree to having their agency on the other side of the river. Campbell, however, told the Indians flatly that the Government would not consent to a trading post on the south side of the Platte, that Raw Hide Buttes was a good location and they should settle on that. Brunot reminded them of all the advantages that would accrue once the agency had been established: the Great Father would send teachers to start schools and show their children how to farm so that they could make a living when the buffalo disappeared. He did not get very far with this line of talk. Red Cloud admitted that the buffalo were decreasing in numbers, but he was sure that if the white men stayed out of their country the Indians would have plenty of game to live without farming. He did not want schools as long as he could raise his children on buffalo. Brunot did not press the point. He simply wanted the Indians to think about such things as schools. Red Cloud said they would; they would talk about these matters that evening.

The second day's council, which opened the next morning at ten o'clock on Colonel Flint's verandah, had not gone far before it became evident that the Commissioners' views had not made much headway among the Indians. Brunot again opened the meeting with prayer, and once again reviewed the situation. He explained that although the Great Father had many soldiers, he did not want to fight with his red brothers, that he wanted peace with all men. For this reason, when Red Cloud told him in Washington that he did not want to trade on the Missouri River, the Great Father had agreed to a trading post in the

Indians' own country, and after thinking about it, he had decided that Raw Hide Buttes was the best place, and he had sent Mr. Campbell and himself to tell them this. Brunot went on to say that when everything was peaceable they would ask the Great Father to send the Oglalas ammunition so they could hunt. Meanwhile, they had been waiting a long time; they wanted to hear what the Oglalas had to say so they could distribute the presents they had brought with them and go home.

Red Cloud arose and walked out into the crowd of Indians in front of the verandah. Not to be outdone by the Commissioner—although he might well have wondered what prayer had to do with the whole business—he raised his right hand to the sky and invoked the blessing of the Great Spirit; he then touched the ground and returned to his seat.

"I have told the Great Father what suited me," he said, "and have very little to say now." He reminded the Commissioners that the Great Spirit had raised him on this land and that he intended to keep it, that Fort Laramie had always been a good place to trade and that he wanted to trade there again, that he did not want to talk about teachers, and that he wished the Commissioners would give them their goods and go back and tell the Great Father to send General Smith to them because he always told the truth.

"When you go back to the Great Father," he concluded, "tell him Red Cloud is not willing to go to Raw Hide Buttes."

The Commissioners tried to point out that there were bad white men on the Platte and that there could not be peace if the Indians associated with them, but it was obvious that they were getting nowhere. Finally, Man-Afraid-of-His-Horse said, "There is too much talk about the trading post. Give us our presents and let the matter stand for a while." Brunot agreed. "We think that the best way," he said, "we want to part friends." Red Cloud agreed, too. He said:

> My young men have picked out the place for a trading post, but I want peace. The Great Father did not tell me he wanted my trading post at the Raw Hide Buttes. I am not mad. Tell the Great Father what I want.

In the afternoon the Commissioners had an inconclusive but friendly interview with Medicine Man, Dull Knife, Little Wolf, and Medicine Arrows of the Cheyennes,[36] and the next afternoon everyone went out

[36] Brunot told the Cheyennes that he was surprised to see them, that he had supposed they would stay on the Canadian River to the south, where there were traders. Presaging the difficulties that were to develop with the Cheyennes, the chiefs told him

to the Sioux camp to distribute the long-awaited presents. It was a gala occasion. As the heavily laden wagon train arrived, Red Cloud pointed out the spot where he wanted the goods unloaded. The Indians, some five thousand of them, congregated in a great circle around the wagons, eagerly watching the bales and boxes tumble out on the ground, anxious to see what the Great Father had sent them. Before the distribution began, the Commissioners made a careful check of the goods to see that all was in order and that the Indians were not being cheated. Red Cloud seemed particularly pleased at this, and on the whole, everyone seemed quite content. Some of the chiefs objected to the tinned kettles, saying that the heavy iron ones used by the soldiers were much better; there was some objection, too, to the white blankets—most of the Indians preferred black—and there was a general feeling that something more useful than hats could have been sent. For the most part, though, objections gave way to pleasure, and as the Commissioners returned to Fort Laramie, they left the Indians happily contemplating their new-found wealth.[37]

Aside from pleasing the Oglalas with presents, however, the Commissioners, for all their praying and all their high hopes, had nothing to show for their efforts. The next morning, in a final attempt to get some sort of an agreement before leaving, they sent John Richard out to bring Red Cloud in for another interview. He came, accompanied by Man-Afraid-of-His-Horse, Red Dog, and American Horse. He said that he was pleased with his presents and would like to receive them on the south side of the river. About locating the agency at Raw Hide Buttes, the Great Father had not mentioned it to him while he was in Washington, and he had not had time to think it over. He might, however, go there for the winter. He wanted Ben Mills for his agent, and he wanted his old traders—Bullock, Ecoffey, Richard, and Brown. But the thing about the agency had not been settled, and he hoped those

---

that they did not like the Canadian country but preferred to live in the north. Brunot suggested that they probably could trade with the Sioux, but Dull Knife said that they did not want to trade with the Sioux because they could not always agree. Red Cloud earlier had told Brunot that he had no contact with the Cheyennes: "I don't know what they intend to do. I made peace with them once but it did not amount to anything." For the Cheyenne troubles, see George Bird Grinnell, *The Fighting Cheyennes* (Norman: University of Oklahoma Press, 1960); Mari Sandoz, *Cheyenne Autumn* (New York: McGraw-Hill, 1953).

[37] They learned the next day that there was some trouble over the division of goods between the Miniconjous and the few Brulés present; in the course of the argument Red Dog's horse was shot, but order was soon restored.

in charge of Fort Laramie would have pity on his people when they came to visit and give them rations; actually, this was the best place to obtain rations, and why could not his people come here for them?

Brunot explained that there would be no rations at Fort Laramie, and they should not come here expecting to receive them. They would have to get their rations on the Missouri, unless they agreed to an agency at Raw Hide Buttes. He could not tell Red Cloud who his agent or traders would be, but they would be good men, Red Cloud could be sure. They would tell the Great Father all that Red Cloud had said; they would also tell him that Red Cloud was working for peace. Meanwhile, he should have his trading post near Raw Hide Buttes; that would be much more convenient. With this, everyone shook hands all around, and the Commissioners left that same day for Cheyenne and the East.

It was apparent that there was some sentiment among the Oglalas for locating near Raw Hide Buttes. Evidently Brunot and Campbell thought that in the end this sentiment would prevail, and before leaving Fort Laramie they wired Secretary Cox: "They [the Indians] insisted upon a trading post on the Platte, but will agree to have it located at Raw Hide Buttes. No depredations have been committed by the Indians for five months, and we are satisfied that they all desire permanent peace and the influence of Red Cloud and all the chiefs will be effectually used to maintain it...."[38]

The Commissioners' optimism was unjustified. In a few days Major Chambers reported from Fort Fetterman: "Red Cloud said the trading point at Rawhide Buttes was sprung on him and he did not have time to consult all of his young men."[39] It was clear that the chief had not agreed to have his agency at Raw Hide Buttes, and as time wore on it became increasingly clear that he would never do so.

The Indian Office, nevertheless, acting in accordance with its Commissioners' optimism rather than with the realities of life in the Indian country, went ahead with plans to locate Red Cloud away from the Platte and, hopefully, at Raw Hide Buttes; the pressure of events would force diversion if not abandonment of those plans before they were well under way.

[38] In their published report (note 31, above), the Commissioners stated that an agreement relating to Raw Hide Buttes had been drawn up, and that Red Cloud was informed that Colonel Flint would have it whenever he was ready to sign. No mention of this is made in the manuscript report of the conference.

[39] Telegram, Chambers to Augur, Omaha, October 25, 1870, NARS, RG 98, TR, Dept. of the Platte.

Following the Fort Laramie conference, Red Cloud and most of his people went off to the Powder River country. By mid-December, however, some of the Sioux were beginning to drift back to Fort Laramie, hungry and clamoring for food. Among them was Red Leaf, who had not been in since the summer of 1869. He reported that he had been all through the Sweetwater, Tongue River, and Powder River regions and had found very few buffalo. He wanted permission to hunt on the Republican where, he understood, game was plentiful. Colonel Flint recommended that the permission be granted, and quickly: it was either let them hunt or feed them.[40] On January 10, Flint, having had no answer to his earlier message and confronted with a growing number of hungry, restless Indians, telegraphed Omaha that unless something was done trouble could be expected—"They [the Indians] say they might as well be killed for fighting as die of starvation."[41]

The delay resulted from inaction in Washington. The Army had referred the matter to the Indian Bureau but had received no answer.[42] General Augur complained to Congressman John Taffe of Nebraska that the Indian Bureau was not aware of the urgency of the situation: "[The Indians] are now in large bodies and can be controlled by their Chiefs, but if not fed, they will soon scatter in search of food and will take it wherever they find it and we will soon have the whole frontier in commotion and trouble about Indian depredations."[43] Finally, after taking the matter to the President, the Army got authority to subsist the Indians temporarily at both Fetterman and Laramie, and $100,000 was made available for the purpose. The President also authorized the issuance of ammunition for small game, as Colonel Flint had recommended.[44] By mid-February, when General Augur visited Fort Laramie to inspect the feeding arrangements, 2,795 Indians, including Red Cloud with seventy-eight lodges, were settled around the post, receiving rations and ammunition.[45] The Indians seemed well disposed

[40] Telegram, Flint to Ruggles, AAG, Omaha, December 18, 1870, NARS, RG 98, TR, Dept. of the Platte.

[41] *Ibid.*, January 10, 1871.

[42] Telegram, Gen W. T. Sherman to Brig. Gen. C. C. Augur, Omaha, January 20, 1871, NARS, RG 98, TR, Dept. of the Platte.

[43] Augur, Omaha, to John Taffe, January 23, 1871, NARS, RG 98, LS, Dept. of the Platte.

[44] Telegrams, AG, USA, to Augur, January 23, 24, 1871, NARS, RG 98, Dept. of the Platte.

[45] Augur to AG, USA, February 21, 1871, NARS, RG 98, LS, Dept. of the Platte. The Indians present, according to General Augur, were the following:

Red Cloud, Oglala, 78 lodges, 390 persons.

toward the whites, but, Augur reported, there was "some wrangling amongst themselves and an effort . . . [was] being made to supersede Red Cloud, . . . as yet . . . unsuccessful." [46]

Red Cloud appears to have been having considerable difficulty maintaining a position of leadership among the Sioux, not only with the northern bands over whom he was trying to develop influence—he had never really had it with these bands—but with his own people as well. In January he told Colonel Flint that he was trying to induce the northern Sioux to abandon the warpath and that until he had accomplished this he could not agree to an agency north of the Platte. If he did, many Indians would say he had sold himself to the whites.[47] It is difficult to determine whether this was a sincere assessment of the situation or simply a ruse to gain time. It has been frequently asserted that Red Cloud lost his influence after his visit to Washington;[48] Lt. William Quintin of the 7th Cavalry reported that in a conference with the Assiniboin and Gros Ventres at Fort Shaw, Montana, he had heard that Standing Buffalo—identified as a "Yankton or Santee"—had told them that Sitting Bull's bands were formerly Red Cloud's but that they had left him after his return from Washington: "Red Cloud returned to his people with wonderful stories of what he had seen and heard while visiting the Great Father at Washington. Red Cloud saw too much. The Indians say that these things cannot be; that the white people must have put bad Medicine over Red Cloud's eyes to make him see everything and anything that they please, and so Red Cloud lost his influence." [49]

Man-Afraid-of-His-Horse, Oglala, 65 lodges, 325 persons.
Lone Wolf, Oglala, 50 lodges, 250 persons.
Cut Forward, Yocopee, 20 lodges, 100 persons.
Big Foot, Oglala, 53 lodges, 265 persons.
Red Leaf, Brulé, 60 lodges, 300 persons.
American Horse, Oglala, 66 lodges, 330 persons.
Swift Bear, Brulé, 20 lodges, 100 persons.
Rocky Bear, Oglala, 17 lodges, 85 persons.
Plenty Bear, Arapahoe, 34 lodges, 170 persons.
Medicine Man, Cheyenne, 26 lodges, 138 persons.
Full Bear, Cheyenne, 76 lodges, 350 persons.

[46] *Ibid.*

[47] Telegram, Flint to Augur, January 27, 1871, NARS, RG 98, TR, Dept. of the Platte.

[48] See, e.g., Charles Lowell Green, "The Indian Reservation System of the Dakotas to 1889," *South Dakota Historical Collections,* XIV (1928), 372–373; Stanley Vestal, *Warpath and Council Fire* (New York: Random House, 1948), pp. 186–194.

[49] 1st Lt. William Quintin to 1st Lt. M. C. Sanbourne, Post Adj., Fort Shaw, May 19, 1871, NARS, RG 75, Montana Superintendency; cf. *History of Montana,* 1739–1885 (Chicago: Warner, Beers & Co., 1888), p. 112.

Whatever Red Cloud's influence with the northern bands, the Army was determined to keep the Indians together under the influence of their chiefs, and until the Indian Bureau established effective agency control the best way to accomplish that was to feed them at Fort Laramie. Indeed, General Augur thought it would be just as well to locate the agency at Fort Laramie because "there the trade can be regulated and contrabandors and liquor sellers kept away."[50]

Feeding the Indians at Fort Laramie constituted a complete reversal of Felix Brunot's position of the preceding October, and he was not at all happy about it. He wrote Secretary Delano from his home in Pittsburgh:

> . . . it will be assumed by Red Cloud and the other Indians as yielding the point and will render it still more difficult, if not impossible, to bring them to consent to any other location. Besides, to yield to Red Cloud's pertinacity in this matter, will make him the more persistent in other demands, such as the vacating of the Old California Road and the abandonment of Fort Fetterman.[51]

Moreover, if the Army were to feed the Indians, it rather than the Indian Bureau would gain control of them. John W. Wham, who, despite Red Cloud's oft-repeated request for Ben Mills as his agent, had been appointed head of the yet-to-be-established Red Cloud Agency,[52] wired Parker from Cheyenne: "Feeding the Indians by the Commissariat robs me of the greatest power to their confidence and will certainly lead to trouble between the military and myself. Can I not control this matter now, as well as at a later date?"[53] The Army had no objection, and in due course the Secretary of War authorized the agent to dispense what remained of the $100,000 of subsistence goods originally made available to the quartermaster for feeding the Indians at Fort Laramie.[54]

Meanwhile, Wham went on to Fort Laramie, where on June 23 Red Cloud's old friend, Col. John E. Smith, who had resumed command of the post, arranged for the agent to have a conference with his

---

[50] Letter cited, note 45 above.

[51] Felix Brunot to Columbus Delano, January 27, 1871, NARS, RG 75, Wyoming Superintendency.

[52] Wham was nominated by the Protestant Episcopal Church, in accordance with the provisions of the peace policy, and seems to have been appointed after Brunot had objected to Mills (Brunot to Parker, November 10, 1870, NARS, RG 75, Upper Platte Agency).

[53] Telegram, John W. Wham to Parker, March 28, 1871, NARS, RG 75, LR, Red Cloud Agency.

[54] Secretary of War to Secretary of the Interior, April 12, 1871, *ibid.*

new charges. Wham came away from the meeting "thoroughly convinced that Red Cloud is working earnestly for the best interests of the Government and with judicious and prompt attention on the part of the department, these Indians can be induced to go north of the Platte River and locate temporarily and by fall they can be induced to go onto the reservations set apart by the Treaty of 1868."[55] On the same day, however, he joined with Colonel Smith in sending the following telegram to Commissioner Parker:

> Red Cloud asks that temporary agency be established 9 miles above this post on the South side of the North Platte. He says he can induce all to go upon their reservation after he gets them together, but if the agency is now established on the reservation, he will lose his influence and all that has been accomplished will be lost. Shall I accede to his views. We recommend it.[56]

In the aforementioned letter, Wham had also urged that Colonel Smith be called to Washington to confer with the Indian Bureau, but before he could get a reply he himself set out for the capital to discuss the matter with Commissioner Parker. Parker was in New York, so Wham took up the matter with H. R. Clum, Assistant Commissioner. By this time, he had changed his mind again and, according to a report which Clum sent Parker, recommended a temporary agency "at some point 30 or 40 miles north of the Platte."[57] Parker was not impressed. He replied that he had a letter from Colonel Smith recommending a temporary agency on the Platte nine miles above Fort Laramie, and that while he himself wanted the Indians to understand that they must select a permanent agency north of Fort Laramie by the beginning of next season, he believed that Smith's recommendation should be followed—"General Smith's information I apprehend is more reliable than agent Wham's as Smith is constantly on the ground and has frequent communications with the Indians." He added: "I am surprised that Wham should come down without authority, for in my judgment, his presence is needed constantly with his Indians."[58]

As soon as Wham returned to Fort Laramie, he had a conference with Red Cloud which convinced him that the greatest cause of Indian unrest was the Government's failure to issue arms and ammunition. Small amounts of ammunition had been issued during the spring, but

---

[55] Wham to Parker, March 24, 1871, *ibid.*
[56] Telegram, Wham and Smith to Parker, March 24, 1871, *ibid.*
[57] H. R. Clum to Parker, April 3, 1871, *ibid.*
[58] Parker to Clum, April 4, 1871, *ibid.*

apparently the Indians wanted guns as well. Wham reported that while at Washington, Red Cloud, "through lying interpreters," had understood that he would have arms and ammunition given him in the fall, and that when Brunot and Campbell had tried to side-step the issue by promising them "by and by," they had left the impression with the chief that they would surely be available at the next issue. The fact that they had not arrived made Red Cloud "ashamed of his great father," and if they did not come soon he would lose his influence for good among his people, which, in Wham's opinion, "would be ruinous."[59] Red Cloud apparently had sold all concerned at Fort Laramie on the idea that peace among the Sioux was dependent upon the maintenance of his influence and he was using it for all it was worth. Wham wanted authority to tell the Indians that "as soon as they select a camp on the north side of the Platte," he would give them fifty guns and some ammunition. The whole cost would not be over six hundred dollars and it would "have a greater effect than all the other goods put together." Wham assured Parker that he would "see that the guns are distributed to the Indians that have long been the friends of the whites."[60]

Although Wham repeatedly inquired about the fate of his request, he received no reply. Meanwhile, he bombarded the Indian Bureau with letters and telegrams describing the growing crisis.[61]

> April 12—The Indians make a great complaint that they are not issued soda. It is an impossibility to make bread out of cold water and flour. . . .
> April 18— . . . a complaint is made by Red Cloud and other chiefs of this agency that they do not get sufficient beef. Can this not be remedied in some way? . . .
> April 21—Indians are coming in here perfectly nude. Grant permission to purchase 400 shirts. May 2—The rations are out and the Indians are clamoring for food.
> May 27—There is a chief now in my office very drunk. This occurs almost daily. . . .

The poor bedeviled Wham did have his problems, and they increased daily as the Indians, learning that the Great Father was dispensing food and clothing at Fort Laramie, congregated about the post in ever greater numbers. Augur had reported 2,795 on February 21;[62] by

[59] Wham to Parker, April 12, 1871, *ibid.*
[60] *Ibid.*
[61] These communications are in NARS, RG 75, LR, Red Cloud Agency.
[62] See above, p. 130.

mid-March the number was put at 3,500;[63] and by mid-May at between six and seven thousand.[64] By this time the Government had decided that at all costs the Indians must be kept at Fort Laramie until a decision had been reached about the agency, and President Grant ordered the Army to re-enter the feeding program.[65]

Meanwhile, Wham continued to work for a decision on the location of the agency. He held a council with the Indians on May 10 and thought he would have a decision by the fifteenth, although, he reported, "They are divided amongst themselves, some being in favor of moving to the north side of the Platte, and others being opposed to it and I fear there will be trouble between them."[66] The fifteenth passed with no decision, and on May 26 Wham wired Parker:

> Every effort has been made to induce these Indians to select an agency North of the North Platte River, without success. No temporary agency yet established. Grant authority to establish one at mouth of Horseshoe Creek 40 miles above here on the Platte. Too many outside conflicting interests at work here.[67]

By this time the Indian Bureau had taken the negotiations out of Wham's hands. Colonel Smith, who had been called back to Washington for consultation, recommended that Felix Brunot be sent again to Fort Laramie to see if he could not get a decision on the matter of the agency. Smith thought that if the Indians were told that rations would be stopped if they had not located their agency by the end of June, it might force a decision.[68] Brunot reluctantly agreed to make the trip, although he felt that feeding the Indians at Fort Laramie after he had told them it would not be permitted had greatly lessened their estimate of his authority and influence.[69]

Brunot arrived at Fort Laramie on the evening of June 9, and at noon on the twelfth he, Smith, and Wham met in the post theater with Red Cloud, the principal chiefs present, and many braves.[70] As on his

[63] Col. John E. Smith to AAG, Dept. of the Platte, March 22, 1871, NARS, RG 75, LR, Red Cloud Agency.

[64] Smith to Parker, May 19, 1871, *ibid.*

[65] Telegram, E. D. Townsend to C. C. Augur, May 3, 1871, NARS, RG 98, TR, Dept. of the Platte.

[66] Wham to Parker, May 12, 1871, NARS, RG 75, LR, Red Cloud Agency.

[67] Telegram, Wham to Parker, May 26, 1871, *ibid.*

[68] Smith to Parker, May 19, 1871, *ibid.*

[69] Brunot to the Secretary of the Interior, May 22, 1871, *ibid.*

[70] The Indians identified as being present, in addition to Red Cloud, were: Red Dog, Sword, Long Wolf, the son of Man-Afraid-of-His-Horse, Quick Bear, Cold Face,

earlier visit, Brunot opened the council with prayer. He was followed
by Great Bear, who at the request of Red Cloud talked to the Great
Spirit. Red Cloud then announced that he wished to speak first.
Calling on Louis Richard and Joseph Bissonette to interpret for him,[71]
he launched into the familiar recital of the wrongs inflicted on his
people, and concluded:

> Whatever the Great Spirit tells me to do I will do. I have not yet done
> what the Great Father told me to do.... I must ask you to wait. I am
> trying to live peaceably. I told the Great Father so. When I went to him I
> asked no annuity goods; all I asked was for my lands—the little spot I left. If
> you have any goods to give, I want you to wait awhile. I will then tell you
> what to do with them. Between here and the railroad is much land. I have
> not been paid for it. I want to think of it.

Ignoring the reference to the railroad, Smith replied that it was
useless to talk about the past, that what was needed now was for Red
Cloud to select a site for his agency at once so that his people would not
suffer; he would probably soon have orders to issue no more rations
at Fort Laramie. Smith was followed by Brunot, who told the Indians
that if they did not move away from Fort Laramie and the river where
bad white men and whiskey were there would be trouble, and if trouble
came the Great Father would put war-houses all through the Indian
country. He and all of Red Cloud's friends did not want that; they
wanted Red Cloud to select a location now, away from the river.

> Do not say for us to wait. Last fall you told Mr. Campbell and me that when
> winter came you would name the place. We told the Great Father what you
> said. You still wait, and we are ashamed, because you are our friends. The
> Great Father said, I want them to locate their agency in their own country

Bran Bear, High Wolf, Full Wolf, Setting Bear, Red Plume, Little Cloud, Spider,
Fire Thunder, Big Crow, Pretty Crow, Big Foot, Little Wound, Pumpkin Seed, Yellow
Beard, Rocky Bear, Bad Wound, Bear Robe, Quick Eagle, Two Buffaloes, Corn Man,
White Eyes, Milk Spotted Horse, Red Leaf, Brave Grass, Buffalo Shed-his-hair, and
Red Buffalo. These names are listed in "Report of a visit to Red Cloud and chiefs of
the Ogallala Sioux, by Commissioner Felix R. Brunot," Com. of Indian Affairs,
Annual Report, 1871, pp. 22–29. Unless otherwise indicated, this report, which includes
all material contained in the Ms. version (NARS, RG 75, LR, Red Cloud Agency), is
the source for my account of the council.

71 Wham, it is interesting to note, had advised the Indian Bureau shortly after he
arrived at Fort Laramie: "there is but one man in this part of the country that Red
Cloud will allow to interpret for him and that is Nicholas Janis." Janis demanded
$1,200 a year for his services rather than the $500 appropriated, and Wham asked,
as he so often did, "What am I to do under these circumstances?" (Wham to Parker,
April 18, 1871, NARS, RG 75, LR, Red Cloud Agency).

now, so that houses may be built, and their goods and provisions given to them there. . . . The Great Father says they cannot come until the houses are ready for them in your own country. I want you to decide while I am here, and the houses will be built at once, and the goods sent there, and your friends can then send teachers, and good men who will help you.

Red Cloud brushed this advice away with poorly concealed contempt. "I ate the provisions of the Great Father long before I was told to have an agency in my country," he replied. "If the rations are stopped we will all go to the north and see our nation, and will then decide what we will do. All that I want is guns and ammunition and pay for the railroad."

Smith said that when the agency was selected and the Great Father saw that the Indians' hearts were good he would send them all they wished. Red Cloud changed the subject. "I have consulted the Great Spirit," he said, "and I do not want a strange man for my agent. There are plenty of men who can read and write, who are married to my people, and they can take care of me and my agency."

And so it went. After much talk about soldiers and whiskey and land and rations, the council broke up with no decision and no prospect of a decision. In a few minutes, however, Red Cloud came forward and told Brunot that he had sent for Black Twin and all the Oglalas, and they would go to their camp and have a council. He was ready to move north of the river, but he wanted all the rest to agree to it. When asked why he had not said that in the council, he replied, "I was afraid to say so, but the rest will come to it."

Later that afternoon, in a private conversation in Smith's headquarters, Red Cloud talked again about the necessity for consulting Black Twin, although he reiterated his willingness to go north of the river. When Brunot reminded him that many of his people were ready to go but were afraid to say so because they thought Red Cloud was opposed, and when he chided the chief for saying one thing in council and another privately, Red Cloud replied, in words that reveal much of his own problem of leadership and much about chieftainship among the Sioux:

> I think I will succeed; I am almost alone here. I want to get all my people together, and I think I will get them to cross the river, but whether I do or not, I will bring General Smith word at once, whether it is yes or no. In every council we consult the Great Spirit. I do not want to be the only chief; at the treaty in 1851, we made one great chief, and the white men killed him. Would you want me to say I am the great chief?

Whether this was an honest statement or simply obstructionism, as George E. Hyde suggests,[72] Brunot accepted it. There was some talk about possible locations. Red Cloud thought White River a good place, but the Brulés had it. The water in Beaver Creek was like physic, it went right through a man. Red Cloud would find a place.

The next day there was another meeting in Smith's headquarters. Smith and Brunot were still trying to press for a decision. Red Cloud said there was no hurry: "The earth will not move away, it will be here for a long time, and there need be no hurry."

Smith agreed. "The earth does not go away, but the sun comes and goes, the seasons pass away, and nothing is done."

Red Cloud admitted this, but it was plain both that he was not going to be moved to prompt action and, that he was still thinking of a location along the Platte. He turned to Wham and said, "You mentioned the bend of the river."

Wham explained to Brunot that before he arrived, he had told Red Cloud that he would ask the Great Father to build the agency at the bend of the Platte and to mark off a reservation, with the understanding that later the agency could be moved back into the country. Brunot, obviously nettled, said, "Such a proposition ought not to have been made to them." Wham replied that he had the authority to so locate the agency if he deemed it desirable.

Brunot did not press the point, but turned the conversation back to Red Cloud. There was some talk about the White River, but nothing was settled. Red Cloud insisted that he must consult his people. Brunot and Smith tried to get a promise out of him that he would be back in fifteen days, but Red Cloud would not set a definite time: "I do not want to tell a lie, and will not name the day, but messengers will come in every few days." Brunot said that unless Red Cloud came back within fifteen days, General Smith and Major Wham would hold a council with the other chiefs and select a location. This was all right with Red Cloud. "It does not make much difference," he said. "Call them up at any time. They will talk, their hearts are not all the same."

After Red Cloud had gone, Brunot met with certain of the other chiefs, telling them that if Red Cloud did not come back in fifteen days, the representatives of the Great Father would meet with them to decide where to put the agency. This seemed satisfactory. Red Dog said that most of the people wanted to go over the river, but there was nothing to say now. They would wait for Red Cloud; if he did not come

[72] *Red Cloud's Folk* (Norman: University of Oklahoma Press, 1957), p. 188.

back they would have a council without him and send word to the Great Father as to what they would do. Brunot left with the "impression . . . that Red Cloud will return and a proper place will be selected with consent of all, or nearly all, the Indians." To help them reach a decision he recommended that the annuity goods be held at Cheyenne until they selected a site for their agency.[73]

The allotted time elapsed and Red Cloud had not returned; indeed, he had not even sent in the promised messages. On June 30, therefore, Smith and Wham held a council with the Indians still at Fort Laramie; this included virtually everyone who had been there before except for Red Cloud and forty lodges. The Indians said they could not go into the interior because the streams all dry up during the summer months and they could find no water. They would remain on the North Platte, and wished their agency located temporarily on the north side of the river, eighteen miles below Fort Laramie. Wham and Smith both recommended that the Government give in. There seemed to be no other way to avoid conflict.[74] Wham also recommended that the order halting the issuance of rations be rescinded immediately—"7,000 Indians now here who will disperse if the issue of rations is not at once resumed and conflict will certainly follow."[75]

For a time it seemed that the Government would hold its ground. On July 5, Parker advised the War Department that the rations were being withheld and asked the Army to be prepared for hostilities,[76] but on the seventh, after receiving another telegram from Wham warning of an outbreak if subsistence was not resumed,[77] he decided not only to resume the issuance of rations but to locate the temporary agency as the Indians wished.[78]

Wham immediately got busy to implement the decision. After some shifting about, the agency was finally located about thirty-two miles downstream from Fort Laramie, approximately a mile west of the present Nebraska-Wyoming border. By fall, Wham had constructed a blacksmith shop, hay corral, issue corral, stables, three storehouses,

[73] Telegram, Brunot to Delano, June 15, 1871, NARS, RG 75, LR, Red Cloud Agency.

[74] Telegrams, Smith to Parker, June 30, 1871; Wham to Parker, June 31, 1871, *ibid.*

[75] Telegram, Wham to Parker, July 2, 1871, *ibid.*

[76] Telegrams, Thomas W. Vincent, AAG, USA, to Lt. Gen. P. H. Sheridan, July 5, 1871; AAG, Military Division of the Missouri, to Augur, July 6, 1871, NARS, RG 98, TR, Dept. of the Platte.

[77] Telegram, Wham to Parker, July 7, 1871, NARS, RG 75, LR, Red Cloud Agency.

[78] Telegram, Parker, Long Branch, N. J., to Clum, July 7, 1871, *ibid.*

and several small employees' quarters.[79] He even went so far as to suggest that as long as the Indians had selected a site north of the river, the arms and ammunition which had been promised them should be delivered![80] A month later, even though the arms and ammunition were not furnished, Wham reported, "Things are working in the most satisfactory manner." Red Cloud would be in from the north "in about 15 days"; Spotted Tail was "perfectly satisfied," and if dealt with properly would permanently establish his agency on the White River.[81]

Actually, Wham was having a good deal of difficulty with Spotted Tail and with Agent James W. Washburn, who accused Wham of trying to undermine his influence over the Brulés.[82] The trouble started in August when a wagon train of goods for the Brulés arrived at Fort Laramie. Wham proposed to send it to the White River, and because of the Oglalas' opposition to having wagon trains across their lands, asked Spotted Tail, who was temporarily at the fort, to provide an escort. Spotted Tail refused to do so. Even though he had agreed to locate on the White River, he spent most of his time hunting on the Republican and wanted his goods issued on the Platte. Wham would not issue the goods there and ordered them held at Fort Laramie. Meanwhile, Spotted Tail wanted to go back to the Republican to hunt. Wham acquiesced but insisted that Frank Yates, a trader, accompany the party as his representative. Spotted Tail was much irritated. He really wanted no white men with him, but if he must have one, it should be his old trader, Todd Randall, described by Wham as "disreputable."[83]

Wham's troubles with Spotted Tail were only a part of his problem. He was receiving no support at all for his activities at the new Red Cloud Agency. Governor J. A. Campbell of Wyoming complained to Parker, "I do not think it would be possible to inflict a greater damage to the Indians themselves. . . ."[84] Felix Brunot wrote the Secretary of

[79] Henry G. Waltmann, "The Subsistence Policy with Special Reference to the Red Cloud and Spotted Tail Agencies" (Master's thesis, University of Nebraska, 1959), p. 46. The station is frequently referred to as the "Sod Agency," but the major buildings at least were constructed of logs (Wham, Annual Report, Red Cloud Agency, Com. of Indian Affairs, *Annual Report*, 1871, pp. 697–703).

[80] Wham to Parker, July 21, 1871, NARS, RG 75, LR, Red Cloud Agency.

[81] Telegram, Wham to Clum, August 29, 1871, *ibid.*

[82] For a good account of the Brulé situation, see Waltmann, "Subsistence Policy," pp. 32–35.

[83] Wham's difficulties with Spotted Tail are described in his annual report, note 79 above.

[84] Campbell to Parker, July 17, 1871, NARS, RG 75, LR, Red Cloud Agency.

the Interior that the agency was poorly located, and that the location was made in opposition to his own views, which were freely stated to Agent Wham in June.[85] Even Colonel Smith, who had supported Wham in the recommendation that the Indians' request be granted, soon was expressing opposition to the precise location selected.[86]

It was obvious that the Platte River location, which represented a complete reversal of the position the Government had maintained since 1868, could not be considered a satisfactory solution to the problem. The Indian Bureau, however, was hardly in a position to take strong and positive action. While Commissioner Parker had been vacillating with respect to Red Cloud's location, he was being investigated by a Congressional Committee in connection with the letting of contracts at the Spotted Tail Agency (the old Whetstone Agency) which had been established on the White River, and in July he resigned under a cloud of suspicion,[87] although his ostensible reason was that "the office had been reduced to a mere clerkship."[88] Henry R. Clum, Parker's assistant, was named Acting Commissioner, and President Grant tried to persuade Felix Brunot to take the post. Brunot, however, decided he would rather remain as chairman of the Board of Indian Commissioners, and Clum continued to serve.[89] Meanwhile, Secretary of the Interior Columbus Delano persuaded Francis A. Walker, who had just completed his great work as Superintendent of the Ninth Census, to accept appointment as a special commissioner to investigate affairs at the Red Cloud and Spotted Tail agencies.[90] Walker (who shortly after his return would be named Commissioner of Indian Affairs)[91] left immediately for the West, and on October 25 had a conference in North Platte, Nebraska, with Spotted Tail, who had been hunting in the Republican River country.[92]

Spotted Tail complained about the treatment he had received from Wham, and about Yates' appointment to supervise his hunt. This

[85] Brunot to Delano, October 21, 1871, *ibid.*

[86] F. A. Walker to Secretary of the Interior, October 28, 1871, NARS, RG 48, LR, Indian Division.

[87] Waltmann, "Subsistence Policy," p. 71.

[88] *The Nation*, XIII (August 17, 1871), 100–101.

[89] Slattery, *Brunot*, pp. 182–185.

[90] Delano to Clum, October 20, 1871, NARS, RG 75, LR, Red Cloud Agency.

[91] For a life of Walker, see James Phinney Munroe, *A Life of Francis Amasa Walker* (New York: Henry Holt and Co., 1923). Chapter VII deals with Indian Affairs.

[92] *New York Times*, October 28, 1871. Walker's report of his trip will be found in F. A. Walker to Secretary of the Interior, October 26, 30, 1871, NARS, RG 48, LR, Indian Division. Unless otherwise indicated, my account is based on these letters.

alarmed Walker, who was rapidly becoming convinced of the importance of conciliating Spotted Tail in every reasonable way: "He is not
only the best Indian in this part of the country, but his power is mani-
festly on the increase, while Red Cloud's influence is somewhat waning."
As a step toward conciliation, therefore, he used his authority as special
commissioner to put Todd Randall in charge of the Republican River
hunt. Randall was "not a saint," but few of the Indian interpreters
were, and in view of Spotted Tail's insistence, his appointment seemed
justified as "a choice between evils."

As for the goods at Fort Laramie, Walker was convinced from talking
to Smith and others that there would have been no problem in getting
them to the White River if Wham had not deliberately stirred up
trouble in an effort to establish control over the Brulés as well as the
Oglalas. Walker felt strongly that it was important to minimize the
contact between the two tribes, and he was particularly concerned
that rations for one group should not go through the agency of the
other. As a solution to the immediate problem, he recommended that
the goods at Fort Laramie destined for Spotted Tail be turned over to
the Red Cloud Agency, and an equal quantity be made available for
Spotted Tail at North Platte or some other convenient point along the
railroad.[93]

As for Agent Wham:

> I will only say now that every word I have heard, whether from Wham's
> friends or his enemies, has gone to convince me that the whole thing here is
> rotten. I shall go into the matter more thoroughly before reporting officially,
> but I think I have enough now to justify an instant removal. At any rate,
> whether there is corruption or not, I am satisfied that there has been intrigue
> carried on here which has seriously compromised the good feeling that at one
> time existed.

Later, Walker submitted evidence that the Government had been
swindled by beef contractors, and that much of the flour issued to the
Indians at Red Cloud had found its way into the hands of John
Richard, who sold it in Cheyenne.[94] As agent, Wham was responsible
for the administration of his agency, but there is no evidence that he
knowingly participated in defrauding the Government or the Indians.
He was inefficient, to be sure, but even the most efficient administrator

---

[93] Walker believed it would be difficult to persuade Spotted Tail to leave the
Republican River country, and he thought that it might be best to allow him to remain
there, establishing a trading post somewhere south of Fort McPherson.

[94] Walker to Delano, November 25, 1871, NARS, RG 48, LR, Indian Division.

would have had difficulty in bucking the system. There were no scales at either Fort Laramie or the Red Cloud Agency, and it was easy for beef contractors to mislead the agent. As for the flour, Wham had protested against its issue—the Indians had no taste for it and did not know how to use it—and it is little wonder that they disposed of it in any way they could. It was clear, though, that Wham was not equal to the task of supervising the agency and the obstreperous Indians. Moreover, he had managed to alienate virtually every man, red and white, with whom he had been in contact. Finally, Wham was saddled with the responsibility for locating Red Cloud's agency on the Platte— although both the Indian Bureau and the Army had agreed to it— thus undermining the Government's efforts to move the Indians away from the river. It was apparent that Wham must go.

Secretary Delano did not even wait for Walker's return, but on October 31 ordered Wham replaced by Dr. J. W. Daniels, an Episcopal nominee then serving as agent for the Indians at Lake Traverse, Minnesota. Until he could arrive at his new post, Colonel Smith would assume charge of the agency.[95]

[95] Delano to Acting Com. of Indian Affairs, October 31, November 1, 1871, NARS, RG 75, LR, Red Cloud Agency.

CHAPTER 9

White River

Francis Walker's appointment as Commissioner of Indian Affairs in December, 1871, temporarily restored public confidence in the office, but there was mounting impatience with a policy which had failed to locate the Sioux and which permitted them to keep the frontier in a state of uneasiness although almost four years had elapsed since they had agreed to accept reservation status. In Dakota, the *Yankton Press* called for the abrogation of the Treaty of 1868,[1] and in Montana, an irate Bozeman editor wrote:

> The humiliating fact stares us in the face that notwithstanding the boast of Fourth of July orators, and the solemn assurances of grave state papers that the protection of the Republic follows her citizens throughout the civilized globe, the government either dare not or will not protect her citizens while extending the boundaries of civilization within its own immediate jurisdiction. . . .[2]

Even though official Army policy was to cooperate with the Indian Bureau to avoid hostilities, many military men shared the West's impatience. General Sheridan wrote the Adjutant General: "Should Red Cloud and his people not be appeased with our humility and submission to his insolence, but still make war, I will . . . make it lively for the squaws, papooses, ponies and villages."[3] The Indian Bureau,

---

[1] March 20, 1872.

[2] *Avant Courier*, Bozeman, April 4, 1872.

[3] Lt. Gen. Philip H. Sheridan to the Adjutant General, March 28, 1872, endorsement to letter, Col. John E. Smith, March 21, 1872, NARS, RG 98, LR, War Dept., AGO.

however, remained determined to avoid hostilities at any cost. Aside from humanitarian considerations, it justified its position by the oft-expressed view that it was cheaper to feed the Indians than to fight them. It was costing $1,500,000 a year to feed the Sioux, but, as Walker pointed out:

> It must be remembered that the Government has, more than once, spent in six months in fighting the Sioux what it would cost at present rates to support them for six years, while the present policy allows our railways and settlements to progress without practical obstruction.[4]

Out at Red Cloud Agency, J. W. Daniels, the newly arrived agent, was optimistic. On February 1 he wrote Walker: "The more sensible portion of the Sioux . . . are disposed to believe that the Agency must be moved to a more favorable place. Their suffering the past winter for the want of fuel, the constant alarm from the evil effects of whiskey . . . has excited their apprehensions as to the wisdom shown in selecting this place to receive their rations."[5] At the end of the month he reported that Red Cloud was on his way in with four hundred lodges, including a few Indians who had never been to a post or agency.[6] Red Cloud himself had never visited the agency on the Platte and he had not been at Fort Laramie since the previous June.

The report was correct. About six P.M. on March 11, Colonel Smith received a message from Red Cloud stating that he was camped five miles from the post and requesting Smith to come out and see him that evening. Smith declined, but the next day he did go to meet the chief and found him crossing the Platte about three miles above the post. He seemed much more reserved than at previous meetings. When they got to the post, he said that he had come in to have a talk, but his people were all too hungry to talk that day. Smith was not sorry, because he wanted Daniels there for the conference and he had not arrived; he was happy to have the Indians spend the balance of the day in feasting. Daniels arrived on the thirteenth, but late in the day, so the council was postponed until the fourteenth.

Smith opened the council by saying that he was glad to see Red Cloud after such a long absence, that Red Cloud had had time to think things over, and that he hoped the chief was prepared to locate his agency where the Great Father desired.[7] If Red Cloud *had* thought

---

[4] Com. of Indian Affairs, *Annual Report*, 1872, p. 46.

[5] Daniels to F. A. Walker, February 1, 1872, NARS, RG 75, LR, Red Cloud Agency.

[6] *Ibid.*, February 29, 1872, *ibid.*

[7] For this visit to Fort Laramie, I am using Smith to AG, USA, March 21, 1872, NARS, RG 75, LR, Red Cloud Agency.

about it, he certainly had not made any progress toward accepting the
Great Father's views. He replied that he would keep his word to the
Great Father and remain at peace, but he would not locate away from
the river; he wanted his agency on the Platte near Fort Laramie. As a
matter of fact, the present agency was too far away; he wanted his
goods sent to Fort Laramie. Smith said that this was impossible; Red
Cloud would have to go to the agency for his goods or else he would not
get any. Red Cloud next complained that his goods had been distributed without his consent, and Smith replied that the goods were not
for him alone but were for all his people, that he had been away for a
long time and they could not let his people starve while waiting for him
to say whether or not he chose to have his goods.

Smith then brought up the depredations committed near Fort
Fetterman, confronting Red Cloud with the fact that certain horses and
mules stolen in the area had been traced to his camp. Red Cloud said
only that the man who had committed the theft did not belong to his
party and he could not be responsible for his acts. He admitted that
the horses and mules had been brought to his camp but many of them
had died. Smith told him that unless he returned the horses, he would
not believe that he wanted to keep his word with the Great Father. At
this, Smith reported, Red Cloud became "very insolent in his de-
meanor" and said that he should not be blamed for the depredations.
Ending the conference, Smith warned Red Cloud that unless he could
control his people the whites would not believe he was a great chief. He
also said that Red Cloud must go to the agency with his people, and that
they must soon make up their minds to have an agency in their own
country or the Great Father would stop sending goods and Red Cloud
would be to blame for it.

Later in the day, Red Cloud came to Smith's quarters to talk matters
over again. He seemed in a much more pleasant frame of mind, assuring Smith that he would try to return the stolen animals. Meanwhile, he
hoped Smith would have his goods delivered to him at Fort Laramie.
Again Smith refused. On the next day Red Cloud returned to Smith's
quarters, repeating his assurances of friendship and his determination
to try to get back the stolen animals. He said he was going to Raw Hide
Creek to await the arrival of Black Twin, after which he would go
down to the agency. He asked Smith to write the agent not to give out
any more of his goods because he had promised to share with Black
Twin; the need for consulting with Black Twin was what had stalled
the negotiations of the previous summer.[8] Smith agreed to his request,

8 See above, p. 137.

but by the next day Red Cloud apparently had forgotten about the necessity for sharing with Black Twin, and he sent a runner in to Smith to ask that his goods be delivered to him at his camp near the fort. Now thoroughly disgusted, Smith replied that Red Cloud had heard his words, and that he must go to the agency or do without his goods.

At this point, trouble broke out at the agency. A rancher named Powell was robbed and murdered, and other whites in the area began to complain about depredations. The Indians became excited, and Daniels called for troops to protect the agency. Smith sent some cavalry and called Red Cloud in for another conference. It was because of such disturbances, he said, that the Great Father wanted him to have his agency away from the Platte River where there was always a chance for trouble. Red Cloud replied that he could see now that all he had been told was true. He understood it now. Smith said that the only way he could remedy the matter was to return the stolen property and give up the man who had murdered Powell, that the soldiers were there to keep peace, and that unless he went down to the agency at once and straightened things out, the whites would not believe that he was a great chief. Red Cloud replied that he should not be held responsible for such things, and complained that when anything happened other Indians were always ready to throw the blame on him. All the more reason for going at once to the agency, Smith rejoined; and after some little demurring Red Cloud agreed to go.

Red Cloud went down to the agency the next day (March 21), and on the twenty-second had a council with Daniels. He soon made it clear what he wanted. He said he had come to get the goods which had been saved for him; he would like to have them delivered at the Raw Hide near Fort Laramie. He said nothing at all about the stolen horses or the murderer of Powell.[9] He wished to trade at Fort Laramie, and the Raw Hide was the most convenient place between the agency and the fort. He wanted the issue made there, "to show the wild Indians the goodness of his great father."[10]

Red Cloud's persistent refusal to accept the idea that he was not to trade at Fort Laramie put Daniels in a quandary. To give in to Red Cloud again might make it all the more difficult to persuade him to accept a location away from the Platte. At the same time, there were seven thousand Indians at the agency, many of them in a menacing

[9] Powell's murderer was never apprehended. F. A. Walker, "The Indian Question," *North American Review*, CXVI (April, 1873), 345–346, treats this episode as an example of the difficulty in dealing with the Sioux.

[10] Daniels to Walker, March 25, 1872, NARS, RG 75, LR, Red Cloud Agency.

mood; even the usually bellicose Sheridan was inclined to be conciliatory.[11] Moreover, Red Cloud was full of assurances. According to
Daniels, the chief "wished to have these wild Indians see the goods, . . .
and then he would speak to them and tell them where to locate the
agency." The agent decided to give in. Red Cloud seemed to be
content. When he came for his goods on the twenty-third, he told
Daniels to move them to the Raw Hide: "Many of those people who
come in will go back North, but I shall stay with you. If I have to
pass through blood ankle deep to get to my white friends, I shall do it
and live with them." [12]

Despite these protestations, Red Cloud was slow to make up his
mind. At the time he secured the concession regarding his goods, he
said that it would take three or four days for him to decide where
he wanted to locate. When at the end of the month he had made no
decision, Daniels told him that he was going to locate the agency on
the White River or on one of the tributaries of the South Fork of the
Cheyenne, and that Red Cloud could have until April 6 to decide
whether or not he wished to join the Indians who were willing to move
to one of these locations.[13]

The decision was to be announced at a council with Colonel Smith.
A snowstorm made it impossible for Smith to be at the agency on the
sixth, and it was April 10 before all were assembled. Present, in addition
to Daniels, Smith, and the chiefs, was Brig. Gen. E. O. C. Ord, who
had succeeded Augur as commandant of the Department of the
Platte.[14] Red Dog, opening the conclave, said, "Today we are going to
look to the welfare of the old people and our children. I want to see if
you all are of the same mind. Last year I located this agency here and
today I look upon you to locate another one."

Red Cloud said, "This is the day to decide. They have asked you to
name the place where the agency shall be and this is the day for you
to say. There are Cheyennes, Arapahoes and Sioux here and I want
to hear from them and hear what they have to say."

Young-Man-Afraid-of-His-Horse spoke for all the Indians. He said
nothing about the agency. Instead, he talked about hunting in the Big

[11] Telegram, Sheridan to AG, USA, March 25, 1872, NARS, RG 98, LR, AGO.
[12] Daniels to Walker, March 25, 1872 (above, n. 10).
[13] *Ibid.*, March 30, 1872.
[14] There is no single full report of the council. My account is taken from the following: Smith to E. D. Townsend, April 13, 1872, NARS, RG 75, LR, Red Cloud
Agency; Daniels to Walker, April 14, 1872, *ibid.*; and E. O. C. Ord to AAG, Military
Division of the Missouri, April 14, 1872, NARS, RG 98, LS, Dept. of the Platte.

Horn country, the times they made peace with Harney and Sanborn, and the trouble they had had with the soldiers. He injected a new element into the discussion by saying that the Indians wanted their own people and the half-breeds to do their work and haul their goods.

Smith, obviously irritated, said to the interpreter, "Tell them they are always looking behind them." Then, to the Indians, he said:

Now I want you all to remember my words. I am getting tired and the Great Father is getting tired of talking to you. . . .

You had better take your agent and go and select a place so that he can have buildings put up to keep your provisions from spoiling. In your treaty you were to have carpenters, blacksmiths and men to do the work you could not do. As soon as you learn, your Great Father will let you do it yourself.

Now I want to tell you why your goods cannot be hauled by the men of the country and half breeds. Your Great Father sends you a great many goods and he wants you to get them; if you do not he makes those who have them pay for all that is lost. He does this to be sure that you get what he sends you.

I want to say again, your chiefs and your head men and your agent ought to go and pick out a place immediately for the agency. If you do not your old people and children will starve. That is all in regard to the agency. . . .

Smith then brought up the Powell murder and the stolen horses. If the chiefs did not bring in the men who had committed the crimes, he would send his soldiers after them.

There was more talk, most of it beside the point, but finally the Indians announced that they had decided on the place; they would go to the White River. It was clear, however, that they hoped to get some concessions as a result of this decision. In the next breath they asked Smith if he would give up his idea about hauling the goods and delivering up the murderer and the stolen horses. Smith refused, but they still kept pressing the point—American Horse, Fire Thunder, and Big Foot all talked about it. Red Cloud had nothing to say on the subject. Although none of the chiefs came out flatly and said so, there was the implication throughout the argument that they could not persuade their young men to move to the White River unless they could wring some sort of concession from the Government. Smith, however, remained adamant. At one point he said, "I hope I am not talking to squaws. . . . I hope I am talking to chiefs and big men." A few minutes later he abruptly closed the conference by saying, "You have heard my words. Bear them in mind and listen to them. Good bye."

Smith's blunt talk put the Indians in a rebellious mood, but by the

end of the month things had quieted down sufficiently to enable Daniels
to take Red Dog and a few others to the White River to select a new site
for the agency. After tramping over the ground they concluded that the
best location was a spot about a mile above the point where the Little
White Clay empties into the river.[15] Red Cloud did not accompany
the group, although he approved of the location and indeed took
credit for selecting it.[16]

Red Cloud's principal interest now was in going to Washington for
another visit with the Great White Father. At the time of the conferences
with Smith he had said to Daniels:

> Tell my Great Father that I wish to go and see him. I want to take some
> of my people and show them the white man's way. I want to be better
> acquainted with him and have a talk about many things. I want to tell him
> what I have done since I saw him.[17]

Red Cloud may have seized upon this as a device for reasserting his
authority, which, it seems clear, had slipped some during his long stay
in the north. Whatever the reasons for the request, Daniels recommended that it be granted,[18] Secretary Delano agreed,[19] and on
May 17 Daniels left for Washington with Red Cloud and twenty-six
of his people.[20] Red Dog was in the group, as were Little Wound,
Blue Horse, High Wolf, Red Leaf, and Big Foot. Jules Ecoffey, Nick
Janis, and Joe Bisonette were along as interpreters. Of the Indians, only
Red Cloud and Red Dog had made the trip before; the others were
all seeing the white man's country for the first time.[21]

On May 27 the Indians gathered at the Department of the Interior
for a conference with Secretary Delano and Commissioner Walker.[22]
Red Cloud invoked the blessing of the Great Spirit and spent some time
talking about the past, recalling his earlier visit and in particular
complaining of wrongs perpetrated by white men in the Indian country.

---

[15] Daniels to Walker, May 1, 1872, NARS, RG 75, LR, Red Cloud Agency.

[16] *Ibid.*; Daniels to Walker, April 11, 1872.

[17] Daniels to Walker, April 11, 1872, NARS, RG 75, LR, Red Cloud Agency.

[18] *Ibid.*

[19] *New York Times*, May 20, 1872.

[20] Telegram, Daniels to Walker, May 17, 1872, NARS, RG 75, LR, Red Cloud
Agency.

[21] *Cheyenne Daily Leader*, May 18, 1872; *New York Times*, May 20, 1872.

[22] Unless otherwise indicated, my source for the Washington conferences is "Report
of Councils held with Red Cloud's band of Ogallalla Sioux by the President of the
United States and Secretary of the Interior, May 27th, 28th, and 29th, 1872," NARS,
RG 75, Old Misc. Records.

He soon got to the point, however: he had located his agency north of the Platte, and now he wanted his goods. "I came down to see the Great Father," he said, "to see if I could not get some ammunition and guns and pistols, and I wanted to get all that is needed. The most of our Nation needs clothing. The reason I want the ammunition and guns is because there is game out in our country and of course we want to go out and hunt and raise our children well." He also wanted the Great Father to give each man in the party a horse at Pine Bluffs, as he did two years ago,[23] "to take us back right."

Little Wound and Red Dog also spoke. Their requests were about the same as Red Cloud's, although Red Dog brought up the matter of having the men of the country haul their goods, and he also hoped that the Great Father would give them a few dollars apiece so they could go anywhere they wished in Washington.

Secretary Delano was most conciliatory. The Great Father would try to get rid of the bad white men in the Indian country. Also, there would be a little money to spend in Washington, and horses to ride home on. Their ammunition had been withheld because of the murder of Powell, but the Great Father was now satisfied that this had been done by bad Indians, and he would let the agent give Red Cloud and his people, and all who wanted to take the right road, some ammunition with which to hunt.[24] The next day, the Secretary said, he would take the Indians to see the Great Father. "It will not be necessary to repeat these speeches to him, as he has not the time," he warned, "but I will tell the President, the Great Father, the words you have spoken."

At the White House the next day, the President told the Indians he did not want them to go beyond the limits set for them. He wondered, however, if they had thought about going south to what was known as the Cherokee country. There the climate was good and the Sioux could have a large tract of land. The Government would build houses for their chiefs and principal men, and give them large herds of cattle and sheep. This, the first of several suggestions that the Sioux consider a move to the south, made no impression at all. Red Cloud ignored it altogether. He said to the President:

> I have but little to tell you—a very few words. There have been many
> Indians in your house; but all these Indians were sent for. This is the second

---

[23] See above, p. 116.

[24] Walker, "The Indian Question" (above, n. 9), 345–346, criticizes the Government for its failure to punish the murderers of Powell, but there is no record that he objected to this decision at the time it was made.

time I have come, and now I come without an invitation—I have come out
of my own will. You have told me that in thirty-five years I shall control
my nation, and I have listened to you. When I went back to my people I
went further north to see the missionary people, and while I was gone they
put the agency across the river; they did it against my will. When they put
the agency across the river I was not there. I was further north. I have
decided a place for my agency. I want it on the White River, and all the
people that are with me want it there. We have found a good creek, and
this man (pointing to Dr. Daniels, the agent) went with me to select that
place, and we came down to let you know of it. That is the only place that is
suitable for our agency. I don't want any other.

The President reminded Red Cloud that the location selected was in
Nebraska, and the Indians might soon have to move. He would let the
Secretary of the Interior decide.

The next day, in the Interior building, Secretary Delano agreed to
let the Oglalas locate on the White River, but he warned them that by
and by the white people would want that country and they would have
to go farther north. He did say that he would try to keep them on the
White River as long as possible, although he suggested that ultimately
they might want to move south to the Cherokee country. Red Cloud
ignored the suggestion, saying only that he did not want to move.
Thus the conference ended. The Government had made its point for
the record, but it is doubtful that the Indians gave much thought to the
possibility that they might have to move from their proposed location
on the White River once they had established themselves.

Back at the agency, Red Cloud busied himself with talking to his
people and presumably urging them to accept the decision to move to
White River. Indeed, he was so busy that he was unable to accompany
Daniels on a trip to Fort Peck, where, it was assumed, he might have a
chance to talk to some of the northern tribes. These tribes had been
counciling at the mouth of the Little Powder and apparently were
divided as to what course they should pursue with respect to the whites
and particularly with regard to the Northern Pacific Railroad. Red
Cloud did give Daniels a message, however, which he was to pass on to
Sitting Bull, No Neck, Red Horse, Fire Horn, and Black Moon, should
he see them. The essence of the message was peace. Red Cloud said:

Friends, I carried on the war against the whites with you until I went to
see my Great Father two years ago. My Great Father spoke good to me. I
remembered his words and came home. I told my people his words and they
have listened to me. I went to see my Great Father a second time; he gave

me good advice. I asked for many things for my people, he gave me those things. All the whites spoke well to me.

I shall not go to war any more with the whites. I shall do as my Great Father says and make my people listen. . . . You must carry on the war yourselves. I am done. . . .

Listen to me and save your country. Make no trouble for our Great Father. His heart is good. Be friends to him and he will provide for you. Your old people and children will not starve. Take his hand and hold it fast. My father (agent) goes to see you. Open your ears and listen to him. His words are good—remember them. . . .[25]

Daniels made very little impression upon the northern Indians and came back convinced that they wanted trouble.[26] But trouble was not confined to the north; he found it brewing at his own agency.

During his absence, some of the Indians had taken to grazing their ponies in large numbers on the south side of the Platte. When the Army's hay contractors complained, Lt. Col. Cuvier Grover, temporarily in command of Fort Laramie because of Colonel Smith's absence, sent troops to force the Indians to take the ponies back across the river. The south side of the river was forbidden territory and the Indians knew it, although apparently they had crossed back and forth all season without interference. When the troops appeared on August 20 and ordered the Indians to remove their ponies to the north side of the river, they refused, and the troops began to round up the ponies, threatening to take them and any Indians who resisted to Fort Laramie. This created much excitement, with the young men threatening to kill the soldiers and all the whites at the agency. Finally, Red Cloud was able to persuade the herders to remove their ponies, and the troops departed.[27] The excitement was a long time dying down, however, and soon Red Cloud became involved in a role other than that of a peacemaker—possibly by design, possibly through the force of circumstances.

At the time of the trouble over the ponies, some of the young men went around saying that they would never consent to moving the

[25] Daniels to Walker, July 6, 1872, NARS, RG 75, LR, Red Cloud Agency.

[26] *Ibid.*, September 4, 1872.

[27] Daniels to Walker, September 2, 1872; endorsement, Lt. Col. C. Grover to AG, Dept. of the Platte, September 27, 1872, to letter, Secretary of War to Sheridan, September 13, 1872, NARS, RG 75, LR, Red Cloud Agency. This correspondence reveals another instance of conflict between the Departments of War and Interior. Daniels blamed the difficulty upon the military and stated that the incident would not have occurred had Colonel Smith been present. Grover, defending his action, appended a telegram from Smith's adjutant expressing complete approval of the manner in which the difficulty was handled.

agency. Red Cloud was definitely on the side of the whites in this difficulty—indeed, he and Blue Nose told the acting agent that if trouble came, "they would defend them with their lives"[28]—and there is no evidence that he sanctioned the talk about refusing to move. On September 11, however, he spoke out in council against moving to White River,[29] and on September 22, when the wagons were all loaded and ready to go, he and Little Wound went to Daniels and said, "they should not go to the White River for 30 years."[30] Daniels faced a difficult decision. Red Dog, Blue Horse, and Red Leaf wanted to move, but they were in the minority and could hardly be expected to take action on their own. Daniels wired Smith at Fort Laramie: "I can see but one way to settle the Red Cloud's party and that is to use force and compel them to do right."[31] Smith concurred and also suggested that further issues of annuity goods be withheld until Red Cloud agreed to move.[32] Commissioner Walker, however, decided not to force the issue at this time or disturb the distribution of Red Cloud's annuity goods,[33] and Smith, complaining that "a golden opportunity to chastize these Indians as they richly deserve has been lost," canceled plans for sending troops to the agency.[34]

It is difficult to determine just why Red Cloud, after all his protestations of the spring and summer, suddenly changed his mind about moving to White River. The only excuses he gave Daniels were that he had been promised in the treaty that he should remain on the Platte River for thirty-five years and that Spotted Tail had received many presents for moving his agency while he had received none. Daniels thought the real cause to be "the natural duplicity of his character and influence of the hostile Sioux."[35] Discounting the "natural duplicity" charge— although one can easily see how the harried Daniels could be moved to make it—the influence of the hostile Sioux probably helps to explain the chief's frequent failures to live up to promises. He was ready to take the white man's road—at least on his own terms—but he desperately

[28] Daniels to Walker, September 2, 1872, *ibid.*

[29] *Ibid.*, September 11, 1872, *ibid.*

[30] Telegram, *ibid.*, September 22, 1872.

[31] Telegram, Daniels to Smith, *ibid.*

[32] Telegram, Smith to Walker, September 22, 1872, *ibid.*

[33] Telegram, Walker to Smith, September 26, 1872, *ibid.*

[34] Smith to AAG, Dept. of the Platte, September 27, 1872, *ibid.* Walker gave no reason for his decision. In view of his complaints against the vacillation of the Government in dealing with the Indians, his action in this instance is interesting, to say the least. See Walker, "The Indian Question" (above, n. 9), pp. 345–346.

[35] Daniels to Walker, September 26, 1872, NARS, RG 75, LR, Red Cloud Agency.

wanted to take all of his people with him, the fighting men as well as the loafers; it is entirely possible that he went back on a promise because he had discovered that he could not carry it out and still retain at least a semblance of leadership among his warriors. He had had difficulty ever since he signed the treaty in 1868; his difficulty had increased after the journey to Washington in 1870 when he had come home to find that many were wondering out loud whether, under the influence of the Great Father, he had sold out to the whites. Agreeing to locate where the white man wanted him to was not an easy thing. Also, there is no question but that jealousy of Spotted Tail played a part in his reluctance to move to the White River. It would not be good to live so close to the Brulé chief.

Although Red Cloud refused to permit the agency to be moved, he did not seem disposed to cause further trouble. Indeed, in October when some of the young men, loaded with whiskey supplied by white traders from across the Platte, threatened to kill the agent and all whites at the agency, Red Cloud, Little Wound, and several others offered protection, and after an uneasy twenty-four hours, during which troops were called from Fort Laramie, the chiefs gradually got things quieted down.[36] Shortly thereafter, Red Cloud went off to Hat Creek, very near the spot selected for the agency, and by November 1 virtually all of the Indians had left the Platte, most of them settling for the winter along the White River, although Little Wound—who had wanted to go south and hunt on the Republican but had been refused permission because he had been unwilling to move the agency—established himself near the site of Fort Mitchell.[37] For a while Red Cloud came to the Platte River for his supplies, but in December Daniels decided to send his goods to the White River. Fifty thousand pounds a month would subsist the Oglalas, and the transportation would not be over two dollars per hundred. The cost was not great, Daniels argued, when the advantages of the plan were considered— "it will give those who, from their bad behavior would not dare come here to stay, a chance to more fully appreciate the advantages of being at peace."[38]

[36] Daniels to Walker, October 25, 1872, *ibid.* Telegram, Smith to AAG, Dept. of the Platte, October 23, 1872, NARS, RG 98, LR, Dept. of the Platte.

[37] Daniels to Walker, October 24, 1872; Telegram, Smith to AAG, Dept. of the Platte, November 1, 1872, *ibid.* Fort Mitchell, near Scotts Bluff, existed as a subsidiary post to Fort Laramie from 1864 to 1867. See Merrill J. Mattes, "Fort Mitchell, Scotts Bluff, Nebraska Territory," *Nebraska History*, XXXIII (March, 1952), 1–34.

[38] Daniels to Walker, December 12, 1872, *ibid.*

Red Cloud had no objection to receiving rations on the White
River during the winter, but he did not want to concentrate his people
there. He was now saying the agency must be located on the Raw
Hide; by the end of February, however, he had changed his mind
again. He told Daniels, "I want you to tell the Great Father that I want
my agency on Hat Creek and I want to have it moved this moon."
The reason for this sudden change was clear. Spotted Tail had moved
over to Whetstone Creek: "I waited for him to move his agency. Now
he has moved."[39] Daniels still favored the White River location, and
he thought that most of the Indians did, too. Hat Creek was not well
adapted for an agency, particularly because of the scarcity of good
water. Weary and irritated, Daniels wrote the Commissioner of
Indian Affairs:

> These same objections were given by Red Cloud last summer and the
> Indians are not loth to call his attention to this fact now. Red Cloud has
> very few friends in this move and has made some very bitter enemies. The
> Indians very generally adhere to White River and would insist upon the
> immediate removal to that place were it not the fear of trouble from the Red
> Cloud party.[40]

Edward P. Smith, who had become Commissioner of Indian Affairs
when Walker decided to abandon government service for a chair in
economics at Yale, was anxious to get the thing settled once and for all.
He was not well-equipped to solve the problem. A minister, his only
prior experience in Indian affairs had been as an agent for the Chippe-
was; as he later admitted, the job of Commissioner was "an enormous
terra incognita."[41] He wrote Felix Brunot for advice, but Brunot was not
particularly helpful. He recalled that two years ago the Indians had
told him that there was a good place for an agency on the White
River, but he had never been more than a mile north of the Platte so
he had no first-hand information. He suggested that perhaps it would
be best to appoint a commission to go out and look over the ground: "It
seems to be very important that the department shall have an account
and accurate knowledge of the points proposed, that there may be
no further mistakes in regard to the supplies of good water, grass and
the capability of cultivation before making a final selection."[42]

[39] Daniels to Walker, February 28, 1873, *ibid.*
[40] Daniels to Com. of Indian Affairs, March 23, 1873, *ibid.*
[41] Henry G. Waltmann, "The Subsistence Policy with Special Reference to the
Red Cloud and Spotted Tail Agencies" (Master's thesis, University of Nebraska,
1959), p. 72.
[42] Brunot to E. P. Smith, April 11, 1873, NARS, RG 75, LR, Red Cloud Agency.

Although it would seem that there had been commissions enough to locate the Red Cloud Agency, Smith decided to appoint still another. He asked Brunot to serve as chairman, accompanied by Henry Alvord, E. C. Kemble, and Governor J. A. Campbell of Wyoming. Brunot could not go west until June, so Kemble and Alvord went on ahead. Red Cloud greeted them very cordially. He shook hands and said that their hearts were the same and that he wanted "only good words." He agreed to participate in a general conference on June 17 of all those who had participated in the Treaty of 1868. He was evasive about the location of the agency, though, and about his responsibility for preventing trouble. He only wanted to talk about the Great Father's failure to keep his promises. Kemble was not impressed. He reported to Smith:

> From all I have seen and can learn of Red Cloud, I conclude that his influence has not been exerted to make friends for the Government and he has clearly not kept his promises repeatedly made to us in the East and at this Agency. The friends which have been made to the Government through the temperate and judicious management of the Agent here, have been made almost in the face of Red Cloud's efforts to the contrary, and now these chiefs and nearly every man of influence here complain openly of his course. . . . I am assured by Agent Daniels that the agency could have been removed at any time during the past eight months if Red Cloud had not withheld his approval.[43]

Brunot and Campbell arrived at the agency on June 19,[44] and on the twentieth the Commissioners met with the chiefs—thirty-five of them, Cheyennes and Arapahoes as well as Oglalas and Brulés. After two days of wrangling, Red Cloud and Little Wound agreed to move to the White River. Red Cloud had insisted that before they would move they must be provided with arms, ammunition, and additional articles of food as promised him in Washington. The Commissioners, as usual, made no promises but said that the Great Father would take care of the Indians' needs if they would do right and follow his instructions; the Indians, as usual, interpreted this as a promise.[45]

Before the Commissioners arrived, Daniels resigned, weary of living in constant jeopardy and frustrated by the refusal of the Government

[43] E. C. Kemble to E. P. Smith, June 2, 1873, *ibid.*

[44] John A. Campbell, "Diary, 1868–1875," *Annals of Wyoming*, X (October, 1938), 161.

[45] For a report of the conference, see Brunot to E. P. Smith, June 28, 1873, NARS, RG 75, LR, Red Cloud Agency.

to supply him with troops with which to enforce his orders.[46] Actually, he had done a good job under the most difficult circumstances, and the fact that Red Cloud finally came around to accepting the White River location must be attributed largely to the skill and patience Daniels had employed in dealing with him during the difficult months just past.[47] He decided to complete the job of removal before his successor, Dr. J. J. Saville, a physician nominated by the Episcopal church, arrived.

He almost failed to do so. On July 25, with the first wagons loaded and on their way, Red Cloud came up and said that the agency must not be moved until the new agent had arrived and they could have a talk with him to see if the Great Father had ordered the things they had asked for when they met with the Commissioners.[48] The wagons were wholly without military protection, so there was nothing to do but order them turned back. In a couple of days Red Cloud relented to the point of suggesting that if the chiefs could have a few presents they would be able to allow the wagons to proceed without waiting for the new agent. Jules Ecoffey, the agency trader, had some goods on hand that seemed to satisfy, and on the twenty-seventh the movement got under way again.[49] On August 2 Daniels, with what must have been great relief, wired Smith: "Agency has gone to place selected."[50]

[46] J. A. Campbell to Columbus Delano, May 5, 1873, NARS, RG 75, LR, Wyoming Superintendency.

[47] He had called for troops a few times, but generally he succeeded without the military force he felt to be essential to the management of the Oglalas. Although the Indian office generally opposed the use of troops, there was a growing feeling even in the Interior Department that a military force would be necessary to keep the Oglalas in hand. Indeed, a special commission consisting of Governor Campbell, Edward P. Goodwin, and S. R. Hosmer reported on August 9, 1873, that the new Red Cloud Agency would be impossible to maintain without military support (Com. of Indian Affairs, *Annual Report*, 1873, pp. 155–156). Daniels said the same thing in his final report as Red Cloud agent (*ibid.*, pp. 243–244).

[48] Daniels to E. P. Smith, July 25, 1873, NARS, RG 75, LR, Red Cloud Agency.

[49] *Ibid.*, August 23, 1873, *ibid.*

[50] Telegram, Daniels to E. P. Smith, August 2, 1873, *ibid.* The entire movement, over seventy-five miles of sandhills trail, was not finally completed until the spring of 1874 (E. S. Ricker, Interview with William Garnett, Ricker Mss., Tablet No. 1, pp. 39–41, Nebraska State Historical Society). The contractor in charge of the move was Dwight J. McCann, prominent Nebraska City, Nebraska, Republican who had been on the scene from time to time since May, 1872, as a special commissioner to help relocate the Red Cloud Agency, and who generally had been a disrupting influence in the long and tedious proceedings (see Waltmann [above, n. 41], p. 47). McCann later was involved in the scandals which brought forth the celebrated investigation of 1875 (see below, pp. 189–198).

The retiring agent thought the new site would provide an excellent home for the Oglalas. In his final report he described the agency as being "in a very pretty valley with good water and all the farming land . . . [the Indians] will require for the next ten years."[51] Although one might question Daniels' estimate of the agricultural potential of the area, on all other scores the new Red Cloud agency standing high on a bluff overlooking the verdant valley of the White River, was handsomely located and indeed could be described as the finest fruit of the peace policy: it had been achieved by patience and negotiation; it had been selected by the Indians themselves. Yet, as we have seen, during the long, weary months of wheedling the negotiations frequently had been interrupted by the threat of force, and Agent Daniels, who more than any of the negotiators was responsible for success, was certain that the temper of the Indians and the disorganized state of the tribes would make it impossible for the new agency to exist without military protection. Time—and very little at that—would prove him right, and within a few months after it was established the new Red Cloud Agency would become the focal point for the disintegration of the policy of peaceful persuasion on which the Government had staked so much in its relations with the Sioux.

There were signs of trouble almost from the beginning. On August 14, 1874, the day after he arrived, Dr. Saville attended a council of the chiefs. Red Cloud told him that now that they had moved to this place as requested by the Great Father, they expected to get the guns and ammunition promised them by the Commission. He had eleven bands and he wanted ten guns for each band. He said further that the chiefs would regulate affairs at the agency and that everything would have to be done as they wished. No white man should cross the White River, and no hay or timber should be cut except within certain bounds, and that would have to be paid for. He wanted regular issues of powder and lead, and finally he said that Spotted Tail's supplies should be shipped in from the Missouri River and not pass through the Oglala country.[52]

Red Cloud was not the only one who was exercising his independence. Almost as soon as the agency was located, large numbers of Miniconjous began to come in from the north. Some of them had never

[51] Com. of Indian Affairs, Annual Report. 1873, pp. 243–244. The site of the agency, located about a mile southwest of the present town of Crawford, Nebraska, is now maintained by the Nebraska State Historical Society as one of the interpretive features of Fort Robinson State Park.

[52] J. J. Saville to E. P. Smith, August 14, 1873, NARS, RG 75, LR, Red Cloud Agency.

been at an agency before, and all of them were described as "impudent and saucy."[53]

So Saville had his work cut out for him—and he was going to have to accomplish it under the most difficult of conditions. His own head-quarters were in a tent; the building supplies and commissary stores were piled on the ground. As he confessed in his first annual report, "Inexperienced in this business myself, and having no one familiar with the forms of the business, and without papers, books, or instructions for guides, I was left in a sufficiently embarrassing position to undertake so complicated a business."[54]

Embarrassed or not, Saville wasted no time commiserating with himself but set to work at once trying to provide some sort of shelter before winter set in. It was not easy. He let a contract for supplying logs to Jules Ecoffey, the agency trader. The Indians, prompted by Louis Richard, who wanted the contract, ordered the work to stop, but after a council they were persuaded to let Ecoffey go ahead.[55] Shortly thereafter Ecoffey threw up his contract and the agent had to make out as best he could.[56] By mid-September he had a warehouse completed and was making progress on the stockade, barn, office, employees quarters, and his own residence.[57] He also seems to have made some progress with Red Cloud and the other chiefs; at least, when he went to Washington in November with a delegation of Arapahoes and Cheyennes (just why the Indian Office thought Saville could be gone for a month at this time is difficult to understand) he took with him messages from Red Cloud, Red Dog, and Blue Horse expressing appro-val of their new agent.[58] Red Cloud said:

> When you get to Washington, I want you to go and see the Great Father and tell him I want to go and see him in relation to farming and stock raising four winters from now. The Ogallala people put the agency here for

[53] Daniels to E. P. Smith, August 1, 1873, *ibid.*

[54] Com. of Indian Affairs, *Annual Report*, 1874, p. 251.

[55] Saville to E. P. Smith, Aug. 22, 1873, *ibid.*

[56] Com. of Indian Affairs, *Annual Report*, 1874, p. 251. Saville had his troubles with Ecoffey and finally revoked his trading license (*ibid.*; cf. George E. Hyde, *Red Cloud's Folk* [Norman: University of Oklahoma Press, 1957], pp. 205–206). Hyde's assertion that Saville fired Ecoffey to replace him with a friend is difficult to credit in view of the fact that the new trader, J. W. Dear, was soon writing to the military in criticism of Saville and with the request that his communication be kept private (J. W. Dear to John E. Smith, February 19, 1874, NARS, RG 94, Doc. File 563, AGO, 1874).

[57] Com. of Indian Affairs, *Annual Report*, 1874, p. 251; Henry M. Baum to H. Dyer [n.d.], in *Yankton Press and Dakotaian*, February 26, 1874.

[58] Messages dated October 26, 1873, NARS, RG 75, LR, Red Cloud Agency.

the purpose of raising their children. . . . It will take some years yet for us to do for ourselves. When that time comes, I will go and see the Great Father and have him give us something to help us make a living the same as the white men do. I have already told the Great Father I did not want anything to do with the soldiers. I can get along with the agent. . . .

I want you to put us on the good road. Everybody knows that we have more Indians here today than ever before. I want you to take this word to the Great Father and get him to give us an answer in writing and you bring the answer back to us. We want you to use your influence and get us guns, ammunition and traders. Get all the different churches that we want to to work for us for I consider them our friends. . . .

I wish you to write this and put it in the hands of the Great Father yourself and then we will know that he gets our word. When we send word to the Great Father, they go through so many ears that they are all lost before they reach him.

Even before Saville returned, however, there were signs that the winter was going to be an uneasy one. There was the perennial problem of guns and ammunition, complicated now by the fact that the Sioux assumed, rightly or wrongly, that they would be furnished guns as soon as they were settled on the White River.[59] There was also the seemingly permanent problem of Little Wound's insistence upon hunting along the Republican. Some of his band had been down there in August and had massacred a party of Pawnees who were on an authorized hunt from their reservation on the Loup.[60] General Sherman argued that by this action the Sioux had forfeited any treaty rights they might have had to hunt on the Republican, and urged that they be prohibited from doing so. Commissioner Smith agreed, and the order went out.[61] Little Wound responded by sending a small party south,

[59] E. C. Kemble had been largely responsible for this assumption (see above, p. 157). Rev. Henry M. Baum, rector of St. Matthew's Church, Laramie, Wyoming, who visited the agency in September, charged that Kemble, who, he declared, "knows nothing about the Indians, and is totally unfit to treat with them," had left the impression that if the Government would not furnish the guns, the church would. Baum, who felt that nothing could be done with the Sioux unless the promises were kept, wrote: "I must respectfully . . . recommend that the guns be given that have been promised to the Indians belonging to the Red Cloud Agency, or that Colonel Kemble be appointed a special commissioner to go and tell them why they are not given to them" (above, n. 57).

[60] The site of the massacre, near Trenton, Nebraska, is marked by a monument. See Addison E. Sheldon, "Massacre Canyon: The Last Nebraska Battlefield of the Sioux–Pawnee," Nebraska History, IV (October–December, 1921), 53–60.

[61] E. P. Smith to Secretary of the Interior, November 14, 1873, NARS, RG 75, LR, Red Cloud Agency.

and in Washington Saville urged the Government to move slowly in enforcing the order. In what would have been a prize *non sequitur* had it not so accurately characterized the confusion in Indian policy, he wrote Smith: "If the department should deem it necessary to use force in compelling obedience ... I respectfully request that it be done without bloodshed, as we are at present defenseless at the agency and such a result would endanger our lives." [62]

Little Wound was left to go his own way, and the question of whether or not he should hunt on the Republican was overshadowed by the larger problem of administering Article 10 of the Treaty of 1868 which provided for the issuance of rations and annuities to the Indians who complied with the treaty and settled on reservations. The Indians constantly complained about both the quality and quantity of the annuities and rations—and frequently with ample justification[63]—but Saville's major problem now was trying to get an exact count of the Indians on which to base the issues.[64] For reasons which puzzled every agent, the Indians strenuously objected to being counted. Some agents attributed this reaction to superstition; Saville believed that they hoped to increase the amounts issued by exaggerating their numbers.[65] At Red Cloud Agency, the problem was complicated by the appearance in the fall of 1873 of many northern Indians who had never been at an agency before and whose presence more than doubled the number of persons to be fed. Saville described his troubles with them in his first annual report:

> Many of these people ... were exceedingly vicious and insolent. They made unreasonable demands for food, and supplemented their demands with threats. They resisted every effort to count them, and as their statements of their numbers were frequently exaggerated, it became necessary to arbitrarily reduce their rations, forming my estimates of their numbers from the best information I could obtain. This caused a constant contention with them; and being unprotected I was compelled to talk with them from morning till night. On one occasion, when attempting to count their lodges, I was arrested by some three hundred of these wild fellows and returned to the agency for trial; but of the older residents of the agency

[62] Saville to E. P. Smith, November 18, 1873, *ibid.*

[63] Waltmann, "Subsistence Policy" (above, n. 41), *passim.*

[64] Article 10 of the Treaty of 1868 provided: "And in order that the Commissioner of Indian Affairs may be able to estimate properly for the articles herein named, it shall be the duty of the agent each year to forward to him a full and exact census of the Indians, on which the estimate from year to year can be based."

[65] Waltmann, "Subsistence Policy" (above, n. 41), p. 86.

about seven hundred, armed and mounted, came to my relief and protected me.[66]

Upon his return from Washington in December, Saville warned that his supply of beef cattle was nearly exhausted. He had been issuing for thirteen thousand—the Indians claimed fifteen thousand—and this required eight hundred thousand pounds of beef per month, more than double the amount estimated. He would make every effort to reduce the number and to try to obtain an exact count of the Indians. Should he fail, he would be compelled to call for troops.[67]

On Christmas Day he gave a feast and called the chiefs and head men together to discuss the census. Inasmuch as Red Cloud, Red Dog, Little Wound, and several others had agreed in advance to having their people counted, Saville thought that finally he would succeed. When the time arrived for the conference, however, Red Cloud had to be sent for twice before he would come; and no sooner had the agent concluded his opening remarks, in which he explained the necessity of a census, than Red Cloud arose and made a long speech, the essence of which was that they would talk about counting their people after the Great Father had sent the guns and ammunition the Commissioners had promised. Red Dog and High Wolf endorsed all that Red Cloud had said, and not a man arose to oppose him. The harried agent, his plans completely awry, adjourned the council, convinced that there was no hope of controlling the issue of rations except by force. He warned his superiors that he might have to call for military assistance at any time, and surely by spring.[68]

On January 14, Saville requested that a military post be established to protect his agency. The Interior Department concurred, but the War Department, acting on advice from General Sheridan, was opposed. Sheridan responded to the request by reiterating his often-expressed opinion that the agency should be located on the Missouri River. There was no point in trying to station troops at the present agency because this would result in hostilities, and in all probability the agency would be moved anyhow. Also, he could not move troops to the White River in the depth of winter; it was too cold to keep the men in

[66] Com. of Indian Affairs, *Annual Report*, p. 251.

[67] Saville to E. P. Smith, December 11, 1873, NARS, RG 75, LR, Red Cloud Agency.

[68] Saville to E. P. Smith, December 29, 1873, *ibid*. Red Cloud's speech was enclosed. In concluding his speech, Red Cloud said, "You can issue rations to these people the same as at present until spring. We will wait that long yet for the guns." Saville took this as a threat of war in the spring.

tents and there was no way at all to protect the animals. He would compromise by sending out a force in late April or early May, "let the consequences be what they may," but even then he thought it best to defer plans for building a post until they could see the results of such action.[69]

The pressure of events soon forced the War Department to reconsider. On February 6 Edward Gray, a teamster en route to the agency, was killed on the Niobrara;[70] about two o'clock on the morning of February 9, Frank S. Appleton, Saville's clerk, was killed by a Miniconjou, and fourteen mules were stolen from a government contractor near the agency;[71] later that same day, out on Cottonwood Creek about twelve miles east of Laramie Peak, Lt. Levi H. Robinson and Corp. James Coleman, who had separated themselves from a Fort Laramie wood train, were ambushed by a large party of Indians and killed.[72] At the Spotted Tail Agency, the Indians drove off the beef herders and did their own issuing, and Agent E. A. Howard, his life threatened, called for military protection.[73] As soon as he got word of the trouble, Sheridan, who was in New York, wired Sherman: "The trouble with the Sioux which for sometime past we have been trying to avoid seems now to be beyond any peaceable solution. . . . I will go home tomorrow and superintend any action which may be necessary."[74] On February 18, he ordered General Ord to send Colonel Smith from Fort Laramie with a force to protect the Red Cloud and Spotted Tail agencies. Smith was to establish his headquarters at Red Cloud and remain there until further orders.

> If, in the accomplishment of these purposes, he should be attacked, he will then strike as hard a blow as possible with the forces at his command, in case he finds such a hostile condition of affairs as would cause him, in his best judgment, to believe an attack was meditated, he, if possible, should strike the first blow, always saving women and children.

[69] Doc. File 511, AGO, 1874, filed with 563, AGO, 1874, NARS, RG 94.

[70] Roger T. Grange, Jr., "Fort Robinson, Outpost on the Plains", *Nebraska History* XXXIX (September, 1958), 195.

[71] *Ibid.*; Saville to John E. Smith, February 9, 1874, NARS, RG 94, Doc. File 563, AGO, 1874.

[72] Telegram, John E. Smith to Ord, February 11, 1874, *ibid.*; Post Return, Fort Laramie, 1874.

[73] Grange, "Fort Robinson," p. 195; Telegram, E. A. Howard to Com. of Indian Affairs, February 9, 1874; Howard to Saville, February 11, 1874, NARS, RG 94,, Doc. File 563, AGO, 1874.

[74] Telegram, Sheridan to Sherman, February 12, 1874, *ibid.*

The government must before long make every portion of its territory safe for its citizens to live in or travel over, and it would be well for Col. Smith to communicate this knowledge to the Indians and those agencies, but he should be specially directed to hold no official counsels with Indian chiefs at the agencies above mentioned. He may, however, notify them, that unless their people behave themselves, he will make them do so.

You will also direct him to hold no correspondence whatever, by mail or telegraph, with the Indian Bureau, except through these or superior headquarters.[75]

Sheridan apparently was anticipating a certain amount of difficulty with the Indian Bureau, and in this he was correct. Even before the order was issued, Felix R. Brunot, Chairman of the Board of Indian Commissioners, having read of the plan in the newspapers, wrote President Grant from his home in Pittsburgh that to send troops to the agencies would "give the Sioux just cause for making war." He attributed the whole trouble to "the strong influence both in the West and elsewhere that is bent on having an Indian war" and hoped that the President would call off the movement.[76] The President did not do this, but he did approve a cautionary letter from Delano to Belknap in which the War Department was warned not to do anything that would provoke hostilities. "While I have no desire or design to dictate the movements of the Army," wrote Delano, "I shall exceedingly regret the occurrence of hostilities with the Sioux, and if they do occur I trust that your department will be able to show clearly that they did not result from this effort to protect Red Cloud's and Spotted Tail's agencies."[77]

The Indian Bureau was sure that the trouble was being caused by the Miniconjous, Sans Arcs, and Hunkpapas, and that Red Cloud and Spotted Tail were both friendly toward the Government. Spotted Tail was always friendly and it seems that Red Cloud, as at other times when serious trouble had threatened, was using his influence for peace. Although Red Cloud thought that the Indians should be paid for doing guard duty,[78] the Oglalas in a general council on February 16 agreed to defend the agency at any cost. Saville was sure that if he could be provided with guns and ammunition and a liberal supply of

[75] Sheridan to Ord, February 18, 1874, *ibid.*

[76] Brunot to the President, February 14, 1874, NARS, RG 48, LR, Indian Division.

[77] Delano to W. W. Belknap, February 26, 1874, NARS, RG 94, Doc. File 563, AGO, 1874.

[78] Saville to E. P. Smith, February 14, 1874, *ibid.*

provisions he could unite them against the northern tribes.[79] Four days later, however, the harried agent wrote Colonel Smith, urging him to hurry:

> Since my last dispatch all has been quiet, but I find there is not the unanimity among the Indians that appeared at the council. Many have left and are leaving the agency for the north; some with unconcealed intentions to join the war party others preferring to be in the interests of peace. But affairs are too complicated among them [the Oglala] to trust to them for protection. . . .[80]

Smith left Fort Laramie on March 2 with eight companies of cavalry and eight of infantry, a total force of 949 men. The cavalry battalion arrived at Red Cloud Agency on the fifth and the infantry battalion on the seventh. Four companies of infantry and one of cavalry were established in camp at Red Cloud and a similar force was sent to Spotted Tail. When it was determined that the agencies would be occupied without resistance, the remaining six companies of cavalry were returned to Fort Laramie.[81] As soon as Smith arrived at the agency he notified Saville that while he did not intend to hold a council with the Indians, he wanted to talk with Red Cloud and some of the other chiefs. Saville, agreeing to call the Indians in, hoped that Smith would "say something soft and sweet to them," to which Smith replied that he "had nothing of that kind to say, but wanted to let them know what they might expect if they did not behave themselves." When Red Cloud and twelve to fifteen chiefs and head men were ushered into the agency building, Smith repeated some of the direct talk he had given them a year before at the old agency on the Platte.[82] He told them that if they could not whip the Northern Indians to let him know and he would do it for them. What's more, he wanted Red Cloud to understand that if any of the Indians at the agency fired into the military camp or took any stock, he would attack them at once. He reminded them that he had often told them if they did not behave themselves they would have soldiers sent to their agency, "but they would not listen . . . and had bad ears, and now the soldiers are here and plenty more are coming."[83]

[79] Saville to E. P. Smith, February 16, 1874, *ibid.*

[80] Saville to John E. Smith, February 20, 1874, *ibid.*

[81] Grange, "Fort Robinson" (above, n. 70), pp. 196–200, discusses the composition and movements of the Sioux Expedition. See also Telegrams, Sheridan to Sherman, March 2, March 7, NARS, RG 75, LR, Red Cloud Agency; letter, Sheridan to Sherman, March 17, 1874, NARS, RG 94, Doc. File 563, AGO, 1874.

[82] See above, pp. 146–149.

[83] Lt. Col. James W. Forsyth to Col. R. C. Drum, AG, Military Division of the Missouri, March 27, 1874, NARS, RG 94, Doc. File 563, AGO, 1874.

Red Cloud seemed sullen and depressed, and refused to reply.[84]
Apparently, however, he took Smith's warning seriously, for on March
24 Saville reported that Red Cloud had apologized for his remarks of
December 25 and had "done much to atone for his hostile speech."[85]
Indeed, things were very quiet at the agency, and Saville was even
making progress on the census.[86]

Things were quiet because the northern Indians had fled at the
appearance of the troops, and those who remained, while perfectly
willing to provoke trouble, had no enthusiasm for a battle with the
soldiers. Any battles that were about to occur, it seemed, would be
between the civilian and military authorities responsible for the
management of the Indians.

Even before the Sioux Expedition had arrived, Saville was demanding
that a commission be sent to relieve him of "the slanders of Gen. John
E. Smith,"[87] and on the day of Smith's arrival the agent, apparently
disregarding the fact that he had been calling for troops all winter, wrote
a long report to the Commissioner of Indian Affairs describing the difficulties he had encountered in reconciling the Indians to the coming of
troops and remarking, "Whether General Smith has done his duty in
thus coming to the relief of the Agency, I leave to his own conscience
to determine."[88] Within a fortnight, Episcopal Bishop William H.
Hare, who was at the agency as head of a special commission appointed
by the President to settle the Sioux problem, telegraphed Secretary
Delano: "We consider it essential that the department shall decide
whether authority of Agent or Commanding Military Officer is superior
on this reservation. We think the situation does not demand that he be
authorized to act independently of the Agent or contrary to his
advice."[89] Delano replied that he had been directed by the President
to say that "the duties of the Military authority and of the Indian
Agent are distinct and independent, and that neither is subordinate
to the other in exercising their several legitimate powers." Should a
difference arise on a specific question, it was to be referred to the
President for settlement.[90]

The Hare Commission was a source of great irritation to the military.

[84] *Ibid.*
[85] Saville to E. P. Smith, March 24, 1874, NARS, RG 75, LR, Red Cloud Agency.
[86] *Ibid.*
[87] Saville to E. P. Smith, March 5, 1874, NARS, RG 75, LR, Red Cloud Agency.
[88] *Ibid.*, March 5, 1874, NARS, RG 75, LR, Red Cloud Agency.
[89] Telegram, William H. Hare to Delano, March 18, 1874, NARS, RG 94, Doc.
File 563, AGO, 1874.
[90] Telegram, Delano to Hare, March 20, 1874, *ibid.*

Sheridan, commenting on the exchange of telegrams between Hare and Delano, hoped that "good hearted but inexperienced men may not disturb the peaceable solution of the troubles at the Red Cloud and Spotted Tail agencies which bid so fair of settlement before their arrival,"[91] Capt. H. H. Lazelle, commanding the military force at Spotted Tail, complained to Colonel Smith that the Commissioners, with their grandiose plans to civilize the Indians immediately, had "simply made mischief . . . by irritating these people."[92] Smith, forwarding Lazelle's letter to General Ord, expressed similar— although not so strongly worded—doubts about the work of the Commissioners; he was particularly unhappy over their failure to settle on permanent locations for the agencies.[93]

It soon became apparent that relocation—much as the Army desired it[94]—would not be a part of the Hare Commission's solution to the Sioux problem. The Commissioners returned to Washington in April to deliver an interim report and to make plans for coming back to the plains to settle upon a permanent location for Spotted Tail; the Red Cloud Agency, the Interior Department had determined, would stay where it was.[95] With this assurance, Smith began to build a permanent camp near the confluence of Soldier Creek and the White River, about a mile and a half from the agency, where he had moved his troops in the spring to get away from the stench of the rotting carcasses from the beef issues, and on July 21 he announced that Camp Robinson had been established.[96] Barracks, warehouses, and two sets of officers' quarters were completed by November,[97] and a wagon road was

---

[91] Telegram, Sheridan to AAG, March 20, 1874, *ibid.*

[92] H. H. Lazelle to John E. Smith, April 6, 1874, *ibid.*

[93] John E. Smith to Ord, April 7, 1874, *ibid.*

[94] Sheridan consistently held that the only satisfactory location for both agencies was on the Missouri River, and he lamented the removal of Spotted Tail from the Missouri (Sheridan to Sherman, March 31, 1874, *ibid*).

[95] B. P. Cowen, Acting Secretary of the Interior, to Secretary of War, May 26, 1874, *ibid.* The Commissioners did not get back to Cheyenne until the end of July, and then Bishop Hare and C. C. Cox became ill and had to return east, leaving the work in the hands of the other two members, Rev. S. D. Hinman and R. B. Lines. After a reconnaissance ranging from the Missouri River to the Black Hills, Spotted Tail was moved ten miles south to West Beaver Creek ("Report of the Sioux Commission," Com. of Indian Affairs, *Annual Report*, 1874, pp. 87–97).

[96] John E. Smith to AAG, Dept. of the Platte, July 21, 1874, NARS, RG 98, Select Documents, Sioux Expedition, 1874. The name was not changed to Fort Robinson until January, 1878 (Grange, "Fort Robinson" [above, n. 70], p. 217).

[97] Grange, "Fort Robinson," p. 203.

opened from Sidney.[98] Red Cloud remained unhappy over the presence of troops at the agency, but he approved of the wagon road, saying it had always been his wish to have his goods come by way of Sidney, that by any other route "they are too long on the road and two-legged mice get into them and some of them are gone." [99]

The wagon road was about the only thing of which Red Cloud approved, however, and if any doubted the necessity of troops at the agency, repeated incidents during the summer and fall should have convinced them otherwise. One such incident was the stir created by the arrest of Toussaint Kenssler, who had escaped from jail in Cheyenne and sought refuge among the Oglalas. When Lieutenants Crawford and Ray went to the agency to arrest him, he tried to flee and Ray shot him in the leg. This upset the Indians, and the chiefs assembled to demand that Kenssler be released; Red Cloud argued that as long as the whites had let him escape, they should allow him to remain in peace among his friends! When their demand was refused, the Indians tried to rescue the prisoner in a midnight attack on the guardhouse. The soldiers repulsed them by forming a skirmish line, but while they were warding off the attackers another group of Indians stole all the quartermaster's beef cattle.[100]

This incident occurred in June. In October there was even more serious trouble when Saville erected a flagstaff at the agency. The Indians had objected to the idea, saying that only soldiers had a flag, that a flag meant war,[101] but Saville dismissed the objections as "purely factious" and went ahead.[102] About noon on October 23, while he was in his office talking to Red Cloud, he noticed a large number of armed,

[98] AAG, Dept. of the Platte, to CO, Sidney Barracks, July 25, 1874, Ord to Senator P. W. Hitchcock, December 19, 1874, NARS, RG 98, LS, Dept. of the Platte. See Norbert Mahnken "The Sidney–Black Hills Trail," *Nebraska History*, XXX (September, 1949) 203–225; Agnes Wright Spring, *The Cheyenne and Black Hills Stage and Express Routes* (Glendale: Arthur H. Clark Co., 1949).

[99] Lt. Charles Morton, Sidney Barracks, to AAG, Dept. of the Platte, August 12, 1874, NARS, RG 98, LR, Dept. of the Platte. Apparently Red Cloud and a number of the other chiefs went to Sidney Barracks for a conference about opening the road. Red Dog, who was also present, was reported as making a speech in which he professed his long friendship for the whites and asserted that Red Cloud had always been opposed to moving to an agency.

[100] Grange, "Fort Robinson" (above, n. 70), pp. 201–202; NARS, RG 75, LR, Red Cloud Agency.

[101] Ricker, Interview with William Garnett.

[102] Saville to E. P. Smith, October 24, 1874, NARS, RG 94, Doc. File 563, AGO, 1874.

breech-clouted Indians running about the flagstaff, shouting and creating a general disturbance; most of them were northern Indians who had recently come into the agency to spend the winter. When one of them began chopping away at the pole, Saville asked Red Cloud to stop them, but the chief refused. The agent then sent a hurried call for troops. Capt. W. H. Jordan, commanding Camp Robinson, had only twenty-eight cavalrymen available, but he rushed Lieutenant Crawford and twenty-two of them over to the agency. When they arrived, they found that the number of Indians, originally reported as about fifty, had swelled to several hundred. The day was saved when Man-Afraid-of-His-Horse and Sitting Bull of the South (not to be confused with Sitting Bull of the Hunkpapas) rushed out and persuaded the Indians to withdraw. Red Cloud, who had averted trouble in similar situations in the past, took no part in this difficulty, being unable or unwilling to do anything with the northern Indians.[103]

These incidents were not serious in themselves—although either of them could have been—but they were symptomatic of the uncertain situation at the agency. Much more serious, and definitely contributory to the unrest, was the Custer expedition to the Black Hills.

---

[103] *Ibid.*; Ricker, Interview with Garnett; Grange, "Fort Robinson," pp. 203–205; William H. Jordan to AAG, District of the Black Hills, October 23, 1874, NARS, RG 94, Doc. File 563, AGO, 1874; Jordan to AAG, Dept. of the Platte, October 29, 1874, *ibid.* Charles W. Allen, "Red Cloud and the U.S. Flag," *Nebraska History,* XXI (October–December, 1940), 293–304, provides an interesting eye-witness account, although Allen has the incident occurring on October 27, 1874.

CHAPTER 10

Fiasco in Washington

There had been rumors of gold in the Black Hills for almost half a century, and from 1833 on occasional exploring parties had ventured into the region. In 1866, Dr. Frederick V. Hayden of the Smithsonian Institution, who had visited the Hills three times in the fifties, made a hurried expedition to the area and returned with seventeen large boxes of specimens and glowing reports of mineral possibilities. This prompted a flurry of activity among would-be prospectors, but the Government, trying desperately to persuade the Sioux to sign a treaty,[1] put a stop to it, and the Treaty of 1868 declared the whole area off-limits to whites.[2] Westerners, it will be recalled, were vehement in their opposition to this clause of the treaty,[3] and Dakota's Delegate Moses K. Armstrong had even introduced a bill to abrogate the offending section (Article 16). Commenting on this, the *Yankton Press* wrote:

> The Indians can make no use of the country which has been set apart for them. The pine lands and mineral deposits are of no value to them, because they neither have the knowledge or inclination to utilize them. The government owes it to the country, and particularly to Dakota, to remove every

[1] See above, Chapter V.

[2] Harold E. Briggs, "The Black Hills Gold Rush," *North Dakota Historical Quarterly* V (1930–31), 71–99; Arthur J. Larsen, "The Black Hills Gold Rush," *ibid.*, VI (1931–32), 302–318.

[3] See above pp. 89–92.

obstacle to the immediate opening up and development of this vast field of untold and incalculable wealth. . . .[4]

The Government continued to prevent entry into the Hills, but pressures against the policy steadily mounted. As the western mines played out or passed into the hands of eastern capitalists, as the Panic of 1873 turned speculative minds toward every possible new source of wealth, the country's attention focused on the Black Hills, endowed by rumor with the greatest wealth-producing potential the world had ever known. By the spring of 1874, companies were forming in all parts of the country for an assault on the Hills whether the Government would permit it or no. Military leaders, faced with the responsibility of enforcing the Treaty of 1868 and of maintaining peace on the frontier, had an explosive situation on their hands. At the same time, there was a growing opinion within the Army that as long as the Indians remained undisturbed in their possession of the Black Hills the hostiles would have a base from which they could conduct forays against the agencies and the lines of communication with Montana. The solution seemed to be a scientific and military expedition which would quiet the clamor by proving once and for all that there was no gold in the Black Hills and provide a basis for determining the Indian posture in the area.

Lt. Col. George A. Custer, commanding the 7th Cavalry at Fort Abraham Lincoln, was eager to lead the expedition, and General Sheridan, apparently with some reluctance, permitted him to do so. Custer was to take with him ten troops of cavalry, two companies of infantry, some Indian scouts, and a small number of civilians, including scientists and newspaper men. If anyone thought the expedition would reduce interest in the Black Hills, he was sorely mistaken; and indeed Custer's every move seemed calculated to have just the opposite effect. The command marched out of Fort Lincoln on July 2 to the strains of "Garry Owen," the newspapermen sent back rhapsodic reports, including assurances that gold existed in large quantities, and Custer disposed of the Indian menace by announcing that the 7th Cavalry could whip all the Indians in the Northwest.[5]

Although the Indians would deal with the 7th Cavalry later in this

[4] March 20, 1872.

[5] There are many accounts of the Custer Expedition of 1874. I have used Briggs, "The Black Hills Gold Rush"; Larsen, "The Black Hills Gold Rush"; W. M. Wemett, "Custer's Expedition to the Black Hills in 1874," *North Dakota Historical Quarterly*, VI (October, 1931—July, 1932), 292–301; and Edgar I. Stewart, *Custer's Luck* (Norman: University of Oklahoma Press, 1955), pp. 61–65.

instance, despite dire predictions that they would resist an invasion of the Black Hills with force, they offered no resistance whatever, and Custer returned to Fort Abraham Lincoln on August 30 with the report that he had seen no Indians at all, and that he would not have known that there were any red men in the country had they not fired the prairie over part of his route of march.[6]

Red Cloud, being interviewed by a reporter from the *New York Herald* on August 16, put Custer's expedition near the head of a long list of grievances, most of which concerned Agent Saville, with whom in a few months he would be engaged in a nationally publicized controversy.[7] As for Custer, Red Cloud simply stated:

> I do not like General Custer and all his soldiers going into the Black Hills, as that is the country of the Ogallala Sioux, and when my men were there cutting lodge poles the Ree Indians fired at them and killed one of my men. General Custer also kept Stabber, one of my Indians, in his camp for five or six days.[8]

If Red Cloud sensed the portentous implications of Custer's activities, he did not show it. Members of the Sioux Commission, however, aware of the Black Hills excitement being generated in the country,[9] were vigorous in their denunciation of the expedition. When Bishop Hare heard that it was being planned, he wrote President Grant that it "would be a violation of the national honor," and urged that it be canceled.[10] After Custer's report had been published, S. D. Hinman wrote Secretary Delano that members of the Commission had read it "with surprise and regret," and declared categorically that there was no gold in the Black Hills.[11] This opinion was confirmed by N. H. Winchell, who had explored the Hills earlier in the year, and by Col. Fred Grant, the President's son, who had accompanied him.[12] Winchell was wrong, of course, and Custer was right. The President announced his intention to keep white intruders out of the Hills,[13] but before long

[6] *New York Herald*, September 1, 1874.

[7] See below, pp. 179, 189–198.

[8] *New York Herald*, August 27, 1874. The Army had denied the killing of Stabber two days before this appeared (*ibid.*, August 25, 1874).

[9] See below, pp. 199–201.

[10] William H. Hare to President Grant, June 9, 1874, in M. A. DeWolfe Howe, *Life and Labors of Bishop Hare, Apostle to the Sioux* (New York: Sturgis and Walton Co., 1912), pp. 124–129.

[11] S. D. Hinman to Columbus Delano, September 18, 1874, NARS, RG 48, LR, Indian Division.

[12] *New York Herald*, September 25, 1874.   [13] *Ibid.*

his determination would falter in the face of an increasing demand that the area be opened for development.[14]

Meanwhile, at Red Cloud Agency the larger issues seemed temporarily to be lost in the petty bickering which had characterized military-civilian relations ever since the arrival of the troops. This time the problem revolved around the question of using troops to arrest Indians suspected of wrongdoing.

In October, Lone Horn's band of Miniconjous came in from the north to draw their annuities, and Saville, suspecting that the band included the man responsible for the murder of his clerk, Appleton, requested Captain Jordan to find and arrest the guilty one. Jordan reported to Headquarters, Department of the Platte, that he was greatly outnumbered and that he doubted his ability to persuade the Miniconjous to surrender the offender.[15] General Ord immediately telegraphed that troops were not to make arrests in the Indian country upon application of the agent; authority for such arrests would have to come from the President or the Secretary of War.[16] Saville had sent this request at the time of the flagstaff trouble, and he did not pursue it. In November, however, he forwarded a request to the Commissioner of Indian Affairs to "arm and pay fifty or a hundred" friendly Indians to provide protection for the agency.[17] This was sent over to the War Department for comment—and comment it received! Sheridan remarked acidly, "What we want at the Red Cloud Agency is more troops instead of more guns for Indians." Sherman, "concurring perfectly in General Sheridan's views," told the Secretary of War: "The Indians have no real use for arms but war—and for us to arm them—when we all know that the time approaches for the battle that is to decide whether they or the United States are sovereign in the land they occupy, is an act of liberality that no man conversant with the subject can dispute." The Red Cloud Sioux already possessed "all the arms needed for game and too many for a people who profess a desire to learn the arts of husbandry and agriculture."[18]

Saville was getting nowhere with the Army, and apparently he began

[14] See below, pp. 199–201.

[15] Capt. W. H. Jordan to AAG, Dept. of the Platte, October 23, 1874, NARS, RG 94, Doc. File 563, AGO, 1874.

[16] Telegram, George D. Ruggles, AAG, Dept. of the Platte, to CO, District of the Black Hills, October 28, 1874, *ibid.*

[17] J. J. Saville to E. P. Smith, November 13, 1874, NARS, RG 75, LR, Red Cloud Agency.

[18] Lt. Gen. P. H. Sheridan to Gen. W. T. Sherman, November 25, 1874, with endorsements, *ibid.*

to lose caste with his own superiors. In December he got off a letter to the Commissioner saying that Red Cloud was demanding to go to Washington and had told him that Captain Jordan had agreed to go with him if the agent would not. Smith sent the letter on to Secretary Delano, urging him to ask the Secretary of War to stop the "unwarrantable interference" of military officers in the agent's affairs. The letter was bucked down to Jordan, who categorically denied having said any such thing to Red Cloud. He added: "I have as good right to believe 'Red Cloud's' repeated assertion that Agent Saville was robbing the Indians as he (Agent Saville) had to believe the absurd and untrue statements of 'Red Cloud' concerning the unwarrantable interference of military officers with Indians affairs." When Delano got the letter back—in March, 1875—he replied, somewhat lamely, that he was forwarding the correspondence to the Commissioner of Indian Affairs, "with instructions to admonish agent Saville against making statements that cannot on investigation be sustained."[19]

By this time, the bickering at the agency was fast being overshadowed by larger problems whose solution ultimately would bring a complete collapse of the peace policy which had seemed so certain of success when the new Red Cloud Agency had been established.

II

Red Cloud's demand that he be allowed to go to Washington—the action which had triggered the conflict between Saville and Captain Jordan—was no idle whim. He pursued the question all through the month of December, and even persuaded Spotted Tail, with whom he seldom cooperated, to join him in urging that the leading men of the Sioux be given an opportunity to visit the Great White Father.

The two chiefs sent their request through Lt. Col. L. P. Bradley, commandant at Fort Laramie. "Red Cloud states as his reason for sending to me," Bradley wrote, "that he thinks his agent unfriendly, and he fears that he cannot get a hearing through him."[20] Bradley recommended that the request be granted, and he was seconded by General Ord, who warned, "Unless something is done for them soon we shall be almost certain between the gold hunters and dissatisfied Indians to have serious difficulties in that country in the spring."[21]

[19] This correspondence is in NARS, RG 94, Doc. File 563, AGO, 1874.

[20] Lt. Col. L. P. Bradley to AG, Dept. of the Platte, January 2, 1875, NARS, RG 94, LR, War Dept., AGO.

[21] William D. Whipple, AAG, Division of the Missouri, to E. D. Townsend, AG, January 9, 1875, *ibid.*

Officials of the Indian Bureau were perfectly willing to have the chiefs come in for a visit, but, as Commissioner E. P. Smith explained in marvelous bureaucratese, they did not have the money to pay for the trip:

> The office fully appreciates the importance of having Red Cloud and Spotted Tail, with some young and influential Ogallala and Brule chiefs, visit this city with a view to procure on the part of the Sioux a better understanding of the wishes of the Government respecting them, and if possible an appreciation of the important changes in their tribal condition which are inevitable at no very distant date, but there are no funds at the disposal of this Office which can be used to defray the expenses of such a visit and therefore their request will have to be denied.[22]

But somehow the money was found, and the decision was made to bring the Indians in.

From the beginning, the Government hoped that the visit might soften up the Indians on the question of relinquishing the Black Hills, and in the West, at least, there was a general assumption that this was the most important if not the sole purpose of the trip. The *Cheyenne Daily Leader* published a letter from Wyoming's delegate to Congress, W. R. Steele, which stated that the Government had decided to bring a delegation of Sioux to Washington "to persuade them to give up the Black Hills";[23] the *Yankton Press and Dakotaian* was happy to note that after "ten long weary years," the Government was finally taking steps to negotiate for the Black Hills;[24] as the date of the trip neared, the *New York Times* reported that "the people of the North-western States and Territories manifest great interest in the negotiations between the Government and the Indians touching the Black Hills country" and stated that senators from Kansas and Nebraska and representatives from a number of the frontier states and territories would be on hand for the meetings.[25] At no time, however, did representatives of the Government specifically indicate to either Red Cloud or Spotted Tail that they were being brought to Washington for this purpose; and when the question of the Black Hills came up, Red Cloud was "quite upset." He had come to Washington to lay his grievances before the Great Father; he had not come to talk about the Black Hills.[26]

[22] E. P. Smith to Secretary of the Interior, January 27, 1875, *ibid.*

[23] *Cheyenne Daily Leader*, March 23, 1873.

[24] *Yankton Press and Dakotaian*, March 25, 1875.

[25] *New York Times*, May 10, 1875.

[26] *Ibid.*, May 27, 1875.

The situation was not that simple. There is no doubt but that Red Cloud's interest in visiting Washington was prompted solely by his desire to go over the agent's head and confer directly with the President, thus enabling him to carry on his conflict with Saville and at the same time reinforce his own position among the Oglalas. Yet for him to be upset or surprised when the Black Hills were brought into the discussion was clearly an act of calculated obfuscation. In submitting their request to Colonel Bradley, he and Spotted Tail had stated that they wished to discuss the sale of the Black Hills; moreover, while preparations for the trip were under way, they discussed the Hills with John S. Collins, post trader at Fort Laramie, who for some unknown reason took it upon himself to try to arrange a cession.[27]

Preparations for the trip revealed almost as much confusion as did various understandings of the reasons for it. Both chiefs wanted large delegations to accompany them. Spotted Tail demanded at least fifty;[28] Red Cloud would settle for twenty, but insisted that Crazy Horse and Black Twin be included in the group.[29] Red Cloud had tried unsuccessfully to involve these two irreconcilables in the decision to locate the agency,[30] and he was equally unsuccessful in this effort—both refused to come in, although Saville had assured Smith in January that both had agreed to join the agency in the spring.[31] Both agents recommended large and representative groups, but the delegations were whittled down to thirteen from Red Cloud Agency and six from Spotted Tail.[32]

[27] The Collins case is a curious one. Apparently without any authority whatever— and certainly over the vigorous objections of Agent Saville—Collins conferred with Red Cloud and Spotted Tail about the Black Hills, reporting to President Grant that the Indians were resigned to losing the region and wanted only to secure as much as possible in payment. Nothing came of these negotiations (Saville to E. P. Smith, March 29, 1875, J. S. Collins to President Grant, April 4, 1875, NARS, RG 75, LR, Spotted Tail Agency).

[28] E. A. Howard to Com. of Indian Affairs, April 13, 1875, NARS, RG 75, LR, Spotted Tail Agency.

[29] Saville to E. P. Smith, April 8, 1875, NARS, RG 75, LR, Red Cloud Agency.

[30] See above, pp. 136, 146–147.

[31] Saville to Smith, January 8, 1875, NARS, RG 75, LR, Red Cloud Agency.

[32] E. S. Ricker, Interview with William Garnett, January 15, 1907, Ricker Mss., Tablet No. 2, Nebraska State Historical Society. Garnett, who accompanied the delegation, said that the following Indians went from the Red Cloud Agency: Red Cloud, Little Wound, American Horse, Scalp Face, Fast Thunder, High Lance, Sitting Bull, Shoulder, Conquering Bear, Black Bear, Young Bad Wound, Iron Horse, and White Tail; and from the Spotted Tail Agency: Spotted Tail, Swift Bear, Crow Dog, He Dog, Good Voice, and Ring Thunder.

There were further difficulties. From Fort Laramie, where the delegation stopped enroute to Cheyenne to take the train, Saville telegraphed that they were being unnecessarily delayed through the influence of Todd Randall and Louis Richard, who were conspiring "to oppose the orders of the government in regard to the visit."[33] Presumably they wanted to be included in the party, and both finally went along as well as Nick Janis, William Garnett, and Leon Palladay.[34] At Omaha, the two chiefs told a reporter from the *New York Times* that the agents had "packed their own interpreters into the party to the utter exclusion of those whom the Indians wanted."[35] Difficulties over interpreters plagued the proceedings throughout the negotiations in Washington. The Government finally selected Rev. Samuel D. Hinman, although the Indians complained that he understood only Santee (which was hardly true), and Todd Randall was allowed to represent the Indians, although he "had to be corrected several times in his very loose translations."[36]

When the Indians arrived in Washington, they were not in a very tractable frame of mind. They even objected to staying at the Tremont House, where they were quartered, and six of them, led by American Horse, went over to the Washington House; they were persuaded to return to their assigned lodgings only after the Government announced that it would refuse to pay any of their bills at the Washington House. The objection to the establishment, as the *New York Times* put it, "was for moral reasons. . . . Delegations of Indians formerly quartered at the Washington House were clandestinely afforded opportunitites to indulge in scandalous excesses, which it is intended shall not be repeated."[37]

[33] Telegram, Saville to Com. of Indian Affairs, May 7, 1875, NARS, RG 75, LR, Red Cloud Agency.

[34] Ricker, Interview with Garnett (above, n. 13).

[35] *New York Times*, May 14, 1875.

[36] *New York Herald*, May 29, 1875.

[37] *New York Times*, May 25, 26, 1875. I have found no evidence to support the implication in George E. Hyde, *Red Cloud's Folk* (Norman: University of Oklahoma Press, 1957), pp. 232–233, and Stanley Vestal, *Warpath and Council Fire* (New York: Random House, 1948), pp. 192–193, that Red Cloud was involved in the questionable conduct. His name is not mentioned in any of the newspaper accounts of this particular difficulty, and surely it would have been had he been involved, in view of the extensive amount of newspaper space given his activities. The only reference I have found which would indicate that Red Cloud fell from grace at any time during his stay in Washington was an editorial in the *Times* which explained that on one occasion (not identified) he failed to make a point, "owing to too much whisky." The editorial went on to say that

Friends, Foes, and Family

V. T. McGillycuddy

H. B. Carrington

Nelson A. Miles

William T. Sherman

Christopher C. Augur

John E. Smith

Spotted Tail

American Horse

Young Man Afraid of his Horses

Red Dog

Sword

Little Wound

Jack Red Cloud

Red Cloud and Wife

To complicate matters still further, just before the delegation arrived a professor of paleontology from Yale threw a bombshell which threatened to blow the Indian Bureau sky-high. The professor was Othniel C. Marsh, who had visited Red Cloud in the fall of 1874 while hunting fossils in the Dakota badlands. Red Cloud had complained at length of the evil treatment he received at the hands of the agent and of the way in which he was being defrauded of the goods and supplies to which he was entitled. He had given Marsh some samples of flour, sugar, coffee, and tobacco to show the low quality of rations being issued his people. George E. Hyde asserts that the samples were fraudulent and that the whole thing was a "pleasing little joke," probably arranged by whites on the agency who had it in for the agent.[38] Whether this was true—and Red Cloud's subsequent conduct tends to give some strength to this comment[39]—Marsh, who had had his own share of difficulties with the testy Saville,[40] took the samples home with him and complained to the Board of Indian Commissioners as well as to the public about the treatment of the Sioux at Red Cloud Agency. On April 28, at the invitation of the Board, he appeared before them in New York, told his story, and presented his samples.[41] The Board members had been reading newspapers accounts all through the fall and winter of irregularities at Red Cloud;[42] they ordered an investigation,[43] with the result that Saville and his superiors in the Indian Bureau, who were bringing the Sioux chiefs in to negotiate possibly for the sale of the Black Hills, found themselves under public attack for defrauding those same Indians.[44]

The first session with the Indians, held May 18 in the Indian

readers could undoubtedly recall the names of politicians in Washington and Albany who had suffered under similar difficulty, and it described Red Cloud as "a redoubtable warrior, of fine presence, great natural abilities, and endowed with a certain eloquence which makes him influential in aboriginal politics" (*ibid.*, June 4, 1875).

[38] Hyde, *Red Cloud's Folk*, p. 227.

[39] See below, pp. 183–184.

[40] Saville tried to dissuade him from taking troops with him and complained that the professor "felt disposed to take the advice of his military friends rather than mine" (Saville to E. P. Smith, November 30, 1874, NARS, RG 75, LR, Red Cloud Agency). For Marsh's side of the story, see Charles Schuchert and Clara Mae LeVene, *O. C. Marsh, Pioneer in Paleontology* (New Haven: Yale University Press, 1940) pp. 139–146.

[41] Board of Indian Commissioners, Minutes, April 28, 1875.

[42] The *New York Herald* and *New York Tribune* were particularly vigorous in their efforts to expose conditions at the agency.

[43] Board of Indian Commissioners, Minutes, April 29, 1875.

[44] See *New York Times*, May 6, 24, 1875.

office, was reasonably satisfactory. Secretary Delano was out of town, so Commissioner Smith did the honors for the Government. He gave the usual speech of welcome, warned the interpreters "to keep their ears open, and if they don't understand, say so on the spot" (which apparently made a favorable impression on the Indians), and promised the chiefs that the Great Father would see them the next day. Red Cloud, responding for the Indians, said:

> When I speak I always call on the Great Spirit to hear me, because I always tell the truth. The white men tell me lies, and I became so troubled I wanted to come to Washington and see the Great Father himself and talk with him. That is why I have come to see you.

After he took his seat, he got up again and relieved the tension somewhat by assuring the Commissioner: "When I spoke of white men telling lies, I did not mean the white men present." Spotted Tail was a little more conciliatory, although he told the Commissioner that he wanted to use his own interpreters because he did not trust those provided by the Government. He also wondered if he could not stay with a friend of his in Washington (by which he meant the Washington House, where he had stayed before) rather than at the hotel. Smith assured him that he could use his own interpreters, but was sorry that the housing arrangements could not be changed. After this, the meeting broke up and the Indians were taken to see the model room of the Patent Office.[45]

The next day they were taken to the White House to see the President. Although they had appeared in European dress at the Indian office, they were now in full paint and feathers, and one of the delegation carried a small "Grant and Wilson" campaign flag. The President was not particularly warm. He was glad to see them, to be sure, but he would not talk business with them. He had two great chiefs, the Secretary of the Interior and the Commissioner of Indian Affairs, and the Sioux would have to deal with them. "It is my duty," he said, "to study your welfare, and I want to do that which will do you good and make you contented and happy. . . . We know what is for your good better than you can know yourselves, and if you will state your business to the Secretary and the Commissioner, you will receive attention, and everything will be done for you that is possible."

The Indians were not at all pleased. Lone Horn said that he was a Great Chief and he wanted to deal only with the Great Father. As for the Black Hills, if the Great Father wanted to talk about that, he

[45] *Ibid.*, May 19, 1875.

wanted him "to talk and settle the matter." It would have been interesting to see what would have happened had Grant taken Lone Horn at his word and started a serious discussion of the Hills, but he simply said," I cannot talk about that matter today," and Lone Horn fell back into his place.[46] Spotted Tail reminded the President that he had talked with the Secretary and the Commissioner before, that they had lied to him, and that he did not want to have any more talks with them. Red Cloud said simply that he had come to Washington to talk to the Great Father, and that he wanted the Great Father to send for him when he was ready to talk. He did not want to talk to any other person.[47]

Following this interview, the Indians killed time for a week, quarreling among themselves, complaining about their housing, and working up a real case of indignation at what they felt was their neglect by the Great Father and his various chiefs.[48] On May 26 Delano returned, and the formal negotiations began. The Secretary got right to the point. He reminded the Indians that certain provisions of the Treaty of 1868 had expired and that it would be necessary to negotiate a new treaty.[49] He suggested that in making a new treaty, they take into account the changed conditions of the country. He recognized that the

[46] *Ibid.*, May 20, 1875. Lone Horn was chief of the Cheyenne River Agency, and was heading a delegation which had been brought to Washington independently of the Red Cloud and Spotted Tail people, but presumably on the same general business. William Garnett had an interesting recollection, which, while not corroborated entirely by the facts, throws some light on the situation: "Now coming back to the Black Hills, the Chiefs Red Cloud, Spotted Tail and Lone Horn were the leaders and their decision finally was adopted by the other chiefs. Red Cloud said in their private council that he did not know anything about this business that was coming up, neither did his people know it, and he could not do anything; Spotted Tail said the same thing, and so did Lone Horn the Miniconjou from the Cheyenne River Agency.... And it was at length decided by the three chiefs that they would end all consultation and go home. Lone Horn was made the spokesman of the delegations to communicate their decision to President Grant. All the other chiefs assented to the agreement that the three had come to" (E. S. Ricker, Interview with William Garnett [above, n. 32]).

[47] *New York Times*, May 20, 1875.

[48] *Ibid.*, May 22, May 26, 1875.

[49] The specific provision of the treaty which had expired was a section of Article 10, which provided that, for a period of four years after settling on a reservation, each member of the tribe was entitled to receive one pound of meat and one pound of flour per day. The same article provided that annuities (clothing and other "articles of necessity") would be furnished in specified amounts for a period of thirty years without the specific requirement of settlement upon the reservation. This created a good deal of uncertainty in the minds of the Indians—and of the whites—who tended to confuse the two provisions of the same article.

Sioux had the right to hunt in parts of Nebraska and on the Smoky Hill side of the Republican in Kansas so long as game could be found, and that they had possession of the Black Hills in perpetuity. The whites, however, were pushing into those areas and the Government would not be able to stop them. Would it not be wise, therefore, for the Sioux to abandon that country, and avoid trouble with the whites? He suggested that they go south to the Indian Territory; they and their children would be happy there, and Congress would continue to furnish them with such help as they would need until they could take care of themselves. Already the Congress had appropriated twenty-five thousand dollars for the Sioux if they would relinquish their hunting rights in Nebraska and on the Smoky Hill. The game had all gone from that country. They should take the money now, and they could talk about the Black Hills later.[50]

All of this came as a great surprise to the Sioux, although Secretary Delano had been nursing the hope that all of the country's Indians could be removed to Indian Territory,[51] and Grant had suggested the possibility during their visit of 1872.[52] Spotted Tail, speaking for the chiefs, said that he did not want to break the treaty, and that he did not want to move; if the Great Father wanted to make a new treaty he would have to send Commissioners to the Indian country, because the chiefs could make no treaty without consulting their people.[53] Smith interrupted to say that the twenty-five thousand dollars appropriated by Congress would lapse unless the Indians agreed to relinquish their hunting rights before the end of June. To this, Spotted Tail replied that they might consider that specific proposal if Congress would provide an additional fifteen thousand dollars; after all, he reminded the Secretary, they were not asking for his money but for the money of Congress, who could get plenty.[54]

Nothing more was accomplished that day. The chiefs met briefly with the President—presumably after their meeting with Delano and Smith—and he told them personally of his desire that they give up the Black Hills and their hunting rights in Nebraska and move to Indian

[50] *New York Times*, May 28, 1875.

[51] *Ibid.*, May 27, 1875.

[52] See above, p. 151.

[53] In making this statement, Spotted Tail told the Secretary that they had as much respect for the opinions of their people as he had for those of the newspapers. This apparently created much merriment; Delano, it should be remembered, was under constant fire from various newspapers, and would shortly resign.

[54] *New York Times*, May 28, 1875.

Territory. The President's remarks were written out by a stenographer and given to the Indians to study. This seemed to please them, but they most certainly were not prepared to give the Great Father an answer until they had had an opportunity to consider the matter in council.[55] Although the Indians seemed complacent enough during their session with the President, after leaving the White House Red Cloud complained that he had presumed that they had been brought to Washington to lay their grievances before the Great Father, and not to talk about the Black Hills.[56]

The opportunity to air grievances came on the twenty-eighth, when the chiefs were invited to the offices of the Indian Bureau to discuss affairs at the agencies. Professor Marsh, who had come to Washington to press his charges, was present, but, much to the irritation of the Indians, neither the President nor Secretary Delano attended the meeting. Red Cloud asked Marsh if he had brought the samples with him. Marsh replied that he had showed them to the Great Father "and told him what you told me to tell him." Red Cloud then said:

> That was the idea of the people of my band in giving you those samples. For two years we were furnished with beef, and when they were weighed some were small and some were large, but they weighed them altogether. I don't want to lay the blame for this on any one in this matter; I don't know who is to blame. I think my Great Father sends me the kind of provisions as he promised to do, and the number that he promised. Last winter we lived very hard. It was a hard winter for us; for one or two months we lived very hard. We had no fresh pork; it was all barreled pork, and we don't like that kind of pork. The tobacco we get is not very good; it does not suit us; we cannot smoke it well; it is sweet and has molasses in it, and is sticky and won't smoke. In regard to blankets, we are a large people, we want large blankets to wear. A great many of our blankets were branded like soldiers' blankets; we don't like to have them branded in this way—like soldiers. That is what I have to say, and I am telling the truth. I call on the Great Spirit to witness that I am telling the truth.

There then followed a long interrogation in which Marsh and B. R. Cowen, Assistant Secretary of the Interior, tried to pin the chief down as to exactly what he was dissatisfied with. This proved to be impossible. On several occasions Samuel Hinman interrupted to say that Todd Randall, who was interpreting at Red Cloud's request, was not translating the chief's remarks accurately, but even when properly translated they did not seem to add up to much. The quality and

[55] *Ibid.*, May 27, 1875.
[56] *New York Herald*, May 27, 1875.

quantity of beef was a particularly difficult question; it turned out that the small beeves of which Red Cloud complained had actually been rejected by the agent and had been killed by the Indians without authority. As for the famous "samples," Red Cloud admitted that they were not characteristic of all the food issued, and had been taken from loads that had got wet en route to the agency. In response to a direct question from Marsh as to whether he was "perfectly satisfied" with his present agent, Red Cloud said:

> When I came first to Washington the President told me he would give me an agent, and I must look out for him; if he didn't please me, to bring him back; that he had a great many men, and would give me a good one. I have brought him back here for you to consider the matter. I want the Great Spirit to hear me, and give me a good and wise man for an agent. I don't want a western man, but a man from the East, and a man that is wealthy. These western men fill their pockets, and when they are full, they fill their hats; and then they say, "good-by," and go away. I know there are a great many good men the Great Father has here, and I want a man for an agent that has a good heart and money, and one that will look after our interest, and take good care of us. I came here with my agent, and didn't mean to say anything about this thing, but have been forced to say it.[57]

Marsh's position was undermined by the Chief's performance but he continued to assert that he was "confident of the substantial truth of the representations first made to him." He also contended, somewhat unconvincingly, that Red Cloud had decided to equivocate because of "the fear that the department might become prejudiced against the Sioux." Officials of the Indian Bureau, on the other hand, argued that Red Cloud was talking about the Marsh charges simply to gain time and to avoid discussing the Black Hills.[58] Whatever the reason— perhaps this was the occasion on which he had had too much whiskey— Red Cloud certainly failed to make his point, and indeed to sustain his oft-asserted reasons for wanting to make the trip. Although, as we shall see, Marsh and others would be successful in pressing for a full-dress investigation of affairs at the agency, Red Cloud's performance was most disappointing.

In the hope that they could get something settled and thus send the Indians home, Delano and Smith met with the chiefs on June 1, Bishop Hare also being present. Smith began by recognizing that the

[57] A transcript of the proceedings of May 28, 1875, will be found in *Report of the Special Commission Appointed to Investigate the Affairs of the Red Cloud Indian Agency, July, 1875* (Washington: Government Printing Office, 1875), pp. 832–837.

[58] *New York Herald*, May 29, 1875; *New York Times*, June 1, 1875.

Sioux did not wish to remove to Indian Territory and suggesting that the matter be dropped. He hoped, however, that they had had time to come to some conclusion about the Black Hills, and he reminded them that they must soon reach an agreement about surrendering their hunting rights in Nebraska or lose the money Congress had appropriated for them. Red Cloud responded with a long speech in which he complained of the rations, of the agent, of the soldiers, and of his treatment generally. He ignored the subject of the Black Hills, but he said that he would take the twenty-five thousand dollars, "although it was so little he could hold it in both hands." Swan, however, said that the sum was entirely too small, and Little Wolf suggested that it should be forty thousand dollars for one hundred years. Delano turned to his colleagues and said, "Well, if all of them are of the same opinion, we may as well stop talking at once."

Spotted Tail and Little Wound agreed with Red Cloud that they should take the money, even though the sum was too small. With this evidence of support, the agreement was brought out and read, after which the chiefs were asked to sign it. But now Spotted Tail had a further reservation:

> When I do business I am accustomed to sign the paper after I get the money. If I sign it today, I shall expect the money this afternoon; otherwise, I won't. I want to wait until I return to my people. If the money is given to somebody here, I am afraid when the presents reach me they will be rather small.

Delano said that they would put the money in the hands of anybody the Indians would select, say Bishop Hare, but the paper would have to be signed before they could draw the money from the Treasury. After consulting among themselves at some length, the Indians replied that they could not accept this, that they would sign the paper only if they could take the money home with them and divide it among their people, rather than receiving presents. Of course, no one expected that the Indians would be given a cash payment, and while Delano, Smith, and Hare were discussing the propriety of this arrangement, Spotted Tail arose and remarked that inasmuch as there seemed to be some difficulty in paying the money after they had indicated a willingness to take it, perhaps they had better wait until they could talk to the President and get his advice.[59]

The President met with the chiefs the next day but got absolutely

[59] *New York Times*, June 2, 1875; *New York Herald*, June 2, 1875.

nowhere with them. He delivered a strong speech, urging the importance of an immediate acceptance of the proposal to surrender the hunting rights. He reminded them that there were no buffalo in the area,
and the Indians would be foolish to refuse payment for what was
actually an empty right, because the white men would soon take over
the territory whether the Indians wanted them to or not. The Indians
were perfectly willing to take the money, but the manner of payment
still bothered them. Spotted Tail suggested that the President draw it
out and hold it for them until they could go home and consult their
people. The President replied that they would have to sign the paper
before even he could get the money. After trying a while longer,
without effect, to persuade the chiefs to sign, the President, his patience
exhausted, left the room, telling them that he would not see them again,
that they would have to conduct the rest of their business with the
Secretary and his subordinate.[60]

By now, all hope of success was gone. The chiefs, already disappointed
at what they felt to be neglect on the part of the Great Father, were
infuriated at his abrupt termination of the council. They would not even
go to the Indian office the next day, and Saville reported that all that
could be done now was to take the chiefs home and see what could be
accomplished at the agency. The next evening Commissioner Smith
went to their hotel and talked with them for a short time. They still
refused to sign the document ceding their hunting rights, but Red Cloud
said that they would be willing to discuss their problems with commissioners appointed by the President. He suggested the appointment of
six men, and nominated Todd Randall and John S. Collins for two of the
places. Smith replied that he would ask the President to consider the
matter.[61]

The next day (June 4), the Indians, somewhat mollified, came to the
Interior Department for another conference. Delano, who was present
in a last-ditch effort to achieve something tangible from the prolonged
and exasperating negotiations, promised the Indians that if they would
sign the paper ceding their hunting rights, he would try to persuade
Congress to appropriate an additional twenty-five thousand dollars.
Even with this bait, however, the Indians refused to bite, and Delano
reluctantly agreed to let them take the agreement for signature after
they returned home. With respect to the Black Hills—which had
been pushed completely into the background by the wrangle over

[60] *New York Times*, June 3, 1875; *New York Herald*, June 3, 1875.
[61] *New York Herald*, June 3, 1875; *New York Times*, June 4, 1875.

hunting rights—the Secretary indicated that a commission would shortly be appointed to visit the agencies to discuss the sale of the territory. The only response, made by Spotted Tail, was not very encouraging. He said that it was not worthwhile talking about the Hills now, as they would demand a very large price for them.[62]

On the morning of the fifth, the Indians called for the last time at the Department; they wanted to shake hands with the Commissioner, and some of the young men wanted to speak. But Red Cloud, rather than any of the young men, came forward to speak, and if he had been ineffective earlier in presenting his peoples' cause, he now gave tragic evidence of the extent to which he had come under the influence of the half-breeds and squaw men whose advice he had so consistently taken and whose interests he had so frequently served. He said:

> My friend, we are going home to-day, and the young men you see here want to shake hands with you and bid you good-bye. We came to ask about something we have not heard about. I would like to ask about the pay for those who came with me—the interpreters and all the Indians.

Smith could hardly contain himself. "There are some things to be said about these men who have come along," he replied, "that I would rather not be obliged to say to you. They have not come by the wish of anybody but themselves, so far as I know, and they have been sources of mischief and trouble ever since they came here. . . . Now they have the impudence to come and ask me to pay them for that sort of service. . . ." As for the Indians, their agents had been authorized to spend twenty-five dollars apiece for presents, and that was all the money he had to spend for them.[63] Red Cloud, unabashed, now requested payment to the proprietor of the Washington House for meals furnished while some of the delegation roomed there, but with no better luck.[64]

Little Wound supported Red Cloud's appeal on behalf of the interpreters, but Smith would hear none of it. He turned to the young men and advised them to shun the half-white, half-Indian men who lived around the agencies: "I am sorry they are white at all. . . . they are only mischief-makers." He hoped the young men would carry the words of the Great Father, of the Secretary, and of himself home to their

[62] *New York Times*, June 5, 1875.

[63] After the Indians departed, some additional money was found, and Inspector J. W. Daniels, former Red Cloud agent who was accompanying the chiefs to look after the agreement on hunting rights, was telegraphed at Omaha to buy a horse and equipment for each member of the delegation (*New York Herald*, June 11, 1875).

[64] *New York Times*, June 6, 1875.

people. If Smith thought that his words would react against the old chiefs, and particularly Red Cloud, he had some cause for hope. When one of the young men (Scalp Face) finally got around to speaking, he turned to Red Cloud and said:

> I told you just how that meeting would be when you commenced it. We came here with divided councils. We have accomplished nothing and we have no one to blame but ourselves. The Red Cloud Agent is a good man, he is a brave, true man. We tried to break him down, but we could not. He is the man we ought to take back with us and keep. . . .[65]

And so the conference ended. What, one might ask, had been accomplished by almost three weeks of wrangling and recrimination? The answer of most of the country was "Nothing."[66] Officials of the Interior Department, however, did not share this opinion. They were sure that the Sioux would soon cede their hunting rights in Nebraska, and they felt that by impressing upon the chiefs the fact that they were no longer guaranteed rations under the treaty of 1868, they had softened them up for the negotiation of a new treaty which would include the cession of the Black Hills.[67] They were correct about the hunting rights—the agreement was signed at both Red Cloud and Spotted Tail agencies on June 23[68]—but they would soon learn that little if anything had been done at Washington to facilitate the negotiation of a new treaty affecting the Black Hills.[69]

Even though the ill-fated negotiations did little to forward the Government's basic Indian policy, it has been suggested that they had a serious effect on Red Cloud's prestige,[70] and it cannot be denied that his conduct was such as to disappoint his most ardent admirers; as Stanley Vestal said, "Before he was through, Red Cloud had managed to enrage or insult most of the officials and friends of the Indians with whom he came in contact." After quarreling with Saville ever since the

[65] *Ibid.*

[66] See, e.g., *New York Herald*, June 9, 1875; *Omaha Weekly Herald*, June 11, 1875. The *New York Herald* commented acidly: "We hope this failure may put an end to the foolish practice of Indian embassies to Washington to negotiate with the government. The time has come when the Indian tribes should no longer be dallied with, but governed. . . ."

[67] *New York Times*, June 10, 1875.

[68] Telegram, Daniels to Com. of Indian Affairs, June 24, 1875, NARS, RG 75, LR, Red Cloud Agency. The agreement will be found in Com. of Indian Affairs, *Annual Report*, 1875, pp. 179–180.

[69] See below, pp. 201–213.

[70] See, e.g., Hyde, *Red Cloud's Folk*, pp. 231–233; Vestal, *Warpath and Council Fire*, pp. 186–194.

agent had arrived, and after having been brought to Washington at his own request so that he could lay his grievances before the President, he backed and filled in such a way as to all but ruin his case. Moreover, his obvious catering to the interests of the hangers-on at the agency lost him the confidence of his own people as well as of the whites who had championed his cause. His name does not appear on the agreement ceding hunting rights in Nebraska, and apparently he was not asked to sign it.[71] Despite this, however, despite his continuing equivocation, and despite an effort on the part of the Government to "depose" him as chief,[72] it was still too early to count him out. He may not have been "the King Bee among the Indians," as Cornelius Craven, herder at the agency, described him,[73] but he still possessed enough of the qualities of leadership to enable him to remain one of the leading figures among his people, and one of the major problems in the politics of Indian affairs.

III

Although the Government moved quickly to negotiate for the Black Hills,[74] it had to deal first with the question of fraud at Red Cloud Agency. Professor Marsh was too well known and his charges were given too much publicity to be ignored by an administration which was deeply involved in scandal and which had been under repeated attack for its careless, if not fraudulent, management of Indian affairs.[75] As has been stated, the Board of Indian Commissioners, to whom Marsh first presented his charges, had ordered an investigation.[76] Shortly after Secretary Delano learned of the action of the Board, he wrote Clinton B. Fisk, its president, requesting him to recommend persons whom he could appoint to a commission "to investigate certain reports put in circulation by a Mr. Marsh relative to the Indian service at the Red Cloud Agency."[77] Apparently he had decided that it would

[71] *Omaha Weekly Herald,* July 23, 1875.   [72] See below, pp. 233–234.

[73] Ricker, Interview with Cornelius A. Craven, October 13, 1906, Ricker Mss., Tablet No. 3.

[74] See below, Chapter 11.

[75] For a good brief account of the growing criticism of Grant's Indian policy, see Henry G. Waltmann, "The Interior Department, War Department and Indian Policy, 1865–1887" (Ph. D. dissertation, University of Nebraska, 1962), pp. 266–275.

[76] See above, p. 179.

[77] Delano to Fisk, May 10, 1875, in *Report of the Special Commission Appointed to Investigate the Affairs of the Red Cloud Indian Agency, July, 1875* (Washington: Government Printing Office, 1875), p. i.

be better to participate in the investigation than to have it conducted independently. Fisk was agreeable, and after some difficulty in finding men who were willing to serve, Thomas C. Fletcher, former governor of Missouri, Congressman Charles J. Faulkner of West Virginia, and Benjamin W. Harris of Massachusetts were appointed to the Commission. Later, Senator Timothy O. Howe of Wisconsin and George W. Atherton, professor of political economy and constitutional law at Rutgers, were added.[78] Fletcher was appointed chairman; Howe did not participate actively in the work of the Commission.

Delano's reference to "a Mr. Marsh" (which was widely ridiculed in the press)[79] may have reflected his irritation with the professor for having gone directly to the President with his complaints.[80] Be that as it may, Professor Marsh proved to be a most difficult person to deal with. He ignored repeated requests for a formal statement of charges, and when, on July 10, he finally filed his complaints, he did so in the form of a pamphlet addressed to the President and furnished in advance to the press.[81] He made ten specific charges:

> 1st. The Agent, J. J. Saville, is wholly unfitted for his position, and guilty of gross frauds upon the Indians in his charge.
>
> 2d. The number of Indians at this Agency has been systematically overstated, for purposes which can only contemplate fraud.
>
> 3d. The last issue of Annuity Goods, which I witnessed, was a suspicious transaction, and, in part, at least, fraudulent.
>
> 4th. The beef cattle given to the Indians have been very inferior, owing to systematic frauds practiced by the agent and beef contractors.
>
> 5th. The pork issued to the Indians during my visit was not suitable for human food.
>
> 6th. The flour was very inferior, and the evidence of fraud in this article is conclusive.
>
> 7th. The sugar and coffee issued were not good, although better than the other supplies.

[78] Sketches of all of the commissioners except Harris will be found in *Dictionary of American Biography*.

[79] See, e.g., Schuchert and LeVene, *O. C. Marsh, Pioneer in Paleontology*, pp. 149–150.

[80] Delano and Marsh developed an intense dislike for each other, and on one occasion engaged in a public argument in the dining room of Wormley's hotel in Washington (*New York Herald*, September 14, 1875). In speaking of Delano's disappointment that the samples had not been given directly to him, Marsh commented that this was "a service which Red Cloud himself, who knew the Honorable Secretary, did not ask me to perform" (O. C. Marsh, *A Statement of Affairs at Red Cloud Agency, Made to the President of the United States* [n.p., n.d.], p. 10).

[81] Marsh, *A Statement of Affairs at Red Cloud Agency*, pp. 4–5.

8th. The tobacco observed was rotten, and of little or no use to the Indians.

9th. In consequence of fraud and mismanagement, the Indians suffered greatly during the past winter for want of food and clothing.

10th. The contract for freight from Cheyenne to Red Cloud Agency was fraudulent, as the true distance is 145 miles, while the contractor was paid for 212 miles.

Secretary Delano responded with a pamphlet of his own, issued for the use of the Commission. In it, he criticized Marsh's handling of the affair, questioned his judgment relative to the matters with which he was dealing—"It will readily be seen that a man of limited general business experience, whose specialty is scientific research . . . might be easily misled by the influences surrounding him, and which he failed fully to comprehend"—and suggested that the whole affair had been trumped up by the *New York Tribune* "in order to secure an object it has long sought to obtain, namely, the injury of the Secretary of the Interior."[82]

Others besides the principal antagonists advised the Commissioners—or rather, passed judgment in advance of the investigation. Delano mentioned only the *Tribune*'s campaign against him, but other New York papers were almost as outspoken. The *Herald* reported Marsh's charges fully and sympathetically, and on July 31 published a long "Matter-of-Fact History About the Frauds at the Red Cloud Agency," laying them at the door of "The Indian Ring," which it identified as "composed of such men as D. W. Clinton Wheeler, G. M. Dodge, J. W. Bosler, R. T. Baldwin, and the official representatives of the Interior Department."[83] It also published a series of letters from William Welsh, former president of the Board of Indian Commissioners, excoriating the administration's Indian policy.[84] The *Times*, while not giving the matter as extensive coverage as either the *Tribune* or the *Herald*, stated flatly that Marsh's charges were "all supported by independent testimony," and declared that the burden of disproving them rested with the Interior Department.[85]

The Commission met for the first time at the Fifth Avenue Hotel in New York on July 19. Between that date and October 16, when it

[82] *Documents Relating to the Charges of Professor O. C. Marsh of Fraud and Mismanagement at the Red Cloud Agency* (n.p., n.d.). A copy of this is at the Nebraska State Historical Society.

[83] *New York Herald*, July 31, 1875.

[84] *Ibid.*, August 13, 16, 25, September 8, 18, 1875.

[85] *New York Times*, July 19, 1875.

submitted its report, it heard eighty-seven witnesses at hearings conducted in New York, Omaha, Cheyenne, Fort Laramie, Red Cloud Agency, Spotted Tail Agency, and Washington, compiling testimony that filled 841 tightly packed pages.[86] Professor Marsh sat with the Commission in New York and Washington, and was permitted to interrogate witnesses. Much of the testimony is complicated, confusing, and contradictory. The Commissioners confined their questioning generally to Marsh's specific charges, although at times the witnesses wandered far afield, and there is hardly a facet of Indian life on the northern plains that was not discussed.

On August 10, the Commissioners met the Oglalas in general council in the store house at Red Cloud Agency. Of approximately eighty chiefs, head men, and warriors present, the following occupied benches across from the Commissioners: Red Cloud, Little Wound, Conquering Bear, Red Leaf, Tall Lance, High Wolf, Old-Man-Afraid-of-His-Horse, Sword, and the Oglala Sitting Bull. The council is interesting both for the divisions it revealed among the Oglalas and for the evidence it supplied relative to Marsh's charges. Red Cloud had hurt himself in Washington, and he had been pushed aside in connection with the Republican River hunting agreement.[87] He still had opposition, but he seems to have recovered some strength, and, in the eyes of the Commissioners, at least, he was definitely recognized as the leading man of the tribe.

Fletcher opened the council with a short address in which he admonished the Oglalas to learn the white man's way of agriculture and husbandry, and assured them that the Commissioners had come not to make treaties or bargains but simply to hear what they had to say. Red Cloud, responding for the Oglalas, delivered a characteristically rambling speech, alternately eloquent and inane. He complained in general about the shortage of rations and the presence of soldiers near the agency, but, aside from wondering when he was to get the new agent the Great Father had promised him, he did not address himself specifically to any of Marsh's charges. When Red Cloud had finished, the Oglala Sitting Bull got up and said to Old-Man-Afraid-of-His-Horse: "If there is anything that Red Cloud has said that you don't

---

[86] *Report of the Special Commission Appointed to Investigate the Affairs of the Red Cloud Indian Agency, July, 1875* (above, n. 77). Unless otherwise indicated, I am following this document throughout the rest of this chapter; when, for the reader's convenience, specific pages are cited, it will be referred to as *Report.*

[87] See above, pp. 188–189.

like get up and speak. These gentlemen have not come here for nothing." Old-Man-Afraid did not reply, and Fletcher intervened to say: "If there are any others who would like to speak to us we will be glad to hear them. . . . The white man regards Red Cloud as a great Sioux, a great warrior, a wise man, and the white man listens to what Red Cloud says, unless somebody else has something more to say. If any have we would like to hear from them too."

Old-Man-Afraid still declined to speak, so Little Wound volunteered to "say a few words for him." He, too, complained of the rations and of the way in which they were issued: "I have not seen it myself, but I have heard complaints by the women and children, that when the issues were given they would throw the corn nearly in their faces. . . . they hear the people at issuing cursing and swearing at them a good deal, and we don't like that, and I hope you will have it stopped." He was also concerned about how the twenty-five thousand dollars that had been given them for their hunting rights was to be spent. They were told that they were to be provided with cattle, wagons, and horses. The wagons had not come yet; the cattle and horses had been delivered, but the cattle were small and the horses were wild and could not be broken. They could not have cost very much; Little Wound wanted to know if they had received the full amount. He also wanted to know when his young men who had gone to persuade the northern Indians to come in for the Black Hills council were going to be paid.

When Little Wound had finished, Fletcher said that the Commissioners wished to have a private talk with "Red Cloud and a few others whom he may choose to bring with him," and later in the day the Commissioners met in Saville's house with Red Cloud, Sitting Bull, Face, Tall Lance, Scraper, Slow Bull, Fast Thunder, Sword, and Old-Man-Afraid-of-His-Horse. For some reason, Little Wound was not included in this gathering.

Sitting Bull spoke first, and he wanted to make it clear that Red Cloud did not speak for all of the tribe:

> We asked Red Cloud to speak for us and he has asked every time for a new agent. This don't please us, we young men sitting in here now. We have this man (Agent Saville) to work for us, and we have helped him, and just about the same time that he is trying to do something for us they are trying to throw him away; this is a fact. Red Cloud asked for another agent, and he will keep doing that, and we don't know where he will find a better one. . . .

The Commissioners did not respond to this. Their principal interest, in this private interview, was to hear from Red Cloud about the rations the Oglalas had been receiving. Were they good or bad? Red Cloud was of no more help than he had been earlier in Washington.[88] The record speaks for itself.

> THE CHAIRMAN. . . . Now, we would like to know if the cattle that we issued to you last fall were small and poor beeves.
>
> RED CLOUD. Yes; they were cows and small yearlings, but they were not counted as beeves.
>
> FAST THUNDER. Once they gave us beef, and out of five there was one yearling. Sometimes we have a full issue, just according to the cattle. They gave me four head of cattle, and then if there was a calf, they would drive it out.
>
> MR. FAULKNER. Was that yearling which was issued to you with the four cattle counted in as one beef?
>
> FAST THUNDER. No; it was not.
>
> MR. HARRIS. [To Red Cloud.] Were the cattle that were issued to you all large cattle—large steers?
>
> RED CLOUD. They were mixed up, small and large cattle, from two to twenty years old—some large and some small. There were eight head of cattle that were seen by some of the officers. I was there and saw them myself. And I suppose that is why they complained about the beef, and those were the cattle they meant.[89]
>
> MR. FAULKNER. Did the eight cattle you saw and speak of now not correspond in size and condition with the cattle that were usually issued?
>
> RED CLOUD. Out of those they issued to us there was only those eight left, and they were left because they were poor. They were kept back and not issued because they were poor. The cattle might have been fat when they bought them, (when the contractor bought them,) but in bringing them here they got poor.

The Commissioners abandoned this line of questioning and turned to a discussion of flour. Fletcher asked Red Cloud, "Did you have flour issued to you last winter that was so bad that you could not use it?" and, in response to this leading question, got this answer:

> Yes. There was bad flour. I am the one that took the flour and the tobacco, and some of the coffee, and I was going to take some of the pork, but it was not good—nasty—and I did not like to put my hands on it. Sitting Bull recollects this, and can tell you the same thing. When I took those samples to Professor Marsh, I said to him: "Take these, and show them to my Great Father, and when you get there tell him I will be there to see him, too;" but I thought that Professor Marsh would throw them away before he got there. . . .

[88] See above, pp. 183–184.
[89] See above, pp. 183–184.

Red Cloud kept insisting that the samples were representative of all the supplies, but even if he had not cut the ground out from under his testimony by his statement that he thought the professor would throw them away, Leon Palladay undermined the whole the next day when he reported that Red Dog had told him that he and Red Cloud had deliberately picked out the bad grains of coffee to give to the professor.[90] After weighing all the evidence, the Commmissioners found themselves completely disenchanted with the celebrated samples. Of the flour, they wrote:

> The sample of this article which Red Cloud placed in the hands of Professor Marsh seems to have been something below the quality of the vilest flour that reached the agency, surreptitiously or otherwise. That wily chief is as distinguished for low artifice as he is for brute courage, and the opportunity which the Professor had for learning his true character should have made him cautious in accepting too implicitly his statements, especially as he availed himself of no opportunity while he was at the agency to compare that sample with even the worst specimens of the flour he saw there. . . .[91]

The same was true of the sugar, coffee, and tobacco; Red Cloud's samples were simply not representative of the products being issued to the Oglalas. This is not to say that the Commissioners approved of the quality of rations being furnished. Far from it. They found all inferior, and some were well below the quality specified in the orders.[92] They recommended that J. W. L. Slavens of Kansas City, who had been furnishing pork for the agency, and J. H. Martin, the flour contractor, be made ineligible for further contracts with the Government, and that E. R. Threlkeld, the Indian Inspector at Kansas City, be fired. In addition, they recommended a general tightening up of all contract procedures, and particularly of inspection.[93] They agreed with Marsh that the Government was being badly defrauded on its freighting contracts, recommending that D. J. McCann, the principal contractor for the agency, be excluded from all further contracts with the Government, and that his accounts be referred to the Department of Justice "for examination and action." They also agreed that Agent Saville should be removed, but not because he was guilty of any fraud. Indeed,

[90] Transcript of conversations with the Oglalas will be found in *Report*, pp. 296–308; Palladay's testimony, pp. 336–337.

[91] *Report*, p. LV.

[92] *Ibid.*, pp. LV–LIX.

[93] For a good account of the difficulties of supplying the Indian agencies, see Henry G. Waltmann, "The Subsistence Policy with Special Reference to the Red Cloud and Spotted Tail Agencies" (Master's thesis, University of Nebraska, 1959).

as they put it, "He may certainly be referred to as an example of at least one Indian agent who goes out of office a poorer man than when he entered it." He was, however, temperamentally unsuited for the responsibilities of his job; and his lax administration, the Commissioners felt, had contributed to conditions which created unrest among the Indians and made fraud easy.[94] The Commissioners concluded their report with some general recommendations for leading the Indians to civilization—virtually no investigating committee could resist the opportunity to sound off in general terms, because it always became apparent that the problem was much larger than the one they had been sent to study. They found no fault with Secretary Delano; Commissioner Smith likewise was adjudged completely honest, although lacking in the "vigilance, astuteness, and decision of character" required by his position.[95]

Reaction to the report was mixed. Commissioner Smith, despite the criticism of his administration, declared the report to be a complete vindication of the Indian Service: "The complaints and alleged grievances of Red Cloud upon which the commission was originated were found to be groundless. The sweeping charges of fraud on the part of the agent and other Government officials were also found to have been made upon hearsay evidence and not in accordance with fact,"[96] A number of newspapers, however, called the report "a white-wash" and criticized the Commissioners for a studied effort to ignore the implications of the testimony they had collected.[97] Professor Marsh, so far as I have been able to determine, made no public comment on the report. Although the Commissioners had shown him every courtesy during their hearings, he was roughly handled in their final report; he could take some comfort, perhaps, in the editorial criticism of the Commissioners' work. Apparently he bore no ill will toward Red Cloud, who had let him down so disappointingly; at any rate, in 1883 he entertained the chief for three days at his home in New Haven.[98]

Actually, very little use was made of the report. On September 22, while the Commissioners were finishing up their work in Washington, President Grant accepted Secretary Delano's resignation, and this was

[94] *Report*, pp. XVII–XVIII.

[95] The Commissioners' findings and recommendations are summarized in *Report*, pp. XV–LXXV.

[96] Com. of Indian Affairs, *Annual Report*, 1875, p. 37.

[97] See, e.g., *New York Herald*, October 23, 1875; *Omaha Weekly Herald*, October 22, 1875. See also Schuchert and LeVene, *O. C. Marsh*, pp. 164–166.

[98] Schuchert and LeVene, *O. C. Marsh*, pp. 167–168.

interpreted in some quarters as a direct outgrowth of the investigation.[99] It may have been, but Delano—surely no sterling Secretary—had long been trying to get out of the Cabinet and had submitted his letter of resignation on July 5. Grant had held it, however, "because of the continued persecution which I believed, and believe, was being unjustly heaped on you through the public press." The President hoped that the future would place the Secretary "right in the estimation of the public" and that he would "continue to enjoy its confidence as you have done through so many years of public and official life."[100] Commissioner Smith stayed on for a while but then resigned under pressure from the House Committee on Indian Affairs, which found him guilty of lax accounting for Indian funds.[101] Saville was removed early in 1876.[102]

The case of D. J. McCann is an interesting one. Although the Commissioners, it will be recalled, had recommended that the Justice Department move against him, he continued to dominate the freighting business at Red Cloud Agency for almost two years. In November, 1878, however, he was brought to trial in the Laramie County District Court in Cheyenne on charges of stealing fifty-two barrels of sugar intended for the Crows and Blackfeet. He was convicted, but on a retrial in December, 1880, the verdict was set aside.[103]

Very little, then, came of the Great Investigation. One cannot escape the conclusion that the Commissioners either played down or failed to see the implications of much of the testimony they heard. Except in a few instances, they seemed perfectly willing—even anxious—to let Red Cloud's failure to carry through settle the case for them. Except for a few editors and a few reformers, people generally seemed to go along with this attitude. As Loring Priest put it:

> Yet these continual revelations did not disturb the public. Even knowledge that Secretary of War Belknap had let Indian trade ships to the highest bidders aroused only momentary criticism. Until President-elect Hayes announced the appointment of Carl Schurz as Secretary of the Interior in 1877, no positive action was taken to check the spread of crimes against the American Indians.[104]

[99] *Ibid.*, pp. 163–166.

[100] *New York Herald*, September 27, 1875.

[101] Loring B. Priest, *Uncle Sam's Stepchildren* (New Brunswick: Rutgers University Press, 1942), p. 67.

[102] See below, p. 216.

[103] Waltmann, "Subsistence Policy" (above, n. 93), pp. 159–162.

[104] Priest, *Uncle Sam's Stepchildren*, p. 68.

Red Cloud, who started the whole thing, probably never heard of the Commissioners' report. He was engaged in a desperate struggle to maintain his leadership among his people—a struggle which involved not only his own role, but a whole way of life.[105] Moreover, even while the Commissioners were at the Agency, Red Cloud's interest was directed primarily toward news that yet another commission was coming out. It had already been organized, and these commissioners were not coming just to talk. They were bringing a paper for the Sioux to sign.

[105] The Commissioners had observed the conflict among the Oglalas, and in their report they wrote: "The iron bond of their tribal organization is rapidly weakening, and the most eminent and distinguished chiefs now hold their positions by a precarious tenure" (*Report,* p. LXX).

CHAPTER 11

Failure of a Commission

Custer's glowing reports[1] turned the eyes of adventurers from all over the West toward the Black Hills. Western newspapers were filled with stories of parties forming or about to be formed at Yankton, Sioux City, Cheyenne, and elsewhere for an assault on the Hills, and despite the Army's effort—admittedly halfhearted—to keep whites out of the area, the spring and summer of 1875 saw a steady influx of prospectors into the forbidden region.[2] The Indian Bureau, caught between the unruly Sioux and the impatient prospectors, tried to maintain the status quo until it could work out some sort of viable solution to the fast-developing problem. Members of the Sioux Commission had categorically denied that there was gold in the Black Hills, and they had been supported by Professor Newton H. Winchell.[3] By the spring of 1875, however, there was no question but that some means would have to be found to persuade the Sioux to give up the Black Hills, and the Government had acceded to the request of Red Cloud and Spotted Tail that they be allowed to visit Washington in the hope that the trip would provide a start, at least, on negotiations for cession.[4] On March 27, while plans for the trip were under way, the Commissioner

[1] See above, pp. 172–174.
[2] For a good account of the excitement, see Harold E. Briggs, "The Black Hills Gold Rush," *North Dakota Historical Quarterly*, V (1930–1931), 71–99.
[3] See above, p. 173.
[4] See above, pp. 176–177.

of Indian Affairs, in an effort to stem the rush of prospectors, asked Professor Walter P. Jenney of the New York School of Mines to visit the Black Hills to determine once and for all whether they really contained any gold. Escorted by Lt. Col. Richard I. Dodge and four hundred men, Jenney spent the summer and early fall in the Hills. He sent back periodic reports, which were duly chronicled in the newspapers; they were not as glowing as Custer's of the year before, but they definitely confirmed the existence of gold,[5] and they were amplified by a correspondent from the *Chicago Inter-Ocean* who accompanied the expedition.[6]

Meanwhile, with or without reference to Jenney's reports, prospectors continued to invade the region. Jenney himself found numerous parties of prospectors, and, curiously enough in view of the Army's orders, Colonel Dodge apparently made no effort to evict them; on the contrary, he specifically authorized some of the intruders to stay[7] and Jenney reported at one time that "about two hundred miners," who had followed him from one point to another, were offering "every assistance in prospecting the country."[8] Late in July, Brig. Gen. George Crook, who had succeeded General Ord as commander of the Department of the Platte, made a reconnaissance of the region, partly to satisfy the Indians that the Army was looking after their interests and partly to see for himself what conditions were like. He found "at least" twelve hundred miners in the area. He ordered them to leave but apparently made no effort to enforce the order.[9] Indeed, he stated in his annual report:

> Now, when I visited the Black Hills country and conversed with the miners in regard to vacating, and reminded them that they were violating a treaty stipulation, it was but natural that they should reply that the Indians themselves violated the treaty hundreds of times every summer by predatory incursions, whereby many settlers were utterly ruined, and their families left without means of subsistence, and this by Indians who are fed, clothed, and maintained in utter idleness by the Government they, the settlers, help support. I respectfully submit that their side of this story should be

[5] See Jenney's report, Com. of Indian Affairs, *Annual Report,* 1875, pp. 181–183.

[6] William S. Waddell, "The Military Relations Between the Sioux Indians and the United States Government in Dakota Territory, 1860–1891" (Master's thesis, University of South Dakota, 1931), p. 49.

[7] E. A. Howard to Com. of Indian Affairs, August 14, 1875, NARS, RG 75, LR, Spotted Tail Agency.

[8] *Ibid.*; see also Briggs, "The Black Hills Gold Rush," p. 84.

[9] Crook to AAG, Military Division of the Missouri, August 16, 1875, NARS, RG 98, LS, Dept. of the Platte.

heard, as the settlers who develop our mines and open the frontier to civilization are the nation's wards no less than their more fortunate fellows, the Indians. . . .[10]

Despite this attitude, Crook's reconnaissance seems to have had a salutary effect upon the Indians. E. A. Howard, Spotted Tail agent, who at the request of Red Cloud and Spotted Tail visited the Black Hills in August with a number of the principal men from both the agencies, found the miners generally preparing to leave in accordance with Crook's orders. As for the Indians, he reported that they "expressed themselves as well pleased with the steps taken by the Government to prevent the whites from invading their country until after the treaty is made."[11]

Back in Washington, Commissioner Smith, trying to salvage something from the Sioux visit to the capital, persuaded the President to accede to Red Cloud's suggestion that a commission be appointed to visit the Indian country, and on June 18 the Secretary of the Interior appointed a commission "to treat with the Sioux Indians for the Relinquishment of the Black Hills." Headed by Senator William B. Allison of Iowa, the other members were Bishop E. R. Ames, Baltimore; Judge F. W. Palmer, Chicago; Brig. Gen. A. H. Terry; Congressman Abram Comingo, Independence, Mo.; Rev. S. D. Hinman, Santee Agency; G. P. Beauvais, St. Louis; W. H. Ashby, Beatrice, Nebraska; and A. G. Lawrence, Providence, Rhode Island. Bishop Ames and Judge Palmer declined to serve, so the work devolved upon the remaining seven. The ubiquitous John S. Collins, post trader at Fort Laramie, was appointed secretary.[12]

The Commission did not exhibit many talents for the job before it. General Terry, of course, was an experienced Indian fighter, but he certainly was no friend of the Sioux. The Rev. Mr. Hinman was well informed and spoke several Sioux dialects, but he was not especially liked by either Red Cloud or Spotted Tail. G. P. Beauvais was a man of vast experience in the West as a trader, but it had been a long time

[10] Crook, Annual Report, Dept. of the Platte, September 15, 1875, 44th Cong., 1st Sess., H. Ex. Doc. 1, pp. 69–70.

[11] Howard to Com. of Indian Affairs, August 14, 1875, NARS, RG 75, LR, Spotted Tail Agency.

[12] "Report of the Commission Appointed to Treaty with the Sioux Indians for the Relinquishment of the Black Hills," Secretary of the Interior, *Annual Report*, 1875, pp. 184–201. Unless otherwise indicated, this report serves as the source for the remainder of this chapter.

since he had been active in the Sioux country. The others, and particularly Senator Allison, seemed to have no qualifications whatever for the assignment. Allison, to be sure, was able and persuasive—even though he was serving his first term in the Senate, he had served four terms in the House, and, as a close friend of President Grant's, was a power to be reckoned with in the Republican party—but he had had no experience in dealing with the Indians. Moreover, in the summer of 1875, his primary interest seems to have been Iowa politics.[13]

The Commissioners' obligations would have been fairly formidable even for the most experienced negotiators, and their instructions were so loosely drawn as to be of little help. They were to procure a cession of "such portion of that country known as the Black Hills, between the North and South Forks of the Big Cheyenne, as the President may determine to be desirable for the Government to purchase for mining purposes." In addition, they were to persuade the Sioux to give up their rights to the Big Horn mountains in Wyoming, and rights of way, to be determined by the President, through country which would still be unceded. No price was mentioned. The Commissioners simply were to "assure the Indians that it is not the wish of the Government to take from them any of their property or rights without returning a fair equivalent therefor," and to state that they had come "representing their Great Father, to fix upon an equivalent which shall be just both to them and to the white people." Finally, the Commissioners were warned to "keep constantly impressed upon the minds of the Indians" that any agreement entered into with them would have to be approved by Congress before it would go into effect; the Indian Bureau had been confronted too often with demands for the fulfilment of stipulations in unratified agreements, and Smith did not want to be caught in this way

---

[13] Leland L. Sage, *William Boyd Allison, A Study in Practical Politics* (Iowa City: State Historical Society of Iowa, 1956), is an excellent biography of Senator Allison, which, unfortunately—but perhaps appropriately in view of the attention which the Senator gave to the matter—devotes little space to his work on the Sioux Commission. Professor Sage has furnished me with some interesting letters from the Allison Papers (Iowa State Department of Archives and History) which throw light on the attitudes and activities of one of Allison's friends, Al Swalm, editor of the *Fort Dodge* (Iowa) *Messenger*, who accompanied the Commission, and, perhaps, by indirection, on the chairman himself. Accepting Allison's invitation, Swalm wrote, "I think I can make myself serviceable to you, if in no other way than to keep up one hand at euchre" (Swalm to Allison, July 20, 1875). Swalm accompanied the expedition in the capacity of a reporter for the *Chicago Tribune*, and on November 29 we find Judge Palmer, an original member of the Commission, wondering how the *Tribune* got exclusive rights to the publication of the Sioux Commission's report (Palmer to Allison, November 29, 1875).

in a matter as crucial as the Black Hills. Reflecting the change in official policy, the Commissioners were not treating with the Sioux as a foreign nation, but, "in negotiating with these ignorant and almost helpless people," they were to keep in mind the fact that they were to "represent them and their interests not less than those of the Government."

The negotiations were to be conducted at Fort Sully or at some other suitable point on the Missouri River, and three of the Commissioners (Hinman, Comingo, and Ashby) were designated to precede the others to make the necessary arrangements. Why anyone—and particularly a person as knowledgeable as Hinman—should have believed that the Sioux would consent to come to the Missouri River for a conference is difficult to understand. In any event, after conferring with both Red Cloud and Spotted Tail, Hinman ruefully reported:

> We regret to say that although they seem kindly disposed and willing to treat for the cession of the Black Hills . . . they express an utter unwillingness to have the grand council held on the Missouri River. We are therefore apprehensive that it will be difficult if not impossible to induce them to meet in general council at that place though the commission will at the appropriate time endeavor to influence them to do so.[14]

Hinman's efforts were wholly unsuccessful, and he finally agreed that the council would be held near the agencies, although he was so vague about the exact spot as to bring on a good deal of confusion. He settled on a location near the Red Cloud Agency, but Spotted Tail assumed that the conference would be held on Chadron Creek, about halfway between the two agencies. As we shall see, this confusion, combined with the competition which inevitably developed between Red Cloud and Spotted Tail even when they were cooperating, almost broke up the conference before it got started.[15]

There was hope, too—surely no better founded than the notion about the location—that the northern bands led by Sitting Bull, Crazy Horse, and Black Twin could be induced to come to the meeting, and Young-Man-Afraid-of-His-Horse and Louis Richard were sent out to try to bring them in. They found possibly as many as nineteen hundred lodges encamped on the Tongue River—Oglalas, Miniconjous, Hunkpapas, Sans Arcs, and Cheyennes. These people were by no means all of one mind. Game was scarce, and the prospect of filling

---

[14] Hinman to Com. of Indian Affairs, July 7, 1875, NARS, RG 75, LR, Spotted Tail Agency.

[15] See below, p. 205.

their bellies at the treaty table must have been alluring. The Cheyennes said they would come in, and so did some of the Oglalas. Crazy Horse and Black Twin said that they might be in after a while, but, as in times past, this expression served only to keep the Commission in a state of unrealized anticipation. Sitting Bull, the Hunkpapa, said that as long as any game remained in his country he would never consent to talk to the white man; the Sans Arcs and the Miniconjous were of the same mind.[16]

Hinman, Ashby, and Comingo went from the Red Cloud and Spotted Tail agencies to Fort Sully to invite the Missouri River Sioux to come out for the conference, and then went down river to Omaha where they met the rest of the Commissioners. After holding an organizational meeting at Omaha on August 26, the group headed west on the Union Pacific Railroad for Cheyenne, whence they journeyed overland to Fort Laramie and Red Cloud Agency, arriving on September 4 with a cavalry escort. Although Hinman had asserted as early as August 2 that "the success of the council . . . is already assured,"[17] the Commissioners were soon to learn otherwise.[18]

Red Cloud immediately objected to the presence of troops, saying it indicated a want of faith in the good will of his people. General Terry, the only experienced Indian fighter in the group, seems to have been perfectly willing to dispense with an escort, but the rest of the Commissioners seemed to feel more comfortable with military protection. Despite Red Cloud's objections, the Commission was accompanied at all sessions of the council with an escort of 120 cavalrymen.

Too much has been made of the hostility of the Indians, the danger to which the Commissioners were exposed, and the effect this had on the negotiations.[19] Certainly there were turbulent spirits, many of them armed, among the vast throng of Indians assembled for the council, and there were times when the Indians seemed belligerent. This was particularly true at the session of September 23, when armed warriors

[16] J. J. Saville to E. P. Smith, August 16, 1875, NARS, RG 75, LR, Red Cloud Agency; *New York Herald*, August 20, 1875.

[17] Telegram, Hinman to Com. of Indian Affairs, August 2, 1875, NARS, RG 75, LR, Dakota.

[18] As indicated in note 12, above, I am relying upon the report of the Commission, except where stated otherwise. For the period while the Commissioners were at Red Cloud Agency, I am supplementing the report with a number of long despatches in the *New York Herald*, September 22, 27, October 1, 6, 7, 1875.

[19] See, e.g., George E. Hyde, *Red Cloud's Folk* (Norman: University of Oklahoma Press, 1957), pp. 242–244; Stanley Vestal, *Warpath and Council Fire* (New York: Random House, 1948), pp. 205–211.

under Little Big Man—who himself was astride his horse stark naked and daubed with warpaint—took up positions directly behind the cavalry. Yet the chiefs seemed to have things under control, and despite understandable apprehension the proceedings continued without incident. Had the Indians been disposed to fight, there is no question but what they could have wiped out the Commissioners and their military escort. It is impossible to say how many were assembled in the vicinity of the Red Cloud Agency—some estimates ran as high as twenty thousand; Allison calculated the number of visiting Indians at 4,490—but the Indians outnumbered the troops available, including those at Fort Robinson and Camp Sheridan who were on alert, by enough to have taken care of the immediate situation. Yet while the restless Sioux were not a very pleasant group to deal with, the Commissioners' basic difficulties stemmed not from any show of hostility but from their own shortcomings and those of governmental policy.

The failure of the Commission was presaged in the preliminary negotiations over the place at which the council would be convened. Wittingly or not, Hinman in his early talks had created the impression, at least among the Brulés, that the council would be held on Chadron Creek, about halfway between the Red Cloud and Spotted Tail agencies; apparently he had asked Spotted Tail where he wanted to hold the council and the chief, assuming that this conveyed authority to name the place had spread the word that the Commissioners would meet the tribes at Chadron Creek. In any event, when the Commissioners arrived at Red Cloud Agency, they found Red Cloud dead set against going to Chadron Creek—he wanted the council held in the stockade at his agency—and they, too, had no desire to go the extra thirty miles to Chadron Creek and convene that far removed from any base of operations. Instead of making a decision, however, the Commissioners referred the question of location to a committee consisting of Red Cloud, Spotted Tail, and four additional chiefs. As might have been expected, this committee could come to no agreement and the matter was thrown back in the laps of the Commissioners, who finally selected a spot on the banks of the White River, about eight miles east of Red Cloud Agency, a site which pleased nobody.

If the Commissioners were indecisive about the location, they were even more so when it came to determining just what sort of a proposition they should lay before the Indians. Senator Allison was concerned about the restriction in Article 12 of the Treaty of 1868 which provided that no treaty for the cession of any part of the reservation could be valid "unless executed and signed by at least three-fourths of all the Adult male Indians, occupying or interested in the same." He urged, therefore, that the Commission negotiate only for the mining rights. Others argued that there was no use letting the Treaty of 1868 stand in the way, that the Indians could not understand the difference between mining rights and a direct cession, and that it would be just as easy to get the latter as it would the former. There was also a difference of opinion as to what should be offered the Indians. Ashby, Comingo, and Lawrence thought that an agreement to pay the current annual appropriation ($1,752,000) for a stated period would be sufficient; the others were inclined to be more generous. The Commissioners finally resolved their difficulties by agreeing to negotiate only for the mining rights and to leave the question of price open for determination as the council proceeded. As soon became apparent, this was probably the poorest solution that could have been adopted.

Finally, on September 20, the first formal session of the council convened at the appointed place. The beginning was not auspicious. When the Commissioners arrived, there were no Indians present, and even the wagons containing the canvas and poles for the council tent were not yet there. The wagons finally showed up, and after about an hour the fifteen soldiers assigned to the task had erected the canopy which was to form the grand tipi. Meanwhile, Spotted Tail had rolled up in a wagon, and a few other chiefs had drifted in. Most of the Oglalas, it turned out, had remained at their agency because rations were being issued. Red Cloud, miffed at the choice of the site, had deliberately stayed away. Senator Allison, however, eventually concluded that a representative body of chiefs had assembled, and began his formal address. The Senator's remarks, haltingly interpreted by Louis Richard, who had to be corrected frequently by Beauvais and Hinman, completely confounded the Indians.

> We have now to ask you [he began] if you are willing to give our people the right to mine in the Black Hills, as long as gold or other valuable metals are found, for a fair and just sum. If you are so willing, we will make a bargain with you for this right. When the gold or other valuable minerals are taken away, the country will again be yours to dispose of in any manner you may wish. . . .

After explaining how difficult it was to keep the whites out of the region, how the Great Father had the same interest in his red children as in his white, and how this proposal would safeguard the interests of both, he suggested that the Government would like to purchase outright the country east of the Big Horns: "It does not seem to be of very great value or use to you, and our people think they would like to have the portion of it I have described."

From the beginning the Indians had refused to consider the cession of the Big Horns, and attention was focused entirely on the proposal to lease the Black Hills. Apparently the chiefs had some difficulty in determining just what the Commissioners had in mind, but Spotted Tail soon concluded that their idea was to have the Indians loan the area to the whites for a while. This, he thought, was little short of preposterous. He turned to Saville and asked jestingly how he would like to loan him a team of mules on the terms proposed by the Commissioners. The Indians saw very clearly that once the whites were in possession of the country they would never leave, and they were sure that the proposal to purchase only mining rights was simply a device to lower the price they would ask. It must be confessed that the Indians can hardly be blamed for seeing it this way, although there is no evidence to justify the charge that Senator Allison and the majority of the Commission acted in anything but good faith in putting this singular proposal to the chiefs.

While Allison was still talking, Red Dog came rushing into the circle, and shortly after the Senator finished his address got up and told the assemblage that he had a message from Red Cloud. The message was: "There have come here a good many tribes to be at the council. It will take seven days for us to study in our minds about this, and we will now hold a council among ourselves."

At this the Oglalas and most of the others got up and prepared to leave. The Commissioners urged them to stay, but only Spotted Tail and his friends complied. The Commissioners then announced that they would hold another council the following day, but postponed it on learning that evening that the Indians would not meet with them again until they had consulted among themselves. Determined nonetheless not to let Red Cloud delay the proceedings for a whole week, the Commissioners declared that on the twenty-third there definitely would be another session and that the Indians would be expected to state their views at this time. The council was held, but some of the young men from the north were so unruly that nothing could be accomplished. Whether they were acting in concert with Red Cloud or entirely on their own, they certainly served the chief's purpose, which was to delay the proceedings as long as possible.

Irksome though it was to the Commissioners, the Indians' desire for delay is perfectly understandable. In the first place, they rather enjoyed these confabs with representatives of the Great Father, and they had all the time in the world. In the second place, in this particular instance there was a strong division between a minority who were determined not to part with the Black Hills at any price, and a majority, including both Red Cloud and Spotted Tail, who were willing to sell if the price was right. This majority, however, was confused by the form in which the Commissioners' proposition had been put, torn by jealousy among the leaders—particularly between the principal leaders—and besieged by conflicting advice from agents, squaw men, interpreters, traders, and others as to what they should demand. As the days dragged on and the Commissioners heard rumors that the Indians would ask a price ranging from thirty to fifty million dollars, they began to despair of any success whatever. On the twenty-sixth they called twenty of the leading chiefs to their quarters at Red Cloud Agency and told them in no uncertain terms that they would have to come to an agreement among themselves, and that the next day they expected to hear what terms the tribes would accept. The chiefs did not demur; they had had their seven days to study the matter and were ready to state their terms.

The Commissioners were hardly prepared for what they heard.

Red Dog said, "We want to be taken care of for seven generations ahead."

Red Cloud was more specific:

> There have been six nations raised, and I am the seventh, and I want seven generations ahead to be fed. . . . These hills out here to the northwest we look upon as the head chief of the land. My intention was that my children should depend on these hills for the future. I hoped that we should live that way always hereafter. That was my intention. I sit here under the treaty which was to extend for thirty years. I want to put the money that we get for the Black Hills at interest among the whites, to buy with the interest wagons and cattle. We have much small game yet that we can depend on for the future, only I want the Great Father to buy guns and ammunition with the interest so we can shoot the game. For seven generations to come I want our Great Father to give us Texan steers for our meat. I want the Government to issue for me hereafter, flour and coffee, and sugar and tea, and bacon, the very best kind, and cracked corn and beans, and rice and dried apples, and saleratus and tobacco, and soap and salt, and pepper, for the old people. I want a wagon, a light wagon with a span of horses, and six yoke of working cattle for my people. I want a sow and a boar, and a cow and bull, and a sheep and a ram, and a hen and a cock, for each

family. I am an Indian, but you try to make a white man out of me. I want some white men's houses at this agency to be built for the Indians. I have been into white people's houses, and I have seen nice black bedsteads and chairs, and I want that kind of furniture given to my people. . . . I want the Great Father to furnish me a saw-mill which I may call my own. I want a mower and a scythe for my people. Maybe you white people think that I ask too much from the Government, but I think those hills extend clear to the sky—maybe they go above the sky, and that is the reason I ask for so much. . . .

Spotted Tail said much the same thing: "As long as we live on this earth we will expect pay. . . . We want some clothes as long as any Indians live; if even only two remain, as long as they live they will want to be fed . . . as long as they live they want tobacco and knives. Until the land falls to pieces we want these things. . . ."

And so it went, as one after another the chiefs—Oglala, Brulé, Arapahoe, Cheyenne—stated their terms. They were being asked to give up their greatest treasure; they must be sure that their people would be taken care of for all time to come: a cow and a horse . . . powder and lead . . . pepper and salt and tobacco . . . for seven generations . . . as long as any Indians live, even if only two remain. . . .

These demands were more than the baffled Commissioners could comprehend—"of so extraordinary a character as to make it manifest that it was useless to continue the negotiations." They continued them, however, for two more fruitless days. The twenty-eighth was spent rehashing the demands of the twenty-seventh. Red Cloud, repeating his requests, also asked for Catholic missionaries and complained about the whiskey being brought on the reservation. Spotted Tail accused the Commissioners of being drunk the day before, although he later apologized, saying that he had spoken only in jest.[20] Finally, he asked the Commissioners to submit their proposal in writing, and this they agreed to do the next day.

The final proposal still reflected the indecision which had characterized the Commission from the beginning. If the Indians would lease mining rights, the Government would give them four hundred thousand dollars a year for as long as the lease should run; if the Indians wanted to sell the Hills outright, the Government would pay six million dollars in fifteen annual installments. Either agreement would have to be ratified by the Congress, and if an outright sale were approved, three-fourths of the adult males of the tribes would have to sign.

[20] The charge of drunkenness was widely circulated in the press.

Neither proposition appealed to the Indians; indeed, several of the important chiefs had not even bothered to come to the final meeting—Red Cloud was off watching an Arapahoe sun dance. Spotted Tail, faithful to the end (despite his occasional jests) responded for the Indians. The amounts offered were too small. It was not the fault of the Commissioners or of the Indians. They had better let the matter rest and postpone the treaty for the moment.

That, then, was that. The Commissioners responded lamely that they would take all of the Indians' words back to the Great Father, that they would depart as friends. Apparently, they did so—"the closing hand shaking was most friendly."

There were many reasons why the Commission had failed so abjectly. In their report, the Commissioners suggested the following:

1. [That] No agreement can be successfully concluded in the Indian country by means of a grand council of chiefs in the presence of a great body of the Indians.

2. No agreement can be made unless accompanied with presents, as presents have invariably been distributed heretofore at the signing of treaties or agreements.

3. The Indians place a value upon the hills far beyond any sum that could possibly be considered by the Government.

4. The Indians are hostile to the presence of whites on the reservation, and they believe that the opening of the hills to the whites would result in the opening of the whole reservation and their final expulsion, which belief induces a strong minority at least to oppose any cession.

5. The determination on the part of persons not Indians but having great influence over them, that no negotiation shall be successful that does not involve a large sum annually for many years, and in case of present failure another commission would be sent, which would deal liberally with them.

The evidence supports some of these conclusions, but not all of them. There is no question but that dealing with the chiefs in the presence of large numbers of their people was fraught with complications, producing a situation which encouraged struggles over precedence and speeches for effect. In this particular case, too, the presence of large numbers of unruly, wild Indians from the north who were suspicious of the agency chiefs as well as of the whites produced an uneasy situation which made calm deliberation almost impossible. There is no doubt, either, but that the failure of the Commissioners to bring presents with them worked against successful negotiations. Commissioners had always brought presents, and on learning that the Allison group had come empty-handed, many of the Indians lost interest in the whole business, drifting away before the negotiations were half over, even though an effort was made to feed them at the agencies. Halfway through the proceedings, Beauvais told a reporter that "if a great feast had been made for all the chiefs and an immense pile of blankets and other presents had been placed in the middle of the council circle, they would have come to terms long ago." [21] Such an approach, which was as old as Indian relations, was patently too cynical for 1875, but one wonders why Beauvais—or, for that matter, Hinman or Terry—did not insist that presents of some kind should be available to facilitate the negotiations.

Also there is no doubt but that contractors and hangers-on around the agencies greatly impeded the negotiations by encouraging the Indians to accept nothing that did not involve a high annual payment. After all, in one way or another they would get a sizable portion of whatever was appropriated for the benefit of the Sioux, and it was to their interest to make this appropriation as large and as long-lived as possible. Yet sincere friends of the Sioux, including Hinman of the Commission, were equally earnest in their desire that the tribes obtain as much as possible for the Hills on the assumption that the region was, indeed, their greatest treasure. Moreover, when word began to filter out from the Jenney expedition about the presence of gold, the region's value in the minds of all concerned inevitably went up. "Evil forces" were at work, but they were by no means the sole determinant of the value the Sioux placed on the Black Hills.

The Commissioner's other conclusions can hardly be sustained. Opposition to any cession whatever was not as great as the Commissioners implied. Most of the agency Indians seem to have been reconciled to parting with the Hills if a high enough price could be secured. Such opposition as did exist was confined almost solely to the northern bands. These people had not been parties to the Treaty of 1868, and they were brought to the council at the behest of the Commission. If Allison and his associates had sought simply to amend the Treaty of 1868 and thus provide a formal justification for white entry into the Hills, they might well have ignored the wild northern bands.

Also, the Commissioners' contention that the price was impossibly high is difficult to credit. Spotted Tail declared before the negotiations began that he would take six million dollars for the Black Hills—

[21] *New York Herald,* October 7, 1875.

which is exactly what the Commissioners offered. To be sure, as the council progressed the price went up, and it was impossible to establish a cash equivalent for the Indians' final demands. At one point, the figure of seventy million dollars was introduced, which was an obvious absurdity. The reporter who covered the council for the *New York Herald* asserted, however, that what was actually meant was seven million dollars and blamed poor interpretation. He wrote:

> I am assured by the best authority that the Sioux do not know the method of counting 1,000,000 but mistakenly suppose it to be 100,000. Their price of $70,000,000 for the Black Hills, therefore, is in reality but $7,000,000, only $1,000,000 more than the offer of the Commission. A competent interpreter should have rendered their demand according to its real significance in English, and a treaty might have been consummated.[22]

Richard, of course, had notable deficiencies as an interpreter, but it seems unlikely that this would have escaped both Hinman and Beauvais.

Whatever the facts relating to this specific aspect of the price— William Garnett said the Indians "did not know a million from the number of stars in the sky"[23]—one cannot avoid the conclusion that the possibility of an agreement, despite all the palaver, was not as remote as the Commissioners implied. The *Omaha Herald*, a close observer of Sioux affairs, insisted that had the Commissioners paid more attention to Red Cloud—"who has more brains than the whole Commission put together"—and less to other chiefs, failure might have been avoided.[24] As has been shown, the Commission had generally ignored and often irritated Red Cloud, but whether another course would have spelled success no one knows. His influence, despite all comments to the contrary, was still great, but it was uncertain; moreover, his own demands, it must be remembered, were fairly unrealistic. It seems clear, at any rate, that had the Commissioners approached their problem with a little more wisdom and with a little more ability, their chances of success would have been greatly enhanced. After Al Swalm returned to his home in Iowa, he wrote to a friend: "The two months rest I had with the Sx Com have made me feel better than I have for several years. . . ."[25] As far as the nation was concerned, it was a fairly expensive cure.

[22] *Ibid.*, October 16, 1875.

[23] E. S. Ricker, Interview with William Garnett, January 15, 1907, Ricker Mss., Tablet No. 3, Nebraska State Historical Society.

[24] *Omaha Weekly Herald*, October 1, 1875.

[25] Swalm to J. S. Clarkson, October 27, 1875, Clarkson papers, Library of Congress, courtesy Leland Sage.

Trying to salvage something from their failure, the Allison Commission recommended that Congress now take the initiative in all aspects of the country's relations with the Sioux, abolish the existing agencies, and reorganize the whole Sioux service. As far as the Black Hills were concerned, Congress should simply "fix a fair equivalent . . . taking into account all the circumstances surrounding them, and the value of the Hills to the United States," with the whole arrangement being "presented to the Indians as a finality."

The country was surely ready for "finality" in solving the Sioux problem, but wishing for it was one thing, achieving it, quite another.

CHAPTER 12

The Army Takes Over

When the Commissioner of Indian Affairs sat down to pen his annual report for 1875, he had not seen the report of the Allison Commission, but he had been advised of its failure. Nonetheless, he was generally sanguine, and particularly so about the Sioux situation. The Bureau had emerged almost unscathed from the investigation of fraud at the Red Cloud Agency, and the people of Nebraska had been mollified by the willingness of the Red Cloud and Spotted Tail people to cede their hunting rights north of the Platte. To be sure, there remained the Black Hills question, and relocation of the Sioux reservations was inevitable since parts of them were in Nebraska, but the Commissioner was confident that these problems could be resolved without undue difficulty. Both the Red Cloud and Spotted Tail Sioux were peacefully inclined, and even if some of the wilder bands were disposed to make trouble, they would be unable to do so. The events of the past year, he believed, had reinforced the accuracy of a statement in the Commissioner's annual report for 1875, and he thought it worth repeating that

> except under extraordinary provocation, or in circumstances not at all to be apprehended, it is not probable that as many as five hundred Indian warriors will ever again be mustered at one point for a fight; and with the conflicting interests of the different tribes, and the occupation of the intervening country by advancing settlements, such an event as a general Indian war can never again occur in the United States.[1]

[1] Com. of Indian Affairs, *Annual Report*, 1875, p. 4.

Even as the Commissioner wrote these optimistic lines, out in the Sioux country events were rapidly building up to a struggle that would culminate in the greatest disaster ever suffered by the United States Army in its long history of warfare with the Indians. The disaster and much of the struggle are outside the scope of this narrative, yet both grew out of and intimately affected the Government's relations with Red Cloud and all of the agency chiefs.

When the Allison Commission departed, it left in the wake of its ignominious failure a good deal of uncertainty and resentment among both whites and Indians. Prospectors who had remained out of the Hills during the summer in the hope that their entry would soon be legalized now began to invade the region in large numbers despite warnings from Army commanders—largely unenforced—that the old prohibitions still prevailed.[2] The northern Indians left the treaty council disgusted with both the Government and their fellow tribesmen, sure that the whites would try to take the Black Hills and more determined than ever to prevent it; and, as we shall see, with the passing weeks, many of the younger men at the agencies began to feel that both their safety and the preservation of their honor lay in joining the hostiles.

Agent Saville reported from Red Cloud on October 11 that many Indians were leaving the agency and going north, but he thought that their purpose was only to hunt, and he assured his superiors that there appeared to be no hostile feeling.[3] Military commanders, however, were unanimous in the opinion that the situation was dangerous, and in his annual report, issued November 22, Secretary of War Belknap warned that there would be trouble in the Black Hills "unless something is done to obtain possession of that section for the white miners."[4] Soon even the Indian Bureau became convinced that something must be done. Inspector E. C. Watkins, who was sent out to study the situation, reported on November 9 that, in his judgment, as long as any of the Sioux were permitted to remain outside the jurisdiction of the agencies, the task of civilizing those on the reservations would be all but impossible. The wild tribes were small in number, but their very

[2] The *Cheyenne Daily Leader*, November 20, 1875, in noting the departure of a party for the Black Hills, commented: "This is but one of an hundred more similar parties, who have gone to the Black Hills from this city, since the failure of the treaty commission."

[3] J. J. Saville to Com. of Indian Affairs, October 11, 1875, NARS, RG 75, LR, Red Cloud Agency.

[4] 44th Cong., 1st Sess., H. Ex. Doc. 1, Pt. 2.

existence posed a threat to the reservation system, and there was always the danger that they would attract enough restless young men from the agencies to comprise a formidable fighting force. Watkins saw no way to bring these wild Indians into the reservations except through the use of force. They roamed over the best hunting grounds still available in the United States; they were well fed and well armed; their leaders were haughty and independent. He recommended, therefore, that they be turned over to the War Department for appropriate action.[5] The Indian Bureau could not be persuaded to take this step, but on December 6 Commissioner Smith ordered the Sioux and Cheyenne agents to notify the roaming bands that they would have to come into their agencies by December 31 or be considered hostile.[6]

Although the Indian Bureau was heartened for a time, as they had been so frequently in the past, by word that Crazy Horse and Black Twin were coming in,[7] the order had no effect whatever on the hostiles and it was greeted with very little enthusiasm by the Indians at the agencies. E. A. Howard reported from Spotted Tail that his young men argued that if the Indians wanted to fight among themselves, the Government should not interfere,[8] and James S. Hastings, who had succeeded Saville as agent at Red Cloud,[9] had to promise a reward before he could persuade anyone to go north with the message.[10] When January 31 came and went and none of the roaming bands had come in—indeed, some of the couriers had not even returned[11]—the non-reservation Indians were turned over to the War Department.

Lt. Gen. Philip H. Sheridan, commanding the Military Division of

[5] 44th Cong., 1st Sess., H. Ex. Doc. 184, pp. 8–9.

[6] *Ibid.*

[7] J. S. Hastings to Com. of Indian Affairs, January 28, 1876, NARS, RG 75, LR, Red Cloud Agency.

[8] Howard to Com. of Indian Affairs, January 3, 1876, NARS, RG 75, LR, Spotted Tail Agency.

[9] Saville had tendered his resignation while in Washington in 1875, but the Indian Bureau decided to hold it until after the investigation of fraud at the agency had been completed.

[10] Hastings to Com. of Indian Affairs, January 28, 1876, NARS, RG 75, LR, Red Cloud Agency.

[11] The couriers were slowed down by the heavy snows and severe cold. Much has been made of the fact that weather conditions would have prevented the Indians from coming in by January 31 even had they wanted to, but, as Edgar I. Stewart points out, both Sitting Bull and Crazy Horse had moved their camps during the winter, despite the cold and snow (Edgar I. Stewart, *Custer's Luck* [Norman: University of Oklahoma Press, 1955], p. 77).

the Missouri and long an advocate of a punitive expedition as the only means of bringing the non-treaty tribes to terms, assumed command of the operation that at last was to accomplish this task. Recalling the success of his "winter campaign" on the southern plains,[12] he hoped to move against the Indians while the snow was still on the ground and have them rounded up or destroyed before the arrival of spring with its good fighting weather. To accomplish this, he planned a three-pronged pincer movement: one column, under Col. John Gibbon, was to move eastward from Montana; another, under Brig. Gen. Alfred H. Terry, was to advance westward from Fort Abraham Lincoln, and a third, under Brig. Gen. George Crook, was to go north from Fort Fetterman through the Powder River country. Gibbon and Terry were delayed by heavy snows and intense cold—why Sheridan thought conditions in Dakota and Montana would be similar to those in Kansas is difficult to understand—and though Crook was able to get his column off, his field commander, Col. J. J. Reynolds, retreated from an initial victory under circumstances that brought him a court-martial conviction and cast a pall over the whole operation.[13]

Crook, disgruntled at Reynolds' failure but still claiming success, fired off a report to Sheridan which was given wide publicity and which diverted public attention temporarily from the war against the Indians to the old war between the Army and the Indian Bureau. Asserting that Reynolds found Crazy Horse's village to be "a perfect magazine of ammunition, war material and general supplies,"[14] he charged that "Every evidence was found to prove these Indians to be in co-partnership with those at the Red Cloud and Spotted Tail agencies, and that the proceeds of their raids upon the settlements have been taken into those agencies and supplies brought out in return."[15]

Both Howard and Hastings responded vigorously to the charge. Howard, declaring the Spotted Tail Indians to be "one of the best-behaved communities in the country," specifically denied that arms, ammunition, or supplies had found their way from the agency to the hostile camps, and stated further that "very few, if any," of his charges

---

[12] See William H. Leckie, *The Military Conquest of the Southern Plains* (Norman: University of Oklahoma Press, 1963).

[13] Reynolds' battle has been rehashed many times. For a good, brief account, which evaluates conflicting evidence and opinion, see Stewart, *Custer's Luck*, pp. 87–95.

[14] There is a question as to whether the village attacked by Reynolds actually was that of Crazy Horse. See *ibid.*

[15] 44th Cong., 1st Sess., H. Ex. Doc. 184, p. 52.

had been with the northern Indians during the winter; he challenged Crook "to produce some of the abundant evidence which he found."[16] Hastings asserted that "five pounds of powder, twenty of lead, and six boxes of percussion-caps comprised all the ammunition that was found in the abandoned camp." He added fuel to the flames by reporting that a half-breed scout who had been with the expedition had told him "that it was a complete failure," and suggested that while the Red Cloud Indians were generally "in good spirits," Crook's failure might "have a tendency to awaken the old feeling of superiority."[17]

Early in May, Crook, determined to see for himself the attitude of the presumedly peaceable Indians, made a hurried trip to the Red Cloud Agency.[18] He found that the agency Indians were far from peaceable. Red Cloud told him:

> The Gray Fox must understand that the Dakotas and especially the Oga al la-las [*sic*] have many warriors, many guns and ponies. They are brave and ready to fight for their country. They are not afraid of the soldiers nor of their chief. Many braves are ready to meet them. Every lodge will send its young men, and they all will say of the Great Father's dogs, "Let them come!"[19]

These were strange words from a man who was supposed to be completely cowed and who was exercising his influence for peace;[20] and, indeed, they were words such as Red Cloud had not uttered since 1868. The *New York Herald*'s correspondent, who had reported Red Cloud's speech, was sure that his attitude had changed, and he accounted for it in this way:

> Long after the treaty of Fort Laramie, by which the government, with folly ever since condemned, abandoned the chain of military posts erected to protect the emigrant road to Oregon and Montana, Red Cloud . . . and the other warriors concerned in the death of Fetterman's brave men showed outward satisfaction and good will. But the corruption and infamy of agents, the perfidy and vacillating duplicity of government and the selfish and persistent encroachments of citizens have gradually changed the wisest

[16] 44th Cong., 1st Sess., S. Ex. Doc. 52, pp. 11–12.

[17] *Ibid.*, p. 12.

[18] John G. Bourke, *On the Border with Crook* (New York: Charles Scribner's Sons, 1892), pp. 285–286. Bourke asserts that Crook also hoped to obtain scouts, but that the Indians were dissuaded from accepting the assignment by Agent Hastings.

[19] *New York Herald*, June 9, 1876.

[20] E.g., see Stanley Vestal, *Sitting Bull: Champion of the Sioux* (New York: Houghton Mifflin Co., 1932), pp. 141–142: "Red Cloud, who had been in Washington, seen countless white men, and measured their big guns with his fan, despaired of victory; he advised his people to cover their ears and sit still."

spirits of the Sioux people, who before have always counselled peace, into brooding genii of malevolence. Their trust in the paternity of the government has been converted into contempt for its professions and its power. The former have never been fulfilled; the latter never adequately exerted. The relinquishment of forts Reno, Phil Kearny and C. F. Smith flattered their sense of prowess, and the failure to punish subsequent violations of the treaty has belittled the army and its officers in their eyes. The miscarriage of the winter campaign has been to confirm them in their vain glory. They ascribe the hasty withdrawal of General Crook from their country to fear instead of its real cause, the consumption of his supplies and the exhaustion of his troops and animals. The better and more prudent Indians have, if constant rumor and report from the agencies are to be believed, imbibed the mad and desperate spirit of the Northern braves. Red Cloud is the type of the best of his race, and it can be guessed, therefore, how widespread among them is the sentiment betrayed by his half warning speech.[21]

Crook returned to Fort Fetterman convinced that Red Cloud was abetting the hostiles and encouraging the young men of his tribe to go out against the whites.[22] There is considerable evidence to support this view. Red Cloud's son Jack went off to join the hostiles, and the military reported a steady exodus of young braves from agencies. On May 28 Lt. James Egan, returning from a scouting expedition through the Powder River country for Crook, reported that he encountered seven to eight hundred warriors all going north, and that at Red Cloud he learned that the agency was almost deserted.[23] On June 2, Col. Wesley Merritt reported that not five hundred warriors remained at the agency,[24] and on the seventh he stated that he had talked with Captain Jordan and Agent Hastings, and was convinced that fifteen hundred to two thousand Indians had left the reservation since May 10. He found Hastings unwilling to believe that this represented a rush to the hostiles or that Red Cloud was abetting the movement; on the contrary, the agent reported that Red Cloud had assured him that those who had departed had done so to recover stock stolen by the northern Indians![25]

Throughout the period of controversy, Hastings had steadfastly maintained that Red Cloud was peaceable and that departures from the agency were not out of the ordinary. On May 5 he reported, "The

[21] *New York Herald*, June 9, 1876.

[22] *Ibid.*, May 29, 1876.

[23] 44th Cong., 1st Sess., H. Ex. Doc. 184, p. 55.

[24] Telegram, Merritt to P. H. Sheridan, June 2, 1876, NARS, RG 94, Doc. File 4163, Sioux War, 1876.

[25] *Ibid.*, June 7, 1876.

Indians here were never more peaceably disposed,"[26] and on June 5
he assured his superiors that not more than four hundred Cheyennes
and four hundred Sioux had left the agency, including women and
children, and that these were people who left every summer to hunt.
He added: "The Agency Indians are all quiet and show no hostile
feeling. There is no foundation for the outrageous false reports in circulation."[27] In this, Hastings was supported by William Vandevere,
United States Indian Inspector, who on June 30 conferred at the Red
Cloud Agency with Red Cloud, Spotted Tail, and the principal chiefs
of their two tribes. He found them all extremely agreeable. They were
willing to continue negotiations for the sale of the Black Hills, and they
were even willing to move from their present locations to the Missouri
River. Vandevere was certain that the only Indians who had joined
the hostiles in significant numbers were the Cheyennes, who really did
not belong to these agencies anyway. He wrote:

> The Sioux, except a very small portion of reckless young men, have
> removed near agencies and kept peace. . . . I have seen the Indians in
> their camps, both now and when I was here in May. I have met large
> numbers of them at the agency, and have been present on issue day, when
> they were assembled by the thousands. I have questioned the chiefs about
> their young men, and, from all I can see or learn, I am constrained to
> believe the agent correct when he says that nearly the entire force of Sioux
> Indians, old men and young, are at home, and that, with the exception
> of 300 or 400, they have not, at any time within the past several months,
> been absent. If anything, there is a less number of Sioux Indians absent
> from home at present than is usual at this season of the year.[28]

The news had not yet reached the outside world, but five days before
Vandevere's council, out on the Little Big Horn River, Lt. Col.
George A. Custer and his entire command had been wiped out. It is
impossible to say how many Indians were involved in the Custer
fight—estimates run from 2,500 to 9,000—and equally impossible to
determine how many of these were from Red Cloud Agency.[29] Merritt
and Egan had reported the agency almost deserted; Hastings and
Vandevere had asserted that its population was virtually at full
strength. Col. R. S. Mackenzie, who made "a careful count" of the

[26] Telegram, Hastings to Com. of Indian Affairs, NARS, RG 75, LR, Red Cloud
Agency.

[27] *Ibid.*, June 5, 1876.

[28] *New York Herald*, July 15, 1876. See also *New York Times*, July 15, 1876; *Omaha
Weekly Herald*, July 21, 1876.

[29] Stewart, *Custer's Luck*, pp. 307–312, discusses the conflicting evidence.

Indians at Red Cloud Agency on September 1, reported a total of 4,760. General Sheridan though this to be "at least 3,000 less than the number alleged to have been there before the count,"[30] but the Allison Commission, the year before, had reported a total of 9,339 residing at the agency. Even though these two counts do not agree, it seems safe to assume that there were only about half as many Indians at the agency in September, 1876, as there were in September, 1875. There had been a similar, although not quite so extensive, exodus from the Spotted Tail Agency.[31]

Of course, not all the Indians who were absent from the agencies had joined the hostiles; some undoubtedly had gone out to hunt, as Hastings asserted. Yet the sum of the evidence from that fateful spring indicates that many of the restless spirits from the agencies had joined their hostile brethren. If you accept the upper estimate of hostile strength (eight hundred),[32] Edgar Stewart put it well when he wrote: "All the malcontents of the prairies were there. In addition, there were hundreds of young men who had spent the winter at the various agencies and streamed out to join the hostiles as soon as the grass was up in the spring and the news of Crook's fiasco on the Powder had emboldened them to the point where they felt that they could safely defy the government."[33]

There was a strong feeling that the hostiles had been supplied and armed from the agencies; the Secretary of War flatly asserted as much in his annual report for 1876,[34] and the newspapers generally seem to have accepted this view. Without a doubt, some agency supplies found their way to the hostiles,[35] but it is easy to overemphasize their

[30] Telegram, Sheridan to W. T. Sherman, September 2, 1876, NARS, RG 94, Doc. File 4163, Sioux War, 1876.

[31] Carl Coke Rister, *Border Command: General Phil Sheridan in the West* (Norman: University of Oklahoma Press, 1944), pp. 210–211, reports that there were five thousand Indians at Spotted Tail on September 1, 1876; the Allison Commission reported eight thousand in September, 1875.

[32] Stewart, *Custer's Luck*, p. 82. This was the estimate accepted by the military; the agents felt that it should be higher.

[33] *Ibid.*, p. 309.

[34] Secretary of War, *Annual Report*, 1876, p. 6, 44th Cong., 1st Sess., H. Ex. Doc. 1, Serial 1742.

[35] George W. Colhoff, who was a clerk at the Red Cloud Agency at the time of the Custer battle, asserted that a trader named Boucher supplied the Indians with arms and ammunition in return for rations, which, in turn, the Indians were drawing on the basis of an excessive enumeration (E. S. Ricker, Interview with George W. Colhoff, November 22, 1906, Ricker Mss., Tablet No. 17, Nebraska State Historical Society).

importance. The Red Cloud Agency was critically short of rations in the spring of 1876, and while this condition undoubtedly inspired desertions it hardly served to make the agency an effective source of supply.[36] Moreover, the sale of arms and ammunition to the Indians at the agency had been stopped in January.[37] Undoubtedly, the hostiles did get some supplies, including arms and ammunition, from the agencies, but (to quote Edgar Stewart's invaluable work again) in the Custer fight "Many of the Sioux and Cheyennes were using bows and arrows, both from necessity and from choice. While a number of them had the latest improved guns, the majority had very inferior guns or nothing more than the usual bow and arrows and a war club."[38]

There still remains the question of Red Cloud's attitude and influence, and in many respects this is the most difficult one to answer. Was he for peace or war? Did the young warriors run off to join the hostiles against his wishes or with his encouragement? Agent Hastings consistently represented him as being peaceably inclined, yet his remarks to General Crook—the only direct statement we have from him during the weeks leading up to the Custer massacre—were anything but peaceable. Moreover, his own son Jack was in the Big Horn fight, and in the absence of evidence to the contrary it seems not unreasonable to assume that he participated with parental approval. Finally, in view of Red Cloud's consistent record of opposition to the policy in which he usually was forced to participate—and again, in the absence of evidence to the contrary—it might be assumed that, whether he had hope of success or not, he did not oppose this effort to upset the system by force.

II

Whatever the precise relationship of the agency Indians to the hostiles, the Custer massacre dramatized the shortcomings of the

[36] Early in May, Hastings had branded a report from Crook that the Indians at the agency were in a starving condition as having "no foundation whatever" (Telegram, Hastings to Com. of Indian Affairs, May 5, 1876, NARS, RG 75, LR, Red Cloud Agency). On June 30, however, Vandevere reported that supplies at the agency "were now nearly exhausted" (*New York Herald*, July 15, 1876).

[37] Hastings had vigorously protested this action, saying, "I am entirely at a loss to know why such an order should be issued at the present time as the Indians here are perfectly quiet and have evinced no disposition to be otherwise" (Hastings to Com. of Indian Affairs, January 24, 1876, NARS, RG 75, LR, Red Cloud Agency).

[38] *Custer's Luck*, pp. 455–456.

Indian Bureau's policies toward the Sioux and convinced the country that a change was needed. As *The Nation* put it:

> The missionary expedient may be said to have failed. . . . The necessity with which the Commission has since found itself of handing over Sitting Bull and his men to the secular arm, marks with painful emphasis the inadequacy of its machinery, particularly when we find that our troops are shot down with the newest breech-loaders furnished at the agencies. . . . If anything can deepen the absurdity of our Indian System in the eyes of the public, this fact surely should do so. . . .[39]

On May 29, General Sheridan had urged that the agency Indians as well as the hostiles be turned over to the Army. He repeated his request on July 18, and this time it found a favorable reception. On the twenty-second, General Sherman telegraphed:

> Mr. Chandler [Secretary of the Interior Zachary Chandler] says that you may at once assume control over all the agencies in the Sioux country. He wants for good reasons both of the agents at Red Cloud and Spotted Tail removed and their duties to be performed by the commanding officers of the garrisons; also that no issues be made at any of the agencies unless the Indians be actually present; that all who are now or may hereafter go outside of the reservation be treated as you propose as enemies, disarmed and their ponies and guns taken away. . . .[40]

On the same day, telegrams went out from the Commissioner of Indian Affairs to Hastings and Howard, ordering them to turn their agencies over to the commanding officers at Camp Robinson and Camp Sheridan, respectively, and advising them that their services would cease with the transfer.[41] A minor hitch developed when someone recalled that under the law of 1870, which the peace advocates had pushed through Congress to prevent President Grant from appointing Army officers as Indian agents, the officers concerned could not officially assume charge of the agencies without forfeiting their commissions. To get around this, it was provided that the officers would take charge of the agencies on a temporary basis and that new agents would be appointed to act under military control.[42]

There was another and more serious problem. The Indians at Spotted Tail seemed reconciled to the military takeover, but there was considerable uncertainty about those at Red Cloud, and Captain

[39] *The Nation*, XXIII (July 13, 1876), 21–22.
[40] Telegram, Sherman to Sheridan, July 22, 1876, NARS, RG 94, Doc. File 4163, Sioux War, 1876.
[41] Telegrams in *ibid.*
[42] Telegram, Sherman to Sheridan, July 25, 1876, *ibid.*

Jordan, commanding officer at Camp Robinson, had only four companies of infantry. Sheridan had proposed to arrest and disarm all Indians as they returned to the agency, but he decided that until the arrival of Col. R. S. Mackenzie, who was being sent from Fort Sill with six companies of cavalry, it would be best to have Jordan sit tight, refrain from trying to make any arrests, and try to keep the Indians reasonably content by feeding them as liberally as possible.[43]

While the Army was marking time, Congress, fired up by the Custer massacre, decided to take the Sioux problem into its own hands. Following the advice of the Allison Commission,[44] on August 15 it enacted legislation directing the President to appoint a commission, not to negotiate with the Sioux but to hand them an ultimatum. They were to be informed that no further appropriations would be made for their subsistence unless they would agree to relinquish all claims to land outside their permanent reservation as established by the Treaty of 1868, and, in addition, all of the reservation lying west of the 103rd meridian (in other words, the Black Hills). Moreover, the Sioux were to permit up to three roads ("Wagon or other") through their reservation, and were to receive their rations and other supplies, as provided by the treaty, only at such places on the Missouri River as the President should designate.[45] The Commission, appointed by the President on August 24, consisted of George W. Manypenny, Columbus, Ohio; Henry C. Bullis, Decorah, Iowa; Newton Edmunds, Yankton, Dakota Territory; Bishop Henry B. Whipple, Fairbault, Minnesota; A. G. Boone, Denver; A. S. Gaylord, Washington; and General H. H. Sibley, St. Paul. General Sibley declined to serve because of ill health, and Dr. J. W. Daniels, former Red Cloud agent, was appointed in his place. Samuel D. Hinman was to serve as official interpreter.[46] Some of the Commissioners brought to their assignment considerable experience in dealing with the Sioux. Manypenny had been Commissioner

[43] Telegram, Sheridan to Sherman, July 30, 1876, NARS, RG 94, Doc. File 4163, Sioux War, 1876. A number of Oglalas, including Jack Red Cloud, slipped back to the agency during this period (*ibid.*, August 3, 1876). Also, it might be noted that the Army had difficulty in providing rations for the Indians at the agency. On July 27, Sheridan complained that only corn and flour were available for issue, and that unless beef could be provided, there would be trouble.

[44] See above, p. 213.

[45] U.S. *Statutes at Large*, XIX, 254–264.

[46] Mary Jane Bowler, "The Sioux Indians and the United States Government, 1862–1878" (Master's thesis, Washington University, St. Louis, 1944), p. 187; see also 44th Cong., 2d Sess., H. Ex. Doc. 1, Pt. 5, p. 393, and 45th Cong., 2d Sess., H. Ex. Doc. 1, Pt. 5, p. 413.

of Indian Affairs, Edmunds had negotiated the treaties of 1865, and Bishop Whipple had long been active on behalf of the western Indians—the *New York Times* stated that "he has done more toward ameliorating their condition than any other missionary excepting Father DeSmet."[47] Possibly now the problem could be solved once and for all.

On August 28, the Commissioners gathered in Omaha for an organizational meeting, electing Manypenny chairman.[48] They arrived at the Red Cloud Agency on September 6, having been escorted on the two-day march from Fort Laramie by a company of cavalry under Captain Egan.[49] Things got off to a good start. Red Cloud welcomed the Commissioners warmly. "We are glad to see you," he told them. You have come to save us from death."[50] Moreover, the Commissioners were able to meet with the chiefs on the day after their arrival—unusual speed for negotiations with the Sioux.

Approximately one hundred and fifty Indians gathered for the first session on September 7, including Red Cloud, Red Dog, Old-Man-Afraid-of-His-Horse, Young-Man-Afraid, Little Wound, and the Oglala Sitting Bull. William Garnett, William Rowland, Leon Palladay, and Todd Randall were on hand to act as assistant interpreters. Bishop Whipple opened the proceedings with a prayer, and then Manypenny laid down the conditions established by Congress.[51] He further announced that the Commissioners had been given authority, within these conditions, to "devise a plan to save their people from death and lead them to civilization." The plan, obviously reflecting the missionary zeal of the Commissioners, for the most part was little more than a re-hash of the conventional Indian Bureau program for the Sioux, through which, it was hoped, they would be led to ways of industry, education, and morality. Aside from a strongly worded reminder to the Sioux that they would have to do as they were told if they were to continue to receive rations and annuities, the only new feature of the "plan" related to the question of location. Congress had specified that the Sioux were to receive rations and annuities only at a point or points on the Missouri

[47] *New York Times*, September 18, 1876.

[48] "Report of the Sioux Commission," 44th Cong., 2d Sess., S. Ex. Doc. 9, pp. 5–18. Unless otherwise indicated, information relating to the work of the Commission is taken from this report.

[49] *New York Times*, September 18, 1876.

[50] This is a far cry from his bellicose speech to Crook; whether it indicated a change of heart or merely a change in tactics, it is difficult to say.

[51] *New York Times*, September 10, 1876.

River to be designated by the President. Manypenny, however, told the chiefs:

> The President believes that the only country where they can hope for permanent improvement is the Indian Territory, inasmuch as the removal of the Indians to the Missouri River will necessarily be temporary. If they shall agree to go directly to the Indian Territory next season, they shall be permitted to remain at the Agency until that time. But before any such removal from their reservation they may select a delegation of five or more from each band to visit the country proposed for them and satisfy themselves of its desirability.[52]

After Manypenny had laid down the terms which the Sioux must accept, both Bishop Whipple and Commissioner Boone lectured the chiefs at some length. The chiefs agreed that they would study the proposal, and Red Cloud suggested that this would be a good time to have the feast the Commissioners had promised. The feast was ordered, but not before the Commissioners warned the chiefs that they would have to have their answer soon because they had no time to lose.[53]

The chiefs then went off to Chadron Creek to council among themselves. The Commissioners, assuming that a week would be long enough for them to come to a conclusion, announced that a second council would be held on the thirteenth. When none of the chiefs appeared on that day, the meeting was put off until the fifteenth.[54] As it turned out, it was the nineteenth before the group could be assembled for a second meeting, and nothing really was accomplished on that day. Red Cloud said that his people were willing to give up the Black Hills, and also to have their young men take a journey to see the country spoken of by the Commission—"if they report it a good country his people will so consider it; if they report it a bad country they will consider it bad." He then led Daniels, Howard, and Joseph Bisonette to a place among the chiefs and told the Commissioners that he wanted them to go south with his young men; he also wanted F. C. Boucher, Antoine Janis, Bill Rowland, Hank Clifford, Todd Randall, Frank Salway, and Nelse Moran to go as interpreters.[55]

Despite Red Cloud's conciliatory attitude, it soon became obvious that the question was far from settled. Young-Man-Afraid-of-His-Horse made a speech saying he was raised in this country and he did

---

[52] *Ibid.* The Commissioners' report contains no indication that this proposition was made to the Sioux.

[53] *Ibid.*

[54] *Omaha Weekly Herald*, September 22, 1876.

[55] *New York Times*, September 22, 1876; *Cheyenne Daily Leader*, September 22, 1876.

not want to leave it; he was willing to have the young men take a look at the southern country, but before signing away the Black Hills he wanted to talk to the Great Father. Red Dog said essentially the same thing. At this point, Bishop Whipple reminded the chiefs that the Great Father required them to sign a paper binding themselves to go to the Missouri River if they did not go to the Indian Territory, and he urged them to do so at once. Gaylord followed with the same advice. While he was talking, however, the Oglala Sitting Bull, who in Washington the year before had been given a handsome rifle by President Grant for his friendship to the whites, broke up the conference by shouting that the Indians wanted to remain where they were, that the document was all foolishness, and that most of their people were in the north and there were not enough present to transact such business. In great fury, he ordered the Sioux to leave the stockade where the conference was being held, and apparently they all followed his command.[56]

This unexplained action on the part of so conspicuous a friend of the whites—William Garnett later said that "the dose in this treaty infuriated him [Sitting Bull]"[57]—temporarily put a damper on the proceedings. But Sitting Bull left the agency and went off to the north (where he was subsequently killed),[58] and by the next day the rest of the chiefs had concluded that they would agree to the demands made upon them. When they learned of this decision about ten-thirty in the morning, the Commissioners told the Indians that they wanted the chief and two head men of each band to be prepared to sign the paper at three o'clock in the afternoon; meanwhile they would have a feast prepared for all the Indians at the agency.

Despite the feast, it was a sombre ceremony. Crow refused to sign altogether; Fire Thunder held his blanket over his eyes and put his mark to the paper blindfolded. Almost every chief made a speech before he signed the document, and the speeches indicated clearly either that they did not understand the terms of the agreement or had no intention of abiding by them. Young-Man-Afraid commented, "I give notice it will take me a long time to learn to labor, and I expect the President will feed me for 100 years, and perhaps a great deal longer." Red Cloud, described as being "grimly meditative . . . his treacherously marked face . . . [betraying] a sullen discontent not consistent with his solid participation in the agreement," said:

[56] *Ibid.*; E. S. Ricker, Interview with William Garnett, January 15, 1907, Ricker Mss., Tablet No. 2.

[57] Ricker, Interview with Garnett.

[58] *Ibid.*

I am a friend of the President, and you men who have come here to see me are chief men and men of influence. You have come here with the words of the Great Father, therefore, because I am his friend I have said yes to what he has said to me, and I suppose that makes you happy. I don't like it that we have a soldier here to give us food; it makes our children's hearts go back and forth. I wish to have Major Howard [E. A. Howard, recently dismissed agent for Spotted Tail] for my agent, and I want to have you send word to Washington so he can come here very soon. If my young men come back and say that the country is bad it will not be possible for me to go there. As for the Missouri River country I think if my people should move there they would all be destroyed. There are a great many bad men there and bad whiskey; therefore I don't want to go there. A great many of my white relatives have no money. If they are employed to go to the Indian Territory to look at the country I hope they will be paid out of the money of the Great Father that you have with you. . . .[59]

Apparently the Commissioners made no effort to correct the misunderstandings reflected in the speeches delivered at the signing ceremony. On the contrary, if William Garnett, who was there as an interpreter, is to be believed, Hinman deliberately misled the Indians by assuring them that provisions of the agreement to which they objected would be removed.[60] Although earlier in the proceedings the Commissioners had been careful to explain that there could be no deviation from the original proposal, once they got the chiefs in a signing mood their only interest seemed to be to collect their "x's" and get away. They went over to the Spotted Tail Agency the next day and after two days of palaver secured a set of signatures there. Then, as quickly as possible, they visited the Standing Rock, Cheyenne River, Crow Creek, Lower Brulé, and Santee agencies. Everywhere they met with success. They reported to the Commissioner of Indian Affairs: "We finished our labors in the Indian country with our hearts full of gratitude to God, who had guarded and protected us, and had directed our labors to a successful issue."

Whether God had had anything to do with it or not—and the Indians would have been hard-pressed to recognize the influence of their Great Spirit in the negotiations—the Commissioners *had* been successful. The Black Hills question was settled, at least on paper. Moreover, in view of the failure of the Allison Commission just a year before and the troubles that had transpired since that failure, it all seemed so easy. One wonders why.

[59] *New York Herald*, September 23, 1876.
[60] Ricker, Interview with Garnett.

No simple answer is available, but a number of possibilities suggest themselves. In the first place, the Commissioners completely ignored Article 12 of the Treaty of 1868 (the article which had so bothered the Allison Commission, providing that no treaty for the cession of any part of the reservation could be valid "unless executed and signed by at least three-fourths of all the Adult male Indians, occupying or interested in the same") and had settled for signatures from the chiefs and two head men of each tribe. The Sioux would argue later that this invalidated the agreement,[61] but after the Custer massacre neither Congress nor the country was prepared to be bound by technicalities; moreover, it could be argued that in the eight troubled years since the signing of the treaty, it had been broken so frequently by both parties as to be little more than a scrap of paper. In the second place, there is every evidence that the Indians really did not understand what was in the agreement. Red Cloud later said that he did not understand that he was signing away the Black Hills.[62] He was an old hand at not understanding what he had signed, but the evidence from the last day of the conference at his agency certainly indicates that if the Indians were not misled, they were seriously confused. Finally, the agency Indians were desperate. Caught between the Army on one side and the hostiles on the other, they knew that they had no choice but to make the best of life at the agencies, and when representatives of the Great Father came with a paper which they must sign or have their rations cut off, they signed.

The Commissioners included in their report a long disquisition on the shortcomings of the nation's past Indian policy with particular emphasis upon the evils of Army administration of Indian affairs, and then wrote:

> In conclusion, your commission respectfully urge that every effort shall be made to secure the ratification and faithful fulfillment of the agreement which we have made by direction of the Government with this hapless people. We entered upon this work by direction of the Government with the full knowledge that those who had heretofore made treaties with these Indians had seen their promises broken. We accepted the trust as a solemn duty to our country, to the perishing, and to God. The Indians trusted us. . . . If we sow broken faith, injustice, and wrong, we shall reap in the future as we have reaped in the past, a harvest of sorrow and blood. We are not simply dealing with a poor perishing race; we are dealing with God. We cannot afford to delay longer fulfilling our bounden duty to those

[61] See below, pp. 337–338.
[62] Ricker, Interview with Garnett.

from whom we have taken that country, the possession of which has placed us in the forefront of the nation's of the earth. We make it our boast that our country is the home of the oppressed of all lands. Dare we forget that there are also those whom we have made homeless, and to whom we are bound to give protection and care? . . .

A great crisis has arisen in Indian affairs. The wrongs of the Indians are admitted by all. Thousands of the best men in the land feel keenly the nation's shame. They look to Congress for redress. Unless immediate and appropriate legislation is made for the protection and government of the Indians, they must perish. Our country must forever bear the disgrace and suffer the retribution of its wrong-doing. Our children's children will tell the sad story in hushed tones, and wonder how their fathers dare so to trample on justice and trifle with God. . . .

One might wonder whether the Commissioners' strictures applied in part at least to their own work; but Indian affairs, particularly where Red Cloud was concerned, were always a blend of fine words and faltering deeds—and out on the reservation there would still be faltering deeds.

III

The Army had little confidence in or patience with the activities of the Sioux Commission. When Congress was considering the bill which would create that body, General Sherman told the Commissioner of Indian Affairs that he "would not for one moment" entertain the idea of an armistice in the struggle with the Sioux.[63] Col. Ranald Mackenzie, who arrived at Camp Robinson with six companies of cavalry late in August, proposed to restrict the Commissioners from dealing at all with the hostiles. Sherman was sympathetic, but he telegraphed that the Secretary of War was opposed to any effort on Mackenzie's part to interfere with the activities of the Commissioners. He was simply to extend them protection and help: "If they succeed, it is well; if they fail, they cannot charge us."[64]

Mackenzie carried out his orders, but as soon as the Commission departed he sent a letter to General Crook, who was at Fort Laramie, asserting that the Commissioners were deluded if they thought the Red Cloud and Spotted Tail Indians would ever become peaceful

[63] Telegram, W. T. Sherman to J. Q. Smith, August 8, 1876, NARS, RG 94, Doc. File 4163, Sioux War, 1876.

[64] Telegram, Sherman to P. H. Sheridan, September 4, 1876, *ibid.*

agricultural people. He declared that both chiefs were still actively aiding the hostiles and that they had signed the agreement merely to gain time. He thought it would be a sad mistake if any of their Indians were allowed to "leave this country with any civil officers of the government to look at the Indian territory, or for any other purpose." Moreover, in view of the situation, he believed himself "justified in preventing at this time, any departure of any Indians under the instruction of any civil officer, no matter what his rank, or any civil official from exercising any authority so far as regard to these Indians, or hold any communication with them." Crook wholeheartedly approved the letter, which he forwarded to Sheridan on September 30. On the same date, Sheridan, who had been at Fort Laramie while the Commission was at Red Cloud, had written Sherman: "The time for transferring the Sioux to the Indian Territory has not come yet, but the time for disarming and dismounting and putting them all on the Missouri River has come." Completely concurring with the views in Mackenzie's letter, he forwarded it to Sherman, asserting, "The action of the Commission can have no other result than to cripple, as it has already done, the action of the military and to produce confusion and calamity." Sherman forwarded the file to the Secretary of War with his full approval, and the latter sent it over to the Secretary of the Interior.[65]

President Grant, however, had approved the Sioux Commission's recommendations, and no action was taken to prevent the visit to the Indian Territory. Daniels and Boone took a delegation of Oglalas and Brulés, including Spotted Tail, south to look over the country. They did not like it, but, as it turned out, even had they found it desirable they would not have been permitted to remove there; Congress, under pressure from railroad and other interests who wanted Indian Territory opened for white settlement, deleted that part of the agreement which provided for removal of the Sioux to the area.[66] Meanwhile, at Red Cloud Agency, the Army went ahead with its plans to disarm and dismount the agency Indians as the best means of isolating them

[65] Mackenzie's letter, with endorsements, is in NARS, RG 94, Doc. File 4163, Sioux War, 1876. The correspondence also is published in George W. Manypenny, *Our Indian Wards* (Cincinnati: Robert Clarke & Co., 1880), pp. 342–372, along with a scathing denunciation of military interference with action which had the President's approval, and a recital of the Army's shortcomings in dealing with the Indians.

[66] Bowler, "The Sioux Indians and the United States Government, 1862–1878" pp. 194–195.

from the hostiles, and General Crook went to Camp Robinson to direct the operation.[67]

Crook remained convinced of Red Cloud's opposition to the Government. The chief was encamped on Chadron Creek, about thirty miles from the agency, and the military were sure that he was in constant communication with the hostiles. Red Leaf, living about a mile from Red Cloud, was another object of suspicion. Deciding that the two men must be located where their movements could be watched, Mackenzie sent William Garnett out to tell Red Cloud that he must move his people into the agency or their rations would be stopped and that ultimately they would be moved in by force. Red Cloud replied that the soldiers could have the buildings at the agency, but that Colonel Mackenzie should send his rations to him on Chadron Creek. When their rations were suspended and the Indians still did not come in, Crook, who had planned to delay direct action until Col. Wesley Merritt's command arrived, decided to act before the bands could move farther away and perhaps join the hostiles.

Under cover of darkness on Sunday evening, October 22, Colonel Mackenzie left Camp Robinson for Chadron Creek with eight companies of cavalry. Enroute, he was joined by Maj. Frank North, North's brother Luther, and forty-two Pawnee Scouts who had been hastily summoned from their camp near Clifford's ranch on the Niobrara River. When about four miles from Chadron Creek, Mackenzie divided his command, sending Maj. George A. Gordon with one battalion of cavalry and half of the Pawnees to Red Leaf's camp, and Capt. Clarence Mauck with the other battalion and the remainder of the Pawnees to deal with Red Cloud. Mackenzie himself accompanied Mauck. At dawn, the Indians in both camps found themselves completely surrounded, and despite Red Cloud's earlier bravado surrendered without firing a shot; perhaps they sensed the utter hopelessness

---

[67] There are numerous accounts of this operation. I am relying primarily upon the following accounts, which have not been used hitherto: Telegram, Sheridan to Sherman, October 24, 1876; Brig. Gen. George Crook to AAG, Military Division of the Missouri, October 30, 1876, NARS, RG 94, Doc. File 4163, Sioux War, 1876 (also published in *New York Herald*, November 10, 1876); Ricker, Interview with Garnett, January 10, 1907. For the participation of the Pawnee Scouts, see Donald F. Danker, ed., *Man of the Plains: Recollections of Luther North, 1856–1882* (Lincoln: University of Nebraska Press, 1961), pp. 194–236; and George Bird Grinnell, *Two Great Scouts and Their Pawnee Battalion* (Cleveland: Arthur H. Clark Co., 1928), pp. 253–256. Of interest also is "Council at Sites of Surround," *Nebraska History*, XV (October–December, 1934), 279–287.

of their situation. While the soldiers disarmed the warriors, the Pawnee
Scouts rounded up their horses. The Indians were well mounted—
Major North collected 722 horses in all—but Crook's fears that they
were well armed proved groundless; apparently they had only a few
old guns and pistols and an insignificant quantity of ammunition.[68]
As soon as the women had the tipis pulled down and the plunder packed,
the troops started the Indians on their way to the agency. The women
were given horses with which to pack the camp, and a few of the old
and feeble were permitted to ride, but the warriors, stripped of their
guns, were forced to walk. When they were caught by darkness, the
women were allowed to stay on the prairie for the night, but the men
were marched on to Camp Robinson and jailed until the women came
in the next day. After they had set up camp near Robinson, they were
forced to take down their tipis and move over to the agency. The
horses they had been permitted to use on the move in were now taken
away. Colonel Mackenzie gave the hated Pawnees a mount apiece,
and Major North took the rest of the herd off to Cheyenne, where they
were sold.[69]

The Army had not yet done with the degraded and demoralized
Sioux. General Crook called the men together in the stockade. There
was no negotiation this time, no prayer, no palaver. The Gray Eagle
simply told Red Cloud that he was no longer to be chief of the Oglalas.
Spotted Tail was to be chief of all the Indians at the Red Cloud Agency
as well as of those at his own.

Red Cloud could hardly believe that the Great Father would permit
him to be treated so badly. "What have I done," he asked, "that I
should receive such treatment from him whom I thought my friend?"[70]

[68] In his official reports, Crook nowhere specified the type or quantity of arms found.
He told a reporter that the troops had captured "seventy or eighty" guns (*New York
Herald*, November 4, 1876). This estimate is from Manypenny, *Our Indian Wards*,
pp. 319–320. Manypenny called the action "a piece of vandalism."

[69] Members of the Sioux Commission were highly critical of the action by which
the Sioux were deprived of their ponies. Prodded by friends of the Indians, the Commissioner of Indian Affairs in 1883–1884 undertook an investigation of the matter and
recommended that $28,200 be appropriated to compensate the Indians for their
losses, the money to be used to purchase cattle, "reserving therefrom, however, a
sufficient amount to be used in the purchase of two horses for the individual use of
Red Cloud." In 1889, Congress appropriated $28,200 to compensate the Red Cloud
and Red Leaf bands for their ponies (Manypenny, *Our Indian Wards*, pp. 307–320;
49th Cong., 1st Sess., H. Ex. Doc. 35, Red Cloud and Red Leaf Bands of Sioux
Indians, January 20, 1886; U.S. *Statutes at Large*, XXV, 899).

[70] Manypenny, *Our Indian Wards*, p. 318.

It was the loss of his horses which Red Cloud felt most keenly. Despite his long-standing rivalry with Spotted Tail, he expressed no particular concern over the Brulé's designation as the chief of his people. As he told a reporter, Spotted Tail could never be chief of the Oglalas except in name. Regardless of what the Government said, his people would follow him.[71] Although much has been made of Crook's action,[72] Red Cloud's confidence in his own position among his people may have been justified. As William Garnett noted, Crook's deposition "little affected him, much less affected the Indians who acknowledged his chieftainship which was not denied in any quarter among them."[73] Joseph Bisonette likewise felt that Crook had made a mistake, asserting that Red Cloud's influence was strong among his people and that Spotted Tail could never take charge of both agencies.[74] It may well be that Crook had actually strengthened Red Cloud's position among his people. In any event, Spotted Tail never attempted to act for the Oglalas, and in a short time Red Cloud had resumed his position of leadership, in name as well as in fact.

Crook, however, was well pleased with himself. In his initial telegraphic report of the dismounting, he told Sheridan, "I feel that this is the first gleam of daylight we have had in this business."[75] Sheridan was equally sanguine. "Go right on disarming and dismounting every Indian connected with the Red Cloud Agency," he replied, "and if Spotted Tail and his Indians do not come up squarely, dismount and disarm them. There must be no half-way work in this matter. All Indians out there must be on our side without question, or else on the side of the hostiles."[76] The disarming and dismounting of Red Cloud's and Red Leaf's bands did have a salutary effect upon the Oglalas,[77] but,

[71] *Cheyenne Daily Leader*, January 17, 1877.

[72] E.g., George E. Hyde, *Red Cloud's Folk* (Norman: University of Oklahoma Press, 1957), pp. 285–286; Stanley Vestal, *Warpath and Council Fire* (New York: Random House, 1948), pp. 256–257; Bourke, *On the Border with Crook*, pp. 387–388.

[73] Ricker, Interview with Garnett.

[74] Bisonette to A. S. Gaylord [n.d.], NARS, RG 75, LR, Spotted Tail Agency.

[75] Telegram, Crook to Sheridan, October 23, 1876, NARS, RG 94, Doc. File 4163, Sioux War, 1876.

[76] Telegram, Sheridan to Crook, October 25, 1876, *ibid.*

[77] Bisonette (above, n. 74), while criticizing the "deposing" of Red Cloud, had admitted that the action had a "good effect on all the Indians." Lt. Col. J. S. Mason, CO at Camp Robinson, reported on November 16: "Since the disarming and dismounting of Red Cloud's and Red Leaf's bands . . . the Indians at Red Cloud and Spotted Tail Agencies have been extremely quiet and obedient and I apprehend no trouble in keeping them in a proper state of subjugation . . ." (Letter to AAG, Military Division of the Missouri, November 16, 1876, NARS, RG 94, Doc. File 4163, Sioux War, 1876).

despite Sheridan's urging, Crook did not pursue the practice further. The rest of the Oglalas, and other bands at the agency, he concluded, were basically loyal, and to take away their guns and their ponies would serve only to alienate them. Instead, he would give them an opportunity to prove their loyalty by serving as scouts in his forthcoming campaign against Crazy Horse. Such service, he solemnly assured Sheridan, would be "the entering wedge by which the tribal organization is broken up, making way for civilizing and christianizing influences":

> As a soldier the Indian wears the uniform, draws rations and pay, and in all respects on equal footing with the white man. It demonstrates to his simple mind in the most positive manner that we have no prejudice against him on account of his race, and that while he behaves himself he will be treated in the same manner as white man. . . .[78]

Whether or not Crook was correct in his estimate of the influence of the military life upon the red men, he was highly successful in recruiting them as scouts. He enrolled approximately four hundred from the Red Cloud Agency and another hundred from Spotted Tail.[79] When Colonel Merritt's cavalry arrived, he was all set for a final assault on Crazy Horse.

IV

After the dispersal of Sitting Bull's band by Col. Nelson A. Miles, the capture of the Northern Cheyennes and Crazy Horse's Oglalas was all that remained before the Sioux war could be brought to a close. As Crook was about to launch the expedition, Sheridan telegraphed Sherman that if Crook should be successful, "which I do not doubt, the Sioux War and all other Indian wars of any magnitude in this country will be at an end forever."[80] Sherman's reply was equally optimistic. The Sioux problem, he predicted, soon "would reduce itself to a simple question of feeding them till they learn to raise some food for themselves. Meanwhile miners and settlers will fill up north of Laramie and about Black Hills so that these troublesome Indians would be hemmed in and would gradually become like those in Minnesota."[81]

[78] Crook to AAG, Military Division of the Missouri, October 30, 1876, NARS, RG 94, Doc. File 4163, Sioux War, 1876.

[79] Ricker, Interview with Garnett.

[80] Telegram, Sheridan to Sherman, November 9, 1876, NARS, RG 75, Indian Office, Dakota.

[81] Telegram, Sherman to Sheridan, November 10, 1876, NARS, RG 94, LR, Military Division of the Missouri.

The operation proved to be more difficult to execute than to plan. Colonel Mackenzie had little trouble with the Cheyenne Village on the Crazy Woman Fork of the Powder River,[82] but Crazy Horse, dividing his people into small bands, led Crook on a merry chase all over the Powder River country. After being struck by a blizzard on Christmas Day,[83] Crook telegraphed from his camp on the Belle Fourche:

> Recent operations have so stirred up the Indians that it is useless to try to catch them with this command. The worn out condition of all the citizen and army transportation in this part of the country makes it an impossibility to keep this command in the field any longer. Will start back for Fetterman in the morning and expect to arrive there in about ten days. . . .[84]

From Fort Fetterman, Crook went on to Cheyenne, where he reported more fully on his failure, complaining particularly about the lack of forage and the meagre appropriation allowed him for transportation.[85] After reading this report, Sherman, impatient with the whole operation, suggested that one officer should be placed in charge of all operations against the Sioux. He thought Colonel Miles was "in the best position and possessed of most mental and physical vigor to exercise this command." Perhaps Miles would be able to get the whole thing cleaned up by June.[86]

Even before Sherman had written, Colonel Miles had gone far toward achieving this objective. After defeating a remnant of Sitting Bull's band near the head of the Ridgewater on December 18,[87] he led the 5th Infantry through sub-zero temperatures in search of Crazy Horse. On New Year's Day he came upon the great war chief's village, some six hundred lodges of Oglalas and Cheyennes stretched out for three miles along the valley of the Tongue River, just below Hanging Woman's Creek. Fighting skirmishes on January 1, 3, and 7, and a five-hour battle on the eighth, Miles, although outnumbered, drove the Indians through the canyons of the Wolf Mountains toward the Big Horn. He was kept from further pursuit by a shortage of supplies and the worn-down condition of his animals, but he was sure that Crazy Horse was desperate: while his warriors had arms, they had fought

---

[82] Telegram, Crook to Sheridan, November 28, 1876, *ibid.*

[83] Bourke, *On the Border with Crook*, p. 395.

[84] Telegram, Crook to Sheridan, December 26, 1876, NARS, RG 94, Doc. File 4163, Sioux War, 1876.

[85] Crook to AAG, Military Division of the Missouri, January 8, 1877, *ibid.*

[86] Sherman to Sheridan, February 2, 1877, *ibid.*

[87] Nelson A. Miles to A. H. Terry, December 20, 1876, copy in NARS, RG 75, Indian Office, Dakota, W-122/1877.

entirely dismounted, they were living on horse meat, and some of them had frozen limbs.[88]

Meanwhile, from Camp Robinson couriers headed north to try to find Crazy Horse and persuade him to give himself up and come into the reservation. They carried word from General Crook that if he would bring his people to the reservation to live, he could expect generous treatment.[89] It was a gamble, but if reports of his desperate plight were true, it might pay off.

The first to go looking for him were Few Tails and Hunts the Enemy (later known as George Sword). Accompanied by thirty men, they set out through the deep January snows with Crook's assurances and a big bag of tobacco for Crazy Horse. They returned in about a month, bringing word that Crazy Horse had received them kindly, that he had smoked the tobacco and found it good. He would come in and join his relatives at the agency.[90] Spotted Tail went out, also, to see what he could do. He did not find Crazy Horse, but he talked to the chief's father, who assured him that his son wanted peace and would soon come into the agency.[91] However, Little Wolf, principal chief of the Cheyennes, told Colonel Mackenzie that he was positive Crazy Horse would not come in.[92] Indeed, Mackenzie was quite certain from what he heard from the Indians around Camp Robinson that Crazy Horse would never come in.[93] Mackenzie could hardly be blamed for his pessimism—on so many occasions in the past, reports that Crazy Horse was coming in had proven false—but, by mid-April, the chief was actually on his way to the agency, and the man who was bringing him in, strangely enough, was Red Cloud.[94]

[88] Sheridan to E. D. Townsend, February 6, 1877, copy in NARS, RG 75, Indian Office, Dakota, A–61. See also Virginia Weisel Johnson, *The Unregimented General: A Biography of Nelson A. Miles* (Boston: Houghton Mifflin Co., 1962), pp. 137–152.

[89] Bourke, *On the Border with Crook*, p. 408.

[90] Ricker, Interview with Garnett; Interview with George Sword, April 29, 1907, Ricker Mss., Tablet No. 16. These two accounts agree in essentials, except for the date of departure. Sword said he left Camp Robinson on January 1; Garnett said he left "about the latter part of January." Garnett probably was more nearly correct. Cf. W. P. Clark to Lt. J. G. Bourke, March 3, 1877, NARS, RG 75, Indian Office, Dakota, W–309.

[91] J. M. Lee to AAG, Camp Robinson, April 5, 1877, NARS, RG 94, LR, AGO. Bourke, *On the Border with Crook*, p. 396, indicates that Spotted Tail visited Crazy Horse himself near the bend of the Powder River.

[92] R. S. Mackenzie to J. G. Bourke, March 17, 1877, NARS, RG 94, Doc. File 4163, Sioux War, 1876.

[93] *Ibid.*, April 1, 1877.

[94] Vestal's statement, "Though Spotted Tail had induced Crazy Horse to come in,

It happened this way. Shortly after Few Tails and Hunts the Enemy returned, Lt. W. P. Clark called Red Cloud to his office at Camp Robinson. He reviewed events since Red Cloud had been stripped of his chieftainship by General Crook, expressing particular dissatisfaction with the failure of Spotted Tail to furnish an adequate number of scouts for the expedition against the northern Indians. He then said:

> Now I want you to go out and bring Crazy Horse and all the people he claims in. Spotted Tail is going out and I think he has already started. I don't want him to get ahead of you. It was your men who studied out this scheme to get him in. Your people are striving to stay in this country and to have an agency of their own. They are dissatisfied with Indian Territory and Missouri River. After you complete your work you people will be going to Washington to try to get an agency. We want to have some of these Northern Indians with Crazy Horse go to Washington with the delegation to let them know that they are at peace; and Gen. Crook is a friend of mine, and if you do as I tell you I'll have him to reinstate you to your place; and I will make you First Sergeant; that is as high as I can place you, for it is the highest office in the Indian Scout Service; I have all the other chiefs on the Agency enlisted; but I will recognize you as the highest officer among the chiefs; so that you can have control of your people. I will assist you with all the rations you think you will need.[95]

Red Cloud was pleased. Of course he would go. Three days later he set out, well equipped and leading a hundred men.[96] He sent word regularly by courier of his progress.[97] General Crook, who had returned to Camp Robinson, was optimistic—Indians were coming in frequently, surrendering their arms and ponies—but he would not assert officially that Crazy Horse was actually coming until he heard from Red Cloud.[98] On April 27 the word arrived. Red Cloud had found Crazy Horse, and he was coming in. His people were moving slowly because of the condition of their ponies; they would be there in eight or nine days.[99]

Red Cloud rode out to meet him and so appear as the one who brought him in to the Oglala Agency" (*Warpath and Council Fire*, pp. 267–272) is hardly fair to Red Cloud and certainly is not supported by the evidence I have. Cf. Hyde, *Red Cloud's Folk*, pp. 289–292; Mari Sandoz, *Crazy Horse* (New York: Hastings House, 1958), pp. 360–369; Harry H. Anderson, "Indian Peace-Talkers and the Conclusion of the Sioux War of 1876," *Nebraska History*, XL (December, 1963), 233–254.

[95] Ricker, Interview with Garnett.

[96] *Ibid.*

[97] Bourke, *On the Border with Crook*, p. 408.

[98] Telegrams, Crook to Sheridan, April 18, 19, 1877; Lt. Col. George A. Forsyth to Sheridan, April 24, 1877, NARS, RG 94, LR, Military Division of the Missouri.

[99] Telegram, Crook to Sheridan, April 27, 1877, *ibid.*

Lieutenant Rosecrans, accompanied by fifty Indian scouts headed by the younger American Horse, was despatched with ten wagonloads of rations and a hundred head of cattle to meet the inbound party. The two groups came together near the Hat Creek stage station on the Laramie–Black Hills road. Rosecrans shook hands with Crazy Horse— the first white man ever to do so—and Crazy Horse gave a pony to the lieutenant and each of the Indian scouts. The starving Indians ate and rested, and then began the final march to Camp Robinson which they reached on May 6. General Crook had gone to Washington, so Lieutenant Clark went out to meet the procession.

It was a solemn moment. Crazy Horse and all the chiefs sat down in a row and asked Lieutenant Clark to come and shake hands with them. They would use the left hand, which is next to the heart; the right hand does all manner of wickedness. If Crazy Horse was in the least offended that only a lieutenant had come out to meet him— Colonel Mackenzie was at Camp Robinson, but he did not participate in the surrender ceremonies—he showed no sign of it. After the hand-shaking, he gave Clark a war bonnet, a pipe, a war shirt, and a beaded sack, and Clark, who handled matters with great good sense, gratified the Indians by putting on his new regalia.[100]

After the Indians were put on the big flat south of the White River (about a mile from the post), the process of disarming and dismounting began. Red Cloud had explained everything to Crazy Horse in advance, so the operation proceeded smoothly. A few of the warriors tried to hide their guns, but they were spotted by the scouts and relieved of their arms without difficulty. All told, the band surrendered two thousand horses and mules and 117 guns and pistols. The people involved totalled 899, including 217 men, 312 women, 186 boys, and 184 girls.[101]

For a time after Crazy Horse arrived at the agency, things seemed to move along as smoothly as could be expected. After Hastings' dismissal,

[100] Ricker, Interview with Garnett. For an estimate of Clark's handling of the Indians, see L. P. Bradley to Crook, July 16, 1877, NARS, RG 94, LR, Military Division of the Missouri.

[101] Ricker, Interview with Garnett; Telegram, AAG, Dept. of the Platte, to Crook, May 9, 1877, NARS, RG 94, Doc. File 4163, Sioux War, 1876; C. A. Johnson, Acting Agent, Red Cloud, to J. Q. Smith, May 6, 1877, NARS, RG 75, LR, Red Cloud Agency. Johnson put the number of horses and mules at 1,700. In his letter he stated: "Red Cloud succeeded in his mission to Crazy Horse and today returned bringing with him Crazy Horse and 145 lodges of hostile Indians." This is further evidence of the role of Red Cloud in Crazy Horse's surrender.

agency affairs had been administered by junior officers of the Army, but on July 1, Dr. James Irwin, who had seen service as Shoshoni agent, took charge of the agency, putting an end to this stopgap arrangement. Irwin got on well from the beginning. Benjamin R. Shapp, a special agent from the Indian Office who visited the agency late in July, reported that the new agent had greatly improved the efficiency of the operation, and that Red Cloud seemed to be happy with him [102]— a pleasing departure from his attitude toward earlier agents. The military, also, seemed to approve of the way Irwin managed affairs. Lt. Col. L. P. Bradley, who had assumed command of Camp Robinson, reported to Crook: "Dr. Irwin has taken charge of the Agency, and I think he will succeed here. The Indians appear to like him and he seems disposed to make them satisfied and contented." Indeed, Bradley assured Crook, "We are as quiet here as a Yankee village on a Sunday." [103] Lieutenant Clark was similarly optimistic. "Dr. Irwin," he wrote, "makes a superior agent, conservative and yet sufficiently firm." The northern Indians were "ravenous for meat," and Irwin had "raised the count a little" to cover an extra issue of beef for them. All this seemed to have its effect; in the same letter, Clark wrote: "Crazy Horse and his people are getting quite sociable, and I reckon I shall have to be considered one of their tribe soon, as I have been invited down to three feasts." [104]

Beneath the calm and the glow of good feeling, however, there lurked a rather dangerous discontent. General Crook, who visited Camp Robinson late in May, held a council with the Indians on the twenty-fifth, discussing with them arrangements for a trip to see the Great Father to settle upon a permanent location for the agency. He made much of the fact that the country now had a new President who wanted an opportunity to get acquainted with his red children. The chiefs had insisted to the Sioux Commission that they must visit the Great Father before selecting a permanent location, and they were happy that arrangements for a trip to Washington were being completed. They assured Crook that they were anxious to do whatever the Great Father wished; however, they did not want to move to the Missouri River! [105] They expressed substantially the same views on July 27, in a council with Inspector Shapp: they would be pleased to

---

[102] Benjamin R. Shapp to Com. of Indian Affairs, August 18, 1877, copy in NARS, RG 94, Doc. File 4163, Sioux War, 1876.

[103] Bradley to Crook, July 16, 1877, *ibid.*

[104] W. P. Clark to Crook, August 1, 1877, *ibid.*

[105] Ricker, Interview with Garnett; C. A. Johnson to Com. of Indian Affairs, June 4, 1877, NARS, RG 75, LR, Red Cloud Agency.

visit the Great Father, they were ready to follow his wishes, but they did not want to move to the Missouri River. More important, at least for the moment, this council revealed serious dissension among the Indians themselves.

At the conclusion of the council, Shapp announced that he would provide a feast. Young-Man-Afraid-of-His-Horse suggested that it should be held at the lodge of Crazy Horse. No one objected, but Red Cloud and one or two others abruptly left the room. About ten o'clock that night, two Indians came to the agent's office and demanded to talk with him saying they represented Red Cloud. When they could not be put off until morning, Irwin sent for an interpreter and listened to their story. They told him that Red Cloud and several others were greatly dissatisfied with the proposal to have the feast at the lodge of Crazy Horse; he had only lately joined the agency and there was no reason at all why the feast should be held at his lodge. In the course of what Shapp described as "a long and earnest conversation," the Indians warned Irwin that Crazy Horse was wholly unreconstructed and would cause trouble at the first opportunity. They prophesied that if he were allowed to take his warriors on a buffalo hunt, as General Crook has promised he could do, he would go on the warpath and never return.[106]

The next day, much to Irwin's surprise, an order arrived from General Crook lifting all restrictions on the sale of ammunition to the Indians at the agency, presumably to allow them to prepare for the buffalo hunt. This whole episode of the buffalo hunt is a curious one. The promise had been made to all the Indians who wished to go—at Spotted Tail as well as at Red Cloud—and not just to the Crazy Horse Indians, as Red Cloud's emissaries implied. Many of the Indians, including all of Crazy Horse's band, had been disarmed and dismounted. Those who had enlisted as scouts had been rearmed and remounted, but Crazy Horse's people were not among this group. One wonders where his warriors were to get their arms and their ponies. Anyhow, the Indians were not of one mind about going on the hunt— Spotted Tail, in particular, was opposed to it; the Crazy Horse people said nothing about it—and in the end apparently there was a general decision not to go, at which time the order permitting sale of ammunition was rescinded.[107]

[106] Shapp to Com. of Indian Affairs, August 18, 1877, copy in NARS, RG 94, Doc. File 4163, Sioux War, 1876.

[107] *Ibid.*; Bradley, endorsement to *ibid.*, September 7, 1877; Bradley to Crook, July 16, 1877, *ibid.*

Hunt or no hunt, it was becoming painfully evident that trouble was brewing at the Red Cloud Agency, and that it was centering around Crazy Horse. Conqueror of Crook on the Rosebud and a leader in the Custer fight, Crazy Horse was easily the most glamorous figure on the reservation. His growing popularity among the young men of the agency and his deferential treatment at the hands of the Army did not set well with the Oglala chiefs, particularly Red Cloud, whose tolerance for rival leadership was never high. Spotted Tail, too, although not so directly affected, gave signs of being jealous of the young war chief.[108] Jealousy undoubtedly contributed to the tension on the reservation and inspired some of the constantly circulating rumors that Crazy Horse was about to break away from the agency and go on the warpath again. But there was much more to the problem than rumors inspired by jealousy. Crazy Horse was in no position to lead a general Indian uprising, even if he cherished the dream—as Patrick E. Byrne put it, "Deprived of firearms, ammunition and horses, Crazy Horse and his people were helpless, and as securely tied down to their fate at Fort Robinson as though they were bound hand and foot"[109]—but he still had the capacity to create a great deal of trouble, and he gave every evidence that he intended to do it. Irwin found him, "silent, sullen, lordly and dictatorial . . . even with his own people." He refused to sign receipts for his rations and annuity goods, and was generally uncooperative.[110] Strangely enough, the officers at Camp Robinson seemed little concerned; as Irwin put it, "The military still had faith in Crazy Horse."[111]

Aside from the fact that Crazy Horse was probably constitutionally unable to adapt to reservation life, his rebelliousness may have derived from a growing feeling that he had been tricked. At some point General Crook apparently gave the chief assurances that he could have his reservation on his old hunting grounds in the Powder River country.[112] But he grew suspicious as the weeks went by and he heard

[108] E. S. Ricker, Interview with Dr. Charles A. Eastman, August 20, 1907, Ricker Mss., Tablet No. 11; Luther Standing Bear, *My People, The Sioux* (Boston: Houghton Mifflin Company, 1928), pp. 86–88; Martin F. Schmitt, *General George Crook, His Autobiography* (Norman: University of Oklahoma Press, 1946), pp. 217–219; Julia B. McGillycuddy, *McGillycuddy: Agent* (Stanford: Stanford University Press, 1941), p. 76.

[109] Patrick E. Byrne, *Soldiers of the Plains* (New York: Minton, Balch & Co., 1926), p. 233.

[110] James E. Irwin to Com. of Indian Affairs, August 31, 1877, NARS, RG 75, LR, Red Cloud Agency.

[111] *Ibid.*

[112] Ricker, Interview with Garnett; Schmitt, *General Crook, His Autobiography*, p. 217.

The Sioux Problem

Indian Peace Commissioners at Fort Laramie

Oglala delegation to Washington, 1880. Seated, left to right, Red Dog, Little Wound, Red Cloud, American Horse, Red Shirt; standing, John Bridgeman

Issue Day at Pine Ridge—Summer

Red Cloud's Home at Pine Ridge

Red Cloud's Bedroom at Pine Ridge

Courtesy of Nebraska State Historical Society

Courtesy of Nebraska State Historical Society

Sun Dance at Pine Ridge, 1883

Camp of Two Strike and Crow Dog, Pine Ridge, December, 1890

nothing but talk of going to the Missouri; and his suspicions were strengthened when Crook's officers at Camp Robinson began enlisting Indian scouts to go on a campaign with the general. The officers said that they were going to round up Chief Joseph and the Nez Perces, but Crazy Horse was sure Sitting Bull, who had fled to Canada, was their quarry. On August 31, as the scouts were preparing to leave, Crazy Horse demanded that they stay home, and threatened to take his people and head north.

This created great excitement. Sensing trouble, Colonel Bradley ordered additional cavalry from Fort Laramie and telegraphed Sheridan: "There is a good chance for trouble here and there is plenty of bad blood. I think the departure of the scouts will bring on a collision here." [113] Sheridan got in touch by telegraph with General Crook, who was on the Union Pacific out of Omaha enroute to Camp Brown to superintend the capture of the Nez Perces, ordering him to get off the train at Sidney and go immediately to Red Cloud Agency; he ordered Bradley to hold the scouts until Crook arrived. [114]

The old-line agency Indians seemed as alarmed as the military. Irwin held a council on September 1 with the leaders (Red Cloud, American Horse, Little Wound, Young-Man-Afraid-of-His-Horse and No Flesh) and was told that they had been counciling together every day for the last ten or twelve days, but that they could do nothing to quiet Crazy Horse. They would see to it, though, that he "did nothing to hurt the Agent's feelings." [115]

General Crook dashed into Camp Robinson on the morning of the second, looked over the situation, ordered Colonel Bradley to take Crazy Horse prisoner, and then headed back to Cheyenne to resume his trip to Camp Brown. [116] On the morning of the fourth, eight

[113] Telegram, Bradley to Sheridan, August 31, 1877, NARS, RG 94, Doc. File 4163, Sioux War, 1876. Bradley's telegram reviewed the events of the day, as described. See also Irwin to Com. of Indian Affairs (above, n. 110).

[114] Telegrams, Sheridan to Crook, Sheridan to Bradley, September 1, 1877, NARS, RG 94, Doc. File 4163, Sioux War, 1876.

[115] Telegram, Irwin to Com. of Indian Affairs, September 1, 1877, NARS, RG 75, LR, Red Cloud Agency.

[116] There is considerable confusion regarding Crook's activities. Bourke, *On the Border with Crook*, p. 420, describes a council which he held with the agency Indians. William Garnett, however, states that after Crook had been informed that Crazy Horse intended to kill him if they met in council (information which later proved to be incorrect) he canceled plans for the session (Byrne, *Soldiers of the Plains*, pp. 235–243). The only contemporary mention of the council or of plans for it which I have seen is this comment in a letter from Lieutenant Clark: "So vicious had this man [Crazy

companies of the 3rd Cavalry, commanded by Lt. Col. John S. Mason, and about four hundred Indians (including Red Cloud, American Horse, Little Wound, and Young-Man-Afraid), led by Lieutenant Clark, left Camp Robinson for Crazy Horse's camp, six or seven miles below the post. When they arrived, they found that the camp had been broken up in the night and the Indians were fleeing. Crazy Horse had slipped off alone to the Spotted Tail Agency; he was arrested there on the fifth and brought back under guard to Camp Robinson, while the agency Indians rounded up the rest of his band.[117] The same day, Crook, who had arrived in Cheyenne, telegraphed Sheridan: "Crazy Horse is now a prisoner and I have ordered Bradley to send him down here. I wish you would send him off where he would be out of harm's way. You can rest assured that everything at the agency is perfectly quiet and will remain so. . . . The successful breaking up of Crazy Horse's band has removed a heavy weight off my mind and I leave here feeling perfectly easy."[118]

Crook did not realize how easily he could rest: that night, at Camp Robinson, Crazy Horse was stabbed to death.

There are many versions of the killing, most of them apparently based upon recollections of persons who were at Camp Robinson on that fateful day.[119] I shall content myself with the contemporary statements of the two Army officers most closely associated with the event.

On September 7, Col. L. P. Bradley, commandant at Camp Robinson, wrote the Adjutant General of the Department of the Platte:

> My orders from Gen. Crook were to capture this chief, confine him, and send him under guard to Omaha. When he was put in the guard house he suddenly drew a knife and struck at the guard and jumped for the door. Little Big Man, one of his own chiefs, grappled with him, and was cut in

Horse] become that on Gen. Crook's arrival here recently, he told his men to go to the council prepared for a fight as he was going to kill him. This calamity was in all probability avoided by the loyalty and prompt action of one of my scouts called Old Womans Dress in informing me a few minutes before the council was to meet" (Clark to Com. of Indian Affairs, September 10, 1877, NARS, RG 75, LR, Spotted Tail Agency). This generally supports Garnett's statement. Cf. Sandoz, *Crazy Horse*, pp. 396–399.

117 Telegram, Sheridan to E. D. Townsend, September 5, 1877, copy in NARS, RG 75, LR, Red Cloud Agency.

118 Telegram, Crook to Sheridan, September 5, 1877, NARS, RG 94, Doc. File 4163, Sioux War, 1876.

119 E.g., Bourke, *On the Border with Crook*, pp. 418–423; Byrne, *Soldiers of the Plains*, pp. 229–243; Hyde, *Red Cloud's Folk*, pp. 297–299, Sandoz, *Crazy Horse*, pp. 399–413; Vestal, *Warpath and Council Fire*, pp. 267–272; W. J. Bordeaux, *Conquering the Mighty Sioux* (Sioux Falls [n.p.], 1929), pp. 94–96.

the arm by Crazy Horse during the struggle, the two chiefs were surrounded by the guard and about this time Crazy Horse received a severe wound in the lower part of the abdomen, either from a knife or bayonet, the surgeons are in doubt which; he was immediately removed, and placed in charge of the surgeons, and died about midnight. His father and Touch the Cloud, Chief of the Sans Arcs, remained with him till he died, and when his breath ceased the chief laid his hand on Crazy Horse's breast and said, "It is good, he has looked for death, and it has come." . . . Crazy Horse and his friends were assured that no harm was intended him, and the chiefs who were with him are satisfied none was intended, his death resulting from his own violence.[120]

Three days later, Lt. W. P. Clark, commandant of Scouts at Camp Robinson, who had accepted Crazy Horse's surrender, and who probably retained faith in him longer than did any other white man, wrote the Commissioner of Indian Affairs, describing Crazy Horse as "remarkably brave, generous and reticent . . . a pillar of strength for good or evil." Of the events leading up to the great war chief's death, he said:

On Sept. 5 having armed a large number of friendly Indians in addition to the Indian Scouts this band was surrounded and dismembered by these friendly Indians and a force of some 400 white soldiers who were in the immediate vicinity to give moral force and if necessary assistance, the lodges joining other bands some few however making their escape to Spotted Tail Agency. Crazy Horse among the rest. The friendly Indians here were ready and would have fought had it been necessary to keep this band from going north, which means war with them, but they did not wish to commence fight.

Crazy Horse was promptly pursued and so earnestly that No Water who had charge of one party killed two ponies in his efforts to overtake and capture him. He reached the camp of the Northern Indians at Spotted Tail and shortly afterwards Big Crow a Brule Indian told him that he understood that Crazy Horse never listened, but now he had got to listen and had got to come with him to the commanding officer and this Indian with White Thunder took him to Maj. Bourke who arranged to send him to this post under Lt. Lee [Lt. J. M. Lee, Spotted Tail Agent]. Starting from Sheridan with only some northern Indians and gradually being joined by scouts who could be trusted Crazy Horse still had his pistol and knife and did not realize he was virtually a prisoner until some distance from Sheridan.

On reaching here he was told he must give up his Pistol and Knives that he was not to be hurt but in attempting to disarm him tho surrounded by

[120] Bradley to AG, Omaha, September 7, 1877, NARS, RG 94, Doc. File 4163, Sioux War, 1876.

white and Indian Soldiers [he] made a violent effort to cut his way out stabbing Little Big Man (who had hold of him) in the arm and in the scuffle that insued himself getting stabbed in the abdomen.

He seemed to think it was done by one of the soldiers bayonets, but is impossible to ascertain about the matter as the Doctors from the appearance of the wound thought it must have been done with his own knife. He died at 11:40 p.m. that night. . . .[121]

Clark reported that the majority of the Indians considered Crazy Horse's death "a real benefit to their people and justify the killing as he first drew his knife."[122] Whatever of justice or injustice there was in the act, the death of Crazy Horse removed the most serious source of significant trouble from the Red Cloud Agency. The older chiefs— Red Cloud, Young-Man-Afraid, Little Wound, American Horse, and others—had had enough of fighting; instead of capitalizing upon the tensions of that troublesome period to lead their followers in an outbreak which would have resulted in disaster, they used their influence to calm the tensions and reassert their leadership.[123]

Red Cloud, notably among them, resumed his old position of leadership. On occasion, he would threaten violence—and from time to time he might even have dreamed of recapturing the glories of the past— but his only really effective weapon would be a type of obstructionism which would yield certain temporary gains, but in the long run would neither restore the old world nor enable him to lead his people into the new.

[121] Clark to Com. of Indian Affairs, September 10, 1877, NARS, RG 75, LR, Spotted Tail Agency.

[122] *Ibid.*

[123] *Ibid.*; James H. Cook, *Fifty Years on the Old Frontier* (New Haven: Yale University Press 1923), pp. 220–221, 230–231.

CHAPTER 13

Missouri River Interlude

Barely three weeks after the death of Crazy Horse, Red Cloud, Spotted Tail, and other leading chiefs arrived at the White House to confer with President Rutherford B. Hayes. When they signed the Black Hills agreement, the chiefs had consented to move either to Indian Territory or to the Missouri River, but had insisted that before they made any move they would have to talk with the Great Father. With Indian Territory soon eliminated from consideration,[1] the Bureau had concentrated its attention on finding a suitable Missouri River site for the tribes. In June a committee consisting of D. J. Jerome of the Board of Indian Commissioners, J. H. Hammond, Superintendent of Indian Affairs for Dakota, and Lt. Col. Pinkney Lugenbeel of the 1st Infantry recommended that Red Cloud's people be located at the junction of the Yellow Medicine and Missouri rivers and that Spotted Tail's move back to the old Whetstone Agency, where they had been from 1868 to 1871.[2]

All summer long the chiefs had said that they did not want to go to the Missouri, but no one seemed to take them seriously except General Crook, who, despite Crazy Horse's suspicions, worked assiduously to persuade Interior and War Department officials that the northern

[1] See above, p. 231.

[2] Lugenbeel to AAG, Dept. of the Dakotas, June 13, 1877, NARS, RG 94, Doc. File 4163, Sioux War, 1876; Com. of Indian Affairs, *Annual Report*, 1877, p. 18.

Indians, at least, should be permitted to live on the Tongue River.[3] Everyone else proceeded on the fatuous assumption that if the chiefs were granted their interview with the Great Father they would agree to anything. It is true that Red Cloud and other chiefs who had visited Washington were intrigued with the idea that they now had a new Great Father and they were curious to hear what he had to say, but these were scarcely grounds for believing that they would be any more amenable to his suggestions than to those of his predecessor.

The Indians were assembled in the East Room of the White House shortly before noon on September 27.[4] The Government had high hopes that one conference would suffice,[5] and to impress the Indians with the importance of the occasion had assembled an imposing array of dignitaries in addition to President Hayes. Secretary of the Interior Carl Schurz, full of ideas for reforming the Indian Service, was there, of course, along with outgoing Commissioner E. P. Smith and incoming Commissioner Ezra Hayt. Other Cabinet officers present included Secretary of State W. M. Evarts, Secretary of War G. W. McCrary, Attorney General Charles Devens, and Postmaster General David M. Key. General Crook and Lieutenant Clark represented the Army, and from outside the Government were Bishop Whipple and William Welsh, formerly chairman of the Board of Indian Commissioners. There were several ladies present, too, including Mrs. Hayes and Mrs. Crook.[6]

If those responsible had expected to settle the question in one meeting, they certainly had not coordinated matters very effectively. Welsh, speaking for the Indians at their request, stated flatly that they did not wish to go to the Missouri River. They were anxious for civilization, but "they could not there become civilized as their women would become corrupt, and other evils follow to the men by the influence of bad white men."[7] When Welsh had finished, Red Cloud came forward,

[3] Martin F. Schmitt, ed., *General George Crook, His Autobiography* (Norman: University of Oklahoma Press, 1946), p. 219; George Crook to Philip H. Sheridan, April 20, 1877, NARS, RG 94, Doc. File 4163, Sioux War, 1876.

[4] The Indians present included: Red Cloud, Young-Man-Afraid-of-his-Horse, Three Bears, Little Wound, American Horse, and Yellow Bear of the Red Cloud Agency; Spotted Tail, Spotted Tail's son, Hollow Horn Bear, and White Tail from the Spotted Tail Agency; Black Coal, Sharp Nose, and Friday of the Arapahoes; and He Dog, Big Road, Little Big Man, and Iron Crow of the northern Indians. Antoine Janis and Leon Palladay were along as interpreters (E. S. Ricker, Interview with William Garnett, January 10, 1907, Tablet No. 1, Ricker Mss., Nebraska State Historical Society).

[5] *New York Times*, September 26, 1877.

[6] *Ibid.*, September 28, 1877.

[7] *Ibid.*

shook hands with the President, and delivered a characteristically long, rambling speech, reciting his difficulties and protesting his friendship for the Great Father and his desire for civilization. Getting to the business at hand, he said:

> There is a rumor of somebody going to the Missouri river. I wish you would not mention that to me; for I do not want to go on the Missouri river. The Missouri river is the whiskey road and if I went there I would not do good; I would come to nothing at all. West of where I am I could raise everything, good grass, fine country for stock, while on the Missouri river I do not see that I could raise anything, and the people there would ask a big price for their stock and would try to get all the advantages they could from me. Another thing, in the winter the river would freeze up and then I could get help from no one, the railroad goes very near where I am now, and I think since the road has been there I have been doing very well; I am not poor; I live very well.[8]

Several others spoke, Oglalas and Arapahoes; they were all opposed to going to the Missouri. Spotted Tail was asked if he had something to say, but replied that he would speak another day; it was apparent by now that there would have to be another meeting. The President did not respond directly to the Indians' plea—he merely said that he had much work to do and would see them all tomorrow—but he was reported to have been deeply impressed with the unanimity with which the chiefs expressed opposition to living on the Missouri and with the reasons they advanced for that opposition. Whatever the President's views, however, he was stymied by congressional action and indeed by the fact that the contracts for furnishing supplies on the Missouri had already been let.[9]

The next morning, when the chiefs assembled again in the White House,[10] Spotted Tail spoke first. As usual, he was more ingratiating than Red Cloud, but the burden of his remarks was essentially the same: he did not want to go to the Missouri River. Moreover, he made it clear that he did not understand that in signing the Black Hills agreement he had agreed to move anywhere:

> All I know is that they are trying to frighten us into this business. That's the way I came to sign the paper that I did. They told me at the time that my Great Father sent the men there for the purpose of treating for the country. If so, I am willing to treat. They told me a good many points not kept up in the old treaty should be given to us in the new, and said if I signed all I wanted would be given according to their promise. They told

[8] *Ibid.*; Ricker Mss., Tablet No. 36.
[9] *New York Times*, September 28, 1877.
[10] For this day's activities, I am following *ibid.*, September 29, 1877; Ricker Mss.

me then if I did not sign they would send me south or across the Missouri River. Although I signed without their telling me exactly what they wanted, I wanted them to tell me how I was to live after I signed the paper; how many cattle and agricultural implements I was to have and other things. That is the way they treated me.

Red Cloud also spoke. He said nothing about the Black Hills agreement, confining himself to a recital of the history of the agencies and of his wants:

> . . . now that I have got to be civilized I want to select a country for my Nation, and that is what I want to say to you today. . . .
>
> Tongue River has four forks, but down by the prairie there is a good place to put an Agency, and there is where I want my Agency. I did not come here to give you anything. The Black Hills is my country, but I gave it to the commissioners, and sent word down here. Suppose you decide now what you are going to give me for the Black Hills. I came here to get it. I want three different kinds of wagons to work with. . . . I want plows and mowing machines. I will not say how many I want, but I want enough for my people. The cattle I want you to give me so that we can raise cattle, and raise them every year. I want two mills, but one is to saw wood with and the other to grind corn. . . . I want you to give me school teachers, so that we will have a good school house, and learn my children how to write and read. Catholic priests are good and I want you to give me one of them also. That Agent [Irwin] is the one I want. I want to stay there with him forever.

After Little Big Man and Sharp Nose had spoken (the latter presenting Hayes with a pipe and a tobacco pouch), General Crook rose "to say a word in behalf of these friends of mine here." The Great Father could be sure that these men spoke the truth, that their hearts were good toward their white brothers, that they wanted to do what was right. He hoped the Great Father would be able to give them the things they asked for. He hoped especially that the Great Father would give particular consideration to the appeal of the Red Cloud and Red Leaf bands, who had suffered much because of the loss of their ponies and arms but had "behaved very well" since the disarming and dismounting. He said nothing about location, not going into it because there was nothing he could do about it.

When Crook finished, the President arose and addressed the Indians. He said that when he took office he was told that their chiefs had agreed to accept their supplies on the Missouri River, and that was what the "Great Council" also believed. Consequently, arrangements had been made to send their supplies to the Missouri, and the Poncas had been removed to Indian Territory so as to provide more room for the Sioux.[11] It was too late to change the arrangements now, but in the spring they could, if they wished, select a location for the agency away from the Missouri. The President thought that somewhere in the vicinity of the White River would be satisfactory; he did not want them to go to the Tongue River; that was too far north.

The Indians seemed pleased, and well they might have been. They had won a major point. Two days later, when they came to the White House for their final interview with the President, they were all wearing the new suits given to them upon their arrival in Washington.[12] At their two previous meetings they had been decked out in feathers, paint, and blankets; they were wearing white man's clothing now, Lieutenant Clark told the President, as a pledge that they would do all things necessary to achieve the white man's civilization. This augured well, but once the session got under way it was clear that the confusion and misunderstanding which had resulted from all previous meetings would characterize the conclusion of this one, too.

Spotted Tail spoke first. He was pleased that the Great Father would permit him to select the location for his agency. He did not need to wait until spring, he would pick the spot now; he wanted to live on Wounded Knee Creek. For the present, he would stay where he was; it would be too difficult to move anywhere this fall—in other words, he did not want to go to the Missouri for the winter. Having made this point, he went on to discuss his needs: wagons, teachers ("we have teachers there, but all they teach us is to talk Sioux and write Sioux, and that is not necessary. I would like to get Catholic priests. Those who wear black dresses. These men will teach us how to read and write English"); cattle ("We don't want cattle with long horns, like elk, but good cattle"); men to work on the farms; seeds, implements, and plows. He wanted these things for all of his people. For himself and those who had accompanied him to Washington, he wanted forty dollars apiece, a trunk, and an overcoat.

Red Cloud was the next speaker. He, too, could tell the Great Father where he wanted his agency: "We have decided that if we cannot get Tongue river, we would like to go to the mouth of White Clay Creek, which runs into White river, above Spotted Tail." He, too, wanted those things which Spotted Tail had requested: forty

---

[11] For a brief account, see James C. Olson, *History of Nebraska* (Lincoln: University of Nebraska Press, 1955), p. 137.

[12] *New York Times*, October 2, 1877; Ricker Mss.

dollars apiece, a trunk, an overcoat, wagons, cattle, implements, and especially Catholic priests to teach his people how to read and write English.[13] In addition, he felt that he should be compensated for the horses he lost the previous fall: "I look upon it this way: the property that was destroyed, and the injury, and the horses should be worth ten thousand dollars, and I would like to get about one-half of it in money, and the other half in things of some use to my people. A good deal of that destroyed was my own." Finally, as for spending the winter on the Missouri, he could not think of it:

> Look at me well, my Great Father, and you will know the fix I am in. I cannot move out there this winter, for I am poor. It is getting cold and near winter, and by the time we get back there, we cannot move over to the Missouri this winter. . . . My Great Father, we have decided where both agencies shall be. . . . I would like to have our provisions and our goods hauled to this place. If they remain too long on the Missouri river there are long-tailed rats there that would go into the boxes, and we would probably lose half of them. We have no means of getting them transported, and I would like to ask you to have them sent to the place where we want our agency.

The President's response was brief and fairly noncommital. He was delighted to see the chiefs in white man's clothing, and he was glad that they wanted agencies within their reservation rather than on Tongue River. He would like to move the supplies from the Missouri, but that was impossible: "We wish you to help get your people nearer to the supplies and General Crook will help you." As for the other things they had asked for, "The great council of my nation has put the money and property which is for you in charge of the Secretary of the Interior. He will be glad to give you what he can, and I think he can suit you very well." He concluded:

> And now this is the end of our present council. I am glad that you came. Let me advise you to move as near the supplies as you can, and General Crook will help you this winter. Next spring you can go to your reservation, and I am glad that you are satisfied with White River. I hope you will all reach home safely and in good health. Before you go, the Secretary of the Interior will give you as many of the things you want as he can. And now I will be glad to shake hands with each one of you, and wish you well.

The chiefs shook hands with the President and with Secretary Schurz and filed out of the White House, apparently well pleased with the

[13] This underscored a point the Catholics had been making for some time. See Peter J. Rahill, *The Catholic Indian Missions and Grant's Peace Policy* (Washington: Catholic University of America Press, 1953), *passim*.

results of their meeting. The next day, however, in a final conference with Schurz, both Red Cloud and Spotted Tail reiterated the reasons for their opposition to spending the winter on the Missouri, and both were more emphatic than they had been in the presence of the President, although neither said outright he would not go. Red Cloud said he did not want to go; Spotted Tail said once during his speech that he would not go, but later that if he did go he should be paid for it. Schurz, like the President the day before, did not press the point; he simply urged the chiefs to move near their supplies for the winter so their people could eat, and assured them that General Crook would help them. He ended the meeting on a pleasant note by providing each of the chiefs with an overcoat, a satchel, and some spending money (thirty dollars, ten less than requested).[14]

The next morning the delegation left for New York, where they spent a day getting rid of their money and taking a ride in a small government steamboat before heading west.[15]

In many respects, the trip must be counted a success. The question of the permanent location of the reservations appeared to have been settled, and the Indians left Washington in a mood of friendliness which contrasted favorably with the sullenness which had characterized their departure after the meetings of 1875. Yet the indefinite state in which the temporary move to the Missouri was left would bring about a winter of cross-purposes and frustration.

Secretary Schurz sensed the possibility of trouble. No sooner were the Indians out of town than he asked the War Department to assemble as large a military force as practicable at the reservations to prevent an outbreak or an escape to join the hostiles.[16] General Sheridan agreed that such action was advisable. For some time he had not been satisfied with conditions at the agencies but had "reluctantly yielded to the judgment of the Department Commander."[17] He thought it would take at least three companies of cavalry at each agency to support the move and urged that rations be despatched immediately; he wanted the matter left in his hands, however, so that he could act when he knew the situation at the agencies after the delegations returned from Washington.[18] To Crook he wired that he shared the anxiety of the

[14] *New York Times*, October 3, 1877.

[15] *Ibid.*, October 6, 1877.

[16] Telegram, E. D. Townsend to Philip H. Sheridan, October 6, 1877, NARS, RG 94, Doc. File 4163, Sioux War, 1876.

[17] Telegram, Sheridan to Townsend, October 7, 1877, *ibid.*

[18] *Ibid.*, October 8, 1877.

Commissioner of Indian Affairs, and urged him to concentrate at Red Cloud Agency every company of infantry which could possibly be spared from other posts in the department, as well as all of the 3rd and 5th Cavalry except for two companies of the 5th at Camp Brown.[19] Dr. Irwin, enroute west with the delegation, was not so apprehensive; he wired the Commissioner: "Indians expressed repeatedly their determination to carry out their promise of going near the Missouri this winter and will do all they can to persuade their young men to submit to the decision and promises of the President. They thought they would be able to keep all quiet."[20]

When General Crook got out to Camp Robinson on October 11, however, he found the Indians unwilling to believe that the President's promises would be kept and resentful of the whole idea of moving for the winter; either the chiefs had not been able to exercise as much influence as they thought they could, or they had weakened in their their determination on their return. After a number of conferences and "many personal assurances," Crook was able to persuade most of the Indians that they should move. Actually, they had little choice. Once the decision had been made to remove the tribes to the Missouri, the flow of supplies to the old agencies was cut off, and by mid-October the stores at both Red Cloud and Spotted Tail were virtually exhausted. The Indians would have to move, and without delay, to avoid starvation.[21]

On October 25, the Red Cloud Indians vacated their agency, and the long, slow trek to the hated Missouri was under way.[22] The Indian Bureau had almost nothing available in the way of food but beef on the hoof, and virtually no transportation. Crook supplied some coffee and sugar from his quartermaster stores at Camp Robinson, and further supported the movement "by scraping together all the available Army transportation within reach, improvising many teams of broken down cavalry horses."[23]

[19] Telegram, Sheridan to George Crook, October 8, 1877, *ibid.*

[20] Telegram, James Irwin to Com. of Indian Affairs, October 10, 1877, NARS, RG 75, LR, Red Cloud Agency.

[21] Telegram, Sheridan to Townsend, October 15, 1877, NARS, RG 94, Doc. File 4163, Sioux War, 1876.

[22] Telegram, Sheridan to Townsend, October 26, 1877, *ibid.* The Spotted Tail Indians left their agency on October 29 (*ibid.*, October 30, 1877). Their trip in many respects was similar to that of the Red Cloud people; this account, however, will be confined to the latter. For an account of Spotted Tail's journey, see George E. Hyde, *Spotted Tail's Folk* (Norman: University of Oklahoma Press, 1961), pp. 254–257.

[23] George Crook to AAG, Military Division of the Missouri, December 6, 1877, *ibid.*

Altogether there were some eight thousand people, including approximately two thousand northern Indians, in the Red Cloud movement. On the march, they made a column stretching eight miles; in camp, they formed a village of tipis more than three miles long. Many of them were sick; all were poorly clad. Early snows combined with sleet and rain made the going difficult and added greatly to the suffering. Moreover, the northern Indians, who reportedly were hauling Crazy Horse's body along with them, were a constant source of trouble, threatening to break away and head north and keeping everyone stirred up. Crook had not waited for the reinforcements Sheridan had proposed to furnish but had started the movement with only two companies of cavalry, relying on the friendlies to keep their wilder brethren in line. Somehow they managed to do it. All but a few of the northern Indians stayed with the main column until they reached the White River at a point about eighty miles from the new agency.[24] Here virtually all of the northern Indians broke away and headed north; and Red Cloud announced that he was going no farther, he would stay on the White River for the winter.[25]

When General Sherman got word, he was furious. He wired Sheridan: "Don't allow them to have a pound of food anywhere except at their proper agency, and consider them as hostile unless they submit to authority."[26] Sheridan agreed fully but wondered if he had the necessary authority. "The Indian Bureau has the right to decide on issues," he replied, "except in case of acknowledged hostilities and I do not know whether I can consider Red Cloud's band as hostile and thus assume the authority to stop supplies." He did not know what promises had been made to the Indians in Washington and thought it would be wise to find out before taking further steps.[27] Sherman wired back that his earlier dispatch had been approved by the Secretary of War. He would show Sheridan's telegram to the Secretary, but meanwhile Sheridan was to construe his message of December first as the general policy of the Government toward the Sioux: "No Indian agent has the right to change the destination of the Red Cloud party."[28] Sheridan immediately telegraphed Crook and Brig. Gen. A. H. Terry, commanding the

[24] Lt. W. P. Clarke to Carl Schurz, November 7, 1877, NARS, RG 75, LR, Spotted Tail Agency; letter, Capt. Joseph Lawson to AAG, Dept. of Dakota, December 4, 1877, NARS, RG 94, Doc. File 4163, Sioux War, 1876.

[25] Telegram, Sheridan to Sherman, December 1, 1877, NARS, RG 94, Doc. File 4163, Sioux War, 1876.

[26] Telegram, Sherman to Sheridan, December 1, 1877, *ibid.*

[27] Telegram, Sheridan to Sherman, December 2, 1877, *ibid.*

[28] Telegram, Sherman to Sheridan, December 3, 1877, *ibid.*

Department of Dakota, that no supplies of any kind were to be issued to the Red Cloud Indians until they came in to their new agency and that this was to be "the general policy of the government to the Sioux." [29]

When A. Bell, Acting Commissioner of Indian Affairs, received copies of the telegraphic exchange between Sherman and Sheridan, he reported to Secretary Schurz that he had authorized Agent Irwin to permit Red Cloud's people to encamp on the White River for the winter and come into the agency once a week for their supplies. This was done out of justice and humanity; the agency simply did not have sufficient timber and water to support the Indian population.[30] Irwin, too, felt that the Indians should be allowed to remain where they were; he charged that Sheridan's order was a direct violation of the President's promises, and that if it could not be revoked or modified, he wanted to be relieved from duty.[31] Sherman did not agree. He told the Secretary of War that concessions to the Indians would be attributed to fear rather than to humanity. Besides, he wrote: "There is more and better water and timber on the Missouri than on the White Earth. On the Missouri they would be under the eye of the agent and the guard. On the White Earth they may concoct mischief. Having been humbugged by these Indians so often I am incredulous of their peaceful intentions." [32] Well before he made these comments, however, Sherman had been overridden, and his order had been revoked.[33]

Although the question of winter location was settled, there still remained the larger issue of a permanent home for both the Red Cloud and Spotted Tail people. General Crook urged strict adherence to the President's promise that the Indians could select the locations for their permanent agencies; otherwise, he was sure, there would be serious trouble in the spring.[34] Indeed, it appeared for a time this would be the case whatever was done, and in the face of the threat the Army and the Indian Bureau relapsed into their old habit of wrangling with each other. On February 20 Irwin wrote Commissioner Hayt

---

[29] Telegrams, Sheridan to Crook, December 4, 1877, Sheridan to Terry, December 3, 1873, *ibid.*

[30] Bell to Secretary of the Interior, December 10, 1877, *ibid.*

[31] Telegram, Irwin to Com. of Indian Affairs, December 13, 1877, NARS, RG 75, LR, Red Cloud Agency.

[32] Sherman, endorsement, January 7, 1878, to letter, Bell to Secretary of the Interior, December 10, 1877 (above, n. 30).

[33] See J. H. Hammond to Sherman, December 14, 1877, with endorsements, NARS, RG 94, Doc. File 4163, Sioux War, 1876.

[34] Crook to AAG, USA, December 13, 1877, *ibid.*

that he was "discouraged with the whole Sioux outfit" and believed that they would "never be cured of their importance and arrogance and willful stubbornness until they are made to feel the power of the government." He was sure that Sitting Bull's Indians would come down from Canada during the summer to raid the Black Hills, and he knew that they would get support and recruits from the agencies; he could not prevent it because an adequate military force had not been furnished as promised by the Army. This letter was sent over to the War Department and down to Sheridan for comment. He wrote that his troops were being deployed as effectively as possible to deal with the trouble which he, too, expected in the spring.

> This is all that can be done. The Indians are in the hands of the Indian Bureau through whose unfortunate management the hard work and great loss of life in the last two or three years have gone for nothing. After the work had been done and in most cases, well done, the Indians had to be turned over to the management of the Indian Bureau and the results of the management are graphically but modestly described by Dr. Irwin. . . .
>
> The Sioux Indians complained of by Dr. Irwin are not under our control. We cannot do anything with them without being called to account for interfering with the Indian Bureau. We do not know what are the views of that Bureau, and I sometimes doubt if it has any views. And therefore the only preparation which can be made is the one already directed, to get everything ready, and when the Indian Bureau has the Indians fixed up to make the best possible resistance and open the ball, to do the best we can with an insufficient force. . . .[35]

Neither Secretary Schurz nor Commissioner Hayt responded to Sheridan's outburst,[36] although Irwin soon found cause to complain about the military, and specifically about the action of Maj. Charles G. Bartlett, commandant of the military post at Cheyenne River Agency. In January, Major Bartlett gave Bull Eagle, one of his Indian scouts, a pass to visit relatives at the Red Cloud Agency; he also asked him to find out what was going on among the Red Cloud Indians. Bull Eagle returned with a story of restlessness to the point of hostility among all the Indians "except the old coffee coolers," and bad management on

[35] Schurz to Secretary of War, February 27, 1878, with endorsements, *ibid.*

[36] Schurz and Sheridan soon would be engaged in an acrimonious public debate over Indian policy as one of the more spectacular features of the conflict between the War and Interior departments over management of the Indians. For an excellent account of this conflict, see Henry G. Waltmann, "The Interior Department, War Department and Indian Policy, 1865–1887" (Ph.D. dissertation, University of Nebraska, 1962).

the part of the agent.[37] Bartlett not only passed this story on to General
Terry but handed it to a reporter for the *Chicago Times*, which gave it a
big play. In due course, Irwin saw a clipping of the story in the *Times*;
he angrily wrote Hayt:

> I am mortified to see an Officer of the U.S. Army promulgating a report
> upon the authority of Bull Eagle, a noted bad Indian kept in the guard house a
> portion of last summer. . . . If I were to make as incriminating a report of
> the official actions of Major Bartlett on the testimony of an Indian whose bad
> character was known to me and furnish a special correspondent of the
> Chicago Times a copy for publication I would expect to be severely cen-
> sured by the department I represent.[38]

Incidents such as this were troublesome, but Irwin's basic problem
during that trying winter and spring was the question of a permanent
location for the agency. Despite the President's promise, the Indian
Bureau still hoped that it could persuade the Oglalas to remain along
the river, where they could be supplied and watched more cheaply
than at any point in the interior of the reservation. In Washington,
Red Cloud had expressed a preference for Tongue River, but when
that seemed to be out of the question he had indicated that he would
like to settle at White Clay Creek. He still talked about Tongue River
during the winter, but Irwin was able to convince him that this was
impossible and he again went back to an acceptance of White Clay.
Irwin was sure that the Government would have to accept this. He
wired Hayt: "Distance from Missouri to White Clay is objectionable,
but I talked them out of Tongue River and now fear if we oppose
White Clay they will get ugly." [39] Hayt's response was to urge Irwin to
use diplomacy. Moreover, he contended that the President's promise
did not contemplate letting the Indians decide the matter for themselves;
at best, a committee of "proper persons" would select the new location
with the consent of the Indians.[40]

Try as he might, Irwin could not persuade the Indians to change
their minds,[41] and after much counciling they agreed that Red Cloud

[37] Bartlett to AAG, Dept. of the Dakotas, January 29, 1878, NARS, RG 94, Doc.
File 4163, Sioux War, 1876.

[38] Irwin to E. A. Hayt, March 4, 1878, in Secretary of the Interior to Secretary of
War, March 23, 1878.

[39] Telegram, Irwin to Com. of Indian Affairs, February 17, 1878, NARS, RG 75,
LR, Red Cloud Agency.

[40] Telegram, Hayt to W. M. Leeds, February 18, 1878, *ibid.* Hayt was in New York
and sent instructions to Leeds in Washington for transmittal to Irwin.

[41] Telegram, Irwin to Hayt, March 18, 1878, *ibid.*

should send a message to the President. That message was clear and to the point:

> Great Father . . . we have done what you asked us to do when we were in Washington, and whatever General Crook has asked us to do since then we have done it the best we could. We were raised in this country and know where we would like to live. We want to live where the country is good, that is good land. We try to do whatever the Great Father through our agents asks us to do. We do not want to work against the Great Father's orders. We have asked for a good place in our country where the land is good, also plenty of timber and good water, where we can settle down and farm and become rich. On this side of Big White Clay, we know all the streams and know that there is not timber enough to build our agency, and we asked you as friends to give us Big White Clay, and ask you as friends again today for the same place, and hope you will give us that place. When I was in Washington you told me to select a place in our country, and this is the only place that I know of that will suit us; it is no use to go to the trouble to hunt the country over for we know it all. We were raised in this country, and know that this is the only good place for our agency in it, and ask you Great Father today as friends to try to let us have this place for our agency. These are my wishes and the wishes of all my people.[42]

Continued efforts to persuade the Oglalas to change their minds brought nothing but antagonism. Inspector J. H. Hammond, who was at the Missouri River agency and out among the Indians in April, reported that further negotiations were useless: nothing short of force would keep the Indians from moving, and the troops at the agency were wholly inadequate to deal with an outbreak, should one occur. He urged prompt and decisive action, one way or another.[43] It was soon evident, however, that nothing would be done until Congress passed the Indian appropriation bill.[44] On June 20 Congress finally acted, authorizing the Secretary of the Interior to appoint a commission to find a permanent location for both the Spotted Tail and Red Cloud Indians.[45] Irwin had warned that the Indians were "not in a mood

[42] This letter was transmitted to the President through military channels by Maj. P. D. Vroom, commanding troops at agency, March 14, 1878, NARS, RG 94, Doc. File 4163, Sioux War, 1876.

[43] Hammond to Com. of Indian Affairs, April 3, 1878; Telegram, Hammond to Com. of Indian Affairs, April 13, 1878, NARS, RG 75, LR, Red Cloud Agency.

[44] Penciled note by Hayt on letter, Irwin to Com. of Indian Affairs, May 7, 1878, *ibid.* The note apparently was the Commissioner's reply to Irwin's letter, which was another plea for prompt action.

[45] Report of the Sioux Commission, Com. of Indian Affairs, *Annual Report*, 1878, pp. 156–161.

to talk with any person or commission"[46] but agreed to go out to their camp and try to quiet their fears until the Commissioners arrived.[47]

The Commission, consisting of Col. D. S. Stanley, J. M. Haworth (a former Kiowa agent), and Rev. A. L. Riggs, and accompanied by Commissioner Hayt, first visited the Spotted Tail people, arriving at their temporary agency on July 5.[48] Spotted Tail had been as adamant as Red Cloud about removing from the Missouri, and the Commissioners found him difficult to deal with. He called Hayt a "bald-headed liar,"[49] and in words which the Commissioners said "were for the Indian populace" declared that he would break up his camps in ten days, burn down the present agency buildings and head for the place he had selected on Rosebud Creek near the south fork of the White River.[50]

After this disappointing conference, the Commissioners moved upriver to the Red Cloud Agency. Red Cloud, who had been persuaded by Irwin to come in and meet the Commissioners, was not as aggressive as Spotted Tail had been—an interesting reversal of the roles of the two chiefs—but he was equally firm in his determination to move. He brandished a paper (apparently a transcript of the proceedings in Washington), which, he said, contained the President's promise that if he would come near the Missouri for the winter, he could select the location he wished for his agency; he had selected White Clay Creek and he would go to no other place.[51] What's more, he wanted five hundred cows and a Catholic priest, and he hoped the Commission would not forget it.[52] Colonel Stanley pointed out that the cost of transporting supplies to White Clay would be very great and would reduce the amount of goods they could receive. Haworth, however, said that Red Cloud had made a good speech, and was absolutely right.[53]

[46] Telegram, Irwin to Secretary of the Interior, June 25, 1878, NARS, RG 75, LR, Red Cloud Agency.

[47] Telegram, Irwin to Com. of Indian Affairs, July 5, 1878, *ibid.* Irwin, incidentally, had submitted his resignation (Irwin to Com. of Indian Affairs, April 27, 1878, *ibid.*) but stated in this telegram that he would withdraw it for the present, "if everything that has been promised the Indians is carried out in good faith."

[48] Report of the Sioux Commission (above, n. 45).

[49] *Omaha Weekly Herald*, July 19, 1878.

[50] Report of the Sioux Commission.

[51] *Ibid.*

[52] *New York Times*, July 15, 1878.

[53] *Ibid.*

The conference ended with matters still up in the air. Hayt left for Washington and the Commissioners made preparations to head west to examine the country chosen by the two tribes for their future homes. Upon inspection, they agreed in general that the areas selected were satisfactory but they found fault with both specific sites. They recommended that Spotted Tail settle on the South Fork of the White River rather than on Rosebud Creek and that Red Cloud locate on Wounded Knee Creek, a short distance from White Clay.[54] A final decision was delayed, however, Hayt apparently believing that the Indians could still be held on the Missouri, though how or why it is difficult to understand.[55]

The Indians now took matters into their own hands. On September 19 they asked Irwin to notify the Great Father that they had waited long and anxiously for permission to move, that the time had come when they must move to avoid cold weather, that they were determined to move themselves the best way possible and would start in two days.[56] On September 25 Irwin, now desperate, telegraphed Hayt:

> I have held the Indians as long as possible; they are starting for White Clay. The unaccountable delay has made them angry and they are not now to be trifled with. As I have repeatedly wired the Department, and as my advice has not been adopted in a single instance, the responsibility does not rest with me. . . . I am intensely exercised over the state of affairs at this agency and earnestly insist that you give me such instructions and privileges as will enable me to act promptly.[57]

This telegram illustrates the confusion and cross-purposes rampant in the Indian Bureau. Commissioner Hayt had acted to expedite the movement of the Red Cloud people by appointing James R. O'Beirne, a clerk in his office, as special removal supervisor—apparently without advising Irwin, and as a means of rebuking the agent for his championship of Red Cloud's insistence upon locating at White Clay. During the visit of the Stanley Commission, Irwin had openly expressed the opinion that the Indians should be allowed to leave the Missouri; after returning from the West, Hayt complained, "There is more trouble

[54] Report of the Sioux Commission

[55] When he got back to Washington, he conferred with General Sherman and the latter telegraphed Colonel Stanley that he agreed fully with the Commissioner that the Indians should remain on the Missouri and urged him to try to persuade them to do so (Telegram, Sherman to Stanley, July 30, 1878, NARS, RG 94, Doc. File 4163, Sioux War, 1876).

[56] Telegram, Irwin to Com. of Indian Affairs, September 19, 1878, NARS, RG 75, LR, Red Cloud Agency.

[57] *Ibid.*, September 25, 1878.

with the Agent than with the Indians. . . . the insinuation of bad faith is simply insulting and it is time it and ringing changes on the President's promises were stopped."[58] Irwin, for his part, charged that Hayt was attempting a "sell-out" of the Sioux.[59]

Special Supervisor O'Beirne did not go to the Missouri but went out to Wounded Knee Creek (actually, he headquartered at Camp Sheridan) to await the coming of the Sioux, who presumably were to start west without authorization (which they did) and were to be received officially when they arrived. O'Beirne, with a great show of energy, got to work at once on the agency buildings, which were located on White Clay Creek, after all, rather than on Wounded Knee. The buildings at the old agency near Camp Robinson provided large quantities of material; additional materials were to come in by wagon from the Union Pacific station at Sidney, Nebraska. O'Beirne had great difficulty in getting transportation, but he assured Hayt, "all mortal energy has been and will be thrown into the work," and despite the opposition of "the railroad and transportation monopolists" he, would push ahead.[60]

O'Beirne telegraphed reports almost daily. Adding to the confusion was the presence in the Nebraska sandhills of a small band of Cheyennes under Dull Knife; they had escaped from their reservation in Indian territory and were heading north, presumably to join the Sioux.[61] There was fear, of course, that the Cheyennes would combine with the Sioux, who were thoroughly disgusted with the Government, to create trouble. This fear, however, was soon allayed. Red Cloud, Little Wound, Red Dog, No Flesh, and Spider arrived at White Clay at noon on October 7; they seemed pleased with the arrangements under way for their people and assured O'Beirne that they would remain friendly to the whites.[62]

Meanwhile the main body of Indians was making its way slowly westward. The Indian Bureau provided ninety-seven wagons for the movement, and the Sioux themselves did the freighting.[63] Irwin got the

[58] Telegram, Hayt to William M. Leeds, August 15, 1878, NARS, RG 75, LR, Red Cloud Agency.

[59] Irwin to Schurz, September 5, 1878, *ibid.*

[60] Telegram, O'Beirne to Com. of Indian Affairs, November 2, 1878, *ibid.*

[61] For an account of the Cheyennes, see Mari Sandoz, *Cheyenne Autumn* (New York: McGraw-Hill Book Co., 1953).

[62] Telegram, O'Beirne to Com. of Indian Affairs, October 8, 1878, LR, Red Cloud Agency.

[63] Telegram, Irwin to Com. of Indian Affairs, November 24, 1878, *ibid.*

last wagon loaded and on its way on November 11 and the next day started west himself with his wife and the families of the agency employees. When they arrived at White Clay on November 18, they had to camp on the prairie because, despite O'Beirne's energetic activities, there was but one small building at the agency and that was occupied by the special removal supervisor.[64] O'Beirne and Irwin kept the wires hot with complaints against each other, but the Indians went into camp for the winter generally content in the thought that at last they had a permanent home; Red Cloud even asked when the Government was going to build his house.[65]

In Washington, too, there was a feeling that the question had finally been settled and that the Oglalas, after ten years of wandering and of wrangling about a location, were finally established at a permanent agency. To lessen the identification with Red Cloud, who had been associated with so much of the trouble over location, the agency was given a new name, "Pine Ridge." Inspector Hammond thought the name incongruous inasmuch as the agency was situated in a wide valley with no ridge and with pines only in the ravines where they did not show. He suggested the name "Oglala." Hayt did not agree—"the name Pine Ridge has been adopted and will be maintained if for no other reason, viz. that not one in a hundred can spell Ogalala [*sic*] correctly."[66]

[64] Telegrams, Irwin to Com. of Indian Affairs, November 11, 19, 1878, *ibid.*

[65] O'Beirne to Com. of Indian Affairs, November 29, 1878, *ibid.*

[66] Endorsement to letter, J. H. Hammond to Com. of Indian Affairs, December 8, 1878, *ibid.*

CHAPTER 14

The Struggle with McGillycuddy

On New Year's Day, 1879, James Irwin submitted his resignation as agent for the Red Cloud Indians, "to take effect as early as may be convenient." He wrote the Commissioner of Indian Affairs:

> I have the honor to represent that I am thoroughly disgusted with your management of the Indian service at this Agency; your crude and impracticable theories so inveterately adhered to; your disregard of my suggestions and entreaties, as well as my rights and duties as an officer of the United States; the failure of your plans causing unnecessary expense to the Government and which may yet cause more serious trouble than you can remedy. I am neither in your confidence or favor. You having tied my hands, while others are by your authority managing the public service, and as I can no longer serve the Department with justice to it or credit to myself, it becomes my duty to retire.[1]

Commissioner Hayt, who had been at odds with Irwin for months, lost no time in accepting the agent's resignation and in finding a successor. His choice fell upon Dr. Valentine T. McGillycuddy, thirty-year-old contract surgeon serving with the military force which had accompanied the Sioux on their journey to the Missouri and back. McGillycuddy had had wide experience in the West and among the Sioux. A topographer as well as a physician, he had served with the Northern Boundary Survey and with the Jenney expedition. He had

---

[1] Irwin to E. A. Hayt, January 1, 1879, NARS, RG 75, LR, Red Cloud Agency.

been with General Crook in 1876, and as post surgeon at Camp Robinson he had attended the dying Crazy Horse. Fearless, hot-tempered, and stubborn, he seemed to be just the man to break the will of Red Cloud and the other recalcitrant old Oglalas, and drive them along the white man's road.[2]

While McGillycuddy remained in Washington to study the Indian Bureau's procedures, Special Supervisor James R. O'Beirne continued to develop the facilities at Pine Ridge. He seems to have won a degree of cooperation from Red Cloud; at least, the chief consented to partici-pate in laying the cornerstone of the agency schoolhouse. O'Beirne regarded this as evidence of "triumph quietly effected over his haughty disposition and inclination to self will," although Red Cloud's brief comments were open to another interpretation. As he placed a gold ring in the box, he said solemnly, "May Almighty God put it into the hearts of the white man not to disturb us in our present home, but allow us to remain here in peace."[3]

McGillycuddy arrived at Pine Ridge on March 10 and immediately got into difficulty, not with Red Cloud, but with Irwin, who refused to turn over the agency until he had been given a receipt for the property. Irwin insisted that he was only following custom, that never had an Indian agent who had not resigned under charges been required to give up his post until he had obtained such a receipt; McGillycuddy demanded that he be permitted to take over the agency and issue a receipt later, after the property had been accounted for. He got tele-graphic support from Hayt, and on the sixteenth Irwin reluctantly stepped down.[4]

Trouble with Red Cloud soon followed. McGillycuddy called a conference of the principal chiefs to explain his hopes for their people and to enlist their cooperation. Red Cloud presided, and at first he seemed disposed to cooperate. He passed the pipe to the new agent and advised the Indians to listen to what their new Father had to say. Encouraged, McGillycuddy got out a map of the reservation. He pointed to many fertile valleys. The Indians, he said, should quit living around the agency and go out into those valleys, plow the land,

[2] For a life of McGillycuddy, see Julia B. McGillycuddy, *McGillycuddy: Agent* (Stan-ford University: Stanford University Press, 1941). This biography, by McGillycuddy's second wife, is far from objective, but it is valuable for presenting McGillycuddy's side of the many conflicts in which he was embroiled during his term as agent, and particu-larly the conflicts with Red Cloud.

[3] O'Beirne to Hayt, February 12, 1879, NARS, RG 75, LR, Red Cloud Agency.

[4] V. T. McGillycuddy to Com. of Indian Affairs, March 17, 1879, *ibid.*

and grow crops. They then would become independent. Red Cloud immediately objected. He rose and said:

> Father, the Great Spirit did not make us to work. He made us to hunt and fish. He gave us the great prairies and hills and covered them with buffalo, deer, and antelope. He filled the rivers and streams with fish. The white man can work if he wants to, but the Great Spirit did not make us to work. The white man owes us a living for the lands he has taken from us.

After a warning that the time would come when the Indians would have to work in order to live, McGillycuddy dropped the subject and proposed the creation of an Indian police force. He would hire fifty young men, give them uniforms, and organize them as a mounted police force. When they were sufficiently well trained, he would try to have the soldiers removed from the vicinity of the agency. Red Cloud replied that he would be happy to have the white soldiers taken away, but there was no need for a special police force; his own soldiers would enforce the law. The two men sparred verbally for a while and the council broke up, with Red Cloud opposing the idea of a police force and McGillycuddy determined to have one.[5]

A few days later, McGillycuddy went over to the Missouri River to inventory government property that had been left there. While he was gone, Red Cloud concluded that he would be unable to live with his new agent, and on May 1, together with twenty-one other chiefs, including Man-Afraid-of-His-Horse, Young-Man-Afraid, and Little Wound, he signed a letter to the President, asking for the removal of McGillycuddy and the reinstatement of Dr. Irwin.[6] O'Beirne was convinced that Irwin, who was still at the agency, had "been tampering with Red Cloud." He suppressed the letter and warned Irwin that he was violating the law in trying to influence the Indians as a private citizen, and that if violation could be proved he would be arrested.[7] Nothing came of either Red Cloud's request or O'Beirne's threats, but the difficulties increased rather than diminished.

On the day before Red Cloud requested McGillycuddy's removal, Father Meinrad McCarthy arrived at the agency with a letter to McGillycuddy from Abbot Martin, Superior of the Benedictine Mission among the Dakotas, requesting permission to establish a mission at Pine Ridge. Red Cloud, who repeatedly had asked for a

---

[5] McGillycuddy, *McGillycuddy: Agent*, pp. 103–104.

[6] Red Cloud and others to the President, May 1, 1879, NARS, RG 75, LR, Red Cloud Agency.

[7] O'Beirne to Hayt, May 14, 1879, *ibid.*

Catholic priest, welcomed Father McCarthy and insisted that he stay at the new house which the Government was building for him and which was nearing completion.[8] O'Beirne was friendly enough—he even gave the visitor twenty dollars to further his work—but he saw very clearly that Father McCarthy's objective was in violation of Indian Bureau regulations which gave the Episcopal Church monopolistic control over the souls of the Oglalas. He asked the priest to wait until Agent McGillycuddy returned and hurried off a letter to Washington, requesting guidance.[9]

By the time McGillycuddy got back, word had arrived from Washington that the priest would have to leave, and on May 17 the agent sent Father McCarthy a terse note informing him that his presence on the reservation could not be allowed, "Ecclesiastically or otherwise."[10] Not wanting to make an issue of the matter, McCarthy pitched his tent about two miles south of the reservation border near Camp Sheridan in Nebraska, and settled down to await further orders from his superiors. Red Cloud urged him to return, saying that he had his permission to re-enter the agency and that he was going to send a petition on his behalf to the Great White Father. McCarthy, however, did not want to create a disturbance which might jeopardize Catholic work among the Sioux; so despite Red Cloud's entreaties, he decided to remain off the reservation until given official permission to enter. After four months, he and his superiors concluded that there was no hope, and he was ordered to withdraw.

In denying Father McCarthy permission to work at Pine Ridge, the

[8] Apparently Red Cloud had been promised in Washington that as soon as he was permanently located, the Government would build a house for him. He kept reminding O'Beirne of the promise, and in February construction was begun on a four-room cottage, one-and-a-half stories high, with kitchen attached. It was completed at a cost of five hundred dollars. It is hard to believe that it was very far along in May, because McGillycuddy did not report its completion until December—at which time, interestingly enough, he requested authority to spend one hundred dollars for "cheap furniture, dishes, etc.," to enable Red Cloud "to live like a white man . . . as he is using every endeavor for the good of the agency and his tribe" (O'Beirne to Com. of Indian Affairs, February 26, 1879; McGillycuddy to Com. of Indian Affairs, December 2, 1879, NARS, RG 75, LR, Red Cloud Agency).

[9] O'Beirne to Com. of Indian Affairs, May 1, 1879, *ibid.*

[10] McGillycuddy to Reverend M. McCarthy, May 17, 1879, copy in *ibid.* McGillycuddy, *McGillycuddy: Agent*, pp. 105–109, reports a very pleasant luncheon conversation between the two men, in which McGillycuddy stated that Father McCarthy could remain on the reservation as long as he wanted to, provided he did not attempt to start a mission. This conversation is dated "One April Sunday," which obviously is incorrect.

Government acted against the expressed wishes of many Oglalas, who from the days of Father DeSmet's early work had preferred Catholic to Protestant missionaries. In a council held May 26, Red Cloud and a number of other leading chiefs insisted that they be permitted to have Catholic teachers. Red Cloud said:

> The Great Father and also the Commissioner told me that whenever and wherever I selected my place for a home, that there I should have school houses and churches with men in them in black gowns. There is one of those men here now and I want him to stay, and if Mr. Robinson [The Reverend John Robinson, Episcopal missionary at Pine Ridge] wants to stay, I have no objections. We want Black Gown and Mr. Robinson also to teach our children. I want you to write a letter and write it strong to the Great Father and the Commissioner telling them these things.

McGillycuddy transmitted the request in a letter addressed to the President, but Commissioner Hayt stopped it in his office. When Secretary Schurz visited Pine Ridge during the first week in September, Father McCarthy appealed directly to him but was told in no uncertain terms that he could not work on the reservation. It was this that ended the matter as far as the Catholics were concerned.[11]

Red Cloud used Schurz's visit as an opportunity to repeat his request for the removal of McGillycuddy. Schurz replied condescendingly: "Red Cloud, the Great Father is a very wise man. He knows everything. If there is anything wrong with your Agent he will know it before either you or I know it."[12] Indeed, Schurz seemed unable to take the old chief seriously. Although Red Cloud complained about a variety of things, including the Indian police which McGillycuddy had organized over his objections, Schurz told a reporter that he had heard only one complaint during his visit, "and that was that the school-teacher talked Dakota, and I was requested to urge upon them to confine themselves to English."[13] Obviously pleased with the way

[11] The council is reported in McGillycuddy to the President, May 26, 1879, NARS, RG 75, LR, Red Cloud Agency. For a general treatment of Father McCarthy's efforts, see Peter J. Rahill, *The Catholic Indian Missions and Grant's Peace Policy, 1870–1884* (Washington, D. C.: The Catholic University of America Press, 1953), pp. 276–284. A contemporary Catholic view of Indian policy will be found in P. Girard, "United States Indian Policy and Religious Liberty," *Catholic World*, XXVI (October, 1877), 90–108.) For a summary view of the Catholic Church's attitude toward the peace policy, see Henry E. Fritz, *The Movement for Indian Assimilation, 1860–1890* (Philadelphia: University of Pennsylvania Press, 1963), pp. 87–108.

[12] McGillycuddy, *McGillycuddy: Agent*, p. 146.

[13] *Chicago Tribune*, October 24, 1879; Ricker Mss., Tablet No. 149.

in which the Sioux were moving along the white man's road, as he had staked it out, Schurz wrote, in his annual report:

> When I entered upon my present duties I was told by men of long experience in Indian affairs that we would never be able to do anything with the Spotted Tail and Red Cloud Sioux "until they had received another thorough whipping." Since that time they have twice been obliged to change their location. A general outbreak was predicted a year ago. When I visited them this autumn I found their freighting wagons by hundreds on the road with their young warriors on the box, their chiefs with their people making hay and cultivating fields on the bottom lands, many of them building houses for their families; anxious to have their children educated; many requesting that their boys and girls be taken to our schools in the East, and the universal wish to be permanently settled and led on "in the white man's way."[14]

McGillycuddy, too, was pleased with the progress his charges had made in the few months he had been responsible for them—progress which had been achieved despite a history of "bribery, fraud, and corruption on the part of some of the former representatives of the government, in the way of contractors, agents, &c." The only serious obstacle to continued progress was the influence of the chiefs. They opposed all efforts to encourage the Indians to work and support themselves because they saw the development of independence as a threat to their authority. If the Government wanted to continue to maintain the Indians as savages "and feed them until they finally die out," McGillycuddy wrote in his first report, "I would recommend the tribal system as the most feasible one." But if the present program, designed to make the Indians self-supporting, was to succeed, the power of the chiefs must be broken. He continued:

> An Indian can no more serve two masters than a white man. He cannot serve his chief and the agent at the same time. The chiefs are men who have as a rule risen to their position by their superior judgment and acuteness, whether on the war path or elsewhere, and they certainly appreciate the fact that they are more important personages, as controlling, without question, a large band of savages, ready for war or peace at their command, than in the, to them, uninteresting position of a quasi-chief over a civilized community, the individuals of which will consult their own interests before they obey orders.[15]

McGillycuddy did not mention Red Cloud by name, but it is clear that he had him in mind: the chief had opposed him at almost every

14 Secretary of the Interior, *Annual Report*, 1879, pp. 23–24.
15 *Ibid.*, pp. 37–40.

turn and had even gone so far as to ask for his removal. This opposition, and—in McGillycuddy's eyes—general obstructionism continued during 1880, both on and off the reservation. In particular, there was difficulty at the Indian Training School at Carlisle, Pennsylvania, where a number of young Brulés and Oglalas had been sent. In June, Red Cloud paid a visit to the school along with several other chiefs. Among them was Spotted Tail, who, despite his long history of collaboration, was developing a reputation for backwardness equal to Red Cloud's.[16] The officer in charge of the school, Lt. R. H. Pratt, complained that both Red Cloud and Spotted Tail made speeches "offensive and prejudical to the discipline of the school."[17] Further evidence of the obstructionist activities of both chiefs was reported shortly after the delegation returned. Charges that T. G. Cowgill, a licensed trader, had been stealing corn were brought before a grand jury at Deadwood, Dakota Territory. The charges were quashed, but McGillycuddy had to go to Deadwood and testify on behalf of the trader. He complained that the whole affair was "a case of malicious prosecution" directed at him and reported that the Indians were "very much disturbed" because of the prominent part taken by Red Cloud and Spotted Tail in presenting the charges. McGillycuddy further reported that the Indians were "holding councils day and night looking toward the final deposing of Red Cloud as chief."[18]

Four months earlier, in March, McGillycuddy, recommending the purchase of a wagon and horses for Red Cloud, had reported that the chief was "behaving himself in an exemplary manner,"[19] but by the end of summer he had obviously taken all he could tolerate from the head man of the Oglalas. In his annual report, submitted September 1, he wrote:

> I have necessarily met much opposition, notably from Red Cloud, who, with the neighboring chief Spotted Tail, form about as egregious a pair of old frauds in the way of aids to their people in civilization as it has ever been my fortune or misfortune to encounter. When these two old men shall have been finally gathered to their fathers, we can truly speak of them as good

[16] It should be borne in mind that Spotted Tail's cooperation with the Government had always been on the basis of maintaining the tribal system as he understood it; he was as much opposed as Red Cloud was to the Schurz policy of civilization.

[17] Pratt to E. J. Brooks, acting Com. of Indian Affairs, June 24, 1880, NARS, RG 75, LR, Spotted Tail Agency.

[18] McGillycuddy to Com. of Indian Affairs, July 27, 1880; Telegram, August 9, 1880, NARS, RG 75, LR, Red Cloud Agency.

[19] McGillycuddy to Com. of Indian Affairs, March 26, 1880, *ibid.*

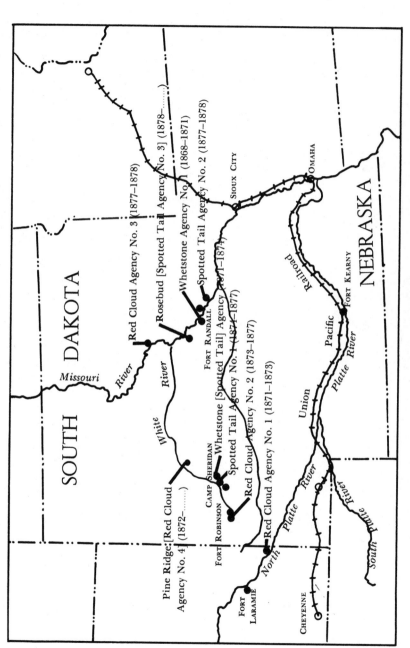

Red Cloud and Spotted Tail Agencies 1865-1880

Indians and only regret that Providence, in its inscrutable way, had so long delayed their departure.[20]

Two days later he called a council of the chiefs and head men for the purpose of deposing Red Cloud and selecting a new head chief. Sensing what was up, Red Cloud refused to come, even after McGillycuddy had sent the head of the Indian police to tell him that his rations would be stopped if he did not obey the summons. There had long been dissatisfaction with Red Cloud's leadership among those who wished to supplant him—Young-Man-Afraid-of-His-Horse, for example, told a reporter that Red Cloud and Spotted Tail were "not fit to be Agency Chiefs; they don't know how to do business"[21]—but McGillycuddy soon learned that when the chips were down most of the Oglalas would stay with their old chief; of more than a hundred chiefs and head men who were asked to vote, all but five placed their sticks in Red Cloud's pile. American Horse, designated to report the results of the council to the President, wrote: "Red Cloud was chosen almost without opposition. . . . He has been our head chief, he is now and always will be, because the Nation love, respect and believe in him." If there was to be a change, it should be in the agent. "We ask and beg of you to take our present Agent from us," American Horse continued, "and give us another in his place so our people can be at peace once more which they will never be as long as he remains with us."[22]

As far as McGillycuddy was concerned, the chiefs' action had no effect; he always referred to Red Cloud thereafter as "the former chief" or "the deposed chief," and kept insisting that the old man was no longer a power to be reckoned with in dealing with the Oglalas. The realities of situation, however, destroyed much of the force of the agent's insistence, and throughout his remaining years as agent at Pine Ridge, McGillycuddy, in one way or another, was preoccupied with the problem of Red Cloud, who symbolized the old way of life and who

[20] Com. of Indian Affairs, *Annual Report*, 1880, p. 40.

[21] *Chicago Tribune*, August 22, 1879, clipping from Ricker Mss., Tablet No. 125.

[22] American Horse to the President, September 4, 1880, NARS, RG 75, LR, Red Cloud Agency. See also Red Cloud to the President, September 4, 1880, *ibid.* These letters apparently were inspired or written by H. C. Dear, a trader whom McGillycuddy banned from the reservation "for disorderly conduct." McGillycuddy, while evidently not reporting the council, later asserted that Red Cloud (and presumably American Horse also) had been persuaded by Dear to write to the President: "Red Cloud is now an old man in his dotage, childish and not responsible for what he does. He acknowledged that he knew nothing of the facts as stated in the letter but was induced to write it" (McGillycuddy to Com. of Indian Affairs, November 15, 1880, *ibid.*).

seemed at every turn to be blocking his people's progress along the white man's road.

In February Red Cloud tried to stop the census. This was a perennial issue, deriving in part from a deeply ingrained dread of being counted and in part from a belief that the whole process was somehow designed to bring about a reduction in rations and annuities. When Saville had first tried to institute the census among the Oglalas in 1874, he had stirred up unrest almost to the point of an outbreak;[23] in subsequent years the annual counting had always produced a degree of tension, but none of the chiefs had openly rebelled. Why Red Cloud decided to make an issue of it at this time is not clear; more than likely he opposed the census simply because McGillycuddy had ordered it taken. Whatever his motives, however, his efforts were unsuccessful. He sent runners to the villages with orders to stop the count, but none of the chiefs were willing to interfere. McGillycuddy met Red Cloud's own refusal by withholding rations from his village, and after a week Red Cloud relented and permitted himself and his twenty-seven families to be counted.[24]

With the inauguration of President Garfield, Red Cloud made yet another attempt to secure McGillycuddy's removal. He wrote the President, saying that he hoped to see him soon and noting that the agent was on his way to Washington. The agent was not a good man. He had never given Red Cloud the ox-teams and wagons which had been promised him, and he was making the agency "more like a military post than an agency to civilize my people." Red Cloud hoped the Great Father would keep the agent in Washington and not let him return.[25] A short time later, Red Cloud and ninety-six chiefs sent a petition to the President formally asking McGillycuddy's removal:

> We as a people have lost faith in him from his unjust treatment of us in many cases. He says we have no rights on our reservation when we differ from his opinion. He has tried to depose our head chief Red Cloud which the nation does not want and we believe he steals our goods and we know he lies to us.[26]

All this happened while McGillycuddy was in Washington. When he

[23] See above, pp. 162–163.
[24] McGillycuddy to Com. of Indian Affairs, March 1, 8, 1881, NARS, RG 75, LR, Red Cloud Agency.
[25] Red Cloud to the President, April 28, 1881, *ibid.*
[26] Red Cloud *et al.* to the President, May 12, 1881, *ibid.*

returned to the agency he found that there had been "secret counselling" during his absence and concluded that members of the Dear family were responsible for it. They may have been—the family had had no love for McGillycuddy since he had taken H. C. Dear's tradership from him—but George Stover had signed the petition as interpreter. In any case, McGillycuddy was able to produce the names of seventeen chiefs who swore that they had not authorized use of their signatures, but of these only five appeared on the petition: Little Wound, Red Dog, High Wolf, Slow Bull, and Man-Afraid-of-His-Horse.[27] Whether these men knew nothing of the contents of the petition, had not authorized the use of their names, or simply had had a change of heart, we will probably never know. Little Wound and Red Dog, particularly the latter, had often worked closely with Red Cloud,[28] but consistency was no more an attribute of the red politician than of his white counterpart, and given the complexities of Oglala politics, anything could happen. Moreover, because of the language barrier, it was always possible—and frequently justifiable—for any Indian to say that he did not understand what was in a paper to which he had put his mark.

At the annual Sun Dance on June 22, Red Cloud and McGillycuddy had it out in the presence of many chiefs and several Army officers, including General Crook's aide, Lt. John G. Bourke. Red Cloud made a long speech, protesting his friendship for the Great Father and reciting his efforts to maintain peace; as for difficulties between himself and his agent, they were mostly the result of women's talk. He concluded: "I hope the Great Father will keep us both still." But McGillycuddy was in no mood to keep still. He wanted Red Cloud to explain the letter he had sent to the President, charging the agent with lying and stealing; he wanted Red Cloud to explain why the chiefs had said that their names were put to the letter without their consent, that they had been stolen by Red Cloud and Mr. Dear. Red Cloud replied: "As to the names you say I stole, I'd like to hear them read so I could find what ones I stole. I want to have a talk about that letter as soon as the Sun Dance is over. I don't think I put anything bad in that letter."

The rest of the conference went like this:

DR. McGILLYCUDDY: Do you deny that you charged that I lied and stole?

---

[27] Red Cloud *et al.* to the President, May 12, 1881, *ibid.*; McGillycuddy to Com. of Indian Affairs, June 2, 1881, *ibid.*

[28] Indeed, Red Dog had gone to the conference at which McGillycuddy had got his seventeen names as an emissary of Red Cloud.

RED CLOUD: Here is the way I wanted that letter written. I never said that you lied or stole. I gave the names of six agents and said that two of them were good agents and this last Agent we have here now, I have nothing against. All that I complained of him for, every time that he or I go to Washington, these words come up. But I wish to ask for, if this talk keeps up, I would like to have our Agent and General Crook and ourselves go to Washington and straighten this thing up.

DR. McGILLYCUDDY: This thing comes down to a question as to who has told a lie—you, Red Cloud, or Mr. Dear? I blame you, Red Cloud, for this thing and so does the Great Father for counselling with Mr. Dear or having anything to do with him. At the council we had last fall, you, Red Cloud, promised the Inspector and me that you would have nothing to do with Mr. Dear. As long as you or your people go to Mr. Dear or have anything to do with Mr. Dear there will be trouble.

RED CLOUD: There is another thing I want to say about the letter which was written last and which Mr. Dear knows nothing about.[29]

DR. McGILLYCUDDY: I'll have nothing to do with you, Red Cloud, until you tell me who has been writing these letters. If you mean what you say, that I am a good man, you ought to trust me and tell me who has been writing those letters, and making this trouble. It is in your hand now to settle all this business.

RED CLOUD: The reason I didn't attend that council, I wanted to see somebody from Washington and also the Commanding Officer from Robinson. I didn't go myself, but I sent Red Dog.[30]

DR. McGILLYCUDDY: You should always attend a council when sent for.[31]

Not very clear, coherent, or conclusive; but such conferences seldom were. Actually, the Sun-Dance confrontation, inconclusive as it was, seems to have been accompanied by a temporary thaw in the relations between Red Cloud and McGillycuddy; at least their personal conflict was subordinated to the problem of the Ponca lands along the Niobrara which had been plaguing the Indian Bureau for several years. These lands had been assigned to the Sioux by the Treaty of 1868, and in 1877, when the Government was making an effort to remove the Sioux to the Missouri River, the Poncas had been sent down to Indian Territory against their will. Some of them, including Standing Bear,

[29] This may have been Red Cloud to "My Great Father," June 4, 1881, NARS, RG 75, LR, Red Cloud Agency, in which he called attention to the earlier petition and asked again for the removal of McGillycuddy as agent. George Stover actually wrote the letter.

[30] This presumably was the council referred to in Note 27, above.

[31] Transcript of conference held at Sun Dance . . . June 22, 1881 . . . transmitted by McGillycuddy to Com. of Indian Affairs, June 23, 1881, NARS, RG 75, LR, Red Cloud Agency.

tried to return; their arrest and ensuing trial created so much public concern that President Hayes appointed a commission to investigate. The Commission recommended that those Poncas who wished to return to their ancestral lands be allowed to do so, and the Government was now anxious to obtain the consent of the Sioux. Accordingly, the Indian Bureau decided to fall back upon the time-honored custom of bringing a delegation of chiefs to Washington, and no matter what agents might say, any delegation of chiefs had to include Red Cloud and Spotted Tail. Since Spotted Tail was killed shortly before the group was scheduled to leave, the Brulé delegation was headed by White Thunder, who was later killed by Spotted Tail's son.[32]

Although White Thunder spoke for the Brulés, Red Cloud clearly dominated the proceedings at Washington. He was in a generous mood; in addition to agreeing that the Poncas should return to their lands, he suggested that if the Cheyennes wanted to leave Indian Territory he would be happy to provide lands for them on his reservation.[33] Red Cloud also looked after a few of his friends, securing permission from the Secretary of the Interior (S. J. Kirkwood, who had replaced Schurz with the inauguration of the Garfield administration) for certain white men who had intermarried with the Indians to remain on the reservation, pending good behavior.

McGillycuddy saw nothing but evil coming of this. In his annual report, penned shortly after his return from Washington, he complained of drunkenness among the Indians as the source of much difficulty and charged that unprincipled white men on the reservation were at the root of the evil. He went on:

> To thoroughly prevent the introduction of liquor into the Sioux country is a difficult matter. It is true that the severe laws enacted by the United States to prevent the traffic should apparently put a stop to it, but when we consider that the noble red men as a people evince a remarkably natural taste for the article, it is not to be wondered at that they should shield the person who may attempt to supply them. This taste and desire for liquor appears not alone among the common Indians; it is not unwelcome to even Red Cloud (whom an editor of one of the philanthropic journals East recently very gushingly termed "the grand old chieftain"), for excessive use of the

---

[32] Both killings were associated with the intense power struggle going on at Rosebud. See George E. Hyde, *A Sioux Chronicle* (Norman: University of Oklahoma Press, 1956), pp. 63–66; Hyde, *Spotted Tail's Folk* (Norman: University of Oklahoma Press, 1961), pp. 276–304.

[33] *New York Times*, August 18, 19, 20, 21, 1881; the Ponca Agreement will be found in Com. of Indian Affairs, *Annual Report*, 1881, pp. xlviii–xliv.

fluid which exhilarates and at the same time intoxicates has had much to do with diminating what grandeur formerly existed in this Indian, and has resulted in his downfall among his people.[34]

On September 5 the agent reported "several cases of drunkenness among the Indians," and charged that they were getting their liquor "through the medium of white men living with Indian women for whose welfare ex-chief Red Cloud was so solicitious."[35] Pursuing the matter with the bulldog tenacity so characteristic of his actions, McGillycuddy charged later that "many of these white men, or as they are more fitly termed 'squaw men'" were not really married to their Indian women but lived with them or not as their desires dictated, and when "tiring of their squaws . . . purchased newer and fresher ones," with the result that they had "several broods of half-breed children, who are illegitimate."[36]

Although McGillycuddy continued to press his case against the squaw men with his superiors in Washington, in view of Secretary Kirkwood's letter and Red Cloud's solicitude, there was little that he could do about them on the reservation, and apparently during the fall of 1881 he did not try to move directly against the offenders or against Red Cloud himself, who seemed to be reasonably content. In November the chief wrote the Commissioner of Indian Affairs to request a flag that had been promised him and photographs of two clerks in the Indian Bureau, who "were particular friends."[37] In January, he reported: "My people are getting along well. The Agent with us is a good Agent. . . ."[38]

This happy state of affairs was not to last long; on April 5 McGillycuddy warned Commissioner Price: "Ex-chief Red Cloud is holding his usual Spring councils with the intention of securing if possible the removal of the present agent." He confessed that "to be eternally harassed by this old man is getting to be somewhat monotonous," and suggested that if Price had any misgivings about the agency, it might be just as well to send an inspector out to investigate.[39] Meanwhile McGillycuddy moved to strengthen his position vis-à-vis the aging

[34] McGillycuddy, Annual Report, September 1, 1881, in Com. of Indian Affairs, *Annual Report*, 1881, p. 45.

[35] McGillycuddy to Com. of Indian Affairs, September 5, 1881, NARS, RG 75, LR, Red Cloud Agency.

[36] *Ibid.*, October 13, 1881.

[37] Red Cloud to the Com. of Indian Affairs, November 26, 1881, NARS, RG 75.

[38] *Ibid.*, January 31, 1882.

[39] McGillycuddy to Com. of Indian Affairs, April 5, 1882, NARS, RG 75.

chief. He called a council of the chiefs and head men and, according to his report, got a vote of confidence in his administration of agency affairs and of censure of Red Cloud. We do not know just who attended the council, but Young-Man-Afraid, Little Wound, American Horse, No Flesh, and Blue Horse all made speeches, presumably in support of the agent.[40]

Despite this vote of confidence, McGillycuddy viewed the approaching Sun Dance with apprehension. The Indians always worked themselves into a fever of excitement at the Sun Dance, and the ceremony was calculated to arouse visions of the glories of the old way of life. Moreover, there were many Sitting Bull Indians on the reservation and some Northern Cheyennes, and most of these were hostile to the agent and the whole reservation system. Red Cloud could easily use the occasion to stir up ill feeling. Apparently he tried to do so. Rigged out in breech cloth, paint, and feathers, he served as "whipper in" during the ceremonies, and counciled with many large delegations.[41] Nothing happened—for which McGillycuddy credited Young-Man-Afraid and the Indian police—and the agent reflected that it was "merely a question of time, pending the death of Red Cloud and a few more of the ancient that the Sun Dance and other barbarous practices will die a natural death."[42]

It was, indeed, "merely a question of time," but McGillycuddy would not see that time during his tenure as agent, and within a few weeks after the Sun Dance of 1882 he found himself locked in combat with his ancient rival and facing the most serious crisis of his stormy career at Pine Ridge.

On Sunday, August 13, Red Cloud and about fifty followers left the reservation without a pass and went down into Nebraska for a feast at the ranch of Louis Shangrau, a half-breed whom McGillycuddy had evicted for bad conduct. Among those present were He Dog, a Sitting Bull chief; Woman's Dress, an enlisted scout from Fort Robinson; Cloud Shield, who recently had been dismissed as lieutenant of the Indian police; and American Horse, who was apt to turn up in any council, and who had earlier supported McGillycuddy. Also present was William J. Godfrey of Colorado, who, McGillycuddy charged, was purported to be an old personal friend of Henry M. Teller, Kirkwood's successor as Secretary of the Interior.[43] Godfrey had a letter all ready

---

[40] *Ibid.*, May 4, 1882.   [41] *Ibid.*, July 10, 1882.   [42] *Ibid.*

[43] McGillycuddy to Com. of Indian Affairs, August 17, 1882, NARS, RG 75, LR. This, and McGillycuddy to W. J. Pollock, September 16, 1882, are the only accounts of the council I have seen. Obviously they are prejudiced, but unless otherwise

for the Indians to sign. Addressed to Secretary Teller, it informed him of "the many acts of petty tyranny and insults we are daily compelled to endure from our Agent here." Reminding the Secretary that two earlier petitions for the removal of the agent had been transmitted without acknowledgment, this one advised him that

> if the incumbent as U.S. Agent is not removed from this Agency within sixty days, or a proper person sent out in the mean time to fully investigate his gross misconduct here, we will upon the expiration of the above stated time take upon ourselves the responsibility of politely escorting him out of our country, and let the consequences be what they may.[44]

The next day Red Cloud threatened to kill the freighters who were preparing to leave for the railroad station at Thatcher, Nebraska, to pick up some six hundred thousand pounds of freight, including a large quantity of bacon, which had been delivered there. Fearing for their lives, the freighters refused to move, and McGillycuddy suspended the issue of coffee, sugar, and bacon. He also got wind of the council at Shangrau's and arrested Woman's Dress for violating his trust as an Indian scout. On Tuesday morning the telegraph line, which had been out of repair for two days, was put in working order, and McGillycuddy wired Commissioner Price of Red Cloud's threat against the freighters, adding, "It depends on your department whether I am to be agent or chief clerk for Red Cloud." That afternoon he received a telegram from Price assuring him that he would be "sustained by this office as agent against the claims of Red Cloud."

Armed with this, and hearing on Wednesday morning that a copy of the petition had been sent to the commanding officer at Fort Robinson, McGillycuddy decided to summon a general council and sent runners to the villages. Freighting was resumed on the same day, and Red Cloud made no effort to carry out his earlier threat.[45] Also on Wednesday George Sword wrote the Commissioner of Indian

---

indicated they are used for the council and the events immediately following. For a brief account of Teller's appointment as Secretary of the Interior and his administration of Indian affairs, see Elmer Ellis, *Henry Moore Teller: Defender of the West* (Caldwell Idaho: The Caxton Press, 1941), pp. 132–144.

[44] Red Cloud *et al.* to Henry M. Teller, Secretary of the Interior, August 13, 1882, NARS, RG 75, LR. On that same day, Red Cloud also sent a letter to the Secretary of the Interior asking that the order banning Shangrau from the reservation be revoked, stating that he would be answerable for his good conduct.

[45] Telegram, McGillycuddy to Com. of Indian Affairs, August 16, 1882, *ibid.*

Affairs, assuring him that white soldiers were not needed, that most of the Indians wished "to live in peace and enjoy the prosperity which has come to them." "Red Cloud," he added, "has been trying hard to make trouble and I think that any foolish Indians who think he can make trouble should be locked up." [46]

McGillycuddy would soon be saying the same thing. On Friday afternoon the Indians assembled in the general council room. McGillycuddy warned them that unless Red Cloud could be stopped his actions would bring white soldiers. He hoped they would take the matter in their own hands and settle it. Sword, Young-Man-Afraid, and Little Wound dominated the proceedings: the agent could rest assured that they would take care of Red Cloud. Yellow Hair, a common Indian who had signed the threatening petition, made a long speech in which he protested his innocence and his desire for peace. American Horse was on hand too, but McGillycuddy refused to shake hands with him. American Horse was hurt. "I have seen nothing wrong at the Agency," he said. "You have refused to shake hands with me. I don't know what for. I simply wanted to explain the present trouble."

"This is no place to explain," McGillycuddy snapped back. "You should have sent your explanation to the Great Father with the letter you signed threatening to make trouble."

At the end of the session, thirty-one of the Indians signed a letter to the Great Father, assuring him that no troops were needed and deprecating Red Cloud's behavior. Numbers are not particularly significant, but fifty-four had signed the threatening petition.[47]

By this time the country was agitated by the perennial fear of an Indian outbreak, and that night McGillycuddy received telegrams from Price and General Crook asking for an investigation of reports that Red Cloud was about to go on the warpath. McGillycuddy replied that while the situation was in hand and no troops were required for the

[46] George Sword to Com. of Indian Affairs, August 16, 1882, *ibid.* This letter has added interest for the light it sheds on Red Cloud's chieftainship. For months, as has been seen, McGillycuddy had been referring to Red Cloud as deposed, presumably by the agent's action. Sword wrote: "This is what I think and say, these old chiefs feel that they must be making trouble. They say that they are the people's choice of chiefs and think that on that account they should be stirring up war. I think it would be well for the department to call in the chiefs commissions and choose new chiefs and give them commissions."

[47] A report of the council and the letter are attached to McGillycuddy to Com. of Indian Affairs, August 20, 1882, NARS, RG 75, LR, which, in addition to McGillycuddy to Pollock, September 16, 1882, cited in note 43, above, I am using for the events of August 18–20, unless otherwise indicated.

present, Red Cloud would be "always a source of trouble and should be removed to Leavenworth, and the continual interference and counseling of white cut-throats prevented." He requested power to act as he saw fit. The next morning (Saturday, August 19), while awaiting an answer, he assembled the friendly chiefs and the police, instructing them to go to Red Cloud's village and demand to know his intentions. They returned about two o'clock with an evasive answer from Red Cloud, who denied that he had made any threats. Sword reported that the chief had assembled his young men under arms, and that many of them "had bad hearts." While McGillycuddy was debating what to do, he received a telegram from Price authorizing him to arrest Red Cloud and hold him prisoner, if necessary to prevent trouble. The agent at once told the chiefs that Red Cloud must report to the office and listen to the telegram. Red Cloud's village was only a mile away from the agency, and the runner sent out with the message returned in a short time. Red Cloud was glad to hear from the Commissioner and hoped that he was well, but he could not come in now to listen to the message because he was tired.

McGillycuddy was in no mood to be trifled with. He told the chiefs that either Red Cloud would come in or he would send the Indian police to bring him in. At this point, Yellow Hair volunteered to see what he could do. While awaiting word from Yellow Hair, McGillycuddy scanned Red Cloud's village with his field glasses. He noticed much excitement: "Indians were flying around in all directions, gathering in their ponies, squaws were leaving and bucks coming in, so that things looked like the old business of 1876 when the Army had to handle Red Cloud for his insolence and hostility." There was excitement at the agency too. Many Indians were leaving, and along with them several traders and employees with their families, all heading south to Nebraska. McGillycuddy issued arms to the fifty Indian police; he also opened up fifty additional rifles, a few of which were issued to friendly Indians and employees who had remained at the agency.

After what seemed like a long absence, Yellow Hair returned with word that Red Cloud was coming. When he did not appear after what would have been a reasonable time for the trip, McGillycuddy asked the chiefs what they proposed to do. They went into council among themselves and after a short time returned with their decision:

Father, send Yellow Hair with these words to Red Cloud. Tell him that we make third and last call. That to prevent bloodshed, if he does not come at once, we will ask our agent to call for troops. We will turn our young men and police in with the troops and disarm and dismount Red Cloud's and Red Shirt's bands. Or, if you say so, we will give you our young men to help your police and bring him anyway. . . .

Yellow Hair went out again, and soon Red Cloud appeared. He was brought into the council room, all arms were laid aside, and McGillycuddy read the Commissioner's telegram. He told the police and the chiefs that he would hold them responsible for Red Cloud's future conduct. Asserting that the Great Father and his government were not to be argued with, he dismissed the meeting without permitting anyone to speak.[48]

Apparently the crisis had passed. Red Cloud went quietly back to his village; the Indian police, except for an agency detail of ten, were permitted to return to their homes. The next day, Sunday, McGillycuddy reported all serene at the agency—"the Church bell is ringing and the flag still floats"—but he warned Commissioner Price that certain whites and half-breeds around the agency were out to force his removal and that they would continue to center their troublemaking on Red Cloud. To Maj. E. V. Sumner at Fort Robinson he telegraphed: "As far as outbreak is concerned, our own Indians will prevent it and kill Red Cloud if necessary, but as long as Red Cloud remains here we will have more or less disturbances. I shall demand that the leaders in the movement be sent to Leavenworth or the Department stand the consequences. . . ."[49]

The next morning McGillycuddy left for Omaha to meet six women who had been hired to teach in the agency boarding school. Commissioner Price was somewhat disturbed that the agent should leave his post at this particular time, but McGillycuddy was certain that everything was in hand, and no valid reason existed for changing his plans; besides, as his wife Julia remarked, "Nothing irked McGillycuddy more than to have his plans upset."[50]

---

[48] McGillycuddy, *McGillycuddy: Agent*, pp. 188–196, presents a much more exciting account of these events than I have, including an attempt by Red Cloud to attack the agent with a knife. McGillycuddy's reports written at the time (which, as indicated above, I have followed), make no mention of this attempt. Hyde, *A Sioux Chronicle*, pp. 88–89, discredits Julia McGillycuddy's story but has Red Cloud incarcerated in the guard house. Again, contemporary accounts make no mention of an incarceration.

[49] Telegram, McGillycuddy to Sumner, August 20, 1882, copy in NARS, RG 75, LR.

[50] McGillycuddy, *McGillycuddy: Agent*, pp. 197–203, describes this trip, but the account is confused and unreliable.

With McGillycuddy gone, his enemies at the agency moved to press their case against him. On August 21, T. G. Cowgill, trader; J. G. Edgar, his clerk; James F. Oldham, chief of police; and Fordyce Grinnell, agency physician, wrote a long letter to the Commissioner, warning that the agent's arbitrary and unjust treatment of Red Cloud might well provoke war: "We are not at all afraid that Red Cloud will make any trouble . . . but we are afraid that the vindictive temper of the Indian Agent will bring it upon us."[51] McGillycuddy, who was keeping in touch by means of a field telegraph with which he could cut in on the line, learned of the letter and immediately ordered his chief clerk, John Alder, to arrest Oldham and maintain a close surveillance of the others. Reporting his action to Price, he stated:

> Red Cloud is a tool, but a dangerous one. This is mutiny, the result of cowardice and conspiracy. I demand that to prevent estrangement of friendly chiefs you positively order Acting Agent Alder to remove offenders from reservation at once. Trader and physician defy the Agent as the Dept. appointed them. This is a criminal disgrace to Indian Service.[52]

The complainants responded by sending another letter to Price (signed by seventeen employees and residents), reasserting that the difficulty was largely the fault of the agent, who had provoked a personal quarrel with Red Cloud, and asking that an inspector be sent out to investigate.[53] Grinnell, who also had signed the petition, sent a separate letter denying that he had ever conversed with Red Cloud in regard to the troubles and asking for an investigation.[54]

McGillycuddy's friends were also active. Trader George F. Blanchard and twenty-nine others signed a letter which repeated McGillycuddy's view that Red Cloud was but a tool in the hands of unprincipled whites and urged the Department to sustain the agent.[55] Little Wound, Young-Man-Afraid, and forty-two other Indians also sent a petition testifying to their satisfaction with the agent and pledging their support of his efforts against Red Cloud.[56]

From Fort Robinson, Colonel Sumner wrote: "Red Cloud is cool but determined; has quite a following which I am informed is daily increasing. Something should be done at once to counteract this influence;

[51] Cowgill, Edgar, Oldham, Grinnell, and others to Com. of Indian Affairs, August 21, 1882, NARS, RG 75, LR.

[52] Telegram, McGillycuddy to Com. of Indian Affairs, August 22, 1882, *ibid.*

[53] T. G. Cowgill *et al.* to Com. of Indian Affairs, August 23, 1882, *ibid.*

[54] Fordyce Grinnell to Com. of Indian Affairs, August 23, 1882, *ibid.*

[55] Blanchard *et al.* to Com. of Indian Affairs, August 22, 1882, *ibid.*

[56] Little Wound *et al.* to Com. of Indian Affairs, August 22, 1882, *ibid.*

otherwise trouble will surely follow, the extent of which cannot be foreseen." He thought "a little more strength" at Fort Robinson and at Fort Niobrara would be desirable.[57]

In Washington, Commissioner Price, thoroughly irritated with McGillycuddy for leaving his post, refused the agent's request to come to the capital and ordered him to return from Omaha as soon as possible. He also decided to send an inspector out to Pine Ridge.[58] The inspector, W. J. Pollock, visited the agency in September. McGillycuddy, quite understandably, did not take kindly to the idea that an investigation was necessary—after all, the call for one had been part of the threatening petition—and he gave Pollock only minimal assistance.[59] He warned him that he should pay no attention to Red Cloud and that under no circumstances should he recommend that the old man be restored to the position of head chief; if this were done, the "younger and more progressive element" would send Red Cloud to "the happy hunting grounds to keep company with his compeer, Spotted Tail."[60]

McGillycuddy's fears about Pollock were soon justified. On the same day that McGillycuddy warned him against Red Cloud, the inspector wrote a letter to Teller, which was to constitute the first part of his report. Red Cloud was by no means blameless, but, in Pollock's judgment, by far the greater share of blame for the controversy lay with the agent:

> It could hardly be expected the old chief would work in harmony with a man who lost no opportunity to humiliate and to heap indignity upon him, who called him liar, fool, squaw, refused to shake hands with, deposed him, ordered the Agency employees not to entertain him in their houses, and no doubt sought to enforce a condition of affairs on August 19th that would result in his death.

Nor was that all. Red Cloud had got along with all of the ten agents who had served his people, "excepting only those who have retired from the service in disgrace." The real reason for the present difficulty, Pollock hinted, was that Red Cloud had discovered irregularities in

[57] Sumner to AG, USA, August 26, 1882, copy in *ibid.*

[58] *New York Times*, August 26, 1882.

[59] McGillycuddy, *McGillycuddy: Agent*, pp. 211–214. This discussion is valuable primarily for presenting McGillycuddy's opinion of Pollock, who, the agent charged, was a disappointed office-seeker and was associated with the "Indian Ring."

[60] McGillycuddy to Pollock. September 15, 1882, NARS, RG 75, LR. By implication, at least, this was another of McGillycuddy's oft-repeated assertions that Red Cloud was no longer chief of the Oglalas.

McGillycuddy's management of the agency and had had the courage to protest them.[61]

The second part of Pollock's report, filed from Sioux City, Iowa, on October 14—the day which, incidentally, marked the end of the sixty-day period of grace granted in the Red Cloud petition which had precipitated the fuss—detailed the irregularities: the agent was living high at the expense of the Indians; he had taken credit on vouchers that were not paid; he had unlawfully deprived Red Cloud of rations while giving the Indian police and other favorites more than they could use; he had permitted agency employees to convert government supplies to their own use.[62] On the same day that Pollock wrote to Teller from Sioux City, E. B. Townsend, another special agent who had recently visited Pine Ridge, reported to Price in Washington, providing advance confirmation of what Pollock would write: not only was McGillycuddy fraudulent in the management of the agency, but the fraud was being perpetrated willfully and as the result of collusion which dated back to 1879, when the agent had assumed his post.[63] Also on October 14, S. S. Benedict, still another inspector brought into the case, was holding a council with the Indians at Pine Ridge. His report, transmitted to Secretary Teller a month later, completely exonerated McGillycuddy of any but "technical irregularities" and asserted that "there would be no trouble if the Department would give Red Cloud to understand that he is not Agent at Pine Ridge and that the Agent must be respected and obeyed." McGillycuddy, in Benedict's opinion, was one of the best agents in the service, and he should not be driven from his post by a chief who stood in the way of his people's progress toward civilization.[64]

Apparently the Indian Bureau felt the same way. The charges against McGillycuddy were not pursued, and he was not even reprimanded for his "technical irregularities," whatever they might have been. Viewed from the perspective of the years, and from the evidence available, those charges do seem fairly flimsy (for example, according to Townsend, the trader, with whom McGillycuddy was supposed to have been in collusion was T. G. Cowgill, a leader of the anti-McGillycuddy faction at the agency) and at the same time it seems clear that they are hardly in keeping with McGillycuddy's reputation, which, despite

[61] Pollock to Secretary of the Interior, September 15, 1882, *ibid.*, Special File 264.

[62] *Ibid.*, October 14, 1885.

[63] Townsend to Com. of Indian Affairs, October 14, 1882, NARS, RG 75, LR.

[64] R. V. Belt to Secretary of the Interior, November 15, 1882, *ibid.*

his many faults, was generally high. As George Hyde wrote, "This agent was armed at every point, with not a chink in his armor through which a weapon might be slipped. His bookkeeping was perfection; his probity above criticism; and not a thing could be found that might be employed as a hook on which to hang charges." [65]

McGillycuddy had ridden out the crisis. There was no sign on October 14 that Red Cloud or anyone else remembered the threat to remove the agent by force if he were not removed by the Government. At the end of the month, writing his annual report, McGillycuddy exulted that the prompt manner in which Red Cloud had been suppressed, "and the peaceful and prosperous condition of affairs here, will, I trust, be an example in the future for ambitious chiefs and designing white men." [66]

Red Cloud had indeed been put down, but he would not stay down for long. His arrest apparently had no significant effect upon his influence among the Oglalas. He still remained a symbol of the old way of life which many of the Sioux hoped would be returned to them, the prating of agents about the progress their charges were making toward civilization notwithstanding. Red Cloud probably had no great hope that the Sioux would walk the old ways again, but he was determined to hold his position of leadership, and even as McGillycuddy was writing of the chief's "suppression" events were transpiring which would thrust him once again to the foreground as a leader of his people, and in the end would let him triumph over the hated agent.

[65] Hyde, *A Sioux Chronicle*, p. 105.
[66] Com. of Indian Affairs, *Annual Report*, 1882, p. 35.

CHAPTER 15

A Temporary Triumph

Although the struggle between Red Cloud and McGillycuddy dominated life at Pine Ridge during the summer of 1882, it was soon overshadowed by the resurging conflict between the whites and the Indians over land. The chief was able to turn this new development to temporary advantage in his feud with the agent, but in the end the train of events it set in motion would bring defeat to Red Cloud and all he represented.

The last time the Sioux had been confronted by demands for their land was in 1876, when, under pressure, they gave up all of their reservation west of the 103d meridian plus the Black Hills country lying between the forks of the Cheyenne River; they also gave the whites permission to build up to three "wagon and other roads" across the remaining reservation.[1] The opening of the Black Hills served to whet rather than satisfy the voracious appetites of land-hungry Dakotans, and they now wanted to occupy the belt of Indian land stretching from seventy to one hundred and fifty miles west of the Missouri. Pursuant to their wishes, Delegate Richard F. Pettigrew, who saw a close relationship between further Indian land cessions and his own role in the politics of impending statehood, managed to get an amendment to the Sundry Civil Act of August 7, 1882, appropriating five thousand dollars to enable the Secretary of the Interior to negotiate such modifications

---

[1] See above, pp. 224–229.

of existing treaties with the Sioux as might seem desirable to him.[2] To conduct the negotiations, Secretary Teller appointed a three-man commission headed by Newton Edmunds, former governor of Dakota Territory, who had negotiated the worthless treaties of 1865–1866.[3] The other two members were Peter Shannon, an elderly Dakota lawyer, former chief justice of the territorial supreme court; and James H. Teller, of Cleveland, Ohio, Secretary Teller's brother and later (by brotherly appointment) secretary of Dakota Territory.[4]

Before they set out on their mission, Edmunds, an old hand at dealing with the Indians, asked for a modification of their instructions. He noted that they were required to follow the provisions of the Treaty of 1868, which provided that three-fourths of all the adult males in the tribe would have to agree to any change in the treaty before it could become valid. Arguing that this would be difficult, if not impossible, he suggested that they be allowed to limit themselves to securing signatures from the principal chiefs and head men, as had been done in 1876. Teller agreed to this—much to his later discomfiture—but he vetoed a related request from Edmunds that the Commission be provided with funds for feasts and trinkets to assist in obtaining the chiefs' signatures. He did, however, permit the Commission to employ Samuel D. Hinman, the missionary interpreter who had frequently participated in councils with the Sioux, and who, if he did not have the confidence of the Indians, possessed an excellent knowledge of their language.

The Commissioners left Yankton on October 16. The agreement they carried presumably was prepared by themselves, but it reflected Secretary Teller's views that many existing reservations were too large,

[2] 48th Cong., 1st Sess., S. Ex. Doc. 70. Unless otherwise indicated, I am following this, which contains the report of the Commission and many related documents. Herbert S. Schell, *History of South Dakota* (Lincoln: University of Nebraska Press, 1961), pp. 316–318, contains a map of Indian land cessions in South Dakota and a good brief account of the negotiations of 1882–1883.

[3] See above, pp. 13–14.

[4] The relations of all three of these men to Dakota politics are discussed briefly in Schell, *History of South Dakota*, *passim*, and Howard R. Lamar, *Dakota Territory, 1861–1889* (New Haven: Yale University Press, 1956), *passim*. See also Elmer Ellis, *Henry Moore Teller: Defender of the West* (Caldwell, Idaho: The Caxton Press, 1941), pp. 19–237, 386. George E. Hyde, *A Sioux Chronicle* (Norman: University of Oklahoma Press, 1956), pp. 107–144, is a detailed and quite hostile treatment of the activities of the Commission, under the title "The Adventures of the Three Musketeers." Hyde apparently relies heavily upon 48th Cong., 1st Sess., Sen. Report No. 283, the "Dawes Report," which I, too, have used extensively (see below, n. 9).

that much Indian land should be made available to homesteaders, and that on the land which remained to them the Indians should be encouraged to engage in stock raising rather than general farming as their basic means of support.[5] It provided that the Sioux were to cede all of their land between the White and the Cheyenne rivers, thus opening a wide corridor from the Missouri to the Black Hills, and, in addition, all of their land north of the Cheyenne and west of the 102d meridian, a total of approximately eleven million acres.[6] There was no longer to be one big reservation: the remaining land was to be divided into five separate tracts, each under the jurisdiction of one of the five agencies already established. In return for relinquishing their land, each Indian who was the head of a family would be allowed to select three hundred and twenty acres as provided by the Treaty of 1868, plus eighty acres for each minor child; and the Government was to provide the Sioux with twenty-five thousand cows and one thousand bulls, to be divided among the reservations in accordance with their population. The cattle were looked upon as foundation herds; they and their progeny were to carry the brand of the Indian Department and none were to be sold or slaughtered without the permission of the agent. Each family which made a selection of land was to be given one good cow and one well-broken pair of oxen, with yoke and chain.

Those who wanted to move along the white man's road might have been able to see some advantage in the proposed agreement, but for the old chiefs it clearly was no bargain—no feasts, no money, no extra food or annuities, just cattle which had to be looked after and which could not be eaten unless the agent gave his permission. Although the Commissioners, by cajolery and not a little misrepresentation, were able to get their signatures, there was serious opposition everywhere.

The Commissioners arrived at Pine Ridge on Sunday, October 22. They had expected difficulty here because of the conflict between McGillycuddy and Red Cloud, and for a time it seemed that they would have it. From Monday through Friday they counciled, with no appreciable results. On Friday Red Cloud told the Commissioners that he and his people had decided not to sign the agreement, and they wished to hear nothing more. Edmunds then asked McGillycuddy, who had taken no part in the proceedings, to see what he could do. Confident that Red Cloud did not speak for a majority, the agent urged the

[5] For Teller's views, see Secretary of the Interior, *Annual Report*, 1882; Ellis, *Henry Moore Teller*, pp. 141–142.

[6] The acreage estimate is from Schell, *History of South Dakota*, p. 317.

Indians to hold another council among themselves and decide to sign the agreement. McGillycuddy's estimate was correct; on Saturday afternoon, after having counciled in the morning, the Indians, including Red Cloud, announced that they were ready to sign. We have no record of the council, but McGillycuddy asserted that the young men had rebelled against Red Cloud and told him, "This nonsense must end." That well may have been the case. The old chief could not hold his people against the wishes of the agent, and all he salvaged from the proceedings was the privilege of signing first.[7]

In due course the Commissioners collected signatures from all the agencies except the Crow Creek and Lower Brulé. While Edmunds and Shannon worked on the chiefs at these agencies, Teller went off to Washington to deliver the agreement to his brother, the Secretary of the Interior. Even though none of the Lower Brulés signed, Secretary Teller persuaded President Arthur to submit the agreement to the lame duck session of the Forty-Seventh Congress, hoping to get it ratified before the Democrats took control of the House of Representatives. Word had got out, however, that the Commissioners had not secured the signatures of three-fourths of the adult males as required by the Treaty of 1868, and though Dakotans and their friends were bringing strong pressures for ratification, various friends of the Indians, including the influential Senator Henry L. Dawes of Massachusetts, began to work against the agreement. In a Congress preoccupied with last-minute maneuvering on the tariff, Dawes was able to block ratification and require the Commission to go back for additional signatures.[8] At the same time, the Senate created a select committee to investigate the whole matter.[9]

[7] Shannon recalled later, in testifying before the Dawes Committee, that after Dr. McGillycuddy had explained the provisions of the treaty "Red Cloud, followed by the majority of his people, and anxious to show his power, came forward to the table to touch the pen," but that Shannon told him to stop, that he could not touch the pen until the agreement had been explained once again. "After that was done Red Cloud again came forward and touched the pen, and it was signed by that numerous body whose signatures you will find to that agreement." Shannon at the time was answering charges that the Commissioners had not adequately explained the agreement to the Indians (see below, p. 294).

[8] Hyde, *A Sioux Chronicle*, pp. 131–137, contains a discussion of the ratification struggle, although he ignores the tariff and tends to overemphasize the relative importance of the matter.

[9] The report of this committee, headed by Senator Dawes, is found in 48th Cong., 1st Sess., Sen. Report No. 283, which, unless otherwise indicated, is my source for the subsequent activities of the Edmunds Commission as well as those of the Committee.

The Commission, regarding acquisition of additional signatures "as a work of detail merely," delegated the responsibility to Hinman. The "detail" turned out to be rather complex. Hinman went first to Pine Ridge, where McGillycuddy assembled the chiefs and head men to listen to what the missionary had to say. After Hinman had explained the object of his visit, Red Cloud spoke vigorously against the agreement and said he would not permit the collection of additional signatures. Hinman reminded him that he and other chiefs had already signed the agreement and that it was now his duty to submit it to all of the people. Red Cloud responded that the ponies were worn out from the winter and the roads were too bad to bring the people in for a council. Finally, under pressure from some of the other chiefs, he said that he would permit Hinman to visit the villages one by one and if a majority of the adult males in each village approved he would call a general council at the agency to ratify the action.

Hinman agreed to make the rounds, and accompanied by George Sword he went to Little Wound's village, the farthest from the agency. Little Wound liked the idea of each family owning its own land and oxen. He hoped, too, that the Government would build him a good house; he recalled that in 1876, good houses had been promised to all of the chiefs, but only Red Cloud and Spotted Tail had received them. With Little Wound's approval, then, Hinman started out to collect his signatures, and immediately bogged down in a quagmire of confusion and uncertainty. In the first place, who was who? Some of the Indians were known by several names. In the second place, who was an adult? The Indians did not figure age or seniority in terms of years, and in some instances a young boy was looked upon as the head of the family. Hinman finally set eighteen as the age of manhood, but found he had only exchanged one problem for another. How was he to determine if a youth was eighteen? "Between sixteen and twenty-one," he lamented, "it is most difficult to determine ages. Their uncouth, bronze, stolid faces are singularly alike, and among the men the youthful appearance is long retained." Moreover, the Indians were hardly cooperating. They refused to tell their ages, the head men consistently tried to pass off boys as adults, and they all objected to being counted. Hinman blamed Red Cloud for part of the trouble, alleging that the chief had sent runners to all the camps, threatening those who signed with banishment from the tribe "and promising all who stood by him to found for them an Indian empire, with no cession of land and a consolidated Dakota nation for its motto."

Early in the game, Hinman abandoned any hope of securing signatures. Instead he and Sword compiled lists of those who indicated their willingness to sign. When he came back to the agency in August, in accordance with his agreement with Red Cloud, he had the names of 633 Indians, which, he asserted, was more than three-fourths of the adult males on the reservation. Whether it was or not, no one knows—McGillycuddy had been feeding 1,226—and even though it had a vital bearing on the administration of rations and annuities, the question is not particularly important in connection with the agreement because by August the whole thing had blown up. Red Cloud had gone off to visit the Shoshonis and the rest of the chiefs would not proceed without him.[10]

For Red Cloud it had been a good summer. The Sun Dance, which he had organized late in June over the agent's objections, had been a great success, with hundreds of Indians coming from Rosebud and the Missouri River, all anxious to council with him.[11] His pass to visit the Shoshonis had come directly from the Great Father.[12] Moreover, it seemed that even the Government did not like the land agreement, and that the Great Council was sending out a committee to talk with the Indians about it; and sure enough, shortly after Red Cloud returned from his visit to Washakie and the Shoshonis, the committee arrived at Pine Ridge.

Red Cloud completely dominated the council with the Dawes Committee. At their first meeting, on Saturday, September 1, he asked for the inevitable postponement so that the Indians could talk among themselves, and his wish was granted. On reconvening Monday morning, Senator Dawes said that they wanted to hear from the young men as well as the old, that they wanted to know how all of them felt about the agreement. He told the interpreter, William Garnett, to ask the Indians which one would speak first. There was no answer; there did not have to be, Red Cloud would speak first. He said:

I will tell you, gentlemen, just how I am situated here. You ask the young

[10] In testifying before the Dawes Committee in September, Red Cloud stated that he and a good many other Indians had signed the agreement during Hinman's second visit: "Mr. Hinman told the Indians that if they did not sign they would not receive any rations or annuities, and, furthermore, they would send them to the Indian Territory; and if I did not sign it I would go to the guard-house." Whether Red Cloud was confused or deliberately lying, or both, this illustrates once again the problem of dealing with the Indians.

[11] McGillycuddy to Com. of Indian Affairs, June 26, 27, 1883, NARS, RG 75, LR.

[12] *Ibid.*, July 1, 5, 1883.

men to speak here. We have no old men; all the old men have died away, and we have none here left. All of these Indians here present are young men, and we claim this land as ours which we are on. There are some things I wish to ask you; I want to know who reported that we gave up our lands to the Great Father: We wish to know who it was.

The dialogue between Senator Dawes and the chief then went on like this:

THE CHAIRMAN. The Great Father says that three men he sent out here made an agreement with the Indians to give the Great Father all the land between the Cheyenne and the White River, and then a strip down to the Nebraska line, and that they agreed to give the Indians 25,000 cows and 1,000 bulls, and then to give the Indians for their reservation the land they are living on. This agreement, the Great Father says, these three men he sent out here made with you Indians, and we have come to know if it is so, and if you understood it to be so. If you do not understand it to be so we want to tell the Great Father it is not so, and if you understand it the other way, why it is all right.

RED CLOUD. I want to know if it is the same party Mr. Hinman was with.

THE CHAIRMAN. Yes, the same men who were here at the council before.

RED CLOUD. I asked Mr. Hinman what he was doing out here, and he said he had a map, and he came to lay out different parts of the reservation for the different agencies, and he said, "That is what I am here for." He told me, as soon as he found out my reservation, that there would be no trouble to bother me hereafter, and no white man would ever come inside of the line. I told him how big a reservation I had. It runs from the Running Water, along this side of the Black Hills, to the mouth of Rapid Creek, to Bad River and from there to the Nebraska line, and I told him it was my reservation, and he told me he had it put down in writing that way; and I never said I would give him any land at that time, and I never did give him anything. When I went to Washington last winter the Great Father showed me my reservation. It runs from this door here to the White River, and I told him it was not right. Hinman came here again and asked some more people to sign this paper, and told them how big the reservation was, and that he had put it down in writing, and he took it off with him again. Hinman lies, and we want to take the names of all the people who signed the paper off of it. The Great Father has given me a map of this country which I have, and I don't want to sell any portion of it at all. If these are the same papers Mr. Hinman had, that you are now talking about, you had better tear them up, for they lie. This is my land and there is a railroad that wants to come through it, and I don't want it to come through, and I want to let you know that.

The dialogue continued, but this was the heart of it: Hinman had lied, the Commissioners had lied, their paper should be torn up; the Oglalas had not understood that they actually were being asked to give up some of their land for the cows and bulls the Commissioners had promised. All the others who testified said essentially the same thing: Red Dog, Little Wound, Torn Belly, Yellow Hair, No Flesh, even George Sword.[13]

McGillycuddy was put in an awkward position. The paper which he had urged his charges to sign was now exposed as a lie, and even his most trusted friends among the Oglalas were lining up with Red Cloud in denouncing it. In testimony which Garnett translated for the Indians, he admitted that no particular mention had been made of that portion of the reservation remaining after the division had taken place, but, he insisted, "I do not think there is an Indian who signed the agreement, or did not sign it, who supposed that the Government would send 25,000 cows and 1,000 bulls out here without getting something in return." At one point, he said that he advised the Indians to sign the agreement because he thought "they would lose a great deal of the reservation unless they signed it." A little later he stated that he knew the agreement would not be approved by Congress and that he had wanted the Indians to sign it "to show that they were willing to do something for themselves to keep them from being paupers."

Over at Rosebud a few days later, McGillycuddy testified again. Out of the hearing of his own Indians, he was considerably more frank than he had been previously. The basic trouble was with the squaw men:

> These Indians, sitting in general council, half the time do not know what they are talking about. They are as a rule giving voice to the advice given them by white men and squaw-men (these are white men who live with squaws). The policy of the half-breeds and squaw-men is not for the Indians to advance toward self-support. The squaw-men realize that as soon as the Indians become self-supporting they will have to support their squaws, just as if they were married to white women, and it has been my experience that the squaw-men are opposed to everything like advancement, and do not want to work; they have taken up with the squaws, and come here because too lazy to work in the East, or they have escaped justice. They as a rule govern the Indians in these treaties, and in everything they desire to do with very few exceptions.

[13] Sword's testimony adds to the confusion. He asserted that he and Hinman had secured the signatures of boys. Hinman, it will be recalled, had declared that they had abandoned the idea of securing signatures and had simply compiled a list of people who had agreed to sign, and that every effort had been made to eliminate boys under eighteen from that list.

Senator Dawes' only comment was that this provided further evidence of the necessity to take great pains to explain everything to the Indians fully and carefully, and McGillycuddy lamely agreed that it did.

At the end of their hearings, which included extended statements from the Commissioners and their friends in Yankton, the Dawes Committee reported that the Indians were virtually unanimous in their opposition to the Edmunds agreement. The Committee recognized that the reservation was larger than the Sioux required and recommended that it be split into separate reservations for the various tribes, with the remainder being paid for by the Government with money rather than with cows and bulls, the whole transaction to require the assent of three-fourths of the adult males as provided by the Treaty of 1868.[14]

As far as Red Cloud personally was concerned, the Dawes Committee was one of the greatest things that had ever happened. Its hearings had put him in the forefront of those who were defending the rights of the Oglalas, had enabled him to gain greater support among his people than he had enjoyed for years—the Dawes Committee wrote that he was a representative of a large portion of the eight thousand Indians at Pine Ridge—and had given him renewed strength for his struggle against McGillycuddy.

Additional support came from Dr. T. A. Bland, founder of the National Indian Defense Association and editor of *The Council Fire*, a journal devoted to the Indians. Bland took the extreme position that the Indians should be let alone and that reform should come only from their initiative.[15] For one holding such views, Red Cloud's struggle with McGillycuddy provided a made-to-order issue—the grand old chief, struggling to preserve his way of life against a tyrannical, ill-tempered agent—and in the pages of *The Council Fire*, Bland maintained a steady barrage of criticism against McGillycuddy.

In June, 1884, at the invitation of Red Cloud and with the permission of Secretary Teller, Bland visited Pine Ridge.[16] Red Cloud, with a retinue of about fifty, went out to meet his friend from Washing-

[14] See below, pp. 313–319.

[15] For discussions of Indian reform movements, see Hyde, *A Sioux Chronicle*, pp. 145–163; Loring B. Priest, *Uncle Sam's Stepchildren: The Reformation of United States Indian Policy, 1865–1887* (New Brunswick: Rutgers University Press, 1942), *passim*.

[16] This account of Bland's visit and the subsequent controversy is reconstructed from documents in NARS, RG 75, Special File 264, containing newspaper clippings, correspondence from Bland and McGillycuddy, and a report by Henry Ward, an inspector sent out to investigate.

ton. Bland had expected him at Valentine, Nebraska, where he left the train, but when the chief did not show up he rode with Todd Randall out to his ranch, where, after a day's wait, the Indians caught up with him. At 11:15 on June 28, amidst great shouting and some talk that the visitor was bringing the Oglalas a new agent, the party arrived at the agency and Dr. Bland went directly to the hotel. Red Cloud said he would be back at two o'clock to take him to see McGillycuddy. Before two o'clock, however, two members of the Indian police arrived and informed Bland that the agent wished to see him without delay. McGillycuddy met him at his office door and told him that he could not remain on the reservation. Bland, producing Secretary Teller's letter, replied that he thought he could. McGillycuddy, according to Bland, after reading the letter aloud and handing it to his clerk for copying, said, "Ordinarily, I take great pleasure in observing the orders of the Secretary, but in this case I shall not. You will leave the reservation this afternoon." He then called in six members of the Indian police and ordered a carriage drawn up in front of the Agency office, telling Bland to get in the carriage or be thrown in. Under this threat, Bland decided to yield.

Just as Bland was getting into the carriage Red Cloud came up. Standing Soldier, one of the police, ordered him to move back while the carriage drove off. Red Cloud then went and sat down in front of Blanchard's store, wondering what to do. After a while he went home and sent Spotted Elk, Afraid of Eagle, and Iron Beaver "to find where Dr. Bland was to see if he had been killed. I told them in case he was killed to bring the body which I was to take to Valentine."[17]

Dr. Bland was very much alive at Jacob Ganow's ranch, just across the line in Nebraska. Red Cloud offered to send a hundred men to escort him back to the reservation and to protect him, but Bland wished to avoid a further encounter with McGillycuddy and suggested that Red Cloud come down into Nebraska. The next day the chief gathered up his pipe and about one hundred and fifty followers and went to a grove not far from Ganow's ranch to see his controversial friend. Here is how Red Cloud described the meeting:

> When we got down to the timber I shook hands, first with Dr. Bland and then all the other Indians shook hands with him. Dr. Bland next said, "Red Cloud if you have anything to tell me say it now." I then said "How. I am ready my friend to let you know something." Dr. Bland spoke next. He pulled out the letter from his pocket. He said this is the Great Father's

[17] Affidavit of Red Cloud taken by Henry Ward, November 19, 1884.

letter. I found today that the Great Father has no power nor you either. The agent has run over both of you." Then he asked me if I was not ashamed over it. Then he continued, "My friend, I don't want you to feel bad over this, as I did not come here to make any trouble. You people have nothing to do with the trouble. It is an affair between us white men." I spoke next. I said, "I have been to Washington and told the Secretary that I would take you as a friend with these Indians and you have come and been put off before you got any square meal. This made me ashamed." Then I talked about treaties that had been made years before. The first treaty made at the mouth of Horse Creek and the Treaty of '68 and another treaty we made giving up the right to hunt on the Republican and Black Hills Treaty of '76. I said, we had had things promised us that had not been given us. Another thing happened to me. The government took some horses away from me. I had then been a peaceable Indian for 7 years. The principal thing I want you to do is to get pay for those horses the government took from me. I do not remember that Doctor Bland said anything more. I told him the next day that I would send my wagon up to take him to Rosebud.

Not much here to get excited about, but when Bland returned to Washington in mid-July he created a sensation through the general press and particularly through the columns of *The Council Fire* by describing in detail his expulsion from the reservation and McGilly-cuddy's persecution of the Indians at Pine Ridge.[18] Later he published a letter from Red Cloud and "700–800 chiefs and head men" which stated that Bland had come to Pine Ridge at their request to explain the Dawes bill, and that they would "cede no portion of their reservation to the United States until this bad and corrupt Agent is removed from this Agency."

McGillycuddy fought back with characteristic vigor. He charged that Bland had lied about conditions at the agency, that he had come to Pine Ridge deliberately to cause trouble, and that, indeed, he had "created more disturbance . . . than a Sun Dance and two or three barrels of whiskey." Long after Dr. Bland had departed, he posted signs around the agency, as follows:

> The following named persons are removed from the reservation in accord-
> ance with the law as provided for in Section 2147 and 2149, Revised U.S.
> Statutes:
> H. C. Clifford, Squawman, Pine Ridge Agency, Dakota.
> T. A. Bland, Philanthropist, Washington, D. C. Todd Randall, Squaw-
> man, Pine Ridge Agency, Dakota.
> Residents of either the Nebraska or the Dakota portion of the Pine

18 See, e.g., *Chicago Times*, July 18, 1884.

Ridge Reserve other than Indians of full blood, harboring any of the above parties subject themselves to removal also.

McGillycuddy, Agent.[19]

McGillycuddy was overexcited, as usual, but in this instance he secured powerful support. Senator Dawes, reading an editorial in the Springfield, Massachusetts, *Republican* praising Bland, wrote to the editor that the supposed friend of the Indians who edited *The Council Fire* was wholly unreliable, and added, "I do not wonder at his being ordered off from the Pine Ridge reservation so much as I do that Mr. Teller let him go there at all." Henry Ward, sent out to investigate Bland's charges, exonerated McGillycuddy completely for removing Dr. Bland from the reservation and concluded that the agent was supported by all but about ten percent of the Indians who were under the influence of Red Cloud.[20]

Red Cloud was clearly disappointed over Bland's failure. He told Inspector Ward that he had hoped his friend would "straighten up the old treaty and fix it so we would not have to sell our land." He remarked that he thought Bland was a great man before he came out from Washington, but when asked what he thought of him after the visit, Red Cloud replied, "I don't think of anything now."

Hope revived with word that there was a new Great Father in Washington and that he belonged to a different party from the old one. Red Cloud counciled with his head men, and decided to go to Washington to ask the new Great Father for a new agent; Todd Randall would go with him as interpreter. The Indians had no money and McGillycuddy would not give them any, but they were able to raise the necessary funds among friends in Valentine, Nebraska,[21] a Democratic stronghold where anti-McGillycuddy sentiment ran high.[22] When the chief got to Washington he found his good friend Dr. Bland ready and able to help him. Indeed Bland, smarting under Dawes'

[19] A copy of the handbill is in NARS, RG 75, Special File 264. Julia B. McGillycuddy, *McGillycuddy: Agent* (Stanford: Stanford University Press, 1941), p. 225, reproduces the text at the end of an account of Bland's visit (pp. 221–225), which dates the event in 1881 rather than in 1884 and differs somewhat in details from the account I have reconstructed from contemporary sources, cited in note 16, above.

[20] Henry Ward to Secretary of the Interior, November 19, 1884, NARS, RG 75, Special File 264. McGillycuddy, *McGillycuddy: Agent*, pp. 226–230, and Hyde, *A Sioux Chronicle*, p. 99, refer to an investigation by a General McNeill, of which I have found no record.

[21] Bland to Secretary of the Interior, March 16, 1885, NARS, RG 75, LR.

[22] See, e.g., *Valentine Reporter*, March 12, 1885, as quoted in *The Council Fire*, VIII (April, 1885), 61.

attack and furious with Teller for his last-minute reappointment of
McGillycuddy to a second four-year term, saw in Red Cloud's visit an
opportunity to get final revenge on McGillycuddy, and he proposed to
make the most of it. Despite his earlier disappointment, Red Cloud
was ready to cooperate.

On March 18, Bland took Red Cloud to see the President. The
chief got right to the point:

> I am head chief of my people. My people made me a chief, and when I
> made a treaty with the Government seventeen years ago the commissioners
> made me a chief. You are chief of the white people and the Indians, so my
> people held a council and told me to come to Washington to see you and
> have a talk with you. My people have been treated very bad, and when we
> heard that a new Great Father had been elected we were all very glad. Our
> agent is a bad man. He steals from us, and abuses us, and he has sent all of
> the good white men out of our country, and put bad men in their places.
> For a long time I have been asking for a new agent, but the other Great
> Father would not hear my words. Now I tell you I want a new Agent . . . .[23]

President Cleveland, though cautious, was sympathetic; he told
Red Cloud he would do everything he could to help him, and he was
sure that the new Secretary of the Interior, L. Q. C. Lamar, would,
too. Lamar was both helpful and cordial. When Commissioner Price,
just going out of office, refused to issue an order to provide Red Cloud
with a new suit of clothes, the Secretary issued it from his own office.
He also invited Red Cloud to be present when John Atkins, the new
Commissioner of Indian Affairs, took the oath of office. With regard to
the agent, however, the Secretary seemed to move rather slowly. He
told Red Cloud that he would have to look at the papers on file in his
office before he could make a decision. On March 24, Red Cloud,
becoming impatient—or prompted by Bland—wrote a letter to the
Secretary:

> I don't want to hurry you; I know you have got a great many things to
> think about; but, my friend, my people are starving. I can't sleep good,
> because I think about them in the night. My heart is sorry for them. I want
> you to take pity on me and my people. You told me you would look at the
> papers Colonel Pollock wrote about my agent. I want you to look at these
> papers as soon as you can, so you can know what I told you is the truth. . . .
>
> My friend, I want you to take this bad agent away and give us an agent
> that me and my people know is a good man . . . .

---

[23] *The Council Fire*, VIII (April, 1885), 52–53. This issue and that of May, 1885,
covered Red Cloud's visit fully, and unless otherwise indicated my account is based
upon them.

While Red Cloud waited for the Secretary to act, he was lionized by Bland and his friends. They had maintained all along that the Indians must be left alone to work out their destiny, and in Red Cloud they had a prime example of the noble chief who could lead his people on the road to progress if only allowed to do so. Unlike certain occasions in the past when his behavior had disappointed his eastern friends, Red Cloud lived up to their highest expectations. His dignified bearing— he was an impressive specimen of manhood even in white man's clothes—his grave remarks, and his obvious sincerity won friends everywhere he went. Bland was delighted.

He was even more delighted when on April 3 Commissioner Atkins ordered McGillycuddy to come into Washington to answer Red Cloud's charges. McGillycuddy was slow about responding to the summons but finally arrived on the twenty-fourth, accompanied by Young-Man-Afraid-of-His-Horse, George Sword, and Standing Soldier. He found himself opposed by an impressive array of talent, including Bland, Judge A. J. Willard, well-known South Carolina lawyer, politician, and brother of Emma Willard, and George W. Manypenny, former Commissioner of Indian Affairs, currently enjoying fame as the author of *Our Indian Wards*. Undaunted by his opposition, McGillycuddy denounced the proceedings as a farce. This brought a sharp reprimand from Atkins, but as the hearing dragged on, it became clear that the problem at Pine Ridge was largely a personal conflict between the agent and the chief. Try as they might, Red Cloud's friends could pin nothing more on McGillycuddy than that he was arbitrary and hot tempered. Red Cloud even admitted that the agent had withheld his rations only because he had not sent his children to school.[24]

[24] McGillycuddy, Annual Report, September 10, 1885, in Com. of Indian Affairs, *Annual Report*, 1885, pp. 33–38. McGillycuddy placed a great deal of emphasis upon education, and one of his complaints against Red Cloud was his opposition to the educational program. Red Cloud, indeed, had always opposed the white man's schools. On November 19, 1884, he told Inspector Ward that he had seven children, the youngest being a girl between twenty-four and twenty-five years old. This child "was once at a boarding school a little while, but she got sick and has been sick ever since. I told the agent we wanted to take her out and brought a grandchild to take her place. The agent consented but the grandchild also soon died." (The word "also" is confusing, implying that the child had died, when Red Cloud spoke of her as being "sick ever since.") Red Cloud also told Ward that he had fourteen grandchildren, ranging in age between one and twenty-seven years, and that none of them were in school (Affidavit of Red Cloud taken by Henry Ward, November 19, 1884, NARS, RG 75, Special File 264). Hyde, *A Sioux Chronicle*, pp. 100-103, refers to a "school war" at Pine Ridge in 1884.

A few days after the hearing concluded, Lamar sent for Red Cloud and told him that he might as well go home. He and the Commissioner would have to examine the evidence, and pending the examination, they were going to send the agent back; he hoped Red Cloud would obey the law and keep the peace. Red Cloud pressed the Secretary to suspend the agent and put a clerk in charge. Lamar declined to do so, but assured Red Cloud that justice would be done. Despite this equivocal response, Red Cloud seemed to be satisfied but he expected action. He told the press, "I shall tell my people that I believe the Great Father and the Secretary and Commissioner are good men, and that they will take our bad agent away from our country." To the President he said, "I am going back to my people, and I leave my cause in your hands."

The Administration was in a dilemma. The President had campaigned for civil service reform, and it would not do to remove an Indian agent for purely political reasons. Moreover, Bland and his friends by no means represented the views of all, or even a majority, of the friends of the Indians who were pushing for reform; others such as Herbert Welsh of the Indian Rights Association and Senator Dawes—who in the Republican-controlled Senate was chairman of the Committee on Indian Affairs—were vociferous in their denunciation of Bland and in their support of McGillycuddy. Cleveland and Lamar, determined to move slowly in the troubled area of Indian affairs, decided to wait a while before taking action on the difficult Pine Ridge question. They had a good excuse; Congress, in the appropriations bill passed March 3, had directed the Speaker of the House to appoint a committee of five to "inquire into and investigate the expenditure of appropriations for the Indians." The Democrats controlled the House in the Forty-Ninth Congress, and the committee, headed by Democratic Congressman William S. Holman of Indiana, included three Democrats and two Republicans.[25] Perhaps this group could provide an acceptable answer to the problem.

The Holman Committee has been represented as designed solely to investigate McGillycuddy,[26] but in fact it was directed to investigate Indian affairs generally. It visited almost every reservation in the

[25] The other Democrats were W. W. Hatch of Missouri and S. W. Peel of Arkansas; the Republican members were Joseph G. Cannon of Illinois and Thomas Ryan of Kansas. The Committee's reports and testimony are contained in 49th Cong., 1st Sess., H. Report No. 1076, which, unless otherwise indicated, I am following.

[26] McGillycuddy, *McGillycuddy: Agent*, pp. 239–247; Hyde, *A Sioux Chronicle*, p. 103. Mrs. McGillycuddy apparently ignored the report of the committee and, using

West and also, according to its charge, investigated the administration of Yellowstone Park. We are, however, concerned here only with the investigation of affairs at Pine Ridge. In the eyes of the Committee, Pine Ridge was important, "not only on account of the large number of Indians under its control, but especially in view of the presence of Red Cloud, claimed by himself, and at least his immediate band, to be the head chief of the Sioux tribe, and of many other prominent and influential chiefs, both of the Sioux and Cheyennes."[27]

The Committee began taking testimony at Pine Ridge on July 22. After questioning Robert O. Pugh, principal of the boarding school, and John Robinson, missionary, largely about educational matters, they came to McGillycuddy. Near the end of a long interrogation, during which all aspects of reservation management were discussed, Holman, who was doing the questioning, brought up the matter of local government on the reservation and the agent's relations with Red Cloud. McGillycuddy explained that about a year before he had organized a council to regulate affairs at the agency and that Young-Man-Afraid-of-His-Horse had been elected president by the Indians themselves. Red Cloud and his followers had refused to participate. McGillycuddy estimated that about three hundred, or approximately one-fourth of the population, remained under the influence of Red Cloud—a much higher figure than McGillycuddy or anyone else had given hitherto. The agent went on to detail Red Cloud's long-standing animosity toward the Government, declaring that he had definitely aided the hostiles during the troubles of 1876 and had not changed his position since that time. Holman was not satisfied. He pointed out that the Commission which had investigated those troubles had exonerated Red Cloud of all responsibility and had found that whatever his Indians had done had been against his strenuous opposition. Holman wondered if the whole trouble did not derive from the agent's unfriendly relations with the chief. The interrogation concluded:

> ANSWER. It is claimed by Red Cloud that if you will give him a new agent he will go in and work, but I have yet to see any solid work on the part of Red Cloud or his people toward progress at the agency. My idea is that he has an idea that he is head chief, and that these people are independent of the Government.
>
> QUESTION. But the Government has found it very desirable in certain

sources of her own (not identified), devoted her account to ridicule of Holman. Hyde apparently bases his brief account upon hers.

[27] Report No. 1076, p. 11.

instances of recent years to recognize the chiefship of Indians for the express purpose of increasing their importance in directing the action of their tribes?

ANSWER. Certainly; if the strong control of the chief is exercised toward progress I presume it would be a good thing, but in setting him up you cannot tell when he may turn around and take the opposite course; my opinion is that if you set him up too strongly he may turn that power against the Government; when they were wild Indians on the war-path, after the fall of Fort Kearny in 1866 it was easier for the Government to control the Indians through one command than each individually, because all we wanted to do was to keep them quiet and subordinate; in these times Red Cloud was useful, but when it got beyond that point in trying to get them into civil pursuits then these men that the Government had set up were stumbling blocks.

QUESTION. Red Cloud wears the costume of the white man?

ANSWER. Yes; within the last two years.

QUESTION. And keeps the American flag floating over his band?

ANSWER. Yes; but in addition to that I have not seen him do any farming; Red Cloud is not a farmer.

QUESTION. Please state what, in your experience and best judgment, are the views of the Indians touching the cession of a portion of their lands to the Federal Government.

ANSWER. The feeling of the Indians, I think, is that it is folly to try to hold out against the Government in case the Government wants to buy the land; I think they would be willing to sell a portion of it; as far as the Pine Ridge is concerned, they are anxious to have a separate reservation, and everything separate from the rest of the Sioux Nation, and Individual property. . . .

QUESTION. Are their local attachments very strong here?

ANSWER. Yes sir. They won't listen to a removal to any other place; one of the strongholds of Red Cloud is that some of these days we will have them removed to the Indian Territory. Indians are like cats, they are attached to localities, and I do not care if they are in a poor country they become attached to it and would not exchange for a good one.[28]

The next day the Committee held a council with the Indians—one of the few occasions during their entire investigation on which they talked with other than agency employees and military men. Red Cloud was in fine fettle; the Committee, he was sure, was bringing him a new agent. He opened the proceedings by saying: "What is your business? Have you anything to tell us by the Great Father's words? And if so, after that I will let you know some things." Holman responded by saying that they had come only to get information. They desired to hear the wants and the wishes of the people of Pine Ridge.

[28] *Ibid.*, pp. 32–33.

Although disappointed, Red Cloud detailed his wants. They were many: plows, mowing machines, oxen, help with farming ("I have an idea that a man claiming that he is a farmer comes around but he does not do anything; I consider it the same as stealing money"), more food and better food ("I ask you to come and see the commissary. I remember a long time ago when I use to catch flat fish; this bacon puts me in mind of it"). The thing he wanted most, though, was a new agent: "I want you to take your agent with you, and take him as far as the railroad, and if you do not do that any trouble arising here I will blame you for not taking your agent away."

After Red Cloud had finished, several others spoke. Young-Man-Afraid said he wanted to live like a white man and the agent was helping him; the agent was a good man. Little Chief of the Cheyennes "had never made a speech yet" but he was going to make one. He was with Red Cloud all the way: "I am for the Ogallalas and Red Cloud for the Cheyennes; me and him draw out of the same commissary and both have equal titles; we have our agency together, me and Red Cloud." As for the agent, "I want you to take him quietly away with you." Wild Hog, No Water, Standing Elk, and Plenty Bear all spoke briefly. They had nothing to say about the agent or Red Cloud. They wanted more food and they wanted to live like white men.[29]

The next day, Red Cloud followed the Committee down to Gordon, Nebraska—whether by invitation or not, we do not know—and had another talk with them. This time, instead of letting the chief make a speech, the Congressmen questioned him closely. Red Cloud, obviously confused, contradicted himself several times. He said that he had asked the agent for plows but had not received them, and later said that he had not asked the agent for anything. Again:

> QUESTION. Do you advise your band to send their children to school?
> ANSWER. No, sir.
>
> . . . .
>
> QUESTION. Did you tell any person that the children of your band should not go to school?
> ANSWER. I do not remember saying that to any person.[30]

The Committee brought in a divided report. The Democratic majority, ducking the question, recommended the appointment of a commission of three Army officers and three civilians to settle the Indian problem once and for all; they were of the opinion that the Government should

---

[29] *Ibid.*, pp. 48–55.
[30] *Ibid.*, pp. 34–36.

go very slowly in disturbing the tribal relation or in breaking up the large reservations, such as that of the Sioux. The Republicans, following the lines staked out by Schurz and Teller, argued that the proper policy was to "cut up the reservation system at its roots," allot the lands in severalty, and sell the remainder. Both favored education. The report, issued on March 16, 1886, did not mention McGillycuddy by name, save in the testimony. The Democrats, however, cited complaints by Indians against their agents and concluded: "A good agent, who displays an interest in the Indians, generally in great degree, secures their respect and confidence." The Republicans disagreed with their colleagues' criteria for a good agent, pointing out that "among some of the tribes there is an insubordinate and turbulent element always antagonizing all civilizing agencies, often with such violence as to intimidate such as are disposed to be orderly and progressive."[31]

Even though the Adminstration received little help from the Holman Committee, it was patent that it would have to act soon on the McGillycuddy matter. Bland and his friends were impatient; Democrats, particularly those in the West, were demanding McGillycuddy's scalp. Western Democrats claimed that to subject Red Cloud longer to McGillycuddy's rule would bring on an Indian outbreak, but this was unlikely, to say the least, and most Republicans generally argued that if it occurred, McGillycuddy could cope with it. Republican Senator Charles F. Manderson of Nebraska, however, warned that Red Cloud could rally every discontented element in the Sioux nation to his standard, and that if an outbreak occurred, "it will be trouble most grave."[32]

The Administration decided to deal with McGillycuddy by indirection; as George Hyde put it: "The Democrats gave up and resorted to Red Cloud tactics. Make McGillycuddy angry and let him hang himself."[33] In May, 1886, the Indian Bureau sent Inspector E. D. Bannister to Pine Ridge with instructions for McGillycuddy to replace his clerk, Donald Brown. When McGillycuddy flatly refused to do so, Bannister, acting under orders of the Secretary of the Interior approved by the President, told McGillycuddy that he was being relieved by Capt. James M. Bell of the 7th Cavalry.[34]

[31] *Ibid.*, pp. X, LXI–LXIII.

[32] *The Council Fire*, IX (May, 1886), 70.

[33] Hyde, *A Sioux Chronicle*, p. 105.

[34] Correspondence from the principals is in NARS, RG 75, LR. See also, Brig. Gen. R. C. Drum, AG, U.S. Army, to Bell, June 22, 1886, NARS, RG 48; McGillycuddy, *McGillycuddy: Agent*, pp. 248–250.

That was all there was to it. Knowing at last that he was licked, McGillycuddy packed his bags and left. Red Cloud, in a joyous mood and apparently employing a much better educated amanuensis than ordinarily was available to him, wrote Dr. Bland: "Well, my friend, the long fight is over at last and the victory is ours, and tyranny and oppression is a thing of the past here. My people, although ignorant, will, I trust, never prove ungrateful to the authorities in Washington that rescued them from long-continued acts of persecution and injustice. We are happy and joyful now, for peace and content reigns, and it makes my heart glad to tell you so. . . ."[35]

On the Fourth of July the people of Chadron, Nebraska, asked the old chief to come down and address their Independence Day celebration. He told them:

> We came here as two nations, with different hearts and different minds, but to-day we must become as one nation with but one heart and one mind. We will build our two houses into one. We have been traveling two different roads, let us from now on travel even.[36]

It was a great day. Reading about it in *The Council Fire* one might have thought that the problem of the Sioux had been solved.

[35] Red Cloud to Bland, May 31, 1886, in *The Council Fire*, IX (July, 1886), 115.
[36] *The Council Fire*, IX (August–September, 1886), 124–125.

CHAPTER 16

The Sioux Bill

Things *were* quiet at Pine Ridge after McGillycuddy departed, although Captain Bell continued his predecessor's policies and in some instances administered them more rigidly. Shortly after Bell arrived he conducted a census—under close guard, with "no possibility of doubling or swapping babies, as had been their custom heretofore"—which trimmed the official population to 4,873, a decrease of 2,776 from McGillycuddy's 1885 figure of 7,649. Strangely enough, there was no opposition, even though the Indians knew that an accurate count might well result in a reduction in their rations. Bell explained their acquiescence by reporting that the Indians recognized that they had been drawing larger rations than they were entitled to, that "they had been drawing rations for all their ghosts." [1] But it was not quite that simple; Bell gained the support of Red Cloud, traditionally an opponent of being counted, by restoring all of the ration tickets which the chief claimed McGillycuddy had stolen from him. [2]

Red Cloud generally approved of Captain Bell. He reported to Dr. Bland that the new agent had "adopted the just and manly course of treating all Indians alike, without regard to former cliques and clans" and that while he was "strict in the execution and performance of his duty," he was "kind and just to us all." [3] Bell appears to have allowed

[1] James M. Bell, Annual Report, Pine Ridge Agency, September 7, 1886, in Com. of Indian Affairs, *Annual Report*, 1886, p. 76.

[2] Red Cloud to T. A. Bland, May 31, 1886, in *The Council Fire*, IX (July, 1886), 115.

[3] *Ibid.*

Red Cloud to do about as he pleased; for example, the chief wanted to visit the Shoshonis, and Bell—unlike McGillycuddy, who would have tried to prevent the trip—cheerfully consented; perhaps he thought it would be a good idea to have Red Cloud out of the way for a while.[4]

Captain Bell's brief tenure ended on October 1, when he was succeeded by H. D. Gallagher, a Civil War veteran and Indiana Democrat, who had been selected by the Cleveland Administration to replace McGillycuddy. Red Cloud approved of him from the beginning. On October 7 he wrote George W. Manypenny:

> Myself and people are very much pleased with our new agent, and I think that the Great Father has at last secured for us the right man, as he is at least approachable and manifests a willingness and kind and friendly disposition towards us all, and in view of this fact I am willing, and with pleasure, to fully cooperate and act in harmony with him in all things, and you may rest assured that you will hear of no more strife and dissatisfaction from Pine Ridge Agency in future.[5]

Although Gallagher was described as "an easy man . . . and satisfied with drawing his salary if affairs went along in orderly fashion,"[6] he pushed ahead along the route that had been charted by Captain Bell— in most respects a continuation of McGillycuddy's program. He did all this quietly and with a saving sense of humor and understanding. As George Hyde put it, "Gallagher . . . [gave] the Pine Ridge Sioux what they most needed: some quiet and an end to the hustling and shouting they had endured in McGillycuddy's day."[7]

Whatever the secret of his success, Gallagher managed to accomplish a good deal during the first few months of his incumbency. He cut the beef ration to correspond with the true population figures, and though there was a good deal of wailing and counciling, the situation was kept well in hand. He even persuaded some of Red Cloud's people to

[4] Thomas M. Jones, the Shoshoni agent, was not particularly happy with his visitors. He wrote the Commissioner of Indian Affairs, September 1, notifying him of the arrival of Red Cloud and 296 Sioux: "Chief Washakie who has often been at war with them gets nervous when they are near him and seems to think their visit is not entirely to trade and be social, but fears they have been elsewhere trying to persuade other Indians to join them in a fight against the whites . . ." (Jones to Com. of Indian Affairs, September 1, 1886, NARS, RG 75, LR).

[5] Red Cloud to Manypenny, October 7, 1886, in *The Council Fire*, IX (November– December, 1886), 171.

[6] E. S. Ricker, Interview with George W. Colhoff, November 25, 1906, Ricker Mss., Tablet No. 25, Nebraska State Historical Society.

[7] George E. Hyde, *A Sioux Chronicle* (Norman: University of Oklahoma Press, 1956), pp. 249–250.

abandon their village on White Clay Creek, near the agency buildings, and locate upon separate farms—something McGillycuddy had vainly tried to bring about.[8] Of great importance was the establishment of Holy Rosary Mission. Red Cloud had repeatedly asked for Catholic teachers, considered himself a Catholic, and at some point had been baptized. Gallagher, an Irish Catholic, got the credit (or blame) for permitting Catholics on the reservation, but the policy which McGilly-cuddy had enforced with such commotion against Father McCarthy[9] had been relaxed to allow the Indians a degree of religious freedom. Anyhow, Red Cloud was pleased. When Father Florentine Digmann arrived in August, 1888, to take charge of the mission, he was welcomed by a delegation of prominent Oglalas led by Red Cloud, who said, "Already years ago, I and Spotted Tail have asked the Great Father for black robes as our teachers, because they were the first ones who brought us the word of the Great Spirit."[10]

Further reflecting the quiet that descended upon the agency after McGillycuddy's departure was the settling of dust that had been stirred up by his constant effort to break the power of the chiefs through developing the spirit of faction among them. Red Cloud and Young-Man-Afraid-of-His-Horse gradually ironed out their differences, and on July 26, 1887, in a council held at the agency, the two men smoked the pipe, shook hands, and agreed to work together to lead their people in the ways of civilization, agriculture, and education. W. B. Waldby, who was visiting the agency at the time on behalf of the Board of Indian Commissioners, reported that Red Cloud told him "that he now considers himself and Young-Man-Afraid-of-His-Horses as one man, and they will pull together and hereafter sit side by side in council as brothers." Waldby commented: "I was exceedingly im-pressed with the earnest manner and noble presence of this old chief. I understand he is very industrious and exemplary."[11]

It was well that the two men had settled their differences, because there was talk of new laws and new commissions which would try to force the Sioux to give up more of their lands. The Oglalas would need to stand together.

The failure of the Edmunds Commission had by no means settled

[8] H. D. Gallagher, Pine Ridge Report, August 26, 1887, in Com. of Indian Affairs, *Annual Report*, 1887, pp. 40–42.

[9] See above, pp. 266–268.

[10] Donald R. Thompson, "A History of the Holy Rosary Indian Mission from its Beginning to the Present" (Master's thesis, Denver University, 1954), pp. 26–27.

[11] Board of Indian Commissioners, *Annual Report*, 1887, p. 23.

the question of the Sioux reservation. Dakotans, now pressing hard for statehood, were as land-hungry as ever and increasingly determined to move into the vast Indian tract lying west of the Missouri. Moreover, most Indian reform groups (except T. A. Bland's National Indian Defense Association) were convinced that the cause of the Indians would be best served by breaking up the tribal relationship, hence the reservations, through establishing a system of individual ownership of land. Senator Dawes had blocked the Edmunds scheme not because he objected to its provisions but because of the fraudulent way in which it had been implemented. Now he was leading the forces of reform, and in 1887 he managed to push through his Severalty Act, which established the principle of private ownership. The act provided that either before or after allotments in severalty, the President could negotiate for the surplus lands, in accordance with procedures prescribed by Congress and the treaties under which the tribe was on the reservation.[12] For the Sioux, this meant that the negotiations would have to be conducted under Article 12 of the Treaty of 1868, which provided that three-fourths of the adult males must approve any cession before it could take effect. The Government had ignored this provision in 1876,[13] but with Indian reformers alert to every possible injustice, no one could hope to do so in 1887.

Congress passed a special Sioux bill on April 30, 1888. Essentially, the measure was the same as that of 1882 under which the Edmunds Commission had worked: the reservation was to be divided into six smaller reserves and the surplus lands were to revert to the public domain; instead of being homesteaded, however, these lands were to be sold for fifty cents an acre, with the proceeds going to an Indian trust fund. While the bill was under discussion, Dr. Bland, Judge Willard, George W. Manypenny, and others in the National Indian Defense Association, not only opposed it in Washington, but made sure that the Sioux would oppose it also. Willard, for example, wrote Red Cloud, urging him to stand fast against sale or division.[14] Gallagher, who got hold of the letter, complained that such influence was doing more "to obstruct progress . . . than all the opposition to be met with on the reservations." [15] Whether that was the case or not, by early summer all

[12] Session Laws, 49th Cong., 1st Sess., Ch. 119. For a general discussion of land policy as it related to the Sioux, see Sister Mary Antonio Johnston, *Federal Relations with the Great Sioux Indians of South Dakota, 1887–1933* (Washington: Catholic University of America Press, 1948).

[13] See above, p. 229.

[14] A. J. Willard to Red Cloud, April 12, 1888, NARS, RG 75.

[15] Gallagher to A. B. Upshaw, April 18, 1888, *ibid.*

of the Sioux agents knew that their Indians were opposed to the bill,[16] and in a short time the Government knew it too.

To secure the consent of the Sioux, William F. Vilas, who had succeeded Lamar as Secretary of the Interior, appointed a commission headed by Richard H. Pratt, Superintendent of the Carlisle Indian School.[17] The Commission went first to Standing Rock, where after more than a month of haranguing they were able to secure but twenty-two signatures out of an adult male population of over a thousand. They had a little more success at the United Crow Creek and Lower Brulé Agency, but while there heard enough to convince them that they would get nowhere with the Indians at Rosebud, Cheyenne River, and Pine Ridge. After a conference with Vilas, Pratt called the agents and certain of the chiefs and head men from all of the Sioux agencies to a general conference at Lower Brulé. What he heard from them confirmed the belief that nothing would be gained by visits to the agencies and convinced Pratt that the only possibility of saving the agreement lay in taking the Indians to Washington for a conference with the Great White Father. Accordingly in October a delegation of sixty-seven, including agents and interpreters, visited the capital city.

Neither Red Cloud nor Young-Man-Afraid-of-His-Horse was in that delegation, and neither had participated in the conference at Lower Brulé. Their being left out was no mere oversight. Pratt, who held that there was no hope for the Indians as long as they remained under the domination of the chiefs, explained that the Commission was trying to go over their heads to the people directly. In any case, the attempt failed—"we had the people together, and they listened with fairly respectful attention, but the chiefs were in front and in open council domineered the people into silent submission to their voice; while outside, and in their own councils, we had the most abundant evidence of their imperious control, extending to acts and threats against the property and the lives of those who should dare to go against their authority." As a result, the Commission resorted to dealing with chiefs and head men, but in the case of Pine Ridge, at least, they still tried to keep the real leaders out of the proceedings. Those brought

[16] Hyde, *A Sioux Chronicle*, p. 189. Hyde, pp. 184–228, discusses in great detail the Sioux bill and negotiations with the Indians. He is very rough on all associated with the Government's case, but aside from that—and in places, because of it, perhaps—his discussion is generally good and in any event is the best available.

[17] For activities of Pratt Commission, see Com. of Indian Affairs, *Annual Report*, 1888.

to Washington from Pine Ridge were Little Wound, American Horse, George Sword, No Flesh, Fast Thunder, Yellow Bear, Standing Soldier, Standing Elk, Little Chief, Pretty Lance, Little Hawk, and Many Bears. Little Chief was the recognized leader of the Cheyennes, but none of the Oglalas, with the possible exception of Little Wound and American Horse, approached Young-Man-Afraid in importance, to say nothing of Red Cloud.

Even the lesser figures proved difficult to handle. According to Pratt, "During their stay in Washington these Indians were constantly beleaguered by persons, male and female, who claimed to be par excellence the friends of the Indians . . . [and who] had abundant opportunity to influence the Indians and did not hesitate to tell them in our hearing that this was a scheme on the part of the Government and your commissioners to rob them." Whatever their coaching, the Indians found much in the agreement to complain about. Essentially, their complaints boiled down to these: (1) the price was not right— why should the Government put a price of fifty cents per acre on Indian land when it asked $1.25 per acre for its own?; (2) many of the promises relating to education and farming were simply repetitions of unfilled promises from the treaties of 1868 and 1876; and (3) the Indians could hardly be expected to divide their lands and negotiate for the cession of some of them when the Government, having failed to survey the reservation as promised, had never really shown them where those lands were. Secretary Vilas was willing to meet the Indians part way, by including a recommendation to Congress that the land be priced at one dollar per acre, graduated downward to seventy-five cents in two years and to fifty cents in five, but the Indians were unwilling to accept these terms. Weary of the negotiations and seeing no hope of success, Vilas sent the Indians home to think it over. "This course," he wrote, "is most likely to bring about their perception of their best interests and a later readiness to deal in a less grasping spirit." [18]

They held a council early in December; the report, signed by Red Cloud, Young-Man-Afraid-of-His-Horse, and Little Wound, and attested to by Gallagher, was little more than a recital of complaints. They had not received what was promised them at the time of the Black Hills treaty; their reservation had not been marked off as had been promised; they had even heard that McGillycuddy was being talked of for agent again. The letter ended: "We want to know what it

[18] *Ibid.*, p. LXVI. See also James McLaughlin, *My Friend the Indian* (Boston: Houghton Mifflin Co., 1910), pp. 276–280.

is that the Great Father has asked us to do that we did not do. We dress like white people and send our children to the schools. We think the Great Father's Indian children pay more attention to what he says than his white children do." [19]

Meanwhile, in Washington, the lame duck session of the Fiftieth Congress passed a new Sioux bill and on March 2, two days before he left office, President Cleveland signed it. The basic provisions were the same as those of the rejected proposal of 1888, providing for division of the reservation, allotments in severalty, and cession of the surplus lands. The terms, however, were much more generous, and in general reflected the demands of the delegation of October, which Vilas had rejected as being unreasonable: purchasers were to pay $1.25 per acre for three years, seventy-five cents for the next two years, and fifty cents thereafter; the Government was to provide for surveys and pay for them; benefits with respect to education and farming were not to be charged to land sales; a $3,000,000 trust fund was to be established. A special provision, inserted possibly as bait for Red Cloud's signature, provided that individual Indians of the Red Cloud and Red Leaf bands were to be paid at the rate of forty dollars a head [20] for the horses taken from them in 1876. [21]

When Red Cloud heard that a new land law was about to be passed, he requested permission to visit Washington to discuss it; he hoped, too, that the Government would pay his expenses, as he was "very poor in money." [22] The new Secretary of the Interior, John W. Noble, trying to put together a commission to go out and collect the necessary signatures, did not want to discuss the matter in Washington with Red Cloud or any other chief, and he turned down the request. [23] Red Cloud, however, accompanied by Nick Janis, had started before receiving a reply to his letter. [24] We know very little about Red Cloud's activities during this trip to Washington. He probably conferred with Dr. Bland and others in the National Indian Defense Association who were opposed to the Sioux bill, but the only record available is a report of a conversation he had with R. V. Belt, Acting Commissioner

[19] Report of Council of Sioux at Pine Ridge held December 10, 1888, NARS, RG 75, LR.

[20] Session Laws, 50th Cong., 2d Sess., Ch. 405. Hyde's otherwise good discussion (see n. 16 above) does not take into account the enactment of the law of 1889.

[21] See above, pp. 230–235.

[22] Red Cloud to Com. of Indian Affairs, March 1, 1889, NARS, RG 75, LR.

[23] Secretary of the Interior to Com. of Indian Affairs, April 2, 1889, *ibid.*

[24] Gallagher to Com. of Indian Affairs, April 10, 1888, *ibid.*

of Indian Affairs. This conversation appears to have been confined to the traders at Pine Ridge; Red Cloud wanted two of them replaced because they cheated him.[25]

On May 19 President Harrison announced the membership of the Commission that was to deal with the Sioux. Unlike the Pratt Commission, it was a high-powered group. Former Governor Charles Foster of Ohio was chairman; the other two members were Senator William Warner of Missouri, National Commander of the GAR, and Maj. Gen. George Crook, who, it was hoped, would be able to bring the Indians into line as he had during the troubles of 1876.[26]

The Commissioners left Chicago on May 29, in a special car on the Northwestern railroad.[27] Their first stop was at Rosebud, where they opened proceedings by providing fifteen beeves for a feast. The Indians put on an Omaha dance, and Bishop William H. Hare, who happened to be at the agency, preached; the Commissioners watched the dance but they skipped the preaching.[28] All of this must have had some effect; despite strenuous opposition on the part of a few leaders, the Commissioners collected 1,455 signatures out of a possible 1,476. When they got to Pine Ridge on June 13,[29] they found a much different state of affairs. Red Cloud was dead set against the agreement, and aided by Young-Man-Afraid-of-His-Horse and Little Wound, he had managed to line many of the Sioux up behind him. The Government could avoid dealing with Red Cloud in Washington, but at Pine Ridge he could not be ignored.[30]

[25] Report of talk between Red Cloud and Acting Commissioner Belt, April 27, 1889, *ibid.*

[26] See above, pp. 230–235. The Indians themselves may have had something to do with the appointment of Crook. At least, the commandant at Fort Robinson reported that he had been visited by "between two and three hundred Sioux," asking whether it was true that their lands were to be taken from them and given to white settlers, and stating that they would not be satisfied with the statement of anyone but General Crook, "in whose words they have unbounded confidence" (Col. Edward Hatch to AAG, Omaha, March 4, 1889, NARS, RG 48, LR, AGO). The Commission's report will be found in 51st Cong., 1st Sess., S. Ex. Doc. 51, which, unless otherwise indicated, I am following.

[27] Schmitt, *General George Crook, His Autobiography* (Norman: University of Oklahoma Press, 1946), p. 284.

[28] *Ibid.*, pp. 284–285.

[29] *Ibid.*, p. 286, gives the impression that Crook at least was at Pine Ridge on June 9.

[30] The Commissioners complained that "the opposing elements had been consolidated and strengthened under the leadership of Red Cloud, assisted by the active influence of the Indian Defense Association. It is proper to say here that not only at

The first Pine Ridge session convened at one-thirty on the afternoon of June 15, with seven hundred Indians spread out in front of the canvas awning or pavilion which shaded the Commissioners. Agent Gallagher began by impressing upon his charges that the men who had come to see them were very important persons. General Crook, he was sorry to say, was sick and unable to leave the house, but the other two commissioners would explain the bill. The Government had decided that the bill was the best thing for the Indians, and he was sure that if they listened carefully, they would see it in that light, too.

Governor Foster and Senator Warner alternated in lengthy explanations of the bill. They dwelt particularly upon the changes that had been made in last year's legislation and upon the benefits the Sioux would receive. They were smiling and conciliatory. They were there to enable the Sioux to become men, to free themselves from their present slavery. Governor Foster said, "I want to live to see the day when the son of Red Cloud, Young-Man-Afraid-of-His-Horses, or your other chiefs, and other Indians, shall occupy a seat in the great council of this State; and instead of having a white man to speak for the Indians, the Indians be able to speak for themselves." Meanwhile, it was important that the Indians sell their land while they could get such favorable terms. Dakota would soon become a state and its people would not tolerate having the state divided by the Great Sioux Reservation, which was like a wall separating the eastern part from the western part: "It does not take much sense to see that the white man is going to break through this wall. We believe it is our duty as friends to advise you of the situation. Unless this act is accepted (and I don't say this in the way of a threat—I say it as a friend), these Senators and these Representatives from Dakota will influence the Congress to get through there in some way."

After the Commissioners had concluded, Red Cloud said: "I have carefully noticed your speech, but there is one thing I did not notice, and that is this: In the treaty of 1868, all of the white men that are incorporated in the tribe have the same right as the Indians."

Warner and Foster both assured him that this was their understanding, too, and after they had promised Young-Man-Afraid that he could have a printed copy of everything that had been said, the council ended. As it broke up, the pavilion was surrounded by a body of mounted warriors who rushed through the assembled Indians, scattering

---

Pine Ridge, but at the other agencies, the agents of this association used every effort to defeat the purpose of the Commission."

them in every direction. No one was going to be permitted to say any more that day.

The next day the Commissioners met separately with the Cheyennes, who complained that they did not understand the Sioux language and wanted a session of their own. On the afternoon of the seventeenth the Sioux came together again, about six hundred of them. Old-Man-Afraid-of-His-Horse got the floor first. He had a copy of the Treaty of 1868 with him. When that paper was given to him at Fort Laramie, he was told that it was to run for eight generations, and then they would make a new treaty; as he calculated—he did not say how, and he may have been confusing 1851 with 1868—the treaty had twenty-one years yet to run. It seemed to him that the Commissioners were in a great hurry.

Red Cloud spoke next. He was obviously irritated with Old-Man-Afraid for intruding himself into the proceedings, but, more than that, he was in no mood to talk about further cessions. This is the Commissioners' report of what he said:

> My friends, I have papers just the same as he has, but I have them at home; but this is the map (exhibiting a small map) that the Great Father laid out for me for a reservation, and I am living on it. My friends, there is an old man (meaning Old-Man-Afraid-of-His-Horses) that has been an Indian chief. That treaty he was talking about he was there at the time the treaty was made. The treaty of 1868, me and Spotted Tail made that treaty. That was nineteen years ago. In the treaty of 1868 we was promised mares, and sheep, and cattle, and hogs, and farming implements that they were going to issue to us right straight along until the treaty run out. Here back we made another treaty, and gave up the right to hunt down at the Republican River, and we got $25,000, and during that time the Government promised to try and get $25,000 more for us.
>
> The next treaty we made was with Colonel Manypenny at my agency and Spotted Tail Agency. At that time we agreed to let him have the Black Hills, just the top of them. In that treaty I asked for pay for seven generations so I have that the map of what I have left, and this is the map (holding up a map) now. Now, my friends, the treaty I made with the Great Father and what has been promised to me has not been fulfilled as promised, and I want that fulfilled first, and now you come and want to get more land before what has been promised has been fulfilled. My friend General Crook knows something about this last treaty of 1876. My friends, when a man owes 10 cents or 50 cents up here at these stores these storekeepers want that paid before he gets any more. Now you come here and ask for more land. You want to buy more land, and I looked around to see if I could see any boxes of money that you brought here to buy more land, and I could not

see any, and now I think this is the talk of sugar again just as this paper was. My friends, my people are going to have another meeting to-morrow and have another talk with you, but this is what has been promised to me before, and I am only saying what has been promised to me in the past.

Little Wound and Young-Man-Afraid also spoke briefly. They, too, dwelt largely on the past, recalling promises that had not been fulfilled. The Commissioners were irritated. They had Red Cloud send for his copy of the Treaty of 1868, and showed the Indians that all of the promises except that about the issue of clothing had long since run out, and that the Government, through the Treaty of 1876 and out of kindness, was doing much more than had been promised in that early document. Senator Warner said, "My friends, that you may have been wronged by agents in the past, I do not question, but that the Great Father has watched over you as you would watch over your children, there is no question. And to-day you come here and slap the Great Father in the face." It was time for the Sioux to forget the past and think of the future. "My friends," he concluded, "there is no death so terrible as that of the man who is talked to death, and I will stop before that occurs and let your old friend, General Crook, talk to you."

Crook, apparently recovered from whatever was ailing him, came forward amid great cheering. He was brief and to the point. He reminded the Sioux that if the Treaty of 1868 had been violated by the white men it had also been violated by them. The old days were gone forever and it was time the Indians started doing for themselves. The new agreement was over at the agency, and they could commence signing right away: "We want every man who is over eighteen years of age on this agency, to come to the agency and say there they will or will not sign." There was only one thing more. The Commissioners had twenty-five head of cattle in the corral, and they were ready to issue them.

Some of the Indians signed that day, but the counciling was far from over. The next day was devoted to the Cheyennes, and on the nine-teenth the Commissioners met with the Sioux again. When the council opened at three o'clock in the afternoon, Red Cloud arose and said, "My friends, I am very sick to-day, and I did not come over to take part in this council, but to sit down and listen to what you have to say. I am not going to say anything, but listen."

For the rest of the council, that is all he did. American Horse took over for the Sioux, and his performance was one of the greatest oratorical efforts in the history of Indian negotiations. He talked almost uninterruptedly until the council had to be adjourned because of darkness, and he went on in the same fashion for two more days. Occasionally, one of the other Indians or one of the Commissioners made a short speech, but the field belonged to American Horse. He was speaking in behalf of the treaty, but he talked about virtually everything: rations, boundaries, former treaties, agents, traders, schools, the past, the present, and the future; he was by turns witty, solemn, and inane. His object was to help his people come to a decision, but his great effort was in vain. Near the end of the third day, he said,

> After my standing here for two days and wasting my energy in talk, and wasting the valuable time of the Commission, hoping that by the many different questions and their answers, would enable you to come to some decision. And what did all my trouble for you amount to? When all the trouble I took to have this thing explained to you, you were sitting there with your eyes shut and ears plugged up, refusing to hear or see.

As for himself, he said, "I will sign this bill, knowing that I have done what is best for my people."

Although American Horse had finally come out for the bill,[31] the Commissioners decided that they were getting nowhere with general councils. For one thing, American Horse was losing their audience with his oratory; the attendance dwindled to around two hundred on June 21, the last day of his great effort. They decided, therefore, to work on the Indians individually and in small groups. In doing so, they resorted to all the old tricks. An eyewitness later reported, "Crook did outrageously in his treaty of 1889. He came and feasted the Indians on beef for two days till he had them full, and then he told them what he wanted. He received anybody as a signer—anyway to get signers."[32] Crook later admitted that he offered Red Cloud, Little Wound, and Young-Man-Afraid two hundred dollars each to feast their bands if they would sign.[33]

Nothing, however, seemed to work, and on June 28 the Commissioners called the Indians together for a final conference. They warned the Sioux against the chiefs who obstructed progress and who lived only in the past; they said they were leaving the agreement with the agent so that any who changed their minds could have an opportunity to sign

[31] Schmitt, *Crook*, p. 286, erroneously states that the opposition to the bill was led by American Horse.

[32] E. S. Ricker, Interview with W. R. Jones, January 23, 1907, Ricker Mss., Tablet No. 2.

[33] Schmitt, *Crook*, p. 288.

before it was too late. Just before the council adjourned, American
Horse stepped forward and signed the agreement in the presence of all.

Two days after the Commissioners left Pine Ridge, Secretary Noble
wrote R. V. Belt, Acting Commissioner of Indian Affairs:

> If there is any existing writing or authority whereby Red Cloud of the
> Sioux Indians had been recognized to any degree as chief I wish you to
> inform me with a view to having it recalled, and I think it would be good
> policy to take some steps in a public nature, so that the Indians may
> understand it, depriving him of any authority from the Government of any
> kind or any recognition as a man of any importance and putting him rather
> in the attitude of an obstructionist. I wish you to consider this and consult
> with me immediately about it, as prompt action is necessary. I wish you
> also to consider the propriety of recognizing "American Horse" an Indian,
> as the Chief of the Sioux, or the one favored by the Government among
> them. I submit to you the form of a letter which I would send to the Agent.[34]

Belt, in a letter which throws light on the whole question of chieftainship among the Sioux, replied:

> I have to say that I have been unable to find any paper on file in this office,
> specifically authorizing the recognition of Red Cloud as Chief—though his
> name appears among the Chiefs and Headmen who signed the treaty of
> 1868 and the agreement of 1876.
>
> The Agent however, in his annual report of 1882, speaks of the deposition
> of Red Cloud as a Chief, and in several later communications, the Agent
> refers to him as the "ex Chief".[35]

He went on to say that "the records of the office show that Red
Cloud has been for years past and is now, a disturbing element among
the Indians." He recommended that the agent "be instructed to give
notice to all the Indians, in the most public manner, that Red Cloud is
not, and will not be recognized as a Chief or in any manner counte-
nanced, consulted or regarded in any way other than an ordinary
individual member of the Sioux Nation of Indians." He agreed that
American Horse should be "recognized as the Headman of the Ogalala
Sioux Indians, and the one with whom and through whom the Government will transact such business as may be necessary or convenient to
be done through a representative Indian of the tribe."[36]

At least three drafts of a letter to the agent were prepared, directing

---

[34] Secretary of the Interior to Acting Com. of Indian Affairs, July 1, 1889, NARS,
RG 75, LR.

[35] This was McGillycuddy. See above, p. 271.

[36] Belt to Secretary of the Interior, July 2, 1889, NARS, RG 48.

him to recognize American Horse rather than Red Cloud as chief of the Oglalas,[37] but on the advice of Inspector W. J. Pollock, who generally took Red Cloud's side, all were withheld.[38] American Horse, however, was chosen to head the delegation from Pine Ridge when various Sioux chiefs were called to Washington in December for a final conference on the agreement with the Secretary and the President.[39] American Horse obviously was not in a very strong position. Despite his support and all of the pressures that had been brought to bear upon the Indians at Pine Ridge, only 684 out of a total of 1,306 eligible adult males had signed the agreement, and many of them were Cheyennes and mixed bloods; almost the only Oglala of importance who signed, in addition to American Horse, was No Flesh, whose name appears first on the list of signers.[40] Moreover, American Horse was worried. He told the Secretary that their beef ration had been cut as soon as the Commissioners had departed and that many felt that it was the signing of the bill that had brought this about.[41] As to chiefs, he said:

> Now, to-day, all of our old chiefs are dead and we have none. We would like if you would give us a head man to every band.

But the old chiefs were not dead, and in the troubled months ahead, both the Sioux and the Government would turn to them, as they had so many times in the past.

[37] The drafts are in NARS, RG 48.

[38] Cyrus Bussey, Assistant Secretary of the Interior, to Secretary of the Interior, July 3, 1889, *ibid.*

[39] 51st Cong., 1st Sess., S. Ex. Doc. 51, pp. 218–233.

[40] The Government, despite the fact that the Commissioners listed the signers by agencies, calculated the signatures on the basis of the entire reservation. The total number of signers was 4,482 out of 5,678 eligibles, or more than the requisite three-fourths of the adult males, and on this basis the agreement was deemed to have the necessary approval.

[41] The Indian appropriation bill for the fiscal year ending June 30, 1890, in cognizance of the reduced populations reported on the reservation, had reduced money available for beef. The Commissioners were as concerned about this as was American Horse, and urged immediate action to restore the cut in rations.

CHAPTER 17

Ghost Dance and Wounded Knee

The council with the Sioux Commission left the Indians dazed and confused. As Bishop Hare put it, "The Indian's state of mind . . . is one of uncertainty and almost consternation."[1] There were many reasons for both the uncertainty and the consternation. The Commissioners had promised much but they had delivered little, and the Sioux, faced with the loss of almost half of their reservation, saw bad times ahead. When they returned to their homes from the counciling they found that their chickens had been stolen, some of their cattle killed, and some of their crops trampled down or eaten up.[2] The crops that remained died from drouth, and many of the surviving cattle were destroyed by the blackleg which ravaged the Sioux herds.[3] To add to their troubles, their government rations, which had been steadily diminishing since 1886,[4] were suddenly decreased by more than half, partly because of reduced appropriations and partly because of mismanagement. Responsible officials disagreed on the effect of the cut. Thomas J. Morgan, the Baptist preacher whom President Harrison had appointed

[1] Board of Indian Commissioners, *Annual Report*, 1889, p. 51.

[2] Statements of American Horse and Bishop W. H. Hare, in James Mooney, *The Ghost-Dance Religion and the Sioux Outbreak of 1890*, Bureau of American Ethnology, *Fourteenth Annual Report*, pp. 840–841. Commissioner of Indian Affairs Thomas J. Morgan put it this way: "There was diminuition and partial failure of the crops for 1889, by reason of their neglect by the Indians, who were congregated in large numbers at the council with the Sioux Commission . . ." (*ibid.*, p. 829).

[3] *Ibid.*, p. 826.

[4] See above, p. 306.

Commissioner of Indian Affairs, admitted that the reduction came at an unfortunate time but denied that it reduced the Sioux to starvation or even extreme suffering.[5] Others were sure that it had. Bishop Hare, for example, delared that the people were often hungry and died when taken sick, "not so much from disease as for want of food."[6] Whatever the situation—and one cannot read the evidence without concluding that the Sioux were desperately hungry[7]—the Indians felt tricked and trapped. As the disillusioned American Horse said, "The commission made us believe that we would get full sacks if we signed the bill, but instead of that our sacks are empty."[8] Adding to their misery, sickness— measles, the grippe, and whooping cough—stalked the reservation, dealing death in almost every village.[9]

The desperate, driven Sioux knew they needed help, but they were at a loss to know where to get it. The Great Father in Washington could not be depended upon; their friends in the East were strangely silent. There was much counciling, and in these councils they turned to their old chiefs. Red Cloud, Young-Man-Afraid, and Little Wound, all of whom had refused to sign the land agreement, dominated the talk-ing.[10] American Horse played his part, too, but his reputation was tarred by his earlier advocacy of the hated agreement which the Sioux somehow associated with all of their troubles. The old chiefs, however, were as confused and uncertain as their people. They could condemn the land agreement, but such condemnation offered little in the way of positive relief from their troubles. Then, in the fall, a ray of hope appeared. George Sword later described it this way: "In 1889 the Ogalala heard that the son of God had come upon the earth in the west. They said the Messiah was there, but he had come to help the Indians and not the whites, and it made the Indians happy to hear this."[11]

[5] Mooney, *The Ghost-Dance Religion*, p. 829.

[6] *Ibid.*, p. 827.

[7] For conditions at all of the agencies, see 52d Cong., 1st Sess., H. Doc. 1, Pt. 2 pp. 132–140.

[8] Mooney, *The Ghost-Dance Religion*, p. 840.

[9] *Ibid.*, p. 826. George E. Hyde, *A Sioux Chronicle* (Norman: University of Oklahoma Press, 1956), quotes George Sword to the effect that in the winter of 1889–1890, the death rate at Pine Ridge was 25–45 a month, mostly among the children.

[10] Hyde, *A Sioux Chronicle*, pp. 234–235, states that a feud had broken out between Red Cloud and a group led by Young-Man-Afraid and Little Wound. He does not document the statement, and I have found no evidence of a sharp break at this time between Red Cloud and the other two.

[11] Mooney, *The Ghost-Dance Religion*, p. 816. Mooney provides a good description of the Messiah movement. See also James H. McGregor, *The Wounded Knee Massacre*

The Sioux at Pine Ridge probably first heard of the new Messiah from their old enemies, the Shoshonis, with whom they had buried the hatchet during Red Cloud's visits of the eighties.[12] Just how they got word we do not know for sure. It may have come by personal contact, but William Selwyn, mixed-blood postmaster at the agency, stated that it came first in letters, written in English, which he translated for the Indians.[13] In any event, by fall there was so much talk about the exciting news from the West that Red Cloud, Young-Man-Afraid, Little Wound, American Horse, and others called a secret council to determine what should be done; they were joined by representatives from the Rosebud and Cheyenne River agencies. Out of the council came a decision to send messengers west to learn more about the Messiah.[14]

The messengers were gone all winter. When they returned in the spring, they brought word that the Messiah really lived and was on earth.[15] The messengers had not seen Him, but those who had said that He could be recognized by the nail prints in His hands and feet and the spear wound in His side, all of which had been put there by the white man many years ago. He spoke the languages of all the Indians and He fed all who came to see Him. He had come to earth to destroy the white men who had crucified Him, and He would destroy all Indians who did not believe in Him. For the believers, however, there would be a new world. All of their dead relatives would be restored to life; the buffalo and the game would all return. Those who believed should go into the ghost lodge and purify themselves.[16] Then they

(Baltimore: Wirth Brothers, 1940), pp. 39–46; Robert M. Utley, *The Last Days of the Sioux Nation* (New Haven: Yale University Press, 1963), pp. 60–83. Utley provides an excellent synthesis of the Ghost Dance and Wounded Knee troubles.

[12] See above, pp. 291, 307.

[13] Mooney, *The Ghost-Dance Religion*, pp. 819–820.

[14] *Ibid.*, p. 820. See also E. S. Ricker, Interview with Philip F. Wells, October 6, 1906, Ricker Mss., Tablet No. 5, Nebraska State Historical Society.

[15] There are many versions of the Messiah story. I am following that of Philip F. Wells, which seems to be as good as any.

[16] This was the sweat lodge, which had long been in use among the Sioux. The term "ghost" was applied to all aspects of the Messiah worship by the whites. The Sioux were thinking of the "spirit," but they probably were satisfied with the term "ghost" because everything connected with the new religion related to the rebirth of spirits of the dead (see Mooney, *The Ghost-Dance Religion*, p. 791.) The Sioux at Pine Ridge were referring to something translated as "ghost lodge" prior to the advent of the new religion. In their council of December 10, 1888, for example, Red Cloud, Young-Man-Afraid, and Little Wound (see above, pp. 311–312) complained of the stopping of the Ghost Lodges.

should put on the ghost shirt, which would protect them from the white man's bullets, and worship the Messiah by dancing.

Here at last was the answer to their problems, and all across the dry, dusty reservation, the starving Sioux took up the Ghost Dance. In many ways it was like the old Sun Dance, but it was much more intense, much more frenzied, much more prolonged. Fields were abandoned and schools were almost deserted as men, women, and children gave themselves up to the worship of their new-found Messiah.

The new religion divided the Indians, as had almost every crisis since the white man first arrived in their country. American Horse and Young-Man-Afraid opposed the Ghost Dance from the beginning, while Little Wound supported it. Red Cloud, as so many times in the past, seemed to embody in his actions the conflict that raged within the Sioux, sensing the inevitability of the new road while looking back to the old. In many respects, his course during the troubles of 1890–1891 was reminiscent of his role in 1876–1877,[17] and similarly it has subject to many interpretations.

Father Placidus Sialm, who was at Holy Rosary Mission early in the twentieth century, wrote: "Red Cloud never O.K.'d the Ghost Dance or the Messiah Craze. He stood aloof, pitying the downfall of the Oglalas into such depths of savagery and deviltry. . . ."[18] On the other hand, Mooney and Hyde both assert that Red Cloud was a firm believer in the new religion.[19] D. F. Royer, who became agent at Pine Ridge in the fall,[20] and who despite his many shortcomings was in a position to observe events first-hand, wrote that "while Red Cloud is not a prominent man in the dance, he is quietly encouraging his people to keep it going."[21] This probably describes his role—encouragement but not involvement; direct involvement came, as it had in 1876, through his son Jack, who was a leader in the dance.[22]

At first the easygoing Gallagher was inclined to dismiss the Ghost Dance as something unimportant which would soon pass away. In response to a request from Commissioner Morgan, asking what he was

[17] See above, pp. 218–222.

[18] Placidus Sialm, S.J., "History, Holy Rosary Mission, Pine Ridge, S. D.," p. 82, Ms., Holy Rosary Mission, made available through the courtesy of Father Lawrence Edwards, S.J.

[19] Mooney, *The Ghost-Dance Religion*, p. 848; Hyde, *A Sioux Chronicle*, pp. 242–250.

[20] See below, p. 325.

[21] Royer to R. V. Belt, Acting Com. of Indian Affairs, October 30, 1890, NARS, RG 75, Special Case No. 188.

[22] *Ibid.*, November 8, 1890.

doing about it, he stated that until he had received the Commissioner's letter he had not been aware of any great excitement among the Indians. He wrote that he had had to deal with the Messiah craze, but that it was dying out:

> The first gathering they [the Indians] had to discuss the matter being called without my authority and at a time when it would seriously interfere with farm work, I ordered the police to disperse the people and to bring to the agency the promoters of the enterprise, three Indians who had just returned from the Northern country, which they had visited without permission during the past winter.
>
> These Indians were given a good lecture upon the mischief they were doing and placed in the guard house for punishment. Later, while the Indians were in council, I explained to them the silliness of what had been told them and cautioned them against being made dupes of by evil disposed persons who would attempt to practice upon their credulity.
>
> I do not believe any serious trouble will result from this excitement, but that in a short time, it will have passed from their minds, possibly to be supplanted by something equally as silly.[23]

Brig. Gen. John R. Brooke, commanding the Department of the Platte, was equally sanguine. Called upon by his superiors in Washington for information, he, too, replied that there was nothing to worry about, and that to send troops would only increase the excitement.[24]

This was mid-June. By mid-July, Gallagher was seriously discussing with agency employees the best means of handling the growing unrest. There seems to have been no agreement, but most of those on the scene were convinced that force ultimately would have to be used against the dancers. There was a minor showdown on Friday, August 22, when some two thousand dancers gathered on White Clay Creek. This was Red Cloud's country, and many of the dancers undoubtedly were Red Cloud's people, although Red Cloud himself was not there, and, indeed, was not even on the reservation.[25] Gallagher instructed the police to disperse the Indians, but they were unable or unwilling to do so. On Sunday the agent visited the dancing grounds himself, accompanied by

[23] H. D. Gallagher to Com. of Indian Affairs, June 10, 1890, NARS, RG 75, LR.

[24] Telegram, Brooke to AG, Washington, June 18, 1890, Copy in NARS, RG 75, LR.

[25] For reasons which we can only surmise, Red Cloud tried to visit the Shoshonis during the summer of 1890. He was ordered back to Pine Ridge before reaching the Shoshoni agency, but he had not returned by August 22 (telegram, Col. J. G. Tilford, CO, Fort Robinson, to AAG, Omaha, July 25, 1890; letter, August 21, 1890; D. F. Royer to R. V. Belt, December 4, 1890, NARS, RG 75, LR).

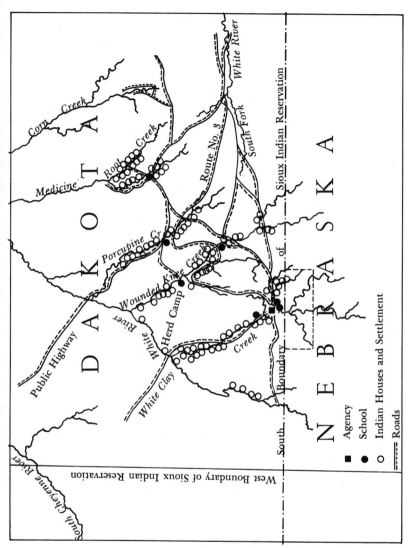

Pine Ridge Agency 1884

twenty policemen; but the dancers, warned of the agent's coming, had disappeared, and there were only a few young men in the area. They were stripped for fighting and stood with their Winchesters in their hands. It is difficult to determine just what happened, but Young-Man-Afraid arrived on the scene and was able to quiet things down before further trouble developed.[26]

At the beginning of October, Gallagher was replaced as agent by D. F. Royer in a wholesale, politically motivated reshuffling of the Indian Service. Gallagher had been slow to appreciate the significance of the Ghost Dance, but all who were in a position to know seemed to agree that he was several cuts above the average Indian agent, that he knew how to handle the Sioux, and that he probably would have been able to deal with the situation if let alone and given adequate support. Royer, on the other hand, was a small-town Dakota politician whose only qualifications appeared to be service in the legislature on behalf of R. F. Pettigrew's election to the United States Senate.[27] As Dr. McGillycuddy, who certainly was no friend of Gallagher's, put it, the new agent was "a gentleman totally ignorant of Indians and their peculiarities; a gentleman with not a qualification in his make-up calculated to fit him for the position of agent at one of the largest and most difficult agencies in the service to manage; a man selected solely as a reward for political services."[28]

Royer was soon crying for help. On November 8 he reported that he had called a council of "all the most prominent chiefs" and had done everything he could "in argument and persuasion" to convince them that they should give up the Ghost Dance, but "they simply laughed and said that they would keep it up as long as they pleased." He did not say who attended this council, but he identified Little Wound, "the most stubborn, head-strong, self-willed, unruly Indian on the Reservation," as the leader of the whole movement. Royer asserted that the situation was completely out of control, and that the only solution now

26 Gallagher, Annual Report, August 28, 1890, in Com. of Indian Affairs, *Annual Report*, 1890, pp. 48–56; Ricker, Interview with Philip F. Wells; E. B. Reynolds, Special Indian Agent, to Com. of Indian Affairs, September 25, 1890, NARS, RG 75, Special Case No. 188.

27 Royer had wanted to be Receiver of the Land Office at Huron but was given the Pine Ridge appointment as a substitute (Alfred Rockefeller, Jr., "The Sioux Troubles of 1890–1891" [Ph.D. dissertation, Northwestern University, 1949], p. 95).

28 Mooney, *The Ghost-Dance Religion* . . . , p. 833. See also Ricker, Interview with Philip Wells; Interview with Robert O. Pugh, Tablet 11; Interview with George W. Colhoff, Tablet No. 25; Hyde, *A Sioux Chronicle*, p. 254; Board of Indian Commissioners, *Annual Report*, 1891, pp. 181–182.

lay in "sending a sufficient number of troops to arrest the leaders and place them in prison under guard and then disarm the balance of the Indians on the reservation."[29]

Royer was not the only one who was alarmed. The whole country was excited, and each day the excitement increased, fanned by sensational press reports from the agencies.[30] Both the Army and the Indian Service had investigators in the field, and Maj. Gen. Nelson A. Miles, commanding the Division of the Missouri, had come west in October to have a personal look at the situation.[31] At Pine Ridge, Royer's control steadily deteriorated. On November 12, when the police tried to arrest an Indian for violation of regulations, the offender brandished a butcher knife and refused to submit, "and in less than two minutes he was reinforced by 200 ghost dancers, all armed and ready to fight."[32] Three days later the agent, frankly scared, telegraphed:

> Indians are dancing in the snow and are wild and crazy. I have fully informed you that employees and government property at this agency have no protection and are at the mercy of these dancers. Why delay by further investigation, we need protection and we need it now. The leaders should be arrested and confined at some military post until the matter is quieted and this should be done at once.[33]

Already, however, President Harrison had decided to turn the situation over to the Army,[34] and on November 20 General Brooke arrived at Pine Ridge with five companies of infantry, three troops of cavalry, a Hotchkiss gun, and a Gatling gun.[35] This strength was soon augmented

[29] Royer to Com. of Indian Affairs, November 8, 1890, NARS, RG 75, Special Case No. 188.

[30] It should be kept in mind, of course, that Pine Ridge was not the only source of trouble, but that all of the agencies were affected. The greatest amount of national attention probably was focused on the Standing Rock Agency, where Sitting Bull was actively participating in the dance. For Sitting Bull's activities, see Stanley Vestal, *Sitting Bull: Champion of the Sioux* (New York: Houghton Mifflin Co., 1932), pp. 271–315.

[31] Royer to Belt, October 30, 1890, reports a personal conference with General Miles.

[32] Royer to Com. of Indian Affairs, November 13, 1890, NARS, RG 75, Special Case No. 188. At this juncture, Royer wanted to go to Washington to discuss matters personally with the Commissioners!

[33] Telegram, Royer to Comm. of Indian Affairs, November 15, 1890, NARS, RG 75, Special Case No. 188.

[34] Benjamin Harrison to Secretary of the Interior, November 13, 1890, *ibid.*

[35] Telegram, Cooper, Special Agent, to Com. of Indian Affairs, November 20, 1890, *ibid.*

by additional cavalry and infantry, a strong force was sent to Rosebud, and troops were stationed at various places throughout the reservation to control the movements of the Indians. General Miles established headquarters at Rapid City, South Dakota.[36] The Nebraska National Guard was called to active duty and distributed at various points along the northern border of the state.[37]

The Army was in control, but no one was sure just how to proceed. As General Miles ruefully admitted, years of peace and inactivity "had, to some extent, impaired the efficiency of the troops." He was not at all sure that they would be a match for the Indians if the tribes were allowed to concentrate against them; his best course seemed to be to keep them separated, to isolate the dancers from the peaceably inclined, and, if necessary, to arrest the principal troublemakers and get them out of the way.[38]

Efforts to implement this policy brought the death of Sitting Bull on December 15 as he resisted arrest in his home at Standing Rock. At Pine Ridge, General Brooke found the Indians sharply divided, with the presence of a large number of hostile Brulés from Rosebud adding to the confusion. Moreover, it was difficult to determine just who was friendly and who was not. Of the principal chiefs, American Horse and Young-Man-Afraid were solidly behind the Government, but the latter was away on a hunting trip in Wyoming; Little Wound, once one of the strongest of the "progressive" chiefs, remained hostile and shortly after the troops arrived was quoted as saying that he wanted to "see all the whites dead."[39] Soon after his arrival Brooke reported to Miles that the disaffected Indians under Little Wound, Big Road, Jack Red Cloud, and others were assembling on White River, and "their attitude is hostile."[40]

Red Cloud finally appears to have been on the side of the Government and doing everything possible to prevent further trouble, despite his son's involvement and despite the fact that as late as November 28

[36] For disposition of the troops, see 53d Cong., 1st Sess., H. Ex. Doc. 1, Pt. 2, pp. 147–148; for Miles' role, see Virginia Weisel Johnson, *The Unregimented General: A Biography of Nelson A. Miles* (Boston: Houghton Mifflin Co., 1962), pp. 261–299.

[37] For an account of the activities of the Nebraska National Guard, see L. W. Colby, "The Sioux Indian War of 1890–91," Nebraska State Historical Society, *Transactions and Reports*, III (1892), 144–190.

[38] 53d Cong., 1st Sess., H. Ex. Doc. 1, Pt. 2, pp. 145–146.

[39] A. T. Lea, Special Agent, to Cooper, Special Agent, November 22, 1890, NARS, RG 75, Special Case No. 188.

[40] Nelson A. Miles to AG, November 22, 1890, NARS, RG 98, LR.

General Miles identified him as one of "the principal incendiaries."[41]
It must be kept in mind that Red Cloud was now old and almost blind,
and his capacity for leadership was nothing like it had been in the past.
On the day before the troops arrived, he wrote the editor of the
Chadron Democrat the following pathetic letter:

> Dear Friend:—I will write a few lines to you this morning to show that I
> remember you as a friend. I have been a friend to the whites that are living
> near the reserve, and I want to have peace all around. I hear something
> yesterday about 2 o'clock, so that is what I want to tell you. I hear that the
> soldiers at Fort Robinson are coming here tomorrow. I tell you this because
> I do not want to have trouble with the soldiers and other good white
> people that are near me. I want you to publish my letter so the people of
> Chadron may know that I am a friend to them. If you can I want you to write
> to the great father at Washington.[42]

Royer, while not acknowledging any help from Red Cloud, exonerated him from complicity in the troublemaking. He wrote to the Commissioner that although it was charged that Red Cloud belonged to the
disturbing element, he had no evidence that the old chief was connected
with the Ghost Dance; on the contrary, he had given "no trouble of any
character."[43]

Red Cloud cooperated to the best of his ability with General Brooke
in trying to persuade the hostiles to give up their dancing and move into
the agency. By early December he had convinced his son Jack that he
should give up, but Short Bull, Two Strike, and Kicking Bear were out
on the White River with their followers, dancing themselves into a
frenzy and afraid of punishment if they came in. General Brooke was
prepared to offer them peace, food, and safety, but he did not know how
to communicate with them. Finally, Father John Jutz, superior of Holy
Rosary Mission, volunteered to see what he could do. He asked Red
Cloud to go with him; the old chief refused but offered the services of
Jack. Father Jutz was not particularly successful. He met with the
Indians on the White River on December 6; Two Strike and about

---

[41] *Ibid.*, November 28, 1890. This does not agree with the statement in Johnson,
The Unregimented General, p. 277, that "American Horse and old chief Red Cloud were
doing their utmost to aid the whites by sending runners to various bands to talk them
into submission."

[42] *Chadron Democrat*, November 20, 1890, clipping in Ricker Mss., Tablet No. 34.

[43] Royer to R. V. Belt, Acting Com. of Indian Affairs, November 25, 1890, NARS,
RG 75, Special Case No. 188.

forty followers agreed to come in, but the others, after a violent quarrel, moved further north into the Bad Lands.[44]

December was a month of growing tension at Pine Ridge. News of the death of Sitting Bull produced great alarm among both friendlies and hostiles. At night, according to Brig. Gen. L. W. Colby, commander of the Nebraska National Guard, "Great lights and signal fires shone from the bluffs and hill tops a few miles distant from Pine Ridge, and the Bad Lands were ablaze with lights that could be seen for miles."[45] Causing further consternation was the appearance in Red Cloud's camp on December 22 of a white man dressed in Indian clothes who claimed to be the Messiah and who wanted to go to the Bad Lands to preach to the Indians. He turned out to be a rural Iowan suffering from millennial and missionary delusions who had come west to save the Sioux. A few of the more credulous believed him, but Red Cloud spat in his face and said, "You go home. You are no Son of God."[46] The old chief had had enough of messiahs.

With each passing day the tension increased. The force at Pine Ridge was augmented, and mounted patrols kept nervous watch over all groups of Indians who had not come into the agency. Then, on December 29, the breaking point was reached and two hundred men, women, and children of Big Foot's band were massacred on Wounded Knee Creek, after they had surrendered and were in the process of giving up their arms.[47]

This senseless slaughter confirmed what the irreconcilables had been saying all along: the white man could not be trusted; better to die fighting than to surrender and be shot down like dogs. Short Bull and Kicking Bear were actually coming in and would have camped the

[44] Sialm, "History, Holy Rosary Mission" pp. 66–67; George Harry Van Huizen, "The United States Government and the Sioux Indians, 1878–1891" (Master's thesis, Washington University, 1950), p. 161. Colby, "The Sioux Indian War of 1890–91," pp. 150–151, states that Short Bull and Kicking Bear actually came into Pine Ridge, and the quarrel occurred there. I have preferred to follow Sialm and Van Huizen. I have no evidence to support Hyde's statement (*A Sioux Chronicle*, p. 282) that Big Road and Kicking Bear were in the friendly camp.

[45] Colby, "The Sioux Indian War of 1890–91," p. 153.

[46] *Ibid.*, p. 154; cf. Hyde, *A Sioux Chronicle*, pp. 282–283.

[47] The tragic story of Wounded Knee has been frequently told. Among the best recent secondary accounts are: Hyde, *A Sioux Chronicle*; McGregor, *The Wounded Knee Massacre*; Utley, *The Last Days of the Sioux Nation*. Mooney, *The Ghost-Dance Religion*, is basic. The Ricker Mss. contain numerous valuable interviews with persons who were at Pine Ridge at the time.

night of December 29 about four miles from the agency; but when they heard what had happened to Big Foot, they wheeled around and moved some seventeen miles up White Clay Creek.[48] Some of Two Strike's people, camped near Red Cloud's house, opened fire on the agency buildings, wounding two soldiers. The troops, under General Brooke's orders, held their fire, but the Indian police killed two of Two Strike's warriors and wounded several others.[49] Two Strike now decided to leave the agency and to force Red Cloud to go with him. The old chief was trapped, and there was nothing he could do. He described his troubles a few days later in a letter to Dr. Bland:

> Chief Two Strike and his people Brule Sioux, 145 family lodges and some Ogalalas was camped near my house, when the news came about Big Foot and his people. Some young men of the Brules on horseback went to fire on the Agency. It caused a great excitement. The Brules and others all stampeded, and the Brules forced me to go with them. I being in danger of my life between two fires I had to go with them and follow my family. Some would shoot their guns around me and make me go faster. . . .[50]

By January 1 at least three thousand Indians had fled the agency; they had burned two school buildings and the Episcopal church; their leaders were preaching violence and threatening to kill any who tried to return.[51] General Miles arrived with fresh cavalry to take personal command. He knew many of the Indians and he was sure that he could induce them to surrender without bloodshed. He addressed a letter to "Red Cloud, Little Wound, Two Strike, Big Road, Little Hawk, Crow Dog, Chief Knife, No Water, Turning Bear, Calico, White Face, Yellow Bear, Kicking Bear, Short Bull, He Dog, and all Indians away from their Agencies." He was their friend. If they would come in and do as he said, they would have no trouble; if they did not, they would have trouble; he had many soldiers on all sides of them.[52] He sent a separate letter to Red Cloud:

[48] 53d Cong., 1st Sess., H. Ex. Doc. 1, Pt. 2, p. 150.

[49] Telegram, Royer to Com. of Indian Affairs, December 29, 1890, NARS, RG 75, Special Case No. 188.

[50] Red Cloud to T. A. Bland, January 12, 1891, in T. A. Bland, ed., *A Brief History of the Late Military Invasion of the Home of the Sioux* (Washington, 1891), pp. 21–22. Johnson, *The Unregimented General*, p. 292, states: "According to friends, Red Cloud hadn't wanted to leave the agency but when the general exodus began his wife threw the old man's belongings into a wagon declaring she was going on the warpath even if her liege lord was not." This is difficult to credit.

[51] Telegram, Royer to Com. of Indian Affairs, January 2, 1891, NARS, RG 75, Special Case No. 188.

[52] Nelson A. Miles to Red Cloud . . . , January 1, 1891, NARS, RG 98, Hq.,

I regret to see your house standing alone. When all the Indians were afraid, and ran away, you were carried with them. I am told no soldier fired at your house, but that it was done by the Indian police.[53] Anything that has been taken from you must be in the Indian camp, and I will order it returned to you when you return, and if not found, will recommend that you be paid for it in time. Since I saw you, I have been twice to Washington to help the Indians. I know all the wrongs that have been done to the Indians and the wrongs the Indians have done. If they do whatever I tell them it will be best for all the Indians. General Brooke is also your friend, but he is now away with many soldiers and I am chief in command.[54]

There was much counciling in the Indian camp, and much confusion. Red Cloud and Little Wound wanted to come in, but Short Bull, Two Strike, and Kicking Bear would have none of it: all would die together; they would kill the first man who tried to escape.[55] Apparently the Indians made some sort of reply to Miles' letter, for on January 2 he wrote again "To all chiefs on or near White Clay Creek," stating, presumably in response to a request that the Secretary of the Interior and the Indian Commissioner come out to see them, that the President had placed him in complete command and that they must do as he said.[56] Red Cloud wrote in reply:

Dear Friend. I received your letter and we had big council around and a crazy boy took it away from us and tore it up, we did not read it. I want you to fix it, that Vice President and others that are helping the Indians to come and fix this trouble, the last letter I wrote it was written mistaken I told you that I don't want any trouble. I want you to send away these soldiers that are around me. I want you to write me and copy, the last letter you and sent it to me and after we read that letter we will come out there.

I want you to sent me another note as quick as you can.

P.S. I will live together again.[57]

Military Division of the Missouri, Letters Sent Field Book, 1890–1891. Copies of letters between Miles and the Indians were furnished me by Robert M. Utley, Regional Historian, National Park Service, Santa Fe, New Mexico.

[53] One report has it that Red Cloud fled because he had heard that the troops were going to shell his home. See Ricker, Interview with William Peano, Ricker Mss., Tablet No. 10.

[54] Miles to Red Cloud, January 1, 1891.

[55] Red Cloud to Bland, January 12, 1891 (above, n. 50); Telegram, Royer to Com. of Indian Affairs, January 2, 1891 (above, n. 51).

[56] NARS, RG 98, Hq., Military Division of the Missouri, Letters Sent Field Book, 1890–1891.

[57] Red Cloud to Miles [n.d.], NARS, RG 98, Box 126.

Miles responded that the soldiers were there only to protect the agency and the friendly Indians from the bad Indians. They would have to remain, but if the Indians would come in and do as he told them, all would be well, and they would have an opportunity to speak to the Secretary and the Great Father.[58] The next day, January 5, a delegation consisting of Big Road, He Dog, Little Hawk, Jack Red Cloud, and High Hawk came in to see what the general had to say. Miles gave them every assurance for their safety; he thought the entire camp would soon surrender.[59]

It would be some time before this happened, but Red Cloud decided to break away from the hostiles. He described his flight this way in his letter of January 12 to Dr. Bland:

> I tried my best for them to let me go back, but they would not let me go, and said if I went they would kill me. But three nights ago I and my family and He Dog and White Hawk and families, all made our escape very late in the night while they all asleep, and we got all right to the Agency, and I reported all about it to General Miles.[60]

Red Cloud hoped that his escape would have a good effect upon the others and induce them to surrender.[61] It may have had; certainly the flight of their oldest and most prominent leader to seek protection at the hands of the Great Father's soldiers must have helped to demonstrate to the Sioux the utter hopelessness of their cause. Seeing soldiers everywhere they looked, the hostiles realized the only end to fighting would be that which had come to Big Foot and his people. On the other hand, they knew that General Miles kept his promises to every Indian who came into the agency, and they all could find food,

[58] Miles to Red Cloud, January 4, 1891, NARS, RG 98, Hq., Military Division of the Missouri, Letters Sent Field Book, 1890–1891.

[59] Telegram, Miles to AG, January 5, 1891, NARS, RG 98.

[60] See note 50 above. Hyde, *A Sioux Chronicle*, p. 308, states: ". . . the old man was delivered by his courageous daughter who led him, blind and helpless, out of the ghost dance camp into a howling blizzard and brought him safely to his own camp at the agency." He does not document the statement, but a generally unsatisfactory work, W. Fletcher Johnson, *Life of Sitting Bull and History of the Indian War of 1890–1891* (Edgewood, S. D., 1891), p. 477, describes the flight similarly, but with more embellishment. Johnson attributes Red Cloud's flight to panic over the killing of Lt. E. W. Casey. This may have been a factor. Casey was killed on January 7 (not on January 27, as Johnson implies), and there is some evidence that Red Cloud had sent a messenger to warn Casey (Lt. S. A. Cloman to Camp Adj., Pine Ridge, February 20, 1891, NARS, RG 75, Special Case No. 188).

[61] Red Cloud to T. A. Bland, January 12, 1891 (above, n. 50).

blankets, and warm clothing there. Moreover, Royer, whose unfortunate administration was associated in the Indians' minds with much of their trouble, had been replaced at Miles' insistence by Captain F. E. Pierce, a soldier whom they knew and trusted.[62]

Slowly the hostiles moved toward the agency. On January 15 they were encamped on White Clay Creek within range of the guns at Pine Ridge, and on the next day they moved in and surrendered. Miles was an easy master. He demanded that the Indians give up their guns, but unlike Colonel Forsyth at Wounded Knee, he did not search their tipis, even though he knew many had not complied with his order.[63] He insisted that he would have to arrest Short Bull, Kicking Bear, and twenty others, and take them to Fort Sheridan, Illinois, for as long as might be necessary to guarantee peace. They gave themselves up without objection; according to George Hyde they were later sent to Europe with Buffalo Bill's Wild West Show![64] Moreover, Miles kept his promise that if the Indians surrendered, some of their chiefs could visit the Secretary of the Interior and the Great Father. The delegation to Washington included, according to Miles, "some of the best and wisest counselors, the ablest and most loyal friends of the Government living upon the Sioux reservations."[65] It did that—Young-Man-Afraid was at the head of the group—but it also included Little Wound, who had been most active in the Ghost Dance, and Two Strike and Hump, two of the leaders in the troubles.[66]

[62] This was part of a complete house-cleaning of the Sioux agencies, in which Harrison's political appointees were removed and replaced temporarily by Army officers (53d Cong., 1st Sess., H. Ex. Doc. 1, Pt. 2, p. 152).

[63] Miles was severely criticized for his leniency. A resident of Rushville, Nebraska, complained: "The settlers feel that the Indians are in worse state of mind towards the whites than when the troops arrived; that they are still armed and plan an uprising in the spring. . . . My candid impression is that the failure of General Miles to disarm the Indians and the withdrawal of all troops will almost depopulate the country" (G. W. Reed to Com. of Indian Affairs, January 28, 1891, NARS, RG 75, Special Case No. 188).

[64] Hyde, *A Sioux Chronicle*, p. 318.

[65] 53d Cong., 1st Sess., H. Ex. Doc. 1, Pt. 2, p. 153. Except where otherwise indicated, my account of the surrender is taken from this document, pp. 152–153.

[66] In addition, the delegation included: American Horse, Standing Elk, Fire Thunder, Big Road, He Dog, High Hawk, High Pipe (Telegram, Lewis, Special Agent, Pine Ridge, to Com. of Indian Affairs, January 26, 1891, NARS, RG 75, Special Case No. 188). The proceedings of the council in Washington—largely a recitation of grievances about food and unkept promises—will be found in Com. of Indian Affairs to Secretary of the Interior, February 4, 1891, NARS, RG 75, Misc. Papers, Box No. 735. See also David Graham Phillips, "The Sioux Chiefs Before the Secretary," *Harper's Weekly*, XXXV (February 21, 1891), 142.

Red Cloud was left at home. On January 26, the day the group left, he wrote the Commissioner:

> A delegation of my people leave today for Washington. Owing to the bad condition of my eyes, I was not able to accompany them. I hope, however, that your office will grant me permission to visit Washington later on when my eyes are in better condition to do so. I feel that in justice to myself and people, I should do so and I promise if you grant me the permission I will give a full and true statement regarding this trouble now existing among my people. I hope you will fully consider my case and that permission will be granted me. Please advise me by letter what your decision is.[67]

The Commissioner's decision is recorded on the letter; he marked it simply "File."

A few days later Red Cloud wrote his old friend W. J. Pollock, who had taken his side years before in his dispute with McGillycuddy. He reported that his eyes were now better, and he would like to come to Washington to explain his role in the recent troubles. He was afraid that his enemies were blaming him for the difficulties and he wanted to set the record straight. In a few words, he summed up much of his career: "I, of course, as many others have done before me, have made mistakes in not doing something I should have done and what I should not have done, but be that as it may, I am constantly on the right side of this great trouble and will continue to be there." Pollock sent the letter on to the Commissioner with this comment: "In this connection I venture to suggest that this old man has been true to the interests of the whites for at least a dozen years to my personal knowledge and his wishes and good will are worthy of serious consideration."[68]

But this letter, too, was filed away, with no action taken. Wounded Knee marked the end of any hope the Sioux might have had of regaining their old way of life; it also marked the end of the active career of the leader who, more than any other, typified the hopeless ambivalence of the Sioux during the long years of transition. Red Cloud's active career ended not in violence, as did that of Crazy Horse or Spotted Tail or Sitting Bull; it was simply lost in a government file.

---

[67] Red Cloud to Com. of Indian Affairs, January 26, 1891, NARS, RG 75, Special Case No. 188.

[68] Red Cloud to W. J. Pollock, February 5, 1891, NARS, RG 75, LR.

CHAPTER 18

The End of the Road

On March 22, 1891, shortly after the Sioux delegation left Washington, Commissioner Morgan addressed a long letter to all the Sioux agents, outlining what the Government was prepared to do for their Indians under the Treaty of 1868, the agreement of 1877, and the act of 1889. The agents were to make sure that the Indians understood fully what they could expect in the way of rations, annuities, educational opportunities, and agricultural assistance; they were to assure their charges that money was available to supply all that had been provided for, and that, in addition, extra money had been appropriated to make up for the shortage of rations in 1890, to pay for losses suffered by friendly Indians during the Wounded Knee troubles, and even to pay members of the Red Cloud and Red Leaf bands for the ponies they had lost in 1876. At the same time, the agents were to "explain very fully and very emphatically . . . that any renewal of trouble will bring upon them severe punishment, great loss, and take away from them the sympathy of their friends and of all the people of the United States."[1] The Government was through with negotiating, through with compromising. As Secretary of the Interior John W. Noble put it:

I think if the Indians are given to understand emphatically that they must obey the law now and keep order and that the government has done

[1] The full text of the letter is in Com. of Indian Affairs, *Annual Report*, 1891, pp. 135–141; see also T. G. Morgan to Capt. Charles G. Penney, March 27, 1891, NARS, RG 98.

everything demanded of it, will be the best course to pursue. I hope I am not wanting in humane feeling toward the Indians and in a disposition to advance them, by all reasonable means, to a state of civilization as rapidly as possible, and to treat them in all matters with magnanimity, but . . . the time has come to make them understand that if any further trouble occurs, it will be an occasion for great severity to them and of punishment, if need be, sufficient to compel obedience. We have done all that we consistently can for them and if this will not serve, they will have to be held by the strong hand of force, be the consequences what they may.[2]

Although the Sioux made very little progress toward "a state of civilization," there was no need to worry about the necessity of force, other than that which could be supplied by the agency police.[3] To be sure, there remained a strong faction of "non-progressives"—sullen, morose, and uncooperative—but they had neither the will nor the strength to try to improve their situation by force. "To themselves," as Capt. Charles G. Penney, who took charge of Pine Ridge early in 1891, put it, "they seem to be fenced in with no future and nothing to do but draw and eat their rations and then die."[4]

Red Cloud lived for almost nineteen of the dreary years following Wounded Knee. Wrinkled, stooped, and nearly blind, he was no longer taken seriously by the whites, and was held in honor among his own people primarily because he was a symbol of a bygone day, one who had been part of the glorious years along the Platte and in the Big Horns. He knew, as much as anyone, how far the glory of those years had departed, and frequently he lamented the fate of his people. Warren Moorehead, the anthropologist, reported in *The American Indian* that one day, while he was standing outside Red Cloud's house at Pine Ridge, the old chief said to him:

> You see this barren waste. . . . Think of it! I, who used to own rich soil in a well-watered country so extensive that I could not ride through it in a week on my fastest pony, am put down here! Why, I have to go five miles for wood for my fire. Washington took our lands and promised to feed and support us. Now I, who used to control 5000 warriors, must tell Washington when I am hungry. I must beg for that which I own. If I beg hard, they

[2] John W. Noble to Com. of Indian Affairs, April 2, 1891, NARS, RG 75, Special Case No. 188.

[3] The agents' reports during the years following Wounded Knee document the lack of progress. For an excellent summary of conditions at Pine Ridge more than half a century after the massacre, see Gordon MacGregor, *Warriors without Weapons: A Study of the Society and Personality Development of the Pine Ridge Sioux* (Chicago: University of Chicago Press, 1946).

[4] Penney to Com. of Indian Affairs, April 7, 1891, NARS, RG 75, LR.

put me in the guard-house. We have trouble. Our girls are getting bad. Coughing sickness every winter carries away our best people. My heart is heavy, I am old, I cannot do much more . . . .[5]

Occasionally Red Cloud took part in a council as he had in the old days, and in 1897 he made a final trip to Washington, but his words were little heeded. In 1892, in a council at Pine Ridge with James Cooper, a special agent of the Indian Service, he complained about the judges of the Indian courts on the reservations, saying that they fined everyone and no one knew what happened to the money the people paid to them; he thought the courts should be abolished. Cooper, however, recommended that they be continued, feeling that to give in on this matter would be a step backward.[6] While in Washington in 1897, Red Cloud joined with American Horse, Clarence Three Stars, and Patrick H. Starr in presenting a long memorial of grievances, and in testifying before the Senate Committee on Indian Affairs, but nothing came of this either.[7] Finally, in September, 1903, Red Cloud spoke briefly at a council which Congressman E. W. Martin of South Dakota held with the Sioux at Pine Ridge. He spoke as an old man who knew the history of his people and of their relations with the Government. In what was the last time he talked in council, he said:

Quite a while ago I used some words with the Great Father. It must have been twenty-six or twenty-eight years ago and I have missed most of the words. There was a man came from the Great Father who told me, "Red Cloud, the Great Father told me to come and see you. So the Great Father told me to come to you because he wants the Black Hills from you." So I asked, "How much money did you bring for the Black Hills?" He answered me, "I brought six million dollars." So I answered him, "That is a little bit of a thing." I told him like this, "The Black Hills is worth to me seven generations, but you give me this word of six million dollars. It is just a little spit out of my mouth." Then he said, "Let me have the Black Hills and the Big Horn both together." But I told him this, "That is too small; so I won't do it." And I kept this land; "So you can go back to the Great Father and say that to me the Black Hills is worth seven generations.

[5] Warren K. Moorehead, *The American Indian in the United States, 1850–1914* (Andover, Mass., Andover Press, 1914), p. 186.

[6] Report of a council held at Pine Ridge, April 30, 1892, transmitted by letter, Capt. George L. Brown, Acting Agent, to Com. of Indian Affairs, April 30, 1892, NARS, RG 75, LR. The Indians also wanted to shoot their beef while running over the prairie, rather than having to kill it in a corral. This, too, Cooper disapproved.

[7] 55th Cong., 1st Sess., S. Docs. Nos. 61, 90. See also Red Cloud *et al.* to the Secretary of the Interior, May 1, 1897, to the President, May 3, 1897, NARS, RG 75, LR.

You can tell the Great Father that I will lend him the top of the hills, if he is satisfied, that is what you can tell him. That is just the rocks above the pines." I would like to tell you this my friend; the rations they give us only last for a day. They should give us the money from the Black Hills treaty, because we need it now. I have been to Washington fifteen times, and this is something like the making of a treaty.

American Horse, Little Wound, Blue Horse, and others also spoke. They all wanted to talk about the Black Hills; they did not like the treaty, and they wanted it changed. Congressman Martin, who had intended to spend only a few hours with the Indians, became impatient as the council dragged into its second day; nevertheless, he heard them out. When they had finished, he said that he was glad that the old men were there and had spoken, but the Indians should know that they did not understand about the treaty. It was a good treaty, and it could not be broken.[8]

In addition to taking part occasionally in a council, the old chief now and then had someone send a letter for him to the Great Father or the Commissioner, complaining about conditions at the agency; in 1898, for example, he tried, unsuccessfully, to prevent the building of fences on the reservation.[9] He was considered to be one of the most intransigent non-progressives among the Sioux, and his efforts generally reflect that attitude. In the important matter of land allotments, however, after holding out for years against taking an allotment, he decided in 1904 to accept his own plot of land—a decision which was credited by the allotting agent with breaking down opposition to the principle of allotments.[10]

For the most part, though, Red Cloud lived in retirement, taking little part in the affairs of his people. He had constant trouble with his eyes and occasionally visited the Shoshoni reservation, where he could

[8] A transcript of the council held at Pine Ridge, September 21–22, 1903, is in Ricker Mss., Tablet No. 16, Nebraska State Historical Society. The memories of the old men may have been faulty, but they had every reason to look back on the Black Hills negotiations as one of the great wrongs committed against their people (see above, pp. 224–230).

[9] These letters are in NARS, RG 75, LR.

[10] Charles H. Bates to Com. of Indian Affairs, December 13, 1904, February 2, 1905, NARS, RG 75, Special Case No. 147. The Sioux had opposed land allotments because the land was not suited to farming and, in their judgment, should be held in common for grazing purposes (see, e.g., Little Wound *et al.* to Secretary of the Interior, March 9, 1896, NARS, RG 75, Special Case No. 147). For a good brief account of the Sioux experience with individual land ownership, see Herbert S. Schell, *History of South Dakota* (Lincoln: University of Nebraska Press, 1961), pp. 329–333.

bathe in the warm springs. On one of these trips, in July, 1894, he was arrested for killing game out of season. Although he stoutly maintained that he was not guilty, the old chief—who thirty years before held sway over the entire area—was lodged briefly in the Casper jail and fined sixty-six dollars, a fine which he paid by giving up two of his horses.[11]

But he had some pleasant experiences, too. Best of all, perhaps, were his visits to the ranch home of his old friend, Capt. James H. Cook, near the fossil beds of northwest Nebraska. With his wife and some of his old people, he would go down and camp for several days on the tree-shaded banks of the Niobrara River, a welcome relief from the desolation of Pine Ridge. There he could enjoy the hospitality of the ranch and talk over the old days with his friend. On one occasion he sat in Captain Cook's study while Bessie Sandes Butler, a family friend and graduate of the Chicago Art Institute, painted his portrait.[12] His last visit, in 1908, lasted for ten days.[13]

During a celebration held at Pine Ridge on July 4, 1903, Red Cloud formally abdicated his chieftaincy in favor of his son Jack,[14] possibly because he remembered how White Hawk years ago had done the same for him. It was an empty gesture. The Sioux had never recognized the concept of the hereditary chief—Red Cloud may have been anointed by White Hawk, but he had won his right to leadership by his own ability—and the Government, which had elevated the position of chief to a status never envisioned by the Indians themselves, was now done with it. Captain Penney, acting agent at Pine Ridge, expressed it well, if cynically, when he forwarded a request from twelve Indians that they be recognized as chiefs. He recommended that they be furnished the papers they asked for—"furnishing these papers can have no effect except to please the vanity of the recipients and keep them in good humor."[15]

[11] James A. George, Washington, to Com. of Indian Affairs, October 15, 1895, NARS, RG 75, LR; Alfred J. Mokler, *History of Natrona County, Wyoming, 1888–1922* (Chicago: Lakeside Press, 1923), pp. 421–426.

[12] Mrs. Margaret A. Cook to the author, September 24, 1963. The portrait hangs in the Cook home, Agate Springs Ranch, Agate, Nebraska.

[13] James H. Cook, *Fifty Years on the Old Frontier* (New Haven: Yale University Press, 1923), *passim.*; conversations with the late Harold Cook, Agate, Nebraska. Shortly after Wounded Knee, Red Cloud tried to secure Captain Cook's appointment as his agent. See *ibid.*, pp. 201, 207; Red Cloud and others to Com. of Indian Affairs, March 10, 1891, Ricker Mss., Tablet No. 13.

[14] Ricker, Interview with Dr. J. R. Walker, Ricker Mss., Tablet No. 25.

[15] Charles G. Penney to Com. of Indian Affairs, June 22, 1891, NARS, RG 75, LR.

Empty though the honor was, Jack apparently made the most of it. Agent John R. Brennan complained in 1906 that Jack spent "most of his time posing as the son of Chief Red Cloud and endeavoring to impress on the other Indians that he will be big chief as soon as the old man passes away."[16] Jack never rose to the heights his father had attained but the aura of the name lingered around him, and when he died in 1918 he was buried with high honors.[17]

Death came to Red Cloud on December 10, 1909.[18] He was buried in the cemetery at Holy Rosary Mission, with the full rites of the Catholic Church administered by Father Eugene Buchel, Superior at St. Francis Mission.[19] Some time later a simple monument was erected over his grave—a monument which remains the principal feature of the little cemetery on the hill above the Holy Rosary Mission.

And so Red Cloud came to the end of the road. For more than forty years it had been the white man's road and he an unwilling traveler. It had been a tragic journey. The tragedy was not that of violence, acute suffering, or sudden death, but of the slow erosion of a way of life. Red Cloud, more than any other of the Sioux chiefs, was associated with that erosion. He was criticized both for giving in too easily to the white man's demands and for obstructing the progress of his people on the white man's road. Both criticisms have some basis in fact; neither is completely accurate. As Captain Cook observed, "During Red Cloud's life he and his people had to meet such conditions as never before had confronted his tribe. . . ."[20] With the old guideposts gone, he made his way along the new road as best he could. As he himself said, "I, of course, as many others have done before me, have made mistakes in not doing something I should have done and what I should not have done. . . ."[21]

Few people have had leaders who could say more.

[16] Brennan to Com. of Indian Affairs, May 26, 1906, *ibid.*

[17] Grace Hebard and E. A. Brininstool, *The Bozeman Trail* (Cleveland: Arthur H. Clark Co., 1922), II, 204.

[18] His death was widely noted in the press. See, e.g., *New York Times*, December 11, 1909, *Omaha Bee*, December 11, 1909.

[19] Placidus Sialm, S.J., History, Holy Rosary Mission, Pine Ridge, S. D., Holy Rosary Mission, p. 83.

[20] Cook, *Fifty Years on the Old Frontier*, p. 215.

[21] See above, p. 334.

Appendix

The Treaty of 1868
(From Charles J. Kappler, comp. and ed., *Indian Affairs, Laws and Treaties* . . . , II, 998–1007.)

Articles of a treaty made and concluded by and between Lieutenant-General William T. Sherman, General William S. Harney, General Alfred H. Terry, General C. C. Augur, J. B. Henderson, Nathaniel G. Taylor, John B. Sanborn, and Samuel F. Tappan, duly appointed commissioners on the part of the United States, and the different bands of the Sioux Nation of Indians, by their chiefs and head-men, whose names are hereto subscribed, they being duly authorized to act in the premises.

ARTICLE 1. From this day forward all war between the parties to this agreement shall forever cease. The government of the United States desires peace, and its honor is hereby pledged to keep it. The Indians desire peace, and they now pledge their honor to maintain it.

If bad men among the whites, or among other people subject to the authority of the United States, shall commit any wrong upon the person or property of the Indians, the United States will, upon proof made to the agent and forwarded to the Commissioner of Indian Affairs at Washington City, proceed at once to cause the offender to be arrested and punished according to the laws of the United States, and also re-imburse the injured person for the loss sustained.

If bad men among the Indians shall commit a wrong or depredation upon the person or property of any one, white, black, or Indian, subject to the authority of the United States, and at peace therewith, the Indians herein named solemnly agree that they will, upon proof

341

made to their agent and notice by him, deliver up the wrong-doer to the United States, to be tried and punished according to its laws; and in case they wilfully refuse so to do, the person injured shall be re-imbursed for his loss from the annuities or other moneys due or to become due to them under this or other treaties made with the United States. And the President, on advising with the Commissioner of Indian Affairs, shall prescribe such rules and regulations for ascertaining damages under the provisions of this article as in his judgement may be proper. But no one sustaining loss while violating the provisions of this treaty or the laws of the United States shall be re-imbursed therefor.

ARTICLE 2. The United States agrees that the following district of country, to wit, viz: commencing on the east bank of the Missouri River where the forty-sixth parallel of north latitude crosses the same, thence along low-water mark down said east bank to a point opposite where the northern line of the State of Nebraska strikes the river, thence west across said river, and along the northern line of Nebraska to the one hundred and fourth degree of longitude west from Greenwich, thence north on said meridian to a point where the forty-sixth parallel of north latitude intercepts the same, thence due east along said parallel to the place of beginning; and in addition thereto, all existing reservations on the east bank of said river shall be, and the same is, set apart for the absolute and undisturbed use and occupation of the Indians herein named, and for such other friendly tribes or individual Indians as from time to time they may be willing, with the consent of the United States, to admit amongst them; and the United States now solemnly agrees that no persons except those herein designated and authorized so to do, and except such officers, agents, and employees of the Government as may be authorized to enter upon Indian reservations in discharge of duties enjoined by law, shall ever be permitted to pass over, settle upon, or reside in the territory described in this article, or in such territory as may be added to this reservation for the use of said Indians, and henceforth they will and do hereby relinquish all claims or right in and to any portion of the United States or Territories, except such as is embraced within the limits aforesaid, and except as hereinafter provided.

ARTICLE 3. If it should appear from actual survey or other satis-factory examination of said tract of land that it contains less than one hundred and sixty acres of tillable land for each person who, at the time, may be authorized to reside on it under the provisions of this treaty, and a very considerable number of such persons shall be disposed to commence cultivating the soil as farmers, the United States agrees to set apart, for the use of said Indians, as herein provided such additional quantity of arable land, adjoining to said reservation, or as near to the same as it can be obtained, as may be required to provide necessary amount.

ARTICLE 4. The United States agrees, at its own proper expense, to construct at some place on the Missouri River, near the center of said reservation, where timber and water may be convenient, the following buildings, to wit: a warehouse, a store-room for the use of the agent in storing goods belonging to the Indians, to cost not less than twenty-five hundred dollars; an agency-building for the residence of the agent, to cost not exceeding three thousand dollars; a residence for the physician, to cost not more than three thousand dollars; and five other buildings, for a carpenter, farmer, blacksmith, miller, and engineer, each to cost not exceeding two thousand dollars; also a school-house or mission-building, so soon as a sufficient number of children can be induced by the agent to attend school, which shall not cost exceeding five thousand dollars.

The United States agrees further to cause to be erected on said reservation, near the other buildings herein authorized, a good steam circular-saw mill, with a grist-mill and shingle-machine attached to the same, to cost not exceeding eight thousand dollars.

ARTICLE 5. The United States agrees that the agent for said Indians shall in the future make his home at the agency-building; that he shall reside among them, and keep an office open at all times for the purpose of prompt and diligent inquiry into such matters of complaint by and against the Indians as may be presented for investigation under the provisions of this treaty stipulations, as also for the faithful discharge of other duties enjoined on him by law. In all cases of depredation on person or property he shall cause the evidence to be taken in writing and forwarded, together with his findings, to the Commissioner of Indian Affairs, whose decision, subject to the revision of the Secretary of the Interior, shall be binding on the parties to this treaty.

ARTICLE 6. If any individual belonging to said tribes of Indians, or legally incorporated with them, being the head of a family, shall desire to commence farming, he shall have the privilege to select, in the presence and with the assistance of the agent then in charge, a tract of land within said reservation, not exceeding three hundred and twenty acres in extent, which tract, when so selected, certified, and recorded in the "land-book," as herein directed, shall cease to be held in common, but the same may be occupied and held in the exclusive possession of the person selecting it, and of his family, so long as he or they may continue to cultivate it.

Any person over eighteen years of age, not being the head of a family, may in like manner select and cause to be certified to him or her, for purposes of cultivation, a quantity of land not exceeding eighty acres in extent, and thereupon be entitled to the exclusive possession of the same as above directed.

For each tract of land so selected a certificate, containing a description thereof and the name of the person selecting it, with a certificate endorsed thereon that the same has been recorded, shall be delivered to the party entitled to it, by the agent, after the same shall have been recorded by him in a book to be kept in his office, subject to inspection, which said book shall be known as the "Sioux Land-Book."

The President may, at any time, order a survey of the reservation, and, when so surveyed, Congress shall provide for protecting the rights of said settlers in their improvements, and may fix the character of the title held by each. The United States may pass such laws on the subject of alienation and descent of property between the Indians and their descendants as may be thought proper. And it is further stipulated that any male Indians, over eighteen years of age, of any band or tribe that is or shall hereafter become a party to this treaty, who now is or who shall hereafter become a resident or occupant of any reservation or Territory not included in the tract of country designated and described in this treaty for the permanent home of the Indians, which is not mineral land, nor reserved by the United States for special purposes other than Indian occupation, and who shall have made improvements thereon of the value of two hundred dollars or more, and continuously occupied the same as a homestead for the term of three years, shall be entitled to receive from the United States a patent for one hundred and sixty acres of land including his said improvements, the same to be in the form of the legal subdivisions of the surveys of the public lands. Upon application in writing, sustained by the proof of two disinterested witnesses, made to the register of the local land-office when the land sought to be entered is within a land district, and when the tract sought to be entered is not in any land district, then upon said application and proof being made to the Commissioner of the General Land-Office, and the right of such Indian or Indians to enter such tract or tracts of land shall accrue and be perfect from the date of his first improvements thereon, and shall continue as long as he continues his residence and improvements, and no longer. And any Indian or Indians receiving a patent for land under the foregoing provisions, shall thereby and from thenceforth become and be a citizen of the United States, and be entitled to all the privileges and immunities of such citizens, and shall, at the same time, retain all his rights to benefits accruing to Indians under this treaty.

ARTICLE 7. In order to insure the civilization of the Indians entering into this treaty, the necessity of education is admitted, especially of such of them as are or may be settled on said agricultural reservations, and they therefore pledge themselves to compel their children, male and female, between the ages of six and sixteen years, to attend school; and it is hereby made the duty of the agent for said Indians to see that this stipulation is strictly complied with; and the United States agrees that for every thirty children between said ages who can be induced or compelled to attend school, a house shall be provided and a teacher competent to teach the elementary branches of an English education shall be furnished, who will reside among said Indians, and faithfully discharge his or her duties as a teacher. The provisions of this article to continue for not less than twenty years.

ARTICLE 8. When the head of a family or lodge shall have selected lands and received his certificate as above directed, and the agent shall be satisfied that he intends in good faith to commence cultivating the soil for a living, he shall be entitled to receive seeds and agricultural implements for the first year, not exceeding in value one hundred dollars, and for each succeeding year he shall continue to farm, for a period of three years more, he shall be entitled to receive seeds and implements as aforesaid, not exceeding in value twenty-five dollars.

And it is further stipulated that such persons as commence farming shall receive instruction from the farmer herein provided for, and whenever more than one hundred persons shall enter upon the cultivation of the soil, a second blacksmith shall be provided, with such iron, steel, and other material as may be needed.

ARTICLE 9. At any time after ten years from the making of this treaty, the United States shall have the privilege of withdrawing the physician, farmer, blacksmith, carpenter, engineer, and miller herein provided for, but in case of such withdrawal, an additional sum thereafter of ten thousand dollars per annum shall be devoted to the education of said Indians, and the Commissioner of Indian Affairs shall, upon careful inquiry into their condition, make such rules and regulations for the expenditure of said sum as will best promote the educational and moral improvement of said tribes.

ARTICLE 10. In lieu of all sums of money or other annuities provided to be paid to the Indians herein named, under any treaty or treaties heretofore made, the United States agrees to deliver at the agency-house on the reservation herein named, on or before the first day of August of each year, for thirty years, the following articles, to wit:

For each male person over fourteen years of age, a suit of good substantial woolen clothing, consisting of coat, pantaloons, flannel shirt, hat, and a pair of home-made socks.

For each female over twelve years of age, a flannel skirt, or the goods necessary to make it, a pair of woolen hose, twelve yards of calico, and twelve yards of cotton domestics.

For the boys and girls under the ages named, such flannel and cotton goods as may be needed to make each a suit as aforesaid, together with a pair of woolen hose for each.

And in order that the Commissioner of Indian Affairs may be able to estimate properly for the articles herein named, it shall be the duty of the agent each year to forward to him a full and exact census of the Indians, on which the estimate from year to year can be based.

And in addition to the clothing herein named, the sum of ten dollars for each person entitled to the beneficial effects of this treaty shall be annually appropriated for a period of thirty years, while such persons roam and hunt, and twenty dollars for each person who engages in farming, to be used by the Secretary of the Interior in the purchase of such articles as from time to time the condition and necessities of the Indians may indicate to be proper. And if within the thirty years, at any time, it shall appear that the amount of money needed for clothing under this article can be appropriated to better uses for the Indians named herein, Congress may, by law, change the appropriation to other purposes; but in no event shall the amount of this appropriation be withdrawn or discontinued for the period named. And the President shall annually detail an officer of the Army to be present and attest the delivery of all the goods herein named to the Indians, and he shall inspect and report on the quantity and quality of the goods and the manner of their delivery. And it is hereby expressly stipulated that each Indian over the age of four years, who shall have removed to and settled permanently upon said reservation and complied with the stipulations of this treaty, shall be entitled to receive from the United States, for the period of four years after he shall have settled upon said reservation, one pound of meat and one pound of flour per day, provided the Indians cannot furnish their own subsistence at an earlier date. And it is further stipulated that the United States will furnish and deliver to each lodge of Indians or family of persons legally incorporated with them, who shall remove to the reservation herein described and commence farming, one good American cow, and one good well-broken pair of American oxen within sixty days after such lodge or family shall have so settled upon said reservation.

ARTICLE 11. In consideration of the advantages and benefits conferred by this treaty, and the many pledges of friendship by the United States, the tribes who are parties to this agreement hereby stipulate that they will relinquish all right to occupy permanently the territory outside their reservation as herein defined, but yet reserve the right to hunt on any lands north of North Platte, and on the Republican Fork of the Smoky Hill River, so long as the buffalo may range thereon in such numbers as to justify the chase. And they, the said Indians, further expressly agree:

1st. That they will withdraw all opposition to the construction of the railroads now being built on the plains.

2d. That they will permit the peaceful construction of any railroad not passing over their reservation as herein defined.

3d. That they will not attack any person at home, or travelling, nor molest or disturb any wagon-trains, coaches, mules, or cattle belonging to the people of the United States, or to persons friendly therewith.

4th. They will never capture, or carry off from the settlements, white women or children.

5th. They will never kill or scalp white men, nor attempt to do them harm.

6th. They withdraw all pretence of opposition to the construction of the railroad now being built along the Platte River and westward to the Pacific Ocean, and they will not in future object to the construction of railroads, wagon-roads, mail-stations, or other works of utility or necessity, which may be ordered or permitted by the laws of the United States. But should such roads or other works be constructed on the lands of their reservation, the Government will pay the tribe whatever amount of damage may be assessed by three disinterested commissioners to be appointed by the President for that purpose, one of said commissioners to be a chief or head-man of the tribe.

7th. They agree to withdraw all opposition to the military posts or roads now established south of the North Platte River, or that may be established, not in violation of treaties heretofore made or hereafter to be made with any of the Indian tribes.

ARTICLE 12. No treaty for the cession of any portion or part of the reservation herein described which may be held in common shall be of any validity or force as against the said Indians, unless executed and signed by at least three-fourths of all the adult male Indians, occupying or interested in the same; and no cession by the tribe shall be understood or construed in such manner as to deprive, without his consent, any individual member of the tribe of his rights to any tract of land selected by him, as provided in article 6 of this treaty.

ARTICLE 13. The United States hereby agrees to furnish annually to the Indians the physician, teachers, carpenter, miller, engineer, farmer, and blacksmiths as herein contemplated, and that such appropriations shall be made from time to time, on the estimates of the Secretary of the Interior, as will be sufficient to employ such persons.

ARTICLE 14. It is agreed that the sum of five hundred dollars annually, for three years from date, shall be expended in presents to the ten persons of said tribe who in the judgment of the agent may grow the most valuable crops for the respective year.

ARTICLE 15. The Indians herein named agree that when the agency-house or other buildings shall be constructed on the reservation named, they will regard said reservation their permanent home, and they will make no permanent settlement elsewhere; but they shall have the right, subject to the conditions and modifications of this treaty, to hunt, as stipulated in Article 11 hereof.

ARTICLE 16. The United States hereby agrees and stipulates that the country north of the North Platte River and east of the summits of the Big Horn Mountains shall be held and considered to be unceded Indian territory, and also stipulates and agrees that no white person or persons shall be permitted to settle upon or occupy any portion of the same; or without the consent of the Indians first had and obtained, to pass through the same; and it is further agreed by the United States that within ninety days after the conclusion of peace with all the bands of the Sioux Nation, the military posts now established in the territory in this article named shall be abandoned, and that the road leading to them and by them to the settlements in the Territory of Montana shall be closed.

ARTICLE 17. It is hereby expressly understood and agreed by and between the respective parties to this treaty that the execution of this treaty and its ratification by the United States Senate shall have the effect, and shall be construed as abrogating and annulling all treaties and agreements heretofore entered into between the respective parties hereto, so far as such treaties and agreements obligate the United States to furnish and provide money, clothing, or other articles of property to such Indians and bands of Indians as become parties to this treaty, but no further.

In testimony of all which, we, the said commissioners, and we, the chiefs and headmen of the Brulé band of the Sioux nation, have here-unto set our hands and seals at Fort Laramie, Dakota Territory, this twenty-ninth day of April, in the year one thousand eight hundred and sixty-eight.

(Signatures omitted.)

Bibliography

1. MANUSCRIPT MATERIAL

National Archives. As the footnotes will indicate, the principal sources for this study have been records in the National Archives of the Bureau of Indian Affairs and the War Department. The following were searched:

RG 75, Records of the Bureau of Indian Affairs.
    Office of Indian Affairs, Letters Sent.
    Office of Indian Affairs, Letters Received.
    Dakota Superintendency, Letters Received.
    Montana Superintendency, Letters Received.
    Wyoming Superintendency, Letters Received.
    Red Cloud Agency, Letters Received.
    Spotted Tail Agency, Letters Received.
    Upper Platte Agency, Letters Received.
    Board of Indian Commissioners, Correspondence.
    Papers Relating to Peace Commission.
    Unratified Treaties File.
    Old Miscellaneous Records.
    Special Case 63, Route No. 3.
    Special Case 96, Pine Ridge.
    Special Case 104, Edmunds Commission.
    Special Case 108, Ghost Dance.
    Special File 219, Red Cloud and Spotted Tail.
    Special File 244, Sioux of 1869.
    Special File 264, McGillycuddy.
RG 94, Records of the Adjutant General's Office.
    Document File 4163, Sioux War, 1876.
RG 98, Records of United States Army Commands.
    Military Division of the Missouri.
    Department of the Platte.
    Fort Robinson.
    Red Cloud Agency.

Nebraska State Historical Society. Of particular value is the Eli S. Ricker collection of interviews with many persons who participated in or observed Sioux affairs. Most of them deal with the Ghost Dance troubles, but a number are useful for the earlier period. The interviews I have found to be particularly useful are those with:

American Horse
Cornelius A. Craven
George W. Colhoff
Dr. Charles A. Eastman
William Garnett
William Girton
Baptiste Pourier
Red Cloud
George Sword
Dr. J. R. Walker
Philip F. Wells

In addition to the Ricker papers, the Nebraska State Historical Society possesses a typescript by Addison E. Sheldon, "Red Cloud, Chief of the Sioux." For a discussion of this, see Chapter II, Note 3. Dr. Sheldon also caused to be collected a considerable number of notes from the records in the National Archives. For the most part, these were from records which I searched, although occasionally these notes fell outside the scope of my search. Locations cited in the footnotes which do not appear in the list above of materials searched in the National Archives indicate that these notes are the source. From a comparison of many of these notes with the originals, I am satisfied that the transcriptions were accurate.

Miscellaneous Manuscripts. I am listing here all manuscript materials, including unpublished theses and dissertations, not listed above.

Albright, Robert E. "The Relations of Montana with the Federal Government, 1864–1889." Ph.D. dissertation, Stanford University, 1933.

Bowler, Mary Jane. "The Sioux Indians and the United States Government, 1862–1878." Master's thesis, Washington University, St. Louis, 1944.

"Diary of Cornelius Hedges on Journey to Montana from Iowa—1864." Montana Historical Society, Helena.

"Diary of the Travels of Richard Owen from Omaha, Nebraska to the Gold Regions of Idaho." Montana Historical Society, Helena.

John Dougherty Papers. Missouri Historical Society, St. Louis.

Hawken, Edward Jay. "The Military Problem on the Powder River Road, 1865–1868." Master's thesis, University of California, 1938.

Maynard, E. A. "My Trip to Montana." Montana Historical Society, Helena.

Parrish, Cora Hoffman. "The Indian Peace Commission of 1867 and the Western Indians." Master's thesis, University of Oklahoma, 1948.

Rockefeller, Alfred, Jr. "The Sioux Troubles of 1890–1891." Ph.D. dissertation, Northwestern University, 1949.

Sialm, Placidus, S.J. "History, Holy Rosary Mission, Pine Ridge, S.D." Holy Rosary Mission.

Thompson, Donald R. "A History of Holy Rosary Indian Mission from its Beginning to the Present." Master's thesis, Denver University, 1954.

Van Huizen, George Harry. "The United States Government and the Sioux Indians, 1878–1891." Master's thesis, Washington University, St. Louis, 1950.

Waddell, William S. "The Military Relations Between the Sioux Indians and the United States Government in the Dakota Territory, 1860–1891." Master's thesis, University of South Dakota, 1931.

Waltmann, Henry G. "The Subsistence Policy with Special Reference to the Red Cloud and Spotted Tail Agencies." Master's thesis, University of Nebraska, 1959.

————. "The Interior Department, War Department and Indian Policy, 1865–1887." Ph.D. dissertation, University of Nebraska, 1962.

2. GOVERNMENT PUBLICATIONS

BOARD OF INDIAN COMMISSIONERS. Annual Reports.

COMMISSIONER OF INDIAN AFFAIRS. Annual Reports.

Congressional Globe.

GILMORE, MELVIN R. "Uses of Plants by the Indians of the Missouri River Region," Bureau of American Ethnology, *33rd Annual Report* (1911–1912), pp. 43–154.

KAPPLER, CHARLES J., comp. and ed. *Indian Affairs, Laws and Treaties.* . . . Vol. 1–2: 57th Cong., 1st Sess., S. Doc. 452; Vol. 3: 62d Cong., 2d Sess., S. Doc. 719.

KEARNY, S. W. "Report of a Summer Campaign to the Rocky Mountains, &c., in 1845," 29th Cong., 1st Sess., S. Ex. Doc. 1.

MALLERY, GARRICK. "Pictographs of the North American Indians," Bureau of American Ethnology, *Fourth Annual Report.*

————. "Picture Writing of the American Indians," Bureau of American Ethnology, *Tenth Annual Report.*

MOONEY, JAMES. *The Ghost Dance Religion and the Sioux Outbreak of 1890.* Bureau of American Ethnology, *Fourteenth Annual Report.*

Report of the Special Commission Appointed to Investigate the Affairs of the Red Cloud Indian Agency, July, 1875. Washington: Government Printing Office, 1875.

RICHARDSON, JAMES D., comp. *Messages and Papers of the Presidents, 1789–1897.* Washington: Government Printing Office, 1896–1899. 10 vols.

SECRETARY OF THE INTERIOR. Annual Reports.

SECRETARY OF WAR. Annual Reports.

SUPERINTENDENT OF INDIAN AFFAIRS, Report, October 29, 1847, 30th Cong., 1st Sess., Ex. Doc. 8.

TAYLOR, EDWARD B. Report of Northern Superintendency, September 15, 1865, 39th Cong., 1st Sess., H. Ex. Doc. 1.

U.S. *Statutes at Large.*

The War of the Rebellion: A Compilation of the Official Records of the Union and Confederate Armies. 130 vols. Washington: Government Printing Office, 1886–1901.

39th Cong., 1st Sess., H. Doc. 58.

40th Cong., 1st Sess., H. Ex. Doc. 97.

40th Cong., 1st Sess., S. Ex. Doc. 13.

40th Cong., 2d Sess., H. Ex. Doc. 97.

44th Cong., 1st Sess., H. Ex. Doc. 1.

44th Cong., 1st Sess., H. Ex. Doc. 184.

44th Cong., 1st Sess., S. Ex. Doc. 52.

48th Cong., 1st Sess., S. Ex. Doc. 70.

48th Cong., 1st Sess., S. Report 283.

49th Cong., 1st Sess., H. Ex. Doc. 35.

49th Cong., 1st Sess., H. Report 1076.

49th Cong., 2d Sess., S. Ex. Doc. 97.

50th Cong., 1st Sess., S. Ex. Doc. 33.

51st Cong., 1st Sess., S. Ex. Doc. 51.

53d Cong., 1st Sess., H. Ex. Doc. 1.

55th Cong., 1st Sess., S. Ex. Doc. 61.

55th Cong., 1st Sess., S. Ex. Doc. 90.

3. NEWSPAPERS

Avant Courier, Bozeman, Montana.

Cheyenne Leader.

The Montana Post, Virginia City, Montana.

New North-West, Deer Lodge, Montana.

New York Herald.

New York Times.

Omaha Weekly Herald.

Yankton Press.

Yankton Union and Dakotaian.

4. BOOKS

ALTER, J. CECIL. *James Bridger.* Salt Lake City: Shepard Book Co., 1925.

ATHEARN, ROBERT G. *William Tecumseh Sherman and the Settlement of the West.* Norman: University of Oklahoma Press, 1956.

BELDEN, GEORGE P. *Belden, The White Chief.* Cincinnati and New York: C. F. Vent, 1871.

BLAND, T. A. *A Brief History of the Late Military Invasion of the Home of the Sioux.* Washington: n.p., 1891.

BORDEAUX, WILLIAM J. *Conquering the Mighty Sioux.* Sioux Falls, n.p., 1929.

BOURKE, JOHN G. *On the Border with Crook.* New York: Charles Scribner's Sons, 1892.

BRADY, CYRUS TOWNSEND. *Indian Fights and Fighters.* Garden City: Doubleday, Page and Co., 1940.

BRININSTOOL, E. A. *Fighting Red Cloud's Warriors.* Columbus: The Hunter-trader-trapper Co., 1926.

BROWN, DEE. *Fort Phil Kearny: An American Saga.* New York: Putnam, 1962.

BURT, STRUTHERS. *Powder River.* New York: Farrar & Rinehart, 1939.

BYRNE, PATRICK E. *Soldiers of the Plains.* New York: Minton, Balch & Co., 1926.

CARRINGTON, FRANCES C. *Army Life on the Plains.* Philadelphia: J. B. Lippincott Co., 1910.

CARRINGTON, MARGARET IRWIN. *Ab-sa-ra-ka, Home of the Crows.* Philadelphia: J. B. Lippincott Co., 1869.

CHITTENDEN, HIRAM M., and A. T. Richardson, eds. *Life, Letters, and Travels of Father Pierre-Jean DeSmet, S.J., 1801–1873.* New York: Francis P. Harper, 1905. 4 vols.

CLOUGH, WILSON O., ed. *Fort Russell and Fort Laramie Peace Commission in 1867.* Sources of Northwest History, No. 14, State University of Montana.

COOK, JAMES H. *Fifty Years on the Old Frontier.* New Haven: Yale University Press, 1923.

COUTANT, CHARLES GRIFFIN. *The History of Wyoming.* Laramie: Chaplin, Spafford and Mathison, 1899.

DANKER, DONALD F., ed. *Man of the Plains: Recollections of Luther North, 1856–1882.* Lincoln: University of Nebraska Press, 1961.

DODGE, RICHARD I. *Our Wild Indians.* Hartford: A. D. Worthington Co., 1890.

EASTMAN, CHARLES A. *Indian Heroes and Great Chieftains.* Boston: Little, Brown, and Co., 1920.

ELLIS, ELMER. *Henry Moore Teller: Defender of the West.* Caldwell, Idaho: The Caxton Press, 1941.

FORD, AMELIA C. *Colonial Precedents of Our National Land System as it Existed in 1800.* Bulletin, University of Wisconsin, No. 352, 1910.

FRITZ, HENRY E. *The Movement for Indian Assimilation, 1860–1890.* Philadelphia: University of Pennsylvania Press, 1963.

GRINNELL, GEORGE B. *The Fighting Cheyennes.* New York: Charles Scribner's Sons, 1915; Norman: University of Oklahoma Press, 1956.

GRINNELL, GEORGE B. *Two Great Scouts and Their Pawnee Battalion.* Cleveland: Arthur H. Clark Co., 1928.

HAFEN, LEROY R., AND W. J. GHENT. *Broken Hand, The Life Story of Thomas Fitzpatrick, Chief of the Mountain Men.* Denver: The Old West Publishing Co., 1931.

————, AND C. C. RISTER. *Western America.* New York: Prentice Hall, 1941.

————, AND FRANCIS M. YOUNG. *Fort Laramie and the Pageant of the West, 1834–1890.* Glendale: Arthur H. Clark Co., 1938.

————, AND ANN W. HAFEN, eds. *Powder River Campaigns and Sawyers Expedition of 1865.* Glendale: Arthur H. Clark Co., 1961.

HANS, FRED M. *The Great Sioux Nation.* Chicago: M. A. Donohue & Co., 1907.

HASSRICK, ROYAL B. *The Sioux: Life and Customs of a Warrior Society.* Norman: University of Oklahoma Press, 1964.

HEBARD, GRACE RAYMOND. *The Pathbreakers from River to Ocean.* Chicago: Lakeside Press, 1912.

HEBARD, GRACE, AND E. A. BRININSTOOL. *The Bozeman Trail.* Cleveland: Arthur H. Clark Co., 1922. 2 vols.

History of Montana, 1739–1885. Chicago: Warner, Beers & Co., 1885.

HOIG, STAN. *The Sand Creek Massacre.* Norman: University of Oklahoma Press, 1961.

HOLMES, LOUIS A. *Fort McPherson, Nebraska, Fort Cottonwood, N.T.* Lincoln: Johnsen Publishing Co., 1963.

HOWE, M. A. DEWOLFE. *Life and Labors of Bishop Hare, Apostle to the Sioux.* New York: Sturgis and Walton Co., 1912.

HYDE, GEORGE E. *Red Cloud's Folk.* Norman: University of Oklahoma Press, 1937, 1957.

————. *A Sioux Chronicle.* Norman: University of Oklahoma Press, 1956.

————. *Spotted Tail's Folk.* Norman: University of Oklahoma Press, 1961.

JOHNSON, VIRGINA WEISEL. *The Unregimented General: A Biography of Nelson A. Miles.* Boston: Houghton Mifflin Co., 1962.

JOHNSON, W. FLETCHER. *Life of Sitting Bull and History of the Indian War of 1890–91.* Edgewood, S. D.: Edgewood Publishing Co., 1891.

JOHNSTON, SISTER MARY ANTONIO. *Federal Relations with the Great Sioux Indians of South Dakota, 1887–1933, with Particular Reference to Land Policy Under the Dawes Act.* Washington: The Catholic University of America Press, 1948.

KELLY, FANNY. *Narrative of My Captivity among the Sioux Indians.* Hartford: Mutual Publishing Co., 1871.

KING, JAMES T. *War Eagle: A Life of General Eugene A. Carr.* Lincoln: University of Nebraska Press, 1963.

LAMAR, HOWARD R. *Dakota Territory, 1861–1889.* New Haven: Yale University Press, 1956.

LAVENDER, DAVID. *Bent's Fort.* New York: Doubleday and Co., 1954.

LECKIE, WILLIAM H. *The Military Conquest of the Southern Plains.* Norman: University of Oklahoma Press, 1963.

LESSER, ALEXANDER. *The Pawnee Ghost Dance Hand Game.* New York: Columbia University Press, 1933.

McGILLYCUDDY, JULIA B. *McGillycuddy: Agent.* Stanford: Stanford University Press, 1941.

McGREGOR, GORDON. *Warriors without Weapons: A Study of the Society and Personality Development of the Pine Ridge Sioux.* Chicago: University of Chicago Press, 1946.

McGREGOR, JAMES H. *The Wounded Knee Massacre.* Baltimore: Wirth Brothers, 1940.

McLAUGHLIN, JAMES. *My Friend the Indian.* Boston: Houghton Mifflin Co., 1910.

MANYPENNY, GEORGE W. *Our Indian Wards.* Cincinnati: Robert Clarke & Co., 1880.

MATTES, MERRILL J. *Indians, Infants and Infantry: Andrew and Elizabeth Burt on the Frontier.* Denver: The Old West Publishing Co., 1960.

MOKLER, ALFRED J. *History of Natrona County, Wyoming, 1888–1922.* Chicago: Lakeside Press, 1923.

MOOREHEAD, W. K. *The American Indian in the United States.* Andover, Mass.: Andover Press, 1914.

MUNROE, JAMES PHINNEY. *A Life of Francis Amasa Walker.* New York: Henry Holt and Co., 1923.

OLSON, JAMES C. *History of Nebraska.* Lincoln: University of Nebraska Press, 1955.

PARKMAN, FRANCIS. *The Oregon Trail.* Boston: Little, Brown and Co., 1891.

PELZER, LOUIS. *Marches of the Dragoons in the Mississippi Valley.* Iowa City: State Historical Society of Iowa, 1917.

PRIEST, LORING B. *Uncle Sam's Stepchildren: The Reformation of United States Indian Policy, 1865–1887.* New Brunswick: Rutgers University Press, 1942.

RAHILL, PETER J. *The Catholic Indian Missions and Grant's Peace Policy, 1870–1884.* Washington, D.C.: The Catholic University of America Press, 1953.

RISTER, CARL COKE. *Border Command: General Phil Sheridan in the West.* Norman: University of Oklahoma Press, 1944.

ROGERS, FRED B. *Soldiers of the Overland.* San Francisco: The Grabhorn Press, 1938.

SAGE, LELAND L. *William Boyd Allison, A Study in Practical Politics.* Iowa City: State Historical Society of Iowa, 1956.

SANDOZ, MARI. *Crazy Horse.* New York: Alfred A. Knopf, 1942; New York: Hastings House, 1958.

———. *Cheyenne Autumn.* New York: McGraw-Hill, 1953.

SCHELL, HERBERT S. *History of South Dakota*. Lincoln: University of Nebraska Press, 1961.

SCHMITT, MARTIN F., ed. *General George Crook, His Autobiography*. Norman: University of Oklahoma Press, 1946.

SCHUCHERT, CHARLES, AND CLARA MAE LeVENE. *O. C. Marsh, Pioneer in Paleontology*. New Haven: Yale University Press, 1940.

SLATTERY, CHARLES LEWIS. *Felix Reville Brunot, 1820–1898*. New York: Longmans, Green, and Co., 1901.

SPRING, AGNES WRIGHT. *The Cheyenne and Black Hills Stage and Express Routes*. Glendale: Arthur H. Clark Co., 1949.

STANDING BEAR, LUTHER. *My People the Sioux*. Boston: Houghton Mifflin Co., 1928.

STANLEY, HENRY M. *My Early Travels and Adventures in America and Asia*. New York: Charles Scribner's Sons, 1895. 2 vols.

STEWART, EDGAR I. *Custer's Luck*. Norman: University of Oklahoma Press, 1955.

TURNER, KATHERINE C. *Red Men Calling on the Great White Father*. Norman: University of Oklahoma Press, 1951.

UTLEY, ROBERT M. *The Last Days of the Sioux Nation*. New Haven: Yale University Press, 1963.

VAUGHN, J. W. *The Battle of Platte Bridge*. Norman: University of Oklahoma Press, 1963.

VESTAL, STANLEY. *Sitting Bull: Champion of the Sioux*. New York: Houghton Mifflin Co., 1932.

———. *New Sources of Indian History, 1850–1891*. Norman: University of Oklahoma Press, 1934.

———. *Warpath*. Boston: Houghton Mifflin Co., 1934.

———. *Warpath and Council Fire*. New York: Random House, 1948.

WADE, MASON, ed. *The Journals of Francis Parkman*. New York: Harper and Brothers, 1947. 2 vols.

YOUNG, OTIS E. *The West of Philip St. George Cooke, 1809–1895*. Glendale: Arthur H. Clark Co., 1955.

5. PERIODICALS

ALLEN, CHARLES W. "Red Cloud, Chief of the Sioux," *The Hesperian*, I (November, 1895, December, 1895, January, 1896), 144–147, 173–178, 211–216.

———. "Red Cloud and the U.S. Flag," *Nebraska History*, XXI (October–December, 1940), 293–304.

ANDERSON, HARRY H. "The Controversial Sioux Amendment to the Fort Laramie Treaty of 1851," *Nebraska History*, XXXVII (September, 1956), 201–220.

———. "Indian Peace-Talkers and the Conclusion of the Sioux War of 1876," *Nebraska History*, XL (December, 1963), 223–254.

The Army and Navy Journal.

ATHEARN, ROBERT G., ed. "From Illinois to Montana in 1866: The Diary of Perry A. Burgess," *Pacific Northwest Quarterly*, XLI (January, 1950), 43–65.

———. "The Montana Volunteers of 1867," *Pacific Historical Review*, XIX (May, 1950), 127–136.

BRIGGS, HAROLD E. "The Black Hills Gold Rush," *North Dakota Historical Quarterly*, V (1930–1931), 71–99.

CAMPBELL, JOHN A. "DIARY, 1869–1875," *Annals of Wyoming*, X (1938), 5–11, 59–78, 120–143, 155–185.

CLARK, GIBSON. "Red Cloud's Prayer," *Annals of Wyoming*, XV (October, 1943), 404–440.

"Council at Sites of Surround," *Nebraska History*, XV (October-December, 1934), 279–287.

The Council Fire.

EDWARDS, ELSA SPEAR. "A Fifteen Day Fight on Tongue River," *Annals of Wyoming*, X (April, 1938), 51–58.

EDWARDS, MARTHA L. "A Problem of Church and State in the 1870's," *Mississippi Valley Historical Review*, XI (June, 1924), 37–53.

FOX, GEORGE W. "George W. Fox Diary," *Annals of Wyoming*, VIII (January, 1932), 580–601.

GIRARD, P. "United States Indian Policy and Religious Liberty," *Catholic World*, 26 (October, 1877), 90–108.

GRANGE, ROGER T., JR. "Fort Robinson, Outpost on the Plains," *Nebraska History*, XXXIX (September, 1958), 191–240.

HAGERTY, LEROY R. "Indian Raids Along the Platte and Little Blue Rivers, 1864–1865," *Nebraska History*, XXVIII (September, December, 1947), 176–186, 229–260.

KING, JAMES T. "The Republican River Expedition, June, July, 1869," *Nebraska History*, IL (September, December, 1960), 165–200, 281–298.

LARSEN, ARTHUR J., ed. "The Black Hills Gold Rush," *North Dakota Historical Quarterly*, VI (1931–1932), 302–318.

McCANN, LLOYD E. "The Grattan Massacre," *Nebraska History*, XXXVII (March, 1956), 1–25.

MAHNKEN, NORBERT. "The Sidney–Black Hills Trail," *Nebraska History*, XXX (September, 1949), 203–225.

MATTES, MERRILL J. "Fort Mitchell, Scotts Bluff, Nebraska Territory," *Nebraska History*, XXXIII (March, 1952), 1–34.

———. "Roubidoux's Trading Post at 'Scott's Bluffs,' and the California Gold Rush," *Nebraska History*, XXX (June, 1949), 95–138.

The Nation.

OLSON, JAMES C., ed. "From Nebraska City to Montana, 1866: The Diary of Thomas Alfred Creigh," *Nebraska History*, XXIX (September, 1948), 208–237.

OLSON, JAMES C., ed. "Along the Trail," *Nebraska History*, XXIX (September, 1948), 294–295.

PENNINGTON, ROBERT. "An Analysis of the Political Structure of the Teton-Dakota Indian Tribe of North America," *North Dakota History*, XX (July, 1953), 143–155.

PHILLIPS, DAVID G. "The Sioux Chiefs Before the Secretary," *Harper's Weekly*, 35 (Feb 21, 1891), 140, 142.

RYAN, BENJAMIN WILLIAMS. "The Bozeman Trail to Virginia City, Montana in 1864: A Diary," *Annals of Wyoming*, XIX (July, 1947), 77–104.

SHELDON, ADDISON E. "Massacre Canyon the Last Nebraska Battlefield of the Sioux-Pawnee," *Nebraska History*, IV (October–December, 1921), 53–60.

SHIELDS, LILLIAN B. "Relations with the Cheyennes and Arapahoes in Colorado to 1861," *The Colorado Magazine*, IV (August, 1927), 145–154.

WALKER, FRANCIS A. "The Indian Question," *North American Review*, 116 (April, 1873), 329–368.

WEMETT, W. W. "Custer's Expedition to the Black Hills in 1874," *North Dakota Historical Quarterly*, VI (July, 1932), 292–301.

6. MISCELLANEOUS

COLBY, L. W. "The Sioux Indian War of 1890–91," Nebraska State Historical Society, *Transactions and Reports*, III (1892), 144–190.

DeLAND, CHARLES E. "The Sioux Wars," *South Dakota Historical Collections*, XV (1930), 8–730.

Dictionary of American Biography.

Documents Relating to the Charges of Professor O. C. Marsh of Fraud and Mismanagement at the Red Cloud Agency.

GREEN, CHARLES LOWELL. "The Indian Reservation System of the Dakotas to 1889," *South Dakota Historical Collections*, XIV (1928), 307–416.

MARSH, O. C. *A Statement of Affairs at Red Cloud Agency, Made to the President of the United States.* n.p., n.d.

ROBINSON, DOANE. "The Education of Red Cloud," *Collections*, South Dakota Department of History, XII (1924), 156–178.

―――. "Tales of the Dakota: One Hundred Anecdotes Illustrative of Sioux Life and Thinking," *South Dakota Historical Collections* XIV (1928), 485–537.

WISSLER, CLARK. "Societies and Ceremonial Associations in the Oglala Division of the Teton-Sioux," *Anthropological Papers of the American Museum of Natural History*, IX (1916), 1–99.

Index